FRENCH THEORY

French Theory

HOW FOUCAULT, DERRIDA, DELEUZE, & CO.

TRANSFORMED THE INTELLECTUAL LIFE

OF THE UNITED STATES

FRANÇOIS CUSSET

TRANSLATED BY JEFF FORT

WITH JOSEPHINE BERGANZA AND MARLON JONES

University of Minnesota Press

Minneapolis

London

The University of Minnesota Press gratefully acknowledges financial assistance provided by the French Ministry of Culture for the translation of this book. Ouvrage publié avec le concours du Ministère français de la Culture—Centre National du livre.

Originally published in French in 2003 as *French Theory: Foucault, Derrida, Deleuze & Cie et les mutations de la vie intellectuelle aux États-Unis.* Copyright 2003 Éditions La Découverte.

English translation copyright 2008 by the Regents of the University of Minnesota

Published by the University of Minnesota Press
111 Third Avenue South, Suite 290
Minneapolis, MN 55401-2520
http://www.upress.umn.edu

Library of Congress Cataloging-in-Publication Data
Cusset, François.
    [French theory. English]
    French theory : how Foucault, Derrida, Deleuze, & Co. transformed the intellectual life of the United States / François Cusset ; translated by Jeff Fort with Josephine Berganza and Marlon Jones.
        p.   cm.
    Includes bibliographical references (p.   ) and index.
    ISBN 978-0-8166-4732-3 (hc : alk. paper)   ISBN 978-0-8166-4733-0 (pb : alk. paper)
        1. Philosophy, French—20th century. 2. France—Intellectual life—20th century.
    3. United States—Intellectual life—French influences. I. Title.
    B2421.C7913 2008
    194—dc22
                                                                        2008000838

Printed in the United States of America on acid-free paper

The University of Minnesota is an equal-opportunity educator and employer.

15 14 13 12 11 10 09 08   10 9 8 7 6 5 4 3

For C.

To L. and Y.

Theory is itself a practice, no less than its object is. It is not more abstract than its object. It is a conceptual practice, and it must be judged in terms of the other practices with which it interacts.

GILLES DELEUZE
Cinema 1: The Movement Image

Contents

PREFACE TO THE ENGLISH EDITION

Why Bother with Theory?

WHY STILL BOTHER with *theory*, French or otherwise? It would take a true rhetorical talent to convince anyone today, even a delusional academic who hasn't left his or her campus for years, that theory and the many debates surrounding it can have *any* impact, say, on technological change, on the leisure industry, on the state of Western democracy or global geopolitics—or on the run-up to the next presidential elections, for that matter. In other words, isn't it simply too late to still be speaking about French Theory *today*?[1] The word *today*, in that sense, conjures up a mix of collective panic and historical changes, an endlessly extended present and an immediate future more blurred than ever, an utterly confused, postcommunist, postcolonial age of global civil war *and* absolute entertainment, religious terrorism *and* state terrorism—the age of a new type of empire unsure as to who its real enemies are and how to identify, much less absorb, its "citizens." In such an unsettling present, one wonders if there is anything left to expect from this weird textual American object known as *theory*, born between the two world wars or in the crazy 1970s, depending on historical accounts, but definable today as a strange breed of academic market rules, French (and more generally Continental) detachable concepts, campus-based identity politics, and trendy pop culture. It seems to many that the gap between real-life politics and theory's guerrillas is much too wide already, after thirty years of academic fever, for the two worlds even to speak a common language. Or for a possible use of Michel Foucault, Gilles Deleuze, or even Jacques Derrida in an attempt to shed some light on today's global disorders—even when Foucault's genealogy of "biopolitics," Deleuze's comments on our "societies of control," and Derrida's concept of "unconditional hospitality," all coined more than two decades ago, appear to be exactly addressing our contemporary situation.

This tendency to relegate theory to a leisurely time when "reality" wasn't really a problem (but did such a time ever exist, even before September 11, 2001?), and to call for more urgent issues to be raised today than just *theoretical* ones, is where old-style liberals or even Marxists and neoconservative watchdogs do collide, or converge. They both agree that theory is perilous today, or at best just patently useless, much as the West German federal police and the East German political police agreed that Michel Foucault was dangerous or useless enough to deserve being arrested twice during his visit to the two sides of Berlin in 1978—as he liked to recall, comparing police stupidity and zeal on both sides of the Berlin Wall in terms not really favorable to the "good cops" of the "free world." This is exactly the kind of consensus that should be tirelessly questioned and disrupted until it no longer holds, today no less than thirty years ago. For in fact, if one takes a closer, more rigorous look, it is easy to see that theory and activism *do* converge today. They do so in certain new forms of social activism, within a new generation of readers on both sides of the ocean who manage to think and write in the lines of these authors, or of others, but always away from their intimidating shadows. New uses of theory's major texts are possible today, they are even necessary, beyond the age-old aporia of theory and praxis as two distinct moments, that old Hegelian dialectics which French Theory was precisely supposed to have refuted, or at least avoided, in favor of what Deleuze and Guattari would call "theoretical practice"—a real practical approach to theory.

But then, how to stick to such theoretical practices when the United States is under direct attack? One of the saddest things about the immediate post-9/11 climate in the United States' public space, beyond blind patriotism and a frustrated virility willing to retaliate as soon as possible, was surely the intellectual field's deliberate *powerlessness*. After decades of rhetorically questioning the imperialistic West, deconstructing America's power, and demonizing the first world's neocolonialism, the various radicals bred in academic quarters this time stood still, muted and schocked. In the aftermath of the attacks on New York City and Washington, D.C., most of these brilliant campus radicals didn't have much to say about Bush, Iraq, terror, national pride, and global democracy, apart from a distant feeling of horror and disarray. Whereas liberals of all sorts in Europe or Asia did expect some sort of awakening from their North American counterparts, or a new inspiration to come from the belly of the beast, perhaps a new tone on American campuses for times of emergency, what they witnessed was mostly self-criticism and a sense of uselessness. When touring campuses right after 9/11, I was astounded to discover that the dominant feeling in academia was one of desperate impossibility, complete with guilt and resentment. Yesterday's tenured radicals were now writing sophisticated articles just to make a note of the insuperable gap between the world and the text, theory and "reality," intellectual leisure and the new state of global emergency. Just when theory was precisely challenged to speak out beyond self-reflection, and lead to other issues inseparable from today's situation—the issues of capitalism and its new social forms, of the media and its industrial production of fear, or of the exhausting of the rhetorics of promise as political horizon—to turn these issues into complete blind spots, all you have to do is to limit theory, again, to a specialized debate for academic experts.

But there *is* another side to the story. Theory is not only what academics do with it in a specific disciplinary and historical context—say, in Ivy League departments of literature around the beginning of the 1990s. Neither identity politics nor textual strategies, the two main currents into which Foucault or Derrida were channeled in the American university over the last three decades, have exhausted the still unidentified flying object known as French Theory. But this represents only two possible readings. In fact, what has been forgotten, or left aside, within French Theory in the process of its American domestication is nevertheless still there, at work in the text, hidden but still available. In this respect, textual politics is still a potentially useful thing, and is not merely that denial of "real" politics which so many off-campus liberals keep deriding. Theory, in short, is *not* a thing of the past, or a vague promise of a better world—which also goes against the grain of a certain nostalgia for those good old days, duly idealized, when theory, politics, and counterculture were best friends, before the nasty academic marketplace tore them apart and left us orphans. In fact, if there is a future for theory, it will start on campus, provided it doesn't die there. But it may even find a suitable nesting place there; for now that theory's passions and controversies are over, now that it has been quietly normalized and institutionalized, it may finally be possible to treat it with a historical approach, a colder eye, rather than with the jargon-filled, decontextualized approach that has been a leading narrative of theory in the United States for more than two decades. When speaking about theory, the choice seems for too long to have been largely whether to mime it (on the part of professional theorists) or to blame it (on the part of conservative columnists), whether to ape it or to denounce it. It is high time that we all go beyond the "with-us-or-against-us" approach, in these matters as in many others.

But if theory is to be of any use nowadays, the many tricks and games implied by its deterritorializations and cultural metamorphoses should be taken seriously. Which is what this book on the *American* invention of *French* theory has tried to achieve, by addressing the American identity of French Theory, or the way it has been displaced and reconstructed to confront specifically American questions, by raising the issue of a "denationalization" of concepts, or of what Pierre Bourdieu would call "a structural misunderstanding," and even by pondering the strange feedback effect of a recent return of French Theory *to France,* where it is now coming back undercover, under the disguise of an American type of threat against France's age-old abstract universalism. This great French–American story deals indeed with the joy of becomings, the power of effects, the surprises of unexpected uses. To put it bluntly, I would summarize this transferring of a body of theoretical texts from 1960s–70s France to 1980s–90s North America along the three following lines: first, the French issue of writing has become the American issue of reading; second, the mystery of late capitalism has been transformed into the enigma of cultural identity; and third, the question of micropolitics has been turned into the very different question of symbolic conflicts—a radical (and triple) displacement typical of today's "denationalizing" of texts in a global academic market. When revolution is reinterpreted as stylized rebellion, when social forces are turned into identity politics, when writing is replaced by reading, when texts published by Gallimard or Éditions de Minuit wind up translated by specialized university presses, when mottos coined during Left Bank marches are being reused in New York art galleries, then indeed one can speak of a "structural misunderstanding," not in the sense of a misreading, an error, a betrayal of some original, but in the sense of a highly productive transfer of words and concepts from one specific market of symbolic goods to another. It takes us back to what Bourdieu calls "the social conditions of the international circulation of ideas," the title of the last article he published during his lifetime. There he insists that "a foreign reading is sometimes more *free* than a national reading of the same text," because it loosens the structure and opens a text onto brand-new uses, but also because it may often be more profitable to base a career on some distant, foreign, exotic body of texts, owing to the "complex network of international exchanges between holders of leading academic positions."[2]

First, then, a shift from writing to reading. A mix of identity politics and an old American tradition of metacommentary *on* education has placed a new stress on the identities and internal diversity of the *readers* themselves (that is, most often, the students). There may even be pragmatic reasons behind such a shift, when the tabula rasa of any subject or intention at the level of writing (which is what theory entails) requires reinstating one at the other end of the spectrum, at least for a reader to be simply able to *use* that same text. And as far as the second and third shifts are concerned, they should probably both stand under the general category of a *denial of market forces*. Which amounts to a case of *double denial*: while campus Marxists derided French Theory as an aesthetics, or a rhetoric, minority experts often mistook it for a theory of cultural symbols. In fact, Marx—and, more broadly, *any* social critique of capital—may be the major blind spot of French Theory's readers and commentators on both sides of the Atlantic, although for opposite reasons: Foucault, Deleuze, and even Derrida enjoyed such a success within American, but also many third-world, universities precisely because of their distance from classical Marxism, or because of what was even seen as their anti-Marxism; meanwhile, they were banned from their home country under the charges of a perverse collusion with the worst of leftist Marxism. Their texts, however, were neither pro-Marx nor anti-Marx. They were, rather, an endless confrontation with, discussion on, reinterpretation of Marxism—best exemplified perhaps by Jean-François Lyotard's delirious suggestion in *Libidinal Economy* that there have always been *two* Marxes, the old, bearded rationalist obsessed with totality, and a young, chesty Bavarian waitress keener on transgression and intensive signs.

In any case, the denial of market forces, of capital and its strategies, helps explain what has been done with French Theory in many universities in the United States for the past twenty-five years under the general label of cultural studies: detailing clothing styles and coded lingos as forms of rebellious expression with little or no consideration of social positions and contexts; debating sex wars and gender norms with hardly a mention of the profitable commodification of femininity as today's ultimate existential product; praising Madonna as a postfeminist icon, or denouncing her as a traitor to feminism, but without ever mentioning her marketing tactics; and, more generally, pointing at symbolic discriminations without analyzing the culture industry as a whole, with its endless ability to absorb negativity, exploit margins, swallow and recycle criticism, and gradually shift from mass promotion to a more timely marketing of differences—as it precisely chose to do around the end of the 1980s. The problem with disregarding the genealogy of capitalism or the critique of market domination in works by Deleuze, Lyotard, or even Paul Virilio, or with splitting Derrida's critique of logocentrism from the political context of France's late 1960s, is that one risks having these works speak the very language of late capitalism. One risks mistaking them for what they clearly denounced: the promotion of relativism, of fluctuating and nonreferential values, that is, a praise of the new virtual, global, financial capitalism. Praising the autonomy of the signifier *for itself*, the death of the subject *for itself*, or a general economics of floating signs and drifting symbols detached from any stable standard, only gives food for thought to management gurus, postmodern sociologists, and the intellectual lobbies of a "self-controlled" society. Maybe such readings of French Theory are also a direct effect of the changing American university, or of what Bill Readings calls the "university in ruins," since the university *too* has to comply with the new dogmas, the dogmas of self-regulation, of a paradigmatic Internet network, and of the ultimate free market. Academia too has no other choice than to favor circulation over production, information over labor, and to break down all barriers to the dissemination of intellectual commodities. Maybe so, but the result, still, is to risk turning real social critics into trendy conservatives.

All "traveling theories," as the late Edward Said once called them, carry with them such a risk, for they have always involved a disconnection from a specific context and reconnection with a new one—in this case, disconnection from a certain Continental notion of writing, from the horizon of Marxism and revolution, and from a timely critique of semiology and the linguistic turn. And reconnection with many American traditions and particularities, to which any import *has* to connect if it wants to become an integral part of the receiving culture. Reconnection with a tradition of textual ontology and literary irony, best represented by the New Critics of the 1940s, against the "fallacies" of psychology and intentionality. Reconnection too with the American tradition of pragmatism, that of William James but also of Emerson, to whom many of Deleuze's ideas sometimes sound like a distant echo. Reconnection with a historical tradition of subversive counterreadings, a quintessentially American tradition that started with the Founding Fathers and their reinterpretation of the Bible. Reconnection again, much closer in time, with the bold new analysis of schizophrenia, therapy, and marginality inaugurated in the 1950s by the likes of Gregory Bateson or Ronald Laing. *Reconnection* may not be the right term: what should be said here, against the fatherly notion of a "filiation," is that there is a historical *convergence* of the two branches, French *and* American, Foucault *and* Bateson, Deleuze *and* Emerson, Derrida *and* Brooks and Warren—or even Félix Guattari *and* John Cage, as Semiotext(e)'s Sylvère Lotringer would have it.

Last, but not least, this exemplary adventure in intellectual dissemination can also shed some new light on the broader epoch in which it took place, on the decisive context of 1980s America. It can renew our understanding of a decade torn between a brutal conservative backlash and a historical crisis of Americanness, between a financial boom and an identitarian fragmentation, or, in a sense, between Ronald Reagan and Leonard Jeffries. A time of tensions on campus culminating in the harsh PC debates of the 1990s, a time of rhetorical and sometimes vainly lyrical conflicts, were it not for its very real and disastrous number one consequence: the cultural rise and final political triumph of the neoconservatives. Indeed, they first capitalized on threats such as the "death of Western culture" and the "balkanization" of education, and, since September 12, 2001, they have been using the very same line of argument to justify the military imposition of so-called free market democracy anywhere in the *rogue* world. They seemed harmless while they were screaming against Martin Bernal; they look scary now that they are advising the White House on Iraq, Israel, or old Europe. In that sense, French Theory as a unified (and simplified) package probably owes much of its North American recognition to the pamphlets of Roger Kimball and Dinesh D'Souza, to its detractors among Boston University humanists or Rand Corporation scholars, even to all these social scientists and analytic philosophers who keep finding in it "nothing but literature," much more to its foes, in a word, than to its official temples—a handful of departments of English and comparative literature. As Paul de Man had seen before anyone else, theory should probably be defined negatively, based above all on the reluctancy it meets, the resistance it triggers, the hatred and disgust it can often arouse. There is no better evidence of this than the phenomenal success of Camille Paglia when she calls Foucault a "bastard," or of Alan Sokal when he tricks *Social Text* with his own version of "fashionable nonsense"—whenever the *"merde* hits the fan,*"* as a British tabloid once had it.

And across the Atlantic, far from such a state of affairs, there was the simultaneous French erasure of French Theory. Around the beginning of the 1980s, right when the works of Foucault, Deleuze, Lyotard, and Derrida were being put to work on American campuses and in some alternative communities as the theoretical foundation for a new type of politics, those very names were being demonized in France as the epitome of an outdated "libidinal" and leftist type of politics. What we are facing here, in other words, is a perfect chiasm, a symmetrically reversed situation: on the one hand, a society run by a new wave of conservatives, but whose intellectual field, limited to isolated campuses, enjoys a proliferation of radical discourses, minority theories, and bold textual innovations, with little effect on the rest of America's public space apart from the controversies of PC and a few radical best sellers; on the other hand, a country run by a new wave of liberals (François Mitterrand's "socialists"), but whose broad intellectual field, occupying a central role in the public space, has just been taken over by a herd of young center-left humanists, with the result of sweeping away leftist and radical tendencies and replacing them with a universalist moral blackmail still on the front stage in today's France. "The politics of difference leads to fascism," warned Bernard-Henri Lévy in 1977, before he and his friends relegated the intellectual liveliness of the 1970s to the Middle Ages, in favor of a few humanitarian catchwords and a journalistic type of philosophy. The de-Marxization of the French intelligentsia can probably be measured in proportion to the overwhelming success of Marxist dogmas in Parisian circles in the 1960s. And we all know that well-trained Stalinists can be equally zealous in their defense of Stalinism as, later, in their labor of de-Stalinization.

But still, it sometimes feels as if social critique in France in the 1980s had been thrown out with the bathwater. Here is the sad part of the story: while Deleuze, Lyotard, and Baudrillard gradually left the political scene after the deaths of Sartre and Foucault, while Althusser turned to psychoanalysis and Derrida moved toward an ethical endorsement of democracy, and while only a handful of individual figures (Jacques Rancière or Alain Badiou, to name two) chose to resist such an across-the-board intellectual counterrevolution, the "nouveaux philosophes" (themselves often ex-students of Foucault and Derrida) and the old-style moralists were patiently deploying their web throughout leading French institutions—from centrist unions to mainstream media, political circles to new European think tanks. More than twenty years later, now that the last survivors of French Theory have disappeared (Derrida in 2004, Baudrillard in 2007), the neo-Kantians and abstract universalists who forged their reputation in the antitotalitarian stand-ups of the late 1970s are still in power in France, they are still advising governments, still appearing on prime-time TV, still filling up the nonfiction best sellers' lists. All in all, they are one major reason, with their unquestioned essentialism and their daunting vision of an apocalypse of civilization, why the proud French République seems so scared, almost life-threatened, by a few schoolgirls wearing a Muslim scarf, or by the very word *communautariste*—the nightmarish promise of a balkanized society made up of selfish and conflicting radical identity groups, in the view of all French columnists and most French citizens, who all keep identifying such a vision with the contemporary United States. And this very argument has just been voiced again, maybe more hysterically than ever (speak of a change in French politics!), during the run-up to the last presidential elections in France, when Nicolas Sarkozy and his new intellectual allies (from André Glucksmann to Pascal Bruckner) urged a national wake-up call against the twin evils of "cultural relativism" and the decline of Western values, evils both associated with the same old student unrest of May 1968, more demonized than ever today.

And yet, behind such bad news, things are starting to change in France. A change of focus, of language, and a change of generation. Such changes extend from legal battles in favor of homosexual couples or male–female equality to a reconsideration of France's immigration "problem" in the light of its long-overlooked colonial history, from a rejuvenated anticapitalism to various new forms of minority movements—long unthinkable in a country whose legal texts and constitution relegate particular identities, whether sexual or ethnic, cultural or religious, to the "private sphere." French society is now at a time when all these American intellectual currents, forbidden for import over the last three decades, can finally be put to use in making sense of an unprecedented situation. Indeed, pioneering universities and independent publishers are working hard these days to make cultural studies, minority theories, "pop" philosophy, gender analyses, and the postcolonial paradigm not only better known in France (the only major country where prominent theorists behind such currents had not been translated yet), but also critically reformulated to better address specifically French issues. In that sense, it could be that an old gap is finally about to be bridged: just as Nicolas Sarkozy and George W. Bush's obvious agreement on many things smells like one sort of French–American reconciliation, common lines of attack and reflection among activists and left-wing academics on both sides of the ocean look like another sort of timely transatlantic alliance, against social regression and intellectual backlash *here and there*, and, joining forces, against the enduring myth of a profound transatlantic discontinuity. We will be able to work and think and act and march together again, not just French and American free-minded citizens, but also their counterparts anywhere in the world, beyond good old national borders.

So that recounting this story of an American *experience with* a few radical French texts may be more timely today than ever—if one is to fight domination not only with the help of media apparatuses, social tools, and real-life weapons, but also with texts and concepts. For nothing may be more essential to political resistance and intellectual autonomy today than *not* taking for granted texts and discourses, from literature to ideological propaganda. Grounds for action and subversion will be found in the undecidability of meaning, in the construction of a text by the ever-changing community of its readers,[3] in the leeway still to be found in interpreting a canonical work, even in the deliberate stretching of the gap between text and context, signifier and uses, the worship of classics, and the tricks of hermeneutical action, whereas reactionary politics and the locking up of the existing social order will always require, on the contrary, a submission to essentialized texts, to unquestioned canons, to interpretation understood as the revelation by others of a one-sided meaning. Where interpretation is obvious, where it is *not* a question, power reigns supreme; where it is wavering, flickering, opening its uncertainty to unpredictable uses, empowerment of the powerless may be finally possible. The authors usually gathered under the label of French Theory have always been obsessed by such issues, and were indeed convinced that protest does entail a reappropriation of texts and other cultural commodities; notwithstanding the fact that they, more than anyone else, found themselves submitted to such interpretative liberties, especially in the United States. Which is why these authors, their texts, and the endless interpretations they inspire (together forming one cultural continuum) can still help us fashion a future of struggles and world making—within but also beyond higher education, in the United States but also throughout the rest of the world.

July 29, 2007

Introduction

THE SOKAL EFFECT

DURING THE LAST THREE DECADES of the twentieth century in the United States, the names of a few French thinkers took on an aura that up to then had been reserved only for the heroes of American mythology or the celebrities of "show business." One might even play the game of casting the American intellectual world in terms of the Hollywood western: these French thinkers, who were often marginalized in their own country, would certainly have the leading parts. Jacques Derrida would be Clint Eastwood, so often cast as the lone pioneer, enjoying unchallenged authority and endowed with the imposing mane of a conqueror. Jean Baudrillard could almost pass for Gregory Peck, a mixture of bonhomie and dark detachment, not to mention an aptitude for always turning up in unexpected places. Jacques Lacan would play an irritable Robert Mitchum, based on their common attraction to murderous traits and undecidable irony. Gilles Deleuze and Félix Guattari would evoke not so much the spaghetti westerns of Terence Hill and Bud Spencer as the disheveled duo, breathless but sublime, of Paul Newman and Robert Redford in *Butch Cassidy and the Sundance Kid*. And why wouldn't Michel Foucault be a kind of unforeseeable Steve McQueen, with his knowledge of prison, his disquieting laughter, and his sharpshooter's independence, appearing in the top spot above all the other players in this cast, the darling of the public? And let's not forget Jean-François Lyotard as Jack Palance, with his rugged heart, Louis Althusser as James Stewart, with his melancholic profile, and, in the female leads, Julia Kristeva as Meryl Streep, mother courage and sister of exile, and Hélène Cixous as Faye Dunaway, a woman unfettered by any models. An improbable western, in which the sets would become characters, the Indians' cunning would lead them to victory, and we would wait in vain for the glistening cavalry to burst onto the scene.

The fact is that throughout American culture, from electronic music to the Internet, from conceptual art to mainstream cinema, from (especially) the academic arena to debates on culture and politics, these French authors, beginning around the early 1980s, reached a level of official notoriety and underground influence in the United States that they never achieved in their own country. Their names, while hardly those of any screen idols, became no less intensely overcoded as they were gradually Americanized and their French accents faded; and these names became inevitable reference points across the Atlantic, whereas in their country of origin the scope of this phenomenon was never truly appreciated. Until one autumn a few years ago, when a short-lived controversy began to play itself out.

At the beginning of October 1997, France found itself in the spotlight of the world media. A few weeks earlier, a beloved English princess had died there in an automobile accident. A few months later, the last World Cup soccer tournament of the century would be taking place there as well, after all the necessary preparations. In the meantime, one of those intellectual debates that frequently divide the editorialists erupted, this time, on the front pages of all the newspapers, marking out an unstable split at the very center of the mediatic-intellectual arena in France, a split that seemed somewhat obsolete insofar as its terms had almost been forgotten. At issue was a book with the French title *Impostures intellectuelles,* published by Odile Jacob and authored by two physicists, the American Alan Sokal and the Belgian Jean Bricmont.[1] The two authors dissect what they call the "jargon" and the "charlatanism," the "veritable intoxication with words," and the "disdain for facts and logic" on the part of an intellectual current which they present, "for convenience" (or as they put it in the French version, "pour simplifier"), as "postmodernism."[2] This current is characterized by "the more or less explicit rejection of the rationalist tradition of the Enlightenment" and "a cognitive and cultural relativism that regards science as nothing more than a 'narration,' a 'myth,' or a social construction among many others." Its targets were almost all French, authors such as "Gilles Deleuze, Jacques Derrida, Félix Guattari, Luce Irigaray, Jacques Lacan, Bruno Latour, Jean-François Lyotard, Michel Serres and Paul Virilio,"[3] to whom they add, as the book progresses, Jean Baudrillard, Julia Kristeva, and Michel Foucault. Sokal and Bricmont denounce "the manifest *irrelevance* of the scientific terminology" sometimes used by these authors, which leads them not only to "confused thinking" but also to "irrationalism or nihilism." The two authors' intention is thus, as stated in a somewhat cursory parenthetical remark, "to defend the canons of rationality and intellectual honesty that are (or should be) common to all scholarly disciplines."[4] They set out to show, with unwavering self-assurance, that "the king is naked" (a phrase they like to repeat): from the "new religion" of Lacanian mathematics to Baudrillard's "hyperspace with multiple refractivity," Sokal and Bricmont judge quite simply that "if the texts seem incomprehensible, it is for the excellent reason that they mean precisely nothing."[5]

To this challenge, pundits and mainstream newspapers responded in battle order. In *Le Monde*, Marion Van Renterghem stigmatized the "old saw" of such an "exercise in scientism"; she was joined by Julia Kristeva, according to whom this "anti-French intellectual enterprise" betrays the "Francophobia" evoked across the Atlantic by the "aura" of the thinkers in question.[6] Following their lead, Roger-Pol Droit scoffed at what he called the "scientifically correct," while in *Libération* Robert Maggiori called rather on the Surrealists, anxious to know if we would soon be "asking if it is scientifically legitimate to say of the earth that it is 'blue like an orange.'"[7] Jean-François Kahn, for his part, sent both sides packing—both the "morgue of scientism" and the "intellectualist logorrhea that hides an utter void beneath scientific jargon"—demanding that "the pre- and post-1968 ideology" (in which he places the thinkers in question) should agree at least to "begin to examine [their] conscience."[8] While Jean-Marie Rouart praised the "invigorating breath of fresh air" blowing over a "rhetoric of verbiage,"[9] Angelo Rinaldi, with his customary verve, made fun of these "doctors à la Molière," as he conceives of our celebrated thinkers, now "caught red-handed in the act of petty theft."[10] Jean-François Revel, for his part, poured out a less ordinary sort of gall, in order to attack, with more virulence than Sokal and Bricmont would have dreamed of, the "postmodern arrogance" revealed by "this foolishness called *French Theory*," that is, the arrogance of "reactionaries [who have] elevated chicanery into a system": erasing the differences "between true and false, good and evil," as Revel accuses Derrida of doing, would amount to nothing less than "falling back into the conceptions of the Nazis . . . and turning one's back on all the victories achieved by the true Left over the past century."[11] This is the same spiteful attack that allowed someone like Jean-Jacques Salomon, in *Le Monde,* to compare the theories of Bruno Latour with those of Mussolini. A more moderate tone was struck in the *Nouvel Observateur;* there everyone took advantage of the "affair" to sort things out and to defend his or her sacred precinct: Pascal Bruckner praised the French style of essayistic writing, as embodied in Jean Baudrillard, for example, over and against the "jargon peddlers of structuralism," whereas Didier Éribon, siding with Foucault against some of his imitators, called on us not to confuse the "constructionism" inherited from these thinkers with its "irrationalist" distortion.[12] Amid all the tumult, two types of remark passed unnoticed. In its usual satirical tone, *Le Canard enchaîné* suggested that the authors targeted by Sokal and Bricmont are, in the United States, "the equivalent in philosophy of what Post-its are in paper supplies: they get pasted up everywhere,"[13] a rare allusion to the whole American machinery of fashionable citations and the splicing together of texts. Significant in another way, but in a mode that was almost as anodyne, was the occasional confession that in France the works in question are dead and buried. *Marianne* announced that "the great postwar debates are finished,"[14] whereas *Le Monde* wondered: "why publish in France . . . a book condemning philosophical vagaries that no longer take place here."[15]

Aside from the transoceanic fortunes of a certain current of French thought, featured from time to time in our magazines under the reductive theme of "the French intellectual [as] an export commodity,"[16] what the polemic suddenly revealed was a French–American divide that was twofold. First, a divide in intellectual history, in terms of which the theoretical battles in France in the 1970s, now long settled in France itself (in favor of the "antitotalitarian humanism" that emerged victorious), still inflame American universities—and have done so for more than twenty years now. Then another divide emerged, a consequence of the first, this time as a split between two fields of knowledge, which explains why so many French commentators falsely interpreted Sokal and Bricmont's project, according to the old transatlantic prism, as a declaration of war against our great thinkers; such commentators were incapable of reading into this project the American intellectual debates of the last twenty years, for Sokal and Bricmont's true targets were, in the end, less the

French thinkers they attacked than the American universities that, in staking a claim on these thinkers, encouraged a double "regression," both identity-based and relativist, as the Canadian Michel Pierssens commented.[17] French readers were able, at best, to hear only indirect or superficial echoes of the terms that loomed behind the "affair," and they were thus unable to decipher these terms in all their implications: cultural studies, constructionism, posthumanism, multiculturalism, canon wars, deconstruction, "political correctness." These words, beyond their falsely familiar resonances, are bound up with the upheavals of the last thirty years not only in the humanities but in the American university as a whole. Even further, they refer back to the problematic articulation that gradually took shape, through various crises and polemics, between the intellectual field and the political arena, between discourse and subversion, but also between the nation and its multiple identities. For better or worse, this larger evolution determines, still today, global intellectual debate; and it explains, as an indirect consequence, both the new imperialist and neoconservative order in the period after September 11, 2001, and the impotence on the part of any left-leaning force that would oppose it. Such are the stakes of this curious category of *French Theory,* and hence of the present book: to explore the political and intellectual genealogy, and the effects, even for us and up to today, of a creative misunderstanding between French texts and American readers, a properly structural misunderstanding—in the sense that it does not refer simply to a misinterpretation, but to differences of internal organization between the French and American intellectual spheres. Thus we will guard against judging this misunderstanding in terms of a "truth" of the texts, preferring to this suspect notion the fecundity of cross-purposes and the unexpected turns of a biased reading, or of what—in a completely different cultural context—the Japanese place under the rubric of "functional beauty" (*yô no bi*). But, in order to understand these divergences and their creative role, we must first recall that before the "Sokal affair" erupted, the "hoax" known by the same name had already been perpetrated—though it caused much less of a stir in France—thus placing the American political stakes more clearly in the foreground.

In 1996, Alan Sokal submitted to the editors of the well-known cultural studies journal *Social Text* a long article titled "Transgressing the Boundaries: Toward a Transformative Hermeneutics of Quantum Gravity."[18] A compendium of pseudoscientific formulas and real quotations from authors (mostly French, in fact, ranging from Derrida to Kristeva) referred to collectively as "postmodernism," the article is a parody that pretends to call into question the reality of the physical world and the postulates of science. But it is a parody that hides behind an argument based on authority, and it is all the more troubling in that it relies on authors and concepts that had long been celebrated in the United States; it is also troubling that the journal's editors, incapable of discerning the scientific countertruths with which Sokal filled the article, accepted it for publication (in a special issue on the "science wars"). In order to demonstrate what he sees as the ravages of "cognitive relativism" inherited from "French theory," Sokal forces the parallels, placing on the same level "equality" in set theory and in radical feminism, "displacement" in the Lacanian unconscious and in quantum physics, or "general relativity" in Einstein and in Derrida—whereas the readers of *Social Text*, and first of all its editor, Andrew Ross, found nothing objectionable in it. One month after the article was published, Sokal revealed the hoax in *Lingua Franca*: his text was nothing but a pastiche aiming to show up "the intellectual arrogance of Theory—meaning postmodern *literary* theory," and to unmask "this silliness . . . emanating from the self-proclaimed Left."[19] The polemic quickly worked its way into the mainstream press—this in a country where the latter rarely pays any notice to intellectual debates, much less academic quarrels. The *New York Times* ran a front-page story, bizarrely giving as examples of the postmodern jargon targeted by Sokal "words like 'hegemonic' and 'epistemological.'"[20] Beyond this, major daily newspapers published a mound of articles, many of a populist and violently anti-intellectual bent, attacking in turn the "gaudy silliness" and the "patois" behind which certain academic charlatans disguise their lack of learning, the "denial of known reality" by "trendy academic theorists . . . whose pretentions obscure their nakedness" and whose critical credentials are those of a "faux Left," or "the corruption of clear thought and clear language" in academic works profusely quoting some French references.[21] More conservative tabloids, in the mold of the *New York Post*, took issue with an entire "pseudo-scholarship" best exemplified by the "dubious factoids in the Afrocentric canon" and accused of perverting the students, making them "waste their precious college years."[22]

Two specifically American aspects of this Sokal *effect* are particularly revealing. On the one hand, reactions on the part of the American universities in question were scarce, as if these institutions were embarrassed at having to translate such a debate into the vulgar language of the mainstream press—with the exception, that is, of a provocative intervention from the famous theorist Stanley Fish, who in the *New York Times* compared the laws of science with the rules of baseball.[23] On the other hand, Marxist intellectuals and journals were particularly virulent, defending Sokal's political pedigree by reminding readers that he had taught mathematics in Nicaragua under the Sandinistas, and denying the high priests of cultural studies or deconstruction any right to call themselves "leftists"—a label, however, with which the Right adorns them much more often than they claim it for themselves. From Brazil to Italy and from Japan to the columns of *Le Monde,* the global press soon began to echo the terms of the affair. Most often it denounced Sokal's "scientism," while also criticizing the excesses of an academic "clique," a local version of which exists in almost all of these countries (with the exception of France), each of which has imported some form of American-style cultural studies or "constructionism." Bruno Latour, in a parable that remains well known, evoked Sokal's vision of France as "another Colombia" with its "hard drug dealers" ("derridium" and "lacanium") threatening American universities with an addiction as bad as crack, making them forget the "joys" of campus life and the "daily dose of analytic philosophy" they had taken before.[24]

What constituted a new discovery for many people in France—namely, that there had been such a penetration of French authors into the tissue of American intellectual life, or that such a battle was raging for the symbolic monopoly of the term "leftist"—was thus, the previous year in the United States, only another episode (albeit one that received greater media coverage) in a conflict that for some twenty-five years had pitted "humanists" against the "masters of suspicion," or "conservatives" against "multiculturalists" in the universities and in certain segments of American society. In a word, it was an epiphenomenon in relation to an ideological polarity that had fully permeated American intellectual life but was absent from the French scene. Constructing a genealogy of this polarity requires that we survey certain American modes of reading the French authors in question—ways of reading that made it possible to decontextualize and appropriate these authors' texts, and to give them an often crucial role in the social and political debates in contemporary American culture. One could thus attempt to grasp the "process of selection . . . a process of labeling and classification," to use Pierre Bourdieu's terms,[25] through which some American academics—not without careerist motivations—were able to draw from these authors the watchwords of the 1980s. And were able, in addition, to mobilize their troops, the rank-and-file readers ready to pounce on their new enemies: the "text" as the product of an "author" and containing a "meaning," the false neutrality of an "imperialist Reason," "universalism" as a weapon of the West, or else the "canon" as a form of literary colonialism. These terms punctuated a certain political radicalization of academic discourse, an approach in which the French authors, or at least those who were aware of it, did not really recognize themselves. It was necessary then to carry out several mediating operations in order to produce a new political discourse on the basis of these French texts. The first of these operations, one of the most difficult to grasp empirically, is one that gradually made it possible to unite the various authors concerned into one homogeneous entity, a veritable naturalized corpus and a source of complicity among its users. It remained only to dub the final package "French theory" (following the appellation that appeared in the second half of the 1970s), "poststructuralism" (for the purposes of intellectual history),[26] or else "French postmodernism," according to the term most often used by its detractors. It is also interesting to note that in France the ephemeral cult of the "high priests of the French university"[27] (who were too close, in a sense, to even require a distinctive rubric), and then their rapid eclipse, prevented them from being united within a single category. Only a gesture of rejection or direct opposition made it possible to assign them a unifying label—whether it was a question of the famous "hermeneutics of suspicion" evoked by Paul Ricoeur at the beginning of *Freud and Philosophy,* or of the myth of a homogeneous and localizable *pensée 68* popularized in a more polemical mode by Luc Ferry and Alain Renaut, who used this term to lump together the authors in question and to denounce their "antihumanism" and "irrationalism," despite the fact that the militants of May '68 referred much more to Marcuse, Henri Lefebvre, or even Guy Debord than to Deleuze, Foucault, or Derrida.[28]

These ten or twelve more or less contemporaneous writers, whose American admirers and French opponents tend to group them into a school of thought and a unified movement, can be associated in this way only at the price of some very debatable rapprochements. A few refrains of the period might lead one to form an exclusively negative community among them: the threefold critique of the subject, of representation, and of historical continuity, a threefold reading of Freud, Nietzsche, and Heidegger, and the critique of "critique" itself, since all of them interrogate in their own way the German philosophical tradition. It would be difficult, then, to spontaneously bring together Foucault's "micro-physics of power," Derrida's "dissemination" of traces, Deleuze's "flows" and "connections" on planes of immanence, and Baudrillard's "hyperreal space" of simulations—except, that is, by default, because one finds in them none of the filiations, whether Kantian, dialectical, or phenomenological, claimed by their predecessors. Not to mention the fact that a great number of disagreements, both intellectual and political, divided them over the years. One need only cite the debate between Derrida and Foucault on madness and reason in Descartes, in which the former denounced what he saw as the latter's "structuralist totalitarianism," and was reproached in turn with exercising his "minor pedagogy" of "textualization."[29] Likewise, in countering the "textualism" with which Derridean deconstruction is often reproached, Deleuze declared: "For me, a text is only a small gear in an extra-textual machine."[30] One might also recall Baudrillard's injunction to *Forget Foucault,* in an essay published under that title in 1977—to which the interested party retorted, "I would have more problems remembering Baudrillard."[31] Or one could evoke the polemical remarks made by the latter, who mocked Lyotard's idea that "only capital takes pleasure" (whereas Lyotard vigorously denounced Baudrillard's theses on "the end of the social"), while at the same time criticizing the "overwhelming versatility of desire in Deleuze."[32]

Rather than forcing open the "black box" of the texts, the approach adopted here in recounting this American adventure in French theory consists rather in a description of the social circulation of signs, the political use of quotations, the cultural production of concepts. But it is nonetheless true that for such a category to exist, one must assume a certain taxonomic violence at the expense of the singularity of the works, as well as of their explicit divergences. Thus the use made here, without quotation marks, of the term French theory refers less to any possible intellectual validity such a grouping may have than to the sheer omnipresence of these two words in the American university since the end of the 1970s—the abbreviated sign for a classification, the seal of an affiliation, and a poorly identified discursive object, but one that was taken up in

concert by thousands of commentators. It is above all a way to acknowledge and address this phenomenon.

After the gesture of gathering these authors together, there came the
operations of labeling and "branding," the reorganization of concepts,
and a redistribution in the practical arena. These operations, too, must
be surveyed, in their audacity and in all their ingenuity. They are what
gave to these texts a political use-value that was specifically American,
and that sometimes—according to the whims of critical rereadings or
productive misinterpretations—reinvented works that in France had become trapped in their editorial and publishing straitjackets. They set up,
in *terra Americana,* an original space of reception for works that were in
no way predisposed to be read more widely there than in France. But this
certainly was the case—to such a degree that they insinuated their traces
into the most unexpected recesses of the dominant culture industry, from
electronic music to Hollywood-style science fiction, from pop art to the
cyberpunk novel. And to the point that allusions to their ideas or their
authors were sprinkled into the subjective references and conversational
codes specific to certain milieus and were thus gradually disseminated
into the various pockets of a constantly changing and process-oriented
culture given over entirely to the laws of the market.

The analysis of a primarily academic phenomenon of intellectual
transference, taking place in the isolated conditions that exist in the university in the United States, does not preclude a search for its curious
avatars among the New York art gallerists or California screenwriters,
in the romans à clef or even the vague and off-base reference to Baudrillard and Virilio by the all-powerful Michael Crichton in denouncing the
Internet in 1997 as a "soul-dissolving hallucination" and a "technology
[whose] false promises make us less human."[33] Moving beyond anecdote, the question becomes how such trenchant texts, often quite difficult to access, could come to be woven so deeply into the American
cultural and intellectual fabric—to the point of inspiring a journalist to
compare this "French invasion" to the "British invasion of pop music
a decade earlier."[34] The answer to this question leads to certain themes
which, regardless of how little known they may be in France, have been
no less influential in the relatively dynamic global and cultural context of
the first few years of this millennium: the recent history and crises of the
university in the United States; the American cultural industry, with all
its resources *and* its limitations with regard to questions of identity; the

inventiveness of a *pragmatics* of the text (its capacity to be used, to operate, as is the case with all cultural products) that a certain French elitism
has for too long judged with contempt; but also the deployment in the interstices of domination—and far from Paris—of a new global discourse
on micropolitical resistance and subalterity, a discourse not necessarily
related to the "antiglobalization" wave that our Left humanists like to
vaunt, a discourse that is deliberately "textualist" and too rarely militant, but a discourse from which some new ideas may be drawn.

It is a question, in the end, of the virtues of decontextualization, or
of what Bourdieu called the "denationalization" of texts. If in leaving behind their country of origin they lose some of the political force that gave
rise to them, these "traveling theories" (to use Edward Said's expression)
can also gain a new power on their arrival in a new place. This power
has to do with an unblocking made possible by the recomposed theories,
and with the enigma of fruitful institutional divergences between the site
of origin and that of reception, which are rarely homologous: the fact
that French philosophers were imported by American *literary* writers
and scholars, that the question of revolution resounded there along with
that of minorities, that authors published by Gallimard and Minuit were
published in the United States by university presses or small alternative
publishers—all these factors make up so many creative dissymmetries. It
is this same force, created by uprooting a discourse from its original context, that made possible a similar transfer in the past, when the French
purveyors of Hegel and Husserl (such as Levinas, Groethuysen, Wahl,
and Kojève) privileged the existential and historical dimensions in Hegel
over the latter's logic and the philosophy of nature, and, in Husserl, the
questions of emotion and imagination (or of a consciousness opened to
things) over the method of transcendental reduction, thus giving birth
to French phenomenology and existentialism—radically innovative at
the time—and to those new "philosophical objects" that came onto the
scene in postwar France: the café waiter and the jazz musician. This inventiveness certainly has its naïvetés and its perverse effects, but it will
be all the more useful to explore it in the case of the American appropriation of French theory because it places us at the crux of the Franco-
American cultural chiasmus. For, at the same moment when Foucault,
Lyotard, and Derrida were becoming ubiquitous in the American university, their names were being systematically eclipsed in France. This
ideologically motivated dismissal, intended to block the path to what

French republicanists see as the identitarian "folklore" and the "crumbling away" of the subject, is not unrelated to the fact that, more than twenty years later, France's fine "universalism" is often no more than a mask concealing the poverty of a certain intellectual provincialism. In 1979, Bernard-Henri Lévy clearly announced the program of this new French "anticommunitarianism," and the dreary transfer of power that was being played out: "Every politics based on the primacy of difference is necessarily fascist,"[35] he thundered, citing (in no particular order) Guy Hocqenghem and neofeminism, after having clearly identified his enemies two years earlier—"technology, desire, and socialism"; hence the necessity to go "against materialism and materialism alone."[36] A few months later, in the leading article of the first issue of *Le Débat*, Pierre Nora stated the new rules, both moral and ideological, of the "regime of intellectual democracy" that the journal envisioned, in order no longer to be a "slave of the masters of suspicion."[37] And five years later, in an essay that was very controversial before this sort of thing became the norm, Luc Ferry and Alain Renaut attacked the "philosophies of difference," their "terroristic methods," and, in formulas anticipating Sokal's complaints, the unreadable "absurdity" of these "philosophists."[38]

Times had changed. It was a change that the American adventure coinciding with French theory will thus allow us to reinterrogate, in order perhaps to draw from it some perspectives on the future. For the detour through this false elsewhere that is America, through the humble history of these (at first) illicit campus purveyors and translators, speaks to us *a contrario* of that "French intellectual landscape" which sociologists and journalists there describe today as a field of ruins—thus enriching their already overstuffed publishers, without ever explaining to us anything about this lunar landscape. In sum, the paths followed by flesh-and-blood Americans and by these overlooked mediators, the micronarratives of the lives of these anonymous purveyors without which no true intellectual *détournements* could ever take place, and all the salutary betrayals that this entails, may well refer the French back to themselves rather than to academic rituals or to the ironies of transference. And they might teach all of us to look again at these bright flashes from three decades ago, labeled by intellectual history, neutralized by the dominant thinking, or quietly turned into museum pieces representing some last avantgarde from a bygone world, whereas those who set off these flashes, the witnesses to the emergence of an era, already described precisely what makes up the present, our present, and its new dangers—power over life, subjectless tribes, faceless terror, an imperial network and its machinations, the reactionary sword, and the identitarian church, but also the forces of microresistance and its less visible interstices. To the invention of *French theory* there might then correspond today—better late than never—a few lessons provided by the *American experience*.

PART I

The Invention of a Corpus

1

PREHISTORIES

American culture as distinct from our own—considered to be
distinct from our own the way that Chinese culture is—this is
purely and simply a European invention.

ANDRÉ MALRAUX, *The Conquerors*

The American adventure with French theory has its deepest roots in a
history that is itself too old, chaotic, and multiple to trace its contours
in only a few pages—much less to exhaust all those contextual factors,
such as political history and the memories of the exiled, with which intellectual history maintains a curious relationship, one that is fragile,
uncertain, and very different from the causalism applied to other parts of
the larger historical narrative. Let it suffice, then, to lay out some markers here, to point out certain passages, in order to evoke the atmosphere
of an uncertain primal scene. And, more specifically, to give some attention to a few examples of contact and influence during the immediately
preceding period (from the 1930s to the 1950s) between the French and
American intellectual traditions and between two triumphalist cultures
whose mutual hierarchical relations, around the middle of the century,
were in the process of being reversed.

There are three histories that must be evoked, however succinctly.
The first is that of the French artistic and intellectual exiles in the United
States between 1940 and 1945, who constitute less an origin than a pre-
figuration; the second is the history of the three great French intellectual exports from the period immediately following the war (Surrealism,
Sartrean existentialism, and the historical investigations of the *Annales*
group); and the third is that of an inaugural date, the conference held at

Johns Hopkins University in October 1966, which—retrospectively—became something of a founding event. This last will also provide an opportunity to touch on some of the broader American paradigms that began to undergo a crisis in the 1960s, in order to understand how the reading of French authors could represent a desired alternative, the only means by which to reconcile an oppositional approach and a faith in the future and to reestablish links with a certain American tradition of freedom—because, in a sense (as Vincent Descombes put it), "the text we fall in love with is the one in which we never cease to learn what we already knew."[1]

From Exile to Export

Until the Japanese attack on Pearl Harbor in December 1941, the United States represented the only viable land of asylum from the Europe of refugees and coups d'état—a provincial antipode, to be sure, but, relatively speaking, an Eldorado of peace and prosperity. In fact, during the ten-year rise of Nazism, the United States gradually became the refuge for European arts and letters. These years of American exile, which marked the de facto end of the United States' cultural isolationism, were decisive in a number of ways: first, for the itineraries of the exiles who, although they rarely evoked this period, composed some of their most important works there; then for the itineraries of certain American artists who were able to directly absorb elements of the European avant-garde; and finally as a kind of hinge, since this period is also that of a historic transfer of artistic and cultural hegemony, from Paris to New York. If New York "stole the idea of modern art" that had been constructed in Europe, according to the polemical thesis of Serge Guilbaut, this transfer of hegemony was less the result of a deliberate overall strategy—despite the antidecadent and soon anticommunist zeal of Clement Greenberg's and Harold Rosenberg's critiques—than the consequence of an unprecedented historical promiscuity. And painting is not the only thing at stake here. In every domain, the inevitable, and more or less felicitous, contacts between the local innovators (who in many cases had themselves visited Europe between the wars) and these exiled "strangers in paradise" helped determine the postwar orientation of several deep tendencies of Western culture—this through a mixture of subterranean influence and critical emulation. There were the ephemeral collaborations between

American social sciences and the exiled thinkers of the Frankfurt School, and the growing divergences that ensued between the functionalist, and soon the cybernetic, approach of the Americans (from Paul Lazarsfeld to Harold Lasswell) and the German critical paradigm. There was the shift from a "logical positivist" school of thought, which before the war was still quite isolated and was bound up with Germanophone emigration, to a new polarity that would be perpetuated during the cold war between "analytic" and "Continental" philosophy. There was the impact that German expressionism, together with the novelists who turned to screen writing (as a way to supplement their income), had on Hollywood film production in the 1940s. And there was, of course—although it was denied by both sides—the influence of Surrealism in exile on progressive young American artists. There are so many intersections and crossings that it is impossible to do justice to them in a few lines, but their living, or even repressed, memory would mark transatlantic intellectual relations for decades to come.

Between Hitler's arrival in power and the definitive occupation of the "zone libre" in France, and between the founding of the first mutual aid organizations and the heroic feats of the Emergency Rescue Committee (and of its representative in Marseille, Varian Fry) in 1941, there were no fewer than 130,000 Germans and twenty thousand French who went to the United States, despite the restrictions on immigration and the dangers inherent in departure. Among them were a large number of major figures of European art and culture: Theodor Adorno, Hannah Arendt, Ernst Bloch, Bertolt Brecht, André Breton, Ernst Cassirer, Marc Chagall, Walter Gropius, Max Horkheimer, Fernand Léger, Claude Lévi-Strauss, Maurice Maeterlinck, Thomas and Heinrich Mann, Jacques Maritain, André Masson, Henri Matisse, Mies van der Rohe, Piet Mondrian, Benjamin Péret, Jules Romains, Denis de Rougement, Saint-Exupéry, Saint-John Perse, Arnold Schoenberg . . . Aside from religious leaders, the only refugees the American administration allowed to enter the country in excess of the quotas were university professors. Thus, from the mid-1930s, American institutions of higher education created lasting ties with European intellectual circles. Columbia University hosted the Institut für Sozialforschung (the future Frankfurt School). Alvin Johnson's New School created a department of social and political science in which some of the most prominent European researchers taught. The University of Chicago supported the work of refugees associated with the Bauhaus.

And the committee established by the Rockefeller Foundation, keenly interested in this exodus of minds, signed agreements with the Institut d'Ethnologie of the Musée de l'homme and the Centre de Documentation Sociale in Paris. It was under the aegis of several universities that, on the initiative of Alexandre Koyré and Louis Rapkine, the École Libre des Hautes Études was founded in New York in November 1941; this was the only French institution of higher learning ever created in the United States. Courses by Georges Gurvitch and Claude Lévi-Strauss, lectures on Baudelaire and Valéry, as well as Denis de Rougemont's seminar on "the idea of power" were avidly attended by many American auditors, curious students, or Left intellectuals taking advantage of the windfall. The school's journal, *Renaissance,* reflected the wealth of research being carried out.

We are aware of the importance that the mass culture industry took on for the thinkers of the Frankfurt School after they had traveled across the Atlantic. It remains difficult, however, to evaluate more broadly the long-term theoretical and aesthetic consequences of an exile that was often hard to come to terms with, rich with encounters and with the strangeness of American cities, but marked also by the end of certain privileges. One thing is certain: the exiled all had the more or less brutal experience of being socially marginalized, culturally uprooted, and normatively dispossessed in ways that left lasting traces in their work. As Edward Said noted, this experience means, "for an intellectual, to be unusually responsible to the traveler rather than to the potentate, to the provisional and risky rather than to the habitual, to innovation and experiment rather than the authoritatively given *status quo.*"[2] This condition of traveling alongside, this self-evacuation, but also this new way of listening, had many echoes among the postwar French intellectuals, though of course in a less dramatic way in a context of peacetime. Whereas Sartre "nowhere felt more free than among the crowds in New York,"[3] Foucault praised the freedom of the "foreigner [who] can ignore all those implicit obligations,"[4] and Julia Kristeva, crossing the ocean for the first time in 1973, celebrated the "therapy of exile."[5] On the other hand, when the Surrealists arrived in New York in 1941, they did not share this enthusiasm. The United States did not yet exist on their world map. Aragon hoped that "America afar [would] crumble with its white buildings amid absurd prohibitions," and Breton, true to himself both before and after the war, went from disgust to abomination in describing their "bargain basement pragmatism" and their "imperialist plans."[6]

And yet, whereas Breton and Max Ernst were more interested in Amer-indian and West Indian art than in the America of Charles Sheeler and Edward Hopper, the young successors of these latter, from Arshile Gorky to Robert Motherwell, and soon Jackson Pollock and Willem de Koon-ing, drew a decisive inflection for their work from these contacts—how-ever distant they may have been.

Links did indeed exist between the Surrealists and American artists such as Calder and Joseph Cornell, between Breton and Gorky (on oc-casion), or between the studios of the French artists (on 11th Street) and those of the Americans (on 8th and 10th Streets), where Roberto Matta initiated the American painters into the techniques of free association and "exquisite corpse"—rebaptized in English "Male & Female." But if the Americans tried their hands at an ephemeral "abstract Surrealism," tensions mounted when, galvanized by Greenberg and his colleagues, they turned against French arrogance, the francophilic favoritism of the city's major museums, and a European formalism they regarded as moribund. Various splits occurred between the different aspects of Surrealism, splits that gave birth to the "abstract expressionism" of the New York School and prefigured, within this earlier phase of artistic activity, the tactics of anamorphic displacement, selection, and recom-bination that would enable a handful of university professors to *invent* French theory some thirty years later. For in 1945 it was a question of distinguishing between "bad painters" (Dalí and Magritte, according to Greenberg) and experimenters whose attitudes could still be of some use (Ernst, de Chirico, Man Ray). And it was a question of realizing on the canvas work that was far more rigorous, in an effort to "replace psychic automatism with plastic automatism," as Motherwell put it. It was a question of appropriating Surrealist strategies, but in the service of what was considered to be a more correct and more youthful ideol-ogy, and a greater aesthetic seriousness, as theorized by Greenberg in the virile terms of a new "American vitalism." To separate the wheat from the chaff: this meant taking from the Surrealists their rich reflection on myth and irrationality, but ridiculing their ludic debauches and commu-nist deviations. As Meyer Schapiro summarized the point: "What the Americans learned from the Surrealists was not automatism, but how to be *heroic*."[7] Between the New York exhibition of 1942, "First Papers of Surrealism," and the first prominent American presence in the Mae-ght Gallery retrospective (in 1947), the artistic avant-garde was shifting from one continent to another.

Far from the Franco-American tensions, this period in New York was the golden age of the well-known heterodox Marxist journal, *The Partisan Review,* which broke with the Soviet Union in 1937. It was the era of an urban far Left made up of a number of enlightened bourgeois referred to collectively as the New York Intellectuals. One of the rare circles of nonacademic intellectuals in American history, the group formed around Dwight McDonald, Mary McCarthy, Lionel Trilling, and Edmund Wilson, and was soon joined by the younger Norman Mailer and William Styron. This intellectual circle was not attached to a party but was energetic in its political engagements. Combining literary verve and political courage, they continually animated debate in postwar New York, inviting major European writers to contribute to their journals, including Sartre, Arendt, and the latter's former husband, Günther Anders. The gradual disappearance of this precious intellectual arena—dispersed as it was by individual trajectories and political reversals and soon finished off by the McCarthyite backlash—opened a void at the heart of American public space. At the same time, the demographic boom of students and the rise of the major research universities around new paradigms of knowledge in the United States (legalism, positivism, functionalism) contributed to the technicalization and compartmentalization of an intellectual field that was becoming more and more specialized and, henceforth, almost exclusively academic. It was in this context that three rather fashionable intellectual currents in postwar France crossed the Atlantic.

Transatlantic Antecedents

Nothing better reflects this evolution than the varying reception given to French Surrealism in the United States before and after the war. Beginning in 1931, the date of the first Surrealist exhibition, this reception took place far from the university campuses. On the one hand, some of the most prominent fashion magazines, including *Vogue* and *Harper's Bazaar,* along with several advertising agencies, mediated by the gallerist and impresario Julian Levy, made "superrealist" fantasies (as they called them in the beginning) part of a persuasive sales pitch. Salvador Dalí, playing a game of one-upmanship, was even invited to Hollywood to paint the portrait of Harpo Marx and ended up on the cover of *Time* magazine in 1936. Such events led the historian Dickran Tashjian to conclude that Surrealism was "the first avant-garde movement" to become the object of "avid mass consumption in the American media,"[8] such that it even inspired, in reaction, a self-styled "socialist Surrealism" movement in New York, as well as—with the addition of a prefix we will often encounter—a "post-Surrealist" school in Los Angeles. But if Surrealism became the hottest new commodity, it registered as quite a scandal among the leagues of virtue, who swore to do everything possible to preserve a pious America. The same defensive posture was taken up among the Left rationalists, but this time against the obscurantism of Breton and his admirers: following the lead of the critic Herbert Muller, they accused them of being "actually in the line of the most reactionary movement of the day" and of "exploit[ing] the dark powers that enslave men."[9]

After 1945, the situation was different: these debates ceased to rage, and the field of reception had changed. Aside from the creation in Chicago in 1965 of an authentic (but very confidential) American Surrealist Movement, the decades that followed were a period in which Surrealism was domesticated academically and institutionalized in the university. The anticlerical and pro-communist virulence of the movement was carefully passed over in silence, much to the dismay of Guy Ducornet, who complains that the Surrealism of the sixties was "squeezed dry, dusted off with care, pinned up on a cork board and made pedagogically programmable," placed "under the label of 'French literature' somewhere between Symbolism and Existentialism."[10] Beginning in the 1950s, the appropriation of Surrealism as a docile object of literary history had opened the age of the specialists. Anna Balakian, Breton's biographer, sees it as a "new mysticism" in French literature. Roger Shattuck, in his foreword to the 1968 translation of Maurice Nadeau's *History of Surrealism*, "reappraises" Surrealism as a solely artistic and literary activity, amputating its cognitive and political dimensions.[11] More interesting are works such as those by J. H. Matthews, who introduced Benjamin Péret to the United States, and Mary-Ann Caws, who edited the journal *Dada/Surrealism*, both of whom proposed a more complete and far more daring approach to the movement.[12] But this was at a time when, after the publication of *Surréalisme et sexualité* by Xavière Gauthier,[13] Breton and his companions became the object of a completely different debate: the feminist critique. From the crude deformations of Gwen Raaberg, railing against the "pimpish" and "homophobic" vagaries of early Surrealism, to the more subtle analyses by Susan Suleiman on the objectification of the body, the Surrealist question was henceforth above all—a sign of the times—that of the exclusion or inclusion of women in the movement, its "essentialist sexism," or else its relation to prostitution.[14] During this time, aside from a few retrospectives in American museums, Surrealism disappeared from the United States—except within the walls of the academy.

It was replaced for a while by existentialism, in conformity with the sequence of fashionable phenomena to which the American observer often reduces European cultural life: "Sartre is automatically fashionable now among those who once found Surrealism automatically fashionable," noted the *New Yorker* at the end of 1945.[15] It is true, nonetheless, that in the United States the case of existentialism resembles that of Surrealism in several ways. There was first of all the paradox of an intellectual elite given over to its fascination with Jean-Paul Sartre, with the man as much as with this very French figure of the "total intellectual"—in sharp contrast with the American heroism of normality, that virtue of the ordinary man which in the United States has made the "simple man," from the revolutionary John Adams to President Reagan, the true hero of the nation. There was a paradox also in the sense that Sartre never hid his deep anti-Americanism, primarily cultural but also ideological, beyond any enthusiasms he experienced while he was there in 1945. He often refused dialogue with any Americans, because for Sartre, as Philippe Roger concludes, "any real intellectual *commerce* with the United States was an impossibility."[16] In addition, there was the same large gap between a brief extra-academic fashion effect—based on the exoticism of Saint-Germain and the vogue of a few journalistic refrains—and a more gradual, and deeper, penetration into the universities, the impetus for which was entirely self-generated. Although American philosophy was becoming more and more distant from the Continental tradition, it nonetheless accorded a small place, here and there, for the study of Sartre, while also reading the master selectively in order to Americanize his propositions—even if this meant in fact playing on the fragility of this discipline in the United States. Bridges were thus extended in many directions: toward deism and the question of religion, by fashioning a subjectivist-spiritualist version of the Sartrean system; toward female students, by including in courses certain texts by Simone de Beauvoir, which had the effect of adding feminine voices to philosophy departments and beginning a theorization of the feminist question; toward the "radical empiricism" of William James, the father of American pragmatism, in the name of their common concern for the way in which consciousness is constructed within a world from which it produces meaning; finally, and more broadly, toward the liberal tradition of a "radical individualism" more acceptable across the Atlantic than Sartre's composite of Marxism and German existentialism.[17] Thus formatted for the American university, where students' interest in Sartre allowed certain philosophy departments to increase declining enrollments, existentialism gradually entered into the academic culture: *Being and Nothingness* was translated in 1956 and has been reprinted many times; the American Philosophical Association has devoted conferences and colloquiums to Sartre; in 1962, the creation of the Society for Phenomenology and Existential Philosophy marked the definitive recognition of the phenomenon. And yet, even in an Americanized version, the existentialist bibliography remains an imported corpus whose American fortunes began to decline in the 1970s under the pressure of changes that went far beyond it—student movements, academic specialization, crises in philosophy as a discipline and in the humanities in general.

As for the *Annales* school, its impact in the United States involved more traditional disciplinary factors. As in France, the pioneering work of Marc Bloch and Lucien Febvre, who founded the sixth section of the École pratique des hautes études along with the journal *Annales* in 1947, brought a renewal of the discipline of history, both through a lateral extension, in terms of the history of mentalities, fields of knowledge, or the *longue durée,* and through a vertical metareflection, inspired in particular by German sociology. Just as the target in France was the chronological history of the diplomats, the American history of patriots and pioneer dates was in turn shaken up. But because it intervened in a period in which American historiography was already undergoing drastic changes, the work of the *Annales* did not so much inspire an analogous "school" in the United States as introduce another element that contributed to the renewal of the discipline. In some cases, this work inspired young researchers, such as Steven Kaplan; in others it provided a theoretical grounding, for Peter Burke, for example; in still others it itself became the object of a metahistory, as in the work of Georg Iggers, or it was combined more broadly with a new current of Anglo-American social history, whose most illustrious representatives at the time were E. P. Thompson and Ira Berlin. It was as much a question of convergence as of influence. Moreover, by historicizing and denaturalizing entire segments of social life, from the conjugal bond to medical institutions, the influence of the *Annales* prepared the way for one of the major importations of the following decade—the work of Michel Foucault.

In the end, a twofold phenomenon characterized the reception in the American university of Surrealism, existentialism, and the "new history," a process of double détente which, for that very reason, distinguished them from the coming *invention* of French theory. First, they were transplanted as is, introduced as products of importation, in all the strangeness of their exotic provenance, a distance that was even expected to attract students; and second, through their contact with the relevant disciplines, all three underwent as many adjustments and adaptations as there were convergences between these French currents and certain American themes of the moment—poetry and mysticism for Surrealism, individualism and pragmatism with existentialism, social history and the history of mentalities in the case of the *Annales*. On the contrary, French theory will constitute a creation ex nihilo of the American university, corresponding to certain precise strategies and, more broadly, to an axiological crisis in the humanities. Thus, more than an adapted import, it was to be an entirely new composite creature; hence its more profound and more lasting impact. It is nonetheless the case that this logic of convergences will in turn play a valuable role in the first successes of French theory, a role requiring that these convergences themselves become the object of a systematic treatment, rather than a fragmentary evocation or a mere collection of traces: more than ten years before they were translated into English, at the moment when Foucault and Deleuze were writing their major works, without their being aware of it (or making any use of it), the theme of the "pluralization of the ego" as against the "politics of representation" and the control exercised by psychoanalysis were already central to the work of Norman O. Brown;[18] questions of alternative therapies and of resistance to asylum institutions occupied the antipsychiatry movement of David Cooper and Ronald Laing;[19] and the pioneering work of Gregory Bateson was exploring the idea of "plateaus" and "continuities" while groundbreaking articles such as Frieda Fromm-Reichmann's were calling for an expanded definition of schizophrenia as a "way of living."[20] Of course, actual connections existed between these almost contemporary works: Deleuze and Guattari refer to Bateson, while Laing and Cooper, under the banner of antipsychiatry, helped to prepare Foucault's first anglophone reception. But the most important factor lies elsewhere. Beyond the convenience of the motif of convergence, for all these authors it was a question of searching for new and similar theoretical tools, as against the political impasses and the disciplinary blockages of intellectual fields that were very different, but both of which were confronted, in Berkeley as in Paris, with the urgency of a world in the process of being born, of shattered certainties, of political reflexes that were suddenly obsolete. In this sense, the difference between the Surrealist or existentialist infiltrations of the 1950s and the emergence of French theory twenty years later is above all historical, bound up with the enigmas of an electrified present.

It was an obvious crisis in the democratic capitalist regimes of the "Western bloc" toward the end of the 1960s—and this crisis has been recounted many times—that inspired, on both sides of the ocean, this simultaneous flourishing of radically different bodies of work, like so many seismographs placed on a shaken system of values. On the American side, because this crisis of paradigms was not muffled or diverted by the type of oppositional political institutions present in de Gaulle's France, it was perhaps even more tangible. It took many forms: A crisis of functionalism, as practiced by sociologists and market researchers, accused of quantifying the *socius* and increasing inequalities. A crisis of legalism, invalidated by the civil rights marches that were attempting to obtain what the law had been unable to provide and by the Vietnam warmongers who were imposing the law of the strongest. A crisis of technocratic legitimacy, which the new generation of the liberal and technical professions suspected of being completely out of control, subjugated to the machine, and devoid of all autonomous decision. A crisis of pioneer-style utopianism, to the extent that the refrains of liberal messianism and of the Founding Fathers were no longer persuasive to the younger generations. A crisis of administrative reason, faced with the latent corruption of proliferating managerial teams. Finally, a political crisis, made manifest in the inanity of the political class—headed by President Nixon—as revealed by the Watergate scandal. More than a context, the elements laid out here are those of a heavily charged environment, an entire framework on the verge of crumbling, within which a university that was renouncing its humanist principles opted for headlong flight—specialization, competition, adaptation to the new constraints of the job market. It was within this agitated political and intellectual landscape, at the beginning of this pivotal decade, that one international conference took place among the many aimed at enhancing the reputation of their host campuses, a conference that would be reinterpreted later, not without reason, as the birth, *avant l'heure,* of French theory.

The Invention of Poststructuralism (1966)

If the students at Nanterre and Columbia spoke a common anti-imperialist language, the French and American intellectual landscapes had never seemed so far apart as they did in 1966. In France this was the "annum mirabile" of structuralism, to use the expression of François Dosse:[21] major texts appeared by Barthes (*Critique et vérité* [*Criticism and Truth*]) and Lacan (*Écrits*); Foucault's *Les Mots et les choses* [*The Order of Things*], published in the spring, enjoyed an unexpected public success, showing up even on the vacation beaches in the summer; and the slogans "death of man" and "paradigm shift" appeared on the front pages of major newspapers. If it was ever possible to spread the image of a coherent school, a concerted structuralist movement, it was indeed during this year. And if there was ever a time when the various projects aiming to *decenter* the question of meaning or to make a certain *de-semanticization* operative within the human sciences—whether in linguistics, history, or psychoanalysis—were for a moment in solidarity with one another, it was at this time. As Deleuze noted three years later, the "authors referred to as 'structuralists' by recent practice may have no essential point in common other than this: sense, regarded not at all as appearance but as surface effect and position effect, and produced by the circulation of the empty square in the structural series."[22] Except that this empty square, which up to then had obsessed only the surveyors of very abstract surfaces, suddenly took on the more romantic colors of a political fire, of aesthetic emotion, of pathic investment. This mad "structuralist passion," as Derrida himself recognized, was a "frenzy of experimentation."[23]

During this time in the United States, divisions remained firm between the student protests, the restrained content of the courses, and the bewildered wait-and-see attitude of civil society. The first were reading Marcuse or Norman O. Brown, the second were ritualistically teaching the logical positivists (in philosophy) or the Russian formalists (in literature), whereas the America of comic books and light romances did not witness the emergence of any frankly subversive best sellers. Although the decisive encounter between Claude Lévi-Strauss and Roman Jakobson took place in the United States, the structuralist vogue did not catch on there, neither in bookstores nor on the campuses. The main translations from French in philosophy and the human sciences, in this latter half of the 1960s, were the essays of Émile Bréhier, Paul Ricoeur, Merleau-Ponty, and Pierre Teilhard de Chardin, who, rather surprisingly, was still being widely read. In 1966, the translation of Lévi-Strauss's *La Pensée sauvage* (*The Savage Mind*) and an issue of *Yale French Studies* devoted to structuralism were met with the most complete indifference.[24] The editor of the latter, Jacques Ehrman, who taught French literature at Yale, was in fact the only American professor at the time to propose an introductory course on structuralism.

It was precisely in order to make up for this lag that two professors at Johns Hopkins, Richard Macksey and Eugenio Donato, had the idea of organizing a conference that would bring together some of the major French figures working at the time. With support from the Ford Foundation, the Baltimore campus hosted, from October 18 to 21, an international gathering under the title "The Language of Criticism and the Sciences of Man"—using a formula so unfamiliar to Americans that it reveals, behind the notion of *sciences humaines,* an object that was still untranslatable in the United States. Among the hundred or so presentations on the program, the most anxiously awaited were those of the ten French guests of honor: Barthes, Derrida, Lacan, René Girard, Jean Hyppolite, Lucien Goldmann, Charles Morazé, Georges Poulet, Tzvetan Todorov, and Jean-Pierre Vernant. Roman Jakobson, Gérard Genette, and Gilles Deleuze had also been invited but were unable to make the trip; they nonetheless took the trouble to send a text or a letter which the organizers communicated to the hundreds of listeners in the audience.

What took place in the course of this conference was not immediately clear to the auditors and the American participants, beginning with the links that were forged behind the scenes: Derrida met Jacques Lacan there for the first time, as well as (and especially) the critic Paul de Man, the future herald of American deconstruction, who at the moment was working on a study of Rousseau's *Essay on the Origin of Languages,* as was the somewhat younger Derrida (this is no doubt what brought them together at the time). In one of the first American gestures aimed at unifying these French authors, the two organizers, in their introduction to the published volume, associated these diverse authors in terms of a French Nietzschean filiation: "Nietzsche has now come to occupy the central position that, since the thirties . . . was held by the Gallic Hegel," such that in "recent works of Foucault, Derrida and Deleuze, the shadow, the 'genealogy,' and the empty spaces are Nietzsche's."[25] But, significantly, they waited for the second edition of the published conference papers to add another formula to the title, "The Structuralist Controversy," and to point out in a new preface that this umbrella term is an "operative concept . . . more evident in the language of its detractors and popularizers than in the express statements of those who are supposed to be its main proponents," and that the event in 1966, although it was expected to be a didactic presentation, was in reality the first public "theoretical deconstruction" of the term.[26] In fact, the debates that followed each lecture revealed unexpected disagreements, as much between the speakers and listeners (among whom were J. Hillis Miller, who would become another major American "Derridean," and Serge Doubrovsky) as between the French participants themselves. Thus, Georges Poulet defended the literary imagination against Barthesian structural analysis; Lucien Goldmann distanced himself from Derrida in the name of the "socialization" of texts; and Jean Hyppolite himself, who began his lecture with a question that became famous ("Isn't it too late to speak of Hegel in our age?"),[27] asked Derrida if it is coherent to speak of a structure's "center." As if this shift into neutral territory liberated the French thinkers for a discussion that in France was constrained by the great notoriety of structuralism, the conference testified to a double translation: from the language of the Hegelians and Marxists into a more open consideration of the question of structure, and from the language of the two speakers most commonly associated with structuralism (Barthes and Derrida) into a first critical distancing from it. Aside from Barthes's lecture "To Write: An Intransitive Verb?" it was Derrida's presentation, which he claimed to have written in ten days, that marked the moment, and that remained the outstanding event of the conference; it is still one of the most often read texts of French theory.

In it Derrida first points to the contemporary "rupture" or "disruption" of the "centered structure"; then, in order to clarify this, he refers to the critiques of "metaphysical complicity," or of the "determination of being as presence," proposed by Nietzsche, Freud, and Heidegger.[28]

There follows a critical reading of Lévi-Strauss, who attempts to separate *"method* from *truth"* and to use an "empiricism" that weakens his theory. Against the "ethics of presence" and the "nostalgia of the origin" that still permeate structuralism, Derrida then introduces the decisive concepts of "supplement" and "play" [*jeu*][29]—which the translators will render as "free play" in an effort to evoke the double dimension of irony and space for movement. Derrida's critique of the dominant semiology of the 1960s begins here: the sign is only an "addition" that is "floating" and that comes to "supplement a lack on the part of the signified"; it cannot replace the absent center but must limit itself to "holding [its] place." Hence this *"overabundance* of the signifier, its *supplementary* character,"* which opens the way to deconstruction as an approach to texts operating on this side of the signified, in the absence of every referent.[30] The concluding formulas will soon become canonical in the United States. There Derrida invites us to go beyond this "structuralist thematic of broken immediacy," the "negative, nostalgic, guilty . . . side of the thinking of play," toward its "joyous" and Nietzschean side, a simple "affirmation of a world of signs without fault, without truth, and without origin": between the "two interpretations of interpretation," it is urgent to substitute, Derrida concludes in a programmatic tone, for the one that "dreams of deciphering a truth . . . which escapes play" one that, on the contrary, "affirms play and attempts to pass beyond man and humanism."[31] The point is clear: this lofty structuralism with its rarefied stakes, which the American university knew only in its narratological version (Genette and Todorov), was something that should be left behind in order to move toward a more playful *post*structuralism. The word will not make its appearance until the beginning of the 1970s, but all the Americans present at Johns Hopkins in 1966 realized that they had just attended the live performance of its public birth.

Thus the conference that was supposed to present structuralism to Americans served rather to invent, a few years later, its designated successor, a far more malleable one with two distinct advantages: it had a much looser, and therefore more accommodating, definition, and it did not exist as a homogeneous category on the Old Continent—where this group of thinkers that had gathered for a moment were soon dispersed. An American critic later concluded, somewhat hastily, that structuralism was a mirage, a kind of ectoplasm, and that it had undergone an immediate self-dissolution in the history of ideas: "Today then no one is a structuralist without really ceasing to be one," claimed Hashem Foda.[32] And yet, aside from a few translations that were still private (including another decisive text by Derrida, "The Ends of Man") and the discreet stirrings of a few French departments, it was necessary to wait another ten years for the theoretical and practical avenues opened by this encounter to be explored more fully and effectively. The only immediate effects of this encounter, which everyone would later read as a liminal scene, a founding moment, involved other less exciting consequences. On the institutional level, it usefully strengthened ties between French and American universities, thanks to programs encouraging exchange students and visiting professors, which were established that fall not only with Johns Hopkins but also with Cornell and Yale, the future "golden triangle" of American deconstruction. On the ideological level, it earned the wrath of the far Left, which deplored the absence of Marxist speakers ("except, perhaps, Lucien Goldmann") and stigmatized the "anti-human ideology" and the "idealistic bourgeois linguistics" behind such "a clique of French intellectuals [playing] spectacular language games for an American audience."[33] For it was precisely Marxism, still firmly ensconced in the American university, that provided the only other introduction to French structuralism at the time, particularly through Fredric Jameson; but this was in fact a highly critical introduction denouncing the "textualism" of a "purely verbal" class struggle.[34]

But the massive upheavals that rocked the American university at the time—protests and repression, financial and moral crises, demographic pressures—would soon alter the situation, giving a second, decisive chance to a few French "ideas" presented for the first time, outside of its context, in Baltimore in October 1966.

2

THE ACADEMIC ENCLAVE

> Two apparently contrary currents, equally harmful in their
> effects and ultimately flowing together in their results, presently
> dominate our educational institutions: the tendency toward
> the greatest possible *extension* and *expansion* of education,
> and the tendency toward the *reduction* and the *weakening* of
> education itself.
>
> FRIEDRICH NIETZSCHE, *On the Future of*
> *Our Educational Institutions*

THE FABRIC OF AMERICAN SOCIAL LIFE owes a great deal to the formidable spatiotemporal isolation of the student milieu. From within this
perspective, the student looks back toward the family cell and a childhood itself defined as a world apart, and forward to the responsibilities
of adult life and the constraints of the job market. Between the extended
fantasy of childhood and the work ethic that will follow, the "college
years" constitute a zone of respite, devoted at once to the reinforcement
of norms and to the possibility, in certain strictly delimited circumstances,
of their subversion. Everything conspires to ensure that this transitional
space—a veritable moratorium between the teenager's insouciance and
the grown-up's struggle for survival—is a world much more distinctly
separate than its counterpart in European societies: the geographic distances of the campuses and the more pronounced break from the familial cocoon that this implies, the establishment for young people of this
particular age of a "student life" with group rules and morals that are
to some extent dispensatory, and the importance of ancestral rites that
still subsist in every university. It is in terms of this isolation that one
can measure the distance maintained in the United States between an

intellectual field almost entirely limited to the academic institution and a civil society that tends to see these few years of initiation as a simple passage, a kind of pit stop, a happy interlude. The relative autonomy of the academic phalanstery also explains the purely rhetorical violence of the academic debates: their terms are all the more caustic for being closely confined, so rarely do they have any occasion to pass beyond the campus gates. Full of insults and exaggeration, and carried out in a much more polemical tone than one finds at the Sorbonne, intellectual debate entrusts the art of its dramatization to an ancient stage in a theater that one attempts to keep isolated from the furors of the street. And yet, these "tempests in a teapot" do not always remain within this separate space, lest one forget the major political role of higher education in a country of immigration, where these few years are also the occasion for social-izing—and therefore Americanizing—the new recruits.

Worlds Apart

If one includes everything from the small and diverse liberal arts col-leges to the academies run by Southern televangelists, and from the large public universities (such as UC Berkeley in the West or the City Univer-sity of New York in the East) to the famous private universities of the Ivy League, there are more than four thousand institutions of higher learning in the United States. But those that are integrated into the cen-tral areas of larger cities, where student life is mixed in with the local urban culture, can be counted on one hand—and for that very reason they are all the more famous: they include New York University, which spills into Greenwich Village; UCLA, which has its larger cultural exten-sion in the ex-hippie neighborhood of Venice; and the Berkeley campus, which merges into the teeming street life of Telegraph Avenue. But the norm in these matters is rather the campus at the edge of the woods, in conformity with the agrarian mythology of nineteenth-century America, according to which a bucolic setting far from the vices of the city will serve to guarantee probity, force of character, and academic excellence. Many of these campuses have a more or less newly built science building or "science center" and a Gothic-style dormitory, a little valley bright with autumn leaves, and seasonal rites that are off limits to strangers. Student societies—fraternities for boys and sororities for girls—proudly display the Greek letters that name their houses (Kappa Alpha, Sigma Phi) and follow strict internal regulations inherited from the first campus literary salons of the 1820s. In the spring, graduation ceremonies proceed according to unchanging codes, caps and gowns imprinted with the emblem of the campus and the discreet color schemes of the disciplines (navy blue for philosophy, sky blue for education, etc.). The almost systematic internment of the students—this too as a result of English influence—in dormitories that were once under close surveillance is supposed to ensure academic camaraderie and ethical community among the students. But this is a form of commingling to which the campuses also owe the tradition of students' demands for better living conditions, on the model of the "Bad Butter Rebellion" that shook Harvard in 1766.

The traditional college has multiplied its specific peculiarities. These go to make up the elements of an extra-academic formation—down to the small pleasures of student life or "collegiate culture"—the means of the student's self-definition as he or she appropriates codes unknown outside the campus. Everything, including transgression, plays such a role: "Distinctive dress marked the collegian; hedonism offered new experiences; rejection of professional standards allowed a sublimated form of adolescent rebellion; and, for some, struggle among peers opened new opportunities," as Helen Horowitz has stated.[1] The American college is more ludic than Stakhanovite. Beyond its English and German influences, the dimensions of play, insouciance, and camaraderie are at the heart of its historical justification. Historically, the existential interlude that it provided had to be above all a pleasant moment, prolonging childhood, deferring the harshness of real life, with no obligation to obtain any results or even to work hard in class—to the point that, as Christopher Lucas reveals (in a chapter describing American undergraduates in the first third of the twentieth century), "it was said of some students that they had contrived never to purchase a textbook through the course of their entire undergraduate careers."[2] If contemporary colleges are somewhat more studious, especially the most prestigious (Vassar, Wellesley, Smith, etc.), the student is never under any obligation to study. Hence, among other factors, the very high rate of students who do not complete their studies ("college dropouts"), since 80 percent of high school students enter college, but only 30 percent of them leave with a bachelor's degree. But such autonomy in their functions, which often borders on autarchy, favors the formations of cliques and intellectual sanctuaries, small schools of thought splintered off from one another and strengthened by ties of solidarity and by the signs of recognition characteristic of a highly coded world. That is how it is possible that, on a given campus, there is a peaceful coexistence between those who share this life apart and its initiate's codes, including "corporate managers side by side with third world Marxists; free market economists with free-form sculptors; mandarin classical scholars with postmodern performance artists; football coaches with deconstructive feminists," to cite the inventory à la Jacques Prévert proposed by Gerald Graff.[3]

More seriously, the isolation of the university system also explains the absence in the United States of that crossover figure of the versatile intellectual who participates both in academic conferences and in the general discussion, that "specialist of the universal" invented by the French literary field in the nineteenth century. Simone de Beauvoir was struck by this phenomenon in 1948, during her first visit to the United States, lamenting the "clear-cut divorce between the university world and the living intellectual world," and the "fatalism" of writers who, for their part, are "unable to have any meaningful effect on public opinion."[4] And yet she could have cited the example of a profession that in certain respects—its literary ethos and its ideological interventions in the mass media—parallels the function of the intellectual as it exists in France, or at least used to, some fifty years ago: I'm referring to the profession of university president, as embodied in the humanist projects like those of Clark Kerr (California), the opinions on the times of a James Conant (Harvard), or the lyrical flights of Robert Maynard Hutchins (Chicago). Beyond the monopoly exercised in this domain by the academic institution, the absence of a public intellectual field also has its origins, of course, in American political history. Because of the interweaving of religious references and democratic principles throughout this history, one does not find the sort of sanctification of the secular intellectual's generalist function that occurs in France. This history also points to the celebration of the ordinary man as a political hero, which renders suspect any too distinctive brilliance or intellectual prolixity—and to the ethnic diversity of a nation of immigrants, bound together by no other cultural norm than the freedom of worship and the freedom of expression, formal freedoms that are more apt to create a patchwork country than an unlikely *common* public debate. Not to mention more recent factors that we will evoke later: in the 1950s, academic specialization and a new polarization of the American intellectual field ended up distancing it from the Western model of the public space of ideas, transversal and unified.

Whatever factors are involved, the result is this: in the United States, intellectual debate, also referred to as "theoretical"—though without any implications concerning the scope of its importance—is only one of the specialized activities in which the university finds its raison d'être. The last generation of American public intellectuals was that of Jack London (1876–1916) and of Edmund Wilson (1895–1972): the former invented a form of socially committed journalism and a body of literature produced in the service of workers' concerns, and the latter, a prolific writer of tremendous energy, who published in *Vanity Fair* and the *New Yorker* and wrote historical novels as well as commentaries on Freud and Marx, made the first half of the twentieth century the last period when it was possible, in the United States, to pursue an intellectual debate accessible to all, and favored by (almost) all. The major figures after World War II, however, were all academics who owed their broader recognition—aside from the strategies pursued by their editors (as with the scientist Carl Sagan)—mainly to the political repercussions of polemics that *first* erupted on college campuses: against racial segregation (Henry Louis Gates Jr., Leonard Jeffries), against the impasses encountered by feminism (Gayle Rubin, Catharine MacKinnon), against the official culture (Susan Sontag), against shortsighted history (Randall Kennedy, Arthur Schlesinger), against propaganda in the media (Noam Chomsky), against orientalist clichés (Edward Said), or against foreign intellectualism (Camille Paglia)—but always from an academic position, in connection with an academic debate, framed in terms of academic legitimacy. Above all, next to the rare names that become known outside the university, how many intellectual stars and campus divas have found that the American university's microsmic function, sequestered from civil society, has limited their recognition—however reverential it might be—to their peers alone? Stanley Fish, himself a formidable heavyweight at Duke University, has often mused over this: "Whatever the answer to the question 'How does one get to be a public intellectual?,' we know that it *won't* be 'by joining the academy,'" he says ironically, before suggesting that the colleges should hire lobbyists so that their stars might have a chance of making it into the mass media.[5] Such a distance, both objective *and* subjective, between the academic sphere and public space in the United States, as well as between the dominant culture and media industries, has its counterpart in the world of publishing.

Thus, alongside the generalist publishers or "trade houses," the subsidiaries of larger conglomerates, and rare independent publishers, the university presses in the United States are the last publishers devoted to the publication of theoretical essays or works in the humanities and social sciences (referred to as "serious nonfiction") and to the translation of their foreign equivalents. And this is in the context of a general decline in translation: the rate of translated works in the United States fell from 8.6 percent in 1960 to 4.95 percent in 1975 and less than 3 percent today of new titles annually, compared to 15 to 20 percent in all the countries of Continental Europe. The roughly 120 university presses in the country (plus those affiliated with the two large British presses, Oxford and Cambridge) have distinct financial structures linked to the research carried out at the campuses that host them, and they often have parallel distribution networks as well, including both bookstores and academic libraries. These presses thus guarantee the circulation of intellectual innovations, but very much on the margins of the general system, that of the "megastores" and the realm of million-copy printings. Moreover, the gradual disinvestment on the part of the universities and the growing number of dissertations to be published (so that their author-teachers will have a chance at securing tenure) have for the past twenty years imposed unheard-of financial pressures on academic presses. More and more, they have had to explore alternatives in the form of regional publications (literature or history of their state) or even more commercial options, called "semitrade books," most often at the expense of titles in the humanities and social sciences, which are the first to be sacrificed.

In sum, the separatism characterizing the American university institution functions at every level: geographically through the isolation of the campuses; demographically by removing 80 percent of a generation (for two to four years) from the larger social structures; sociologically by submitting the students to partially dispensatory norms; intellectually by assigning entirely to the academic realm the task of stirring debate over ideas; and, on the level of communications and publishing, by managing, in a space set apart from the mainstream American cultural market, the distribution of intellectual productions—including the digital networks of the universities, which were set up for use twenty years ago. Despite this isolation, however, the university is a focus of national concern in the United States, and is often the sounding box, or the dramatic relay point, for some of the most pressing questions of American society. To use Gramsci's distinction, one could even say that, although it is separated from *civil society*, the university nonetheless maintains a closer link with American *political society*, because of its role as an ideological crossroads and in the formation of elites. Hence the far-reaching echoes, resounding well beyond the bucolic campuses, of the polemics set off there by French theory.

Gentlemen and Scholars

A historical ambiguity lies at the heart of the American university system: the hesitation that has characterized it since its beginnings between different approaches, universalist or professionalist, generalist or technical, or, in the terms of American pedagogy, between "humanism" and "vocationalism." To see this double tendency at work, and to understand the place that certain French authors came to play in this debate, we must look for a moment at the history of the American university. From Harvard College (founded in 1636) to Dartmouth College (in 1769), colonial America opened nine premier institutions designed on the British model, whose functions of civic morality and public utility were deemed all the more precious in this land of pioneers. Attended by Quakers, Baptists, and Catholics, the goals of these institutions were to foster tolerance of religious diversity and to transmit a knowledge of classical learning—Latin, Greek, rhetoric, logic, astronomy—as a way to unify these various communities. Then, during the revolutionary period there was a brief French influence. Before the return of strict religious orthodoxy in the nineteenth century, deism, rationalism, and the ideals of the Enlightenment flourished for a few years on the campuses, where the alliance against England favored the teaching of French (which began at Columbia, then known as King's College, in 1779) and made it possible for a few expatriate physiocrats such as Quesnay de Beaurepaire to have an impact on the programs.[6] From 1776 to 1860, the number of colleges rose from nine to 250, but the quality of the teaching did not keep pace with this expansion. In 1828, the *Yale Report* expressed alarm and recommended the adoption of a generalist curriculum: "Our goal is not to teach what is peculiar to each profession, but to expose the foundations common to all of them," the report concludes.[7] But then the pendulum swung back in the other direction. The mid-century educators, who demanded that the college be useful above all "for the manufacturer, the merchant, the gold-digger," asked in a polemical mode whether the recent "great advances of civilization" have taken place in "literature or science."[8] The period of Reconstruction that followed the Civil War then saw the transition from the traditional college to the modern university, under pressures that took several forms: industrialization and urbanization, the progress of science, a demography that enriched the sons of the bourgeoisie, and, shining all the way across the ocean, the aura of the great German academic model.

Here too there is a double evolution, at once scientific and industrial: toward the university as a site of research, concerning which the philosopher Charles Sanders Peirce went so far as to assert that (in Christopher Lucas's paraphrase) it "had nothing whatsoever to do with instruction"; and, in Andrew Carnegie's words, toward a "relevant" knowledge, referring to the "school of experience" as "the very knowledge required for [the] future triumphs" of the captains of industry to come.[9] This period saw the development not only of land-grant colleges, but also of black colleges and women's colleges. These last were intended by educators to "spare" young women from being subjected to the same instruction as boys, in the belief that this would prevent nervous crises and mental corruption. As for the large universities, whose presidents were paying visits to Berlin and Tübingen, it was the German example that began to triumph. This example involved the establishment of the principles of a diverse curriculum (*Lernfreiheit* or freedom of learning) and of the priority of research over the teaching career (*Lehrfreiheit,* or freedom of teaching), the development of the doctorate (the first Ph.D. was given by Yale in 1860) and of graduate studies (the graduate schools, which come after college), private financing of basic research on campus, and even the division into departments and disciplines—which Johns Hopkins University was the first to organize in a competitive mode, in order to attract the best professors and students. After the shift from the paternalist but not very studious college, where dead languages and a knowledge of the classics were imposed, to the large research university, liberal and impersonal, expected not only to transmit knowledge but also to produce it, American higher education was no longer the same.

The beginning of the twentieth century was the time of the great university presidents, the ones whom Thorstein Veblen called "captains of erudition,"[10] but it was also a time when the patrons of industry truly took hold of the university system. They had already preempted it in part during the preceding period by giving their names to the new universities they were financing, as Johns Hopkins did in Baltimore, James

Duke in North Carolina, and Leland Stanford near San Francisco. Now the new philanthropic foundations, those of Rockefeller or Carnegie, implicated themselves in the content of the programs and the management of the campuses, which they contributed to bureaucratizing, while they opposed anything that could harm their industrial interests—even demanding the dismissal of leftist professors such as Scott Nearing of Chicago who, in 1915, had dared publicly to denounce the use of child labor in coal mines. Control of the large trusts would never again be relinquished—and these trusts were responsible for the budgetary favors given to certain disciplines over others judged to be less useful, for the orientations of scientific research, for attempts at standardizing university procedures, and often, also, for the recruitment of high-level administrative personnel. The new "corporate culture" filtered into the university, dictating its utilitarian morality and its focus on specialization, and securing the good and loyal service of the professional pedagogue: "Where the philosopher once said that all of life is a preparation for death, the educational careerist now thinks that all of life is a preparation for business," the sociologist Benjamin Barber concluded.[11] To this power wielded by the managers, two world wars and the economic Depression of the 1930s added new incursions by the federal government that were unthinkable the preceding century. The pacifist teachers were taken to task by Washington in 1917, whereas Roosevelt's New Deal forced professors to declare their official loyalty to the governor as well as to the president. But it was World War II that turned out to be truly decisive. The mobilization of research centers, from radio transmitters to nuclear physics, and of the curriculum in general, in order to explain the European peoples to their future liberators, led to what the historian Clyde Barrow called "building a military-academic complex."[12] Although it was necessary to wait until 1973 for the establishment of the first broad system of federal aid for the payment of tuition, the law established upon the return of soldiers from World War II—the famous GI Bill of Rights (which provided social protection, financial advantages, and educational funding for the heroes of the Allied victory)—subsidized at that time their reintegration into the university system. The large number of demobilized soldiers thus added to the baby boom and tended to lengthen the duration of studies, provoking a demographic explosion in the universities: from 1950 to 1970, the student population more than doubled, its share of the total population increasing from 15.1 percent to 32.5 percent (during the same period in France, it increased from 4 percent to 10 percent), while the average size of the institutions increased as well.[13] The McCarthyite witch hunt marked the 1950s with the pursuit of "reds" and "pinkos," while university libraries got rid of their "subversive" titles, and "academic freedom" itself was presented as "the major Communist Party line for American higher education"[14]—in other words, as a dangerous Soviet deviation that had to be contained. But McCarthyism changed nothing in these more fundamental developments. The modern American university, on the eve of the student rebellions of the 1960s, claimed to provide an egalitarian preparation for the life of business and the duties of the citizen, torn between its two antagonistic historical vocations: moralization and specialization. This is confirmed by debates that occurred between 1961 and 1963 between the technological priorities of the Kennedy administration, which involved training experts and winning the space race against its enemy, the USSR, and the contrary calls rather "to strengthen general knowledge," calls made by a few prominent figures after the example of Daniel Bell in his manifesto *The Reforming of General Education*.

This ancestral conflict in the United States became focused on certain significant issues. In 1869, the president of Harvard, Charles Eliot, set off a lively debate by establishing a system of individual choices between the different disciplines ("elective curriculum"), thus eliminating the principal subjects that had been imposed ("core curriculum"). The idea of a fixed body of knowledge, absolute and ahistorical, was gradually replaced by the sole principle of a "curricular egalitarianism." The unchanging canons of liberal culture, that indispensable ingredient in making a "respectable man," had to start making room for the myriad combinations of a personalized course of study. The classical humanists opposed this, but they did so less in the name of general culture as an end in itself than by recalling the practical *relevance* of teaching it. "Even now, in this day of practicality, a little wider sprinkling of theorists, book worms, pedants, even, would do our land no harm," the president of Middlebury College, C. B. Hulbert, affirmed in 1890, without bothering to conceal his contempt.[15] The compromise that became widespread at the turn of the twentieth century, which consisted in associating one or several in-depth disciplines ("majors") and the dispersal of the other chosen subjects ("minors"), did not satisfy either party. For the philosopher John Dewey, the unity of different types of knowledge, which was at the center of the debate, had to be at once referential and methodological. Thus, in 1902 he proposed a historical and logical synthesis under the name of "general education"—in the form of innovative courses, oriented toward methodology, but that would nonetheless remain experimental.[16] Erudition and know-how seemed decidedly irreconcilable. After the war, applied research flourished thanks to federal funds from the years 1942–45, as did the functionalist and quantitative paradigms in the social sciences, all of which reinforced the pole of specialization. And yet, in the land of the business university and of knowledge-for-use, two even older historical factors constituted the last ramparts against triumphant professionalization.

In the first place, even if in 1936 Harvard dared to replace "Christo et Ecclesiae" on the official seal with the sole word "Veritas," religion—without any required courses or explicit sermons—continued to play the role in the United States that *Raison* or *Wissenschaft* played as the keystone of educational doctrine in France and in Germany. In a country where the relation to the state as the primary instance of authority has not entirely replaced the relation to the church, the truth is not essentially scientific but theological. And the only course that ever had the function of a crossover discipline in the United States was the course of moral philosophy, a barely secularized version of Protestant dogma. As the English critic Jonathan Culler states with some astonishment, in the literature departments of American universities (and we will see what ideological cauldrons these became), one finds Marxists, Lacanians, or radical feminists, but "seldom anyone who seriously attacks religion."[17] The religious specter is found again, finally, in the literary theoreticians' obsession with the question of the interpretation of texts, as well as in the contrary mistrust shown by traditional humanists toward the fashion of the "theorists," this time in the tradition of the evangelical anti-intellectualism of the early pastors. In short, in the absence of a transversal knowledge that could provide an account of all the particular areas of competence, the regime of ultimate ends remains the only viable opposition to limitless specialization. But another impediment remained. This was the task entrusted to the university, beginning with the advent of the nation-state model in the European countries, to inculcate, to define, and to preserve a national consciousness and a cultural identity that would be specifically American. Unlike in Germany, where philosophy constituted *the* national tradition (and unlike in France, where this role fell to history), in the United States the mission of a "reflection on cultural identity" was entrusted by "the nation-state," at the beginning of the twentieth century, to the discipline of literature: henceforth, as Bill Readings summarizes, "culture becomes literary."[18] In the name of the civic and ethical virtues of literature, the great critic Matthew Arnold fervently defended such an orientation. But it would soon become problematic, for a number of reasons: because literature (unlike philosophy) is in conflict with the values of science, even as it evolved as a discipline toward a technical and scientific ideal; because the literary canon in the United States refers back to British rather than American classics; and, more broadly, because the decline of the nation-state, and with it of the task of cultural unification, would eventually submerge the literary field into a kind of normative void, and a latent crisis in its traditions was soon revealed.

Excellence and the Market

After the years of student protest, as the American university entered the 1970s—a decade marked by a return to order and by economic recessions—it saw itself more and more simply as a kind of funnel feeding into the job market. Of its 8.5 million registered students (today the number is 15 million), divided among 2,550 institutions, a majority were female. Graduate studies themselves grew at a faster pace than higher education as a whole. And those who had a Ph.D. were not always assured of finding a job. For establishments that thought of themselves on the model of the new "service economy," it was a matter of assuring their "clients" the best chances of employment, treating the knowledge they dispensed as a commodity whose beneficial virtues had to be optimized (and that had to be formatted and packaged in a way that could be measured in discrete units, in grades, in semesters), and managing their institutions according to the principles then dominant in large businesses: profitability, by increasing the return on the investment in these "knowledge factories"; productivity, by teaching more and more quickly; reduction of time frames, by assuring professional success as quickly as possible; and "downsizing," if necessary, by turning to layoffs in order to check rising expenses. Above all, each university followed an unrestrained rhythm of competition. It was imperative to have the best students, to obtain federal funds, to recruit the best professors, to raise the rankings of the basketball or football team, to have every department listed at the top of the annual rankings, and its research centers among the preferred partners of the large local businesses. This development was summarized in one short phrase: "Learn to earn!" This was the informal motto of the students of the 1970s, and the neologism "multiversity" for designating a compartmentalized institution that no longer has much to do with the precepts of the unity and universality of the traditional university. It was the emergence of the "university of excellence," according to an expression fashionable at the time among the first gurus of management.

"Intellectual activity and the culture that it revived are being replaced by the pursuit of excellence and performance indicators,"[19] Bill Readings notes in summarizing the arrival of this "posthistorical university" without any referent—since here excellence itself is, in this logic, a notion with no content. Hence its porosity in relation to nonnormative elements, its power of integration, and its new capacity to absorb what in the past would have threatened its "values": the university of excellence is the very one that would soon develop feminist studies in order to attract female students, and research on ethnic or sexual minorities in order to win points with these new fringes of the student clientele; it is even the one that, more broadly, will soon integrate into its programs the critique of ideology and the new discourses of opposition, as its own traditional function of ideological surveillance was declining. For it was necessary to develop the products that would sell best. The absorption of the enemy for the purpose of turning its energy to profit is a theme interrogated at the time, in a completely different context, in the new theories of power developed by Deleuze and Foucault. This motif of excellence, which Bill Readings also calls "dereferentialization,"[20] because of its very elasticity, also plays the functional role that had been played by philosophy in the German university of the nineteenth century, as the only element of transversality under which the particular areas of knowledge that were taught could be organized. Except that in the latter case this transversality also guaranteed a certain autonomy for academic knowledge in relation to the social market; whereas in the American university, despite its separatism, this transversality was the tool for an unprecedented alliance between the transmission of knowledge and the economic order. As sociologist Alain Touraine notes in an analysis of the American academic system at the beginning of the 1970s, its sociocultural function seems to have given way to a directly economic role: "The academic system is less concerned with the reproduction of the social order and participates much more directly in its production."[21] Such a development, while it depended also on factors that were both circumstantial (the tightening of the job market) and ideological (the counterrevolutionary reaction against the disorder of the sixties), nonetheless had three basic consequences for the academic institution that turned out to be decisive for the imminent transferral of French "poststructuralism."

The first effect of this model of excellence was that the social isolation of the university was paradoxically reinforced, whereas the new economic and professional realism might have led one to expect the opposite. Indeed, the emphasis placed on the functions of research and professionalization, and therefore on disciplinary divisions, to the detriment of the transversal civic and political functions of the university, in fact distanced it even further from civil society. In the second place, this *excellence* without referent also led to an increase of pedagogical methods and meta-educative discourses *in place of* the knowledge to be transmitted: under the influence of the type of psychology and behaviorist pragmatism that was fashionable among the "experts," as Hannah Arendt observed in her diagnosis of the crisis in education in the United States, "pedagogy developed into a science of teaching in general in such a way as to be wholly emancipated from the actual material to be taught."[22] Teaching becomes a technique without object, rather than the mastery and transmission of a content. The programs themselves, as will be the case with the reading of French philosophers in literature courses, become the theater for a reflection on pedagogy; one latches onto texts that have no relation to the theme of education in order to reinforce the principles of an education that is itself without any predetermined object. Finally, in an ultracompetitive landscape, the humanities—and literary studies, which occupies a central place—submit to these new conditions much more painfully than the exact sciences, management, law, or the social sciences. What is called generalist education, traditionally associated with the field of the humanities, even became "a disaster area," according to the conclusions of the Carnegie Council report in 1977.[23] Likewise, all the statistics from the 1970s show that the liberal arts colleges saw their enrollments decrease in favor of specialized colleges, that courses in philosophy, history, and literature were being chosen less and less, except when they "technicalized" their program, and that both public and private financial aid was drastically reduced in these disciplines, leading to a more precarious professoriat and even the closing of some research institutions.[24] If the Carnegie report did not specify what it means by the "technicalization" of literary studies, the crisis that the latter underwent at the time involved a double and contradictory orientation toward a "science of texts" with variable definitions and toward a more general politico-cultural reflection. These questions require that we go back to the middle of the century—and interrogate the specifically American current of New Criticism, whose contributions were decisive for the future French theory.

The New Criticism and Literary Modernism

At the beginning of the twentieth century, the field of literary studies exhibited on a smaller scale the same tension as the American university as a whole—between a liberal English tradition, which had passed down humanist values and an approach focused on style and themes, and a more scholarly German tradition. The latter became manifest both in a question concerning national identity, when it was a matter of isolating a specifically American literature from the general English-language corpus, and in an approach that was more theoretical than the French *explication de texte* that was being taught during the same period. At the heart of the discourse on literature pursued by the American university, one finds in effect, beginning in the second half of the nineteenth century, a systematic investigation of the procedures of reading and interpreting works, an investigation that will become increasingly refined. Thus, even before Nazism brought European philologists and literary theoreticians to American campuses, the landscape of literary criticism and theory in the United States was remarkably rich and diverse. This was so much the case that, in comparison, the France of Sainte-Beuve and Gustave Lanson came to seem like a country that did not *interrogate* literature. After World War I, critical discourses and new schools of thought thus flourished on college campuses, promoting debates concerning both the critical tradition and the future of literature.

The already classic arguments of Matthew Arnold on the moral function of literature against the ravages of technology and industry were still the object of heated debates. As were the earlier remarks of John Henry Newman in *The Idea of a University*, on literature as the mother of all disciplines. At the same time, the political function of literature was at the heart of Edmund Wilson's reflections, and its larger epistemological function (which was to engage all forms of knowledge) pervades the essays of Kenneth Burke, whereas the role of classical erudition as the foundation of collective life was passionately defended by T. S. Eliot and F. R. Leavis, who in this sense were more "Arnoldian" than their older contemporary. All were agreed in giving the work of Shakespeare, which remained a constant reference, a role as important in the formation of the West as Greek philosophy and Roman law. The less normative school of "neo-Aristotelianism" founded by Ronald Crane at the University of Chicago was interested in questions of literary genres and their historicity, of composition and narration, but also of reading as a construction of meaning. Likewise, the idea of literary "appreciation," put forth in the seventeenth century by the Englishman John Dryden, was reintroduced as a way to understand the role of reading in the aesthetic construction of the work. From the 1920s to the 1950s, every possible avenue was explored: social readings and psychological readings in Lionel Trilling; the literary formation of Americanness in F. O. Matthiessen and Alfred Kazin; a first form of literary structuralism, with its schemes of formal invariants and narrative patterns drawn up after the war by Northrop Frye; and even more theoretical questions of aesthetic representation and literary realism in Erich Auerbach's *Mimesis* (1946), the masterwork of another great refugee. These different orientations, despite the ideological divergences of their defenders, coexisted peacefully within the academic literary landscape. The latter already functioned as an agora of critical discourses, accumulating innovations and bringing together new approaches, rather than privileging one school over another. It was in this rich intellectual context that the New Criticism appeared at the end of the 1930s. It would soon give a central place and confer an unequaled prestige to literary criticism within the American intellectual world.

The approach was first formulated by Cleanth Brooks and Robert Penn Warren in their 1938 classic *Understanding Poetry*, then systematized by René Wellek and Austin Warren in 1942 in *The Theory of Literature*, a textbook for graduate students. The short didactic essay *The New Criticism*, published by John Crowe Ransom in 1941, and the ambitious retrospective by Wellek, *History of Modern Criticism*, are two other influential titles. Central to the New Criticism is the notion of "intrinsic criticism": its method is that of "close reading," and its aim is to bring to light the ontological status of the text (according to the motto "a poem should not mean but be")[25] and the intransitive horizon of its language (against the theories of communication emerging at the time). But to accede to the work as a closed and stable system, it is first necessary to be rid of three "heresies" of extrinsic criticism, targeted by W. K. Wimsatt and Monroe Beardsley in three famous eponymous essays: "The Intentional Fallacy," which consists in reading the text as the direct product of an author's plan; "The Affective Fallacy," which limits the text to a series of subjective emotions—and thus limits criticism to being no more than a tremulous paraphrase; and "The Personal Fallacy," which adds to the first two fallacies the biographical and historicist deviations of traditional criticism. What the New Critics thus denounced was less the idea of the author's subjectivity, which they did not deny, than the psychologism of biographical determinants and the simplistic notion of an "intention" fully realized in the text. More broadly, they substituted an autonomous "internal history" of texts for the habitual recourse to general history, reduced in their essays to "an affair of porridge and wearing apparel" and thus to no more than a "matter of footnotes identifying a few local allusions," to quote Gerald Graff's summary.[26] The emphasis falls rather on an irreducible polysemy as the criterion of literariness, and on the structuration of major texts on the basis of their very ambiguities, the tensions and contradictions that traverse them—even speaking, thirty years before Derrida, of a structural "irony" inherent to the literary work. On the disciplinary level, three major issues are at stake: the professionalization of academic literary criticism, a respect for the great critical texts in continuity with the respect owed to the works of the corpus, and an integration of the most noble functions of criticism into the core of English departments, those beacons of the modern university. In the name of the omnipotence of texts, the literature course must win out over the history course, which sees them as no more than a reflection, and over the philosophy course, which speaks of them in terms of a mere narrative and linguistic "content." Yale University, cradle of the New Criticism, would become the model of this *literary* university.

The influence of the New Criticism did not begin to decline until the 1960s, partly because, in privileging the recognized modern and classical corpus (up to Marcel Proust and Virginia Woolf), it remained deaf to the literary innovations of the "beat" counterculture and of the new formalism. Similarly, it was of course unable to embrace the anti-academicism of the sixties, in a culture that was leaving the ivory tower and calling—also on the theoretical level—for collective movements and for what Susan Sontag (in *Against Interpretation*) would call "the erotics of art." Sensing the imminent eclipse of New Criticism, the leftist critic Irving Howe in 1958 gave an enthusiastic homage, already expressing nostalgia for a golden age: "The most intense moment in the history of modern criticism, the moment of its greatest hold upon the imagination of serious young people, has probably just come to an end."[27] And yet it was less the New Criticism as a critical approach that disappeared in the last forty years from the American university, where some of its books have remained major references, and where deconstruction would in fact take up some of its propositions, than the broader ethos of American intellectual "high modernism." For this liberal ethos, which smacked of elitism and was perfectly embodied by the major figures of the New Criticism, has since been supplanted by a mixture of irony and specialization, the two approaches privileged by mass culture and "postmodern" life. By "modernism," the Americans designate in fact their few great writers of the half century, from the right-leaning Arnoldians to the leftist New York intellectuals, all of whom practiced a cult, both tragic and aesthetic, of high culture as an autonomous sphere, and saw in it the last resistance to the dominant conformism of industrial society. From that point of view, the New Criticism is no more.

In the meantime, in the wake of the allied victory, the new current represented a historical turning point for literary studies in the United States. The rupture with the European traditions of philology and literary history that it represented, in favor of a more up-to-date rhetoric and poetics, corresponded to a fundamental redefinition of literary studies. It was a question of replacing its national political function (in forging a literary identity) with a general cognitive function that was much more ambitious, and of opposing to the traditional dichotomy between primary and secondary texts the principle of a newly conceived community between the work and its critique, between literature and theory. This latter word is at the heart of the project of the New Critics: "Literary theory, an *organon* of methods, is the great need of literary scholarship today," Wellek and Warren claimed in 1949.[28] This theoretical exigency even contributed to familiarizing students in literature during that time—the future professors of the 1980s—with some of the key concepts of Continental philosophy. But the New Critics' insistence on autonomous mechanisms in criticism and literature, on their irreducibility to history and to social structures, also translated into an ambivalence in their relation to the political field. The antireferentialism of

an objectless beauty, which had haunted modernity since the Flauber-
tian project of writing a "book about nothing," announced as though
in advance the American exaggerations of the Derridean watchword of
1967: "there is no outside-the-text."[29] What is taking shape here is a
withdrawal of literature from the affairs of the world, the refusal of an
intellectual generation to sully the Text by mixing it too closely with the
spirit of its times—even if they sincerely wished for a great literature
accessible to all.

For this project of a universal critical methodology was also derived
from a democratic principle. The only knowledge required is a knowledge of language and its function, which is more accessible to the under-
privileged classes, the New Critics thought, than literary history, cultural
allusions, biographical knowledge, all of which are elitist. As the soldiers
returning from the European front made their way to the college campuses, after the passage of the GI Bill of Rights, the New Critics vaunted
the effectiveness of their approach in the transmission of literary values to all.[30] And yet, they watched in silence as the McCarthyite purges
swept over the campuses, transforming their departments into formalist refuges far from the political struggles. One scandal in particular is
indicative of this attitude. In 1949, a jury made up of T. S. Eliot and
two well-known New Critics conferred the prestigious Bollingen Prize
on the *Pisan Cantos* by Ezra Pound, an author whose anti-Semitic and
pro-Mussolini errors were by this time widely known. This provoked
a furor among the entire intellectual Left, to whom the jurors retorted,
by way of justification, that "consideration of anything other than the
sheer quality of the poetic work" would be a serious threat "against
civilized society"[31]—an extreme limit, if there ever was one, of the political disengagement displayed by the New Critics. The emergence of
new literary and political forms on the campuses throughout the 1960s
eventually placed the New Criticism in an awkward position, underlining its untenable indifference to the *politics* of texts. Old adherents and
young disciples of the New Criticism, from Wellek to Paul de Man, thus
preferred to explore the few alternatives available. Some opted for a belated militantism, others for European academic life, but the majority,
by reading the French structuralists and founding the first departments
of comparative literature, moved toward a political critique of the Enlightenment and of ordinary language *on the basis of* theory. This was a
way to extend the study of the "ambiguities" and "tensions" of the text

through the more politically legitimate study of the "displacements" and "slippages" of writing. French theory, which did not yet bear this name, would thus be, for the young scholars interested in New Criticism, the figure of a third way between the dead ends of formalist criticism and the political blockages of a university institution subjected to the state as much as to the market—and caught in the trap of an old Thelemite dream (Rabelais's "Do what you will") in the process of turning into a nightmare.

And yet, beyond any continuities there may have been between one "revolution" and another in the American literary field, the predominant focus was on the differences between the New Criticism of the 1940s and the type of deconstruction that would soon be triumphant in the 1980s. Unlike their Derridean successors, the New Critics always dreaded mixing literature with the vulgarity of "intellectual history." And the formalist exaggeration, by analyzing, for example, the function of a newspaper article in the same way that one can analyze a sonnet by Shakespeare, would lead, according to them, to textual relativism and to the disappearance of the canon, compromising the ahistorical aesthetic universalism they so avidly defended. Above all, they never laid a foundation for *the critique of critical reason* that would soon be deployed by Derrida and his American followers in an effort to reveal the rationalist illusions of ordinary reading—in relation to the totality of the text, its autonomy, its semantic articulation. Paul de Man reproached them with having "mistook their own projection of the totalization characteristic of interpretation for a property of the text which they then had to see as a unity," as Wlad Godzich summarized the point.[32] The text can be totalized only if its coherence is presumed to prevail, but it is a coherence reconstructed from out of the ruins of its primary meaning. On the contrary, by concentrating on the aporias of the text and its irremediable incoherencies, deconstructionists came to believe that they were engaging in an even "closer reading"—closer, that is, to the text in its opacity.

In the end, like the evolution of the American university in general after the war, the experience of the New Criticism revealed in its ambivalences the same inextricable tension between expertise and general relevance, pure knowledge and historical engagement, culture and politics. These antagonisms, although they have been at the heart of the academic project from its origins, were reinforced in the American situation by the isolation of the institutions of higher learning, and their frantic rush toward specialization, even in literature and philosophy, as the progressive horizon of the model country—a country devoted to winning the peace after having liberated the world. This series of contradictions will be brought out into the open in explosive forms by the student movements of the 1960s—followed by the strange decade of the 1970s, which was both highly studious and wildly freethinking—thus transforming the American university and its incessant discourses about itself into one of those knowledge/power spirals, delirious and unstable, that Foucault had described.

3

THE SEVENTIES: A TURNING POINT

> How could a historian come to believe that a fashion, an
> enthusiasm, an infatuation, or even exaggerations do not
> reveal, at a given moment, the existence of a productive nodal
> point in a culture?
>
> MICHEL FOUCAULT, unpublished text

From college campuses to ashrams, from the political party office to the
business office, from revolution to counterrevolution, caught between
a new fear and its actually existing antidotes, the "wild seventies" were
decidedly a paradoxical decade. This is true for French theory as well,
which was making its first appearances in the United States, at a time
when it had not yet been situated within a specific territory. This was
the decade of French theory's countercultural temptations, its anarchic
expansion, by way of alternative journals and rock concerts, but it was
also the decade of the first academic uses of French theory, if only as the
instrument of a (purely discursive) subversion of the university institution. Except that what was being put into place, through deviations and
false turns, would thoroughly shake up the American intellectual field in
the last part of the century.

From Militancy to Existence

In ten years of activism, from the first civil rights marches in 1962 to the
sleep-ins at the beginning of the 1970s, the vast American student movement gradually evolved from an organized political opposition into a spontaneous mode of behavior whose aims were above all existential—from

militant anticapitalism to a mystical celebration of "free bodies" and hallucinogenic drugs. These shifts were mirrored in songs of Bob Dylan, who around this time was moving from anti-imperialist folk music to psychedelic spiritualism. This metamorphosis of the student rebellion, which was losing its luster also because of the brutal repressions of the 1970s, was one of the sociological factors determining the reception, and the *détournement,* of French theory. But this was only indirectly the case: through the displacement of struggles onto the terrain of discourse alone, through the oppositional nostalgia left by the passing of the 1960s, through the romanticism of liberated forms of life, through the ideological chasm opened, finally, at the core of the university by the apparent good behavior of the 1970s. This change of perspective was more than anything the first stage of a new intellectual adventure, one that would lead to the identity politics and radical multiculturalism of the 1980s. From the last riots of the 1960s up to the election of Ronald Reagan in November 1980, it was a question of understanding how social life in America went from student contestation to radicalized communitarianism, or from a transversal but sporadic struggle to continuous but henceforth segmented battles. In this perspective, it is necessary to go back and examine the history of the humanist and existential dimensions constitutive of the American student movement—those that also favored its communitarian or identity-based splintering.

In February 1960, a protest in response to the exclusion of four black students from a whites-only cafeteria in Greensboro, North Carolina, launched the civil rights movement in the university. In 1961 and 1962, the first "cultural rebels" mobilized on the campuses. They were inspired as much by the nebulous notion of a beat generation as by the writings of Paul Goodman, who compared American society at the time with a rat race in a windowless room,[1] and by the sociologist C. Wright Mills, who denounced the power of elites hidden under the veil of democracy. We are still very far from the 350 student strikes and the 9,500 demonstrations that took place in the year 1969–70 (around 30 percent of the 8 million students stated that they took part that year in at least one of these).[2] The year 1962 saw the creation in Michigan of the leftist group SDS (Students for a Democratic Society), whose young twenty-two-year-old leader, Tom Hayden, clarified their political positions in the Port Huron Statement: in addition to a call for "participatory democracy" and for small-scale egalitarian communities, it was a matter of replacing "power rooted in possession, privilege, or circumstance by power and uniqueness rooted in love, reflectiveness, reason, and creativity."[3] Keeping in mind the theses of C. Wright Mills (who died that same year) on the political mission of the leftist intelligentsia, Hayden stressed the necessity of reducing the distance between "our technical concepts [which] are highly esoteric and our moral concepts [which] are too simplistic." In October 1964, two thousand students blocked a police car that had come to arrest a student activist, propelling the Berkeley campus into the forefront. Inspired by young leaders like Mario Savio, the coalition of the Free Speech Movement was created—as was, in 1965, the Free University of Berkeley, which gave improvised courses in "radical politics" but also in "personal development" and "self-help."[4] As the nature of the American involvement in Vietnam was becoming more and more apparent, the student movement adopted a pacifist and patriotic rhetoric, so that the great tradition of "American humanism" would not give way to "anti-Communist corporate liberalism," in the terms used by the young Carl Oglesby.[5] After the example of these sons of democratic teachers who had become militant activists, the reference to one's life story began to predominate over ideology, and personal engagement won out over abstract ideas.

Beginning in 1965, the gap gradually widened between a minority of radicalized students, linked with the Black Power movement (which would soon exclude whites) and calling for nonparticipation in the "capitalist university," and the majority of students made up of very sporadically involved activists, interested mostly in the new alternative forms of life and the surest methods for evading the draft. The year 1968 was marked by a double split: Black Power and SDS ceased cooperating and, within SDS, a rupture occurred between reformists who wanted to move more slowly and extremists who advocated direct and immediate action. That same year, *The Strawberry Statement* by the young James Simon Kunen became a great success; it was a symptom of the desire to prolong the party rather than to take up arms: its author vindicates above all the right to wear long hair and to sleep late, under the pretext that "my revolutionary fervor takes about half an hour longer than the rest of me to wake up," before assuring his readers (if any assurance was needed) that "since the First Republic of the United States is one hundred ninety-two years old and I am nineteen, I will give it one more chance."[6] But in April, the occupation of a building at Columbia University by black students, the subsequent occupation of four other buildings, and then the violent intervention of the police, finally lit the powder keg. Riots broke out on hundreds of campuses, often to the cries of "two, three, many Columbias!" In Washington, Nixon continued to call the protesters "bums," while his vice president spoke of "impudent snobs." In May 1970, when spontaneous marches took place at sixty universities against the American bombing of Cambodia, the National Guard shot real bullets at nonviolent protesters at the universities of Kent State and Jackson State, killing six and wounding dozens more. Despite the national uproar, such a cold and determined military reaction marked the end of an era. It brought with it the rapid decline of the movement—the return to classes in the fall of 1970 took place in the midst of an astonishing calm—and ended by isolating the radical minority. This abrupt demonstration of force occurred alongside the other violent political events of the period, which was marked by the assassinations of Malcolm X, Robert Kennedy, and Martin Luther King. The fun was over: guilty of having brought about bloodshed—according to the old paradox by which the nonviolent must "disarm," so to speak, by blaming themselves for the brutality of the repression directed against them—the political impetus of the 1960s stopped cold.

But the existential enthusiasm from which it drew its energy managed to continue in other forms. The struggles against imperialism and commodification were followed by demands for sexual liberation and the affirmation of psychedelic drugs, bound up as much with the defense of a radical individualism as with experimental forms of desubjectification—to die psychologically in order to be reborn in the unexplored regions of the cosmos, in a deformed and reformatted version of a kind of shamanistic Buddhism. Drugs, which no one suspected the CIA of having spread on campuses in order to neutralize the student movement, were consumed very liberally in the "counterrevolutionary" university of the 1970s: joints or acid brought no punishment to their users, and in 1979 half of all students favored the decriminalization of marijuana.[7] "Protest songs" and the tactics of occupation, for their part, gave way to sessions of spontaneous expression and to frenetic weekend parties. The old conflict between humanities students and science students or athletes, which had been transferred for some years onto ideological terrain (the former generally taking up positions of protest, as against the conservatism of the latter), returned to the space of academic disciplines where it had always flourished, in the form of mutual mockery and budgetary competition. Media attention did not let up, but stories of campus life no longer filled the "society" and "culture" pages of the major newspapers. If these issues of lifestyle were a continuation, as the students saw it, of the political utopias of the preceding decade, the press for its part was not taken in—the danger was past. For the fact is that the student movement was tied less to the conflict than to the continuity between generations. In 1965, as in 1975, it was rather a question of "living out their parents' ideals," those of urban middle-class households that, as sociological surveys showed, were also focused on values of health, moral freedom, and personal growth.[8] Nothing in any of this required a revolution in the social order. In a significant way, during the 1970s the only themes of common action on the campuses, divided more and more into communities based on self-identified affinities (ethnic or sexual), consisted in a rather vague interest in the third world and an even vaguer call to generalize Woodstock ("Woodstock Nation")—plus a few studious demands for longer library hours, more competent TAs, and lower registration fees.[9]

The elements of continuity dominated, then, from one decade to the next, as much when it came to the ethos of contestation, about which Alain Touraine noted already in 1969 that it "brings to mind Eastern monachism or 13th century Italian Joachism rather than political struggles,"[10] as on the level of the themes of contestation themselves—alienated human relations, destruction of natural resources, media manipulation of the imagination. From James Kunen's *Strawberry Statement,* in 1968, to contemporary fanzines, the art of benign provocation and ludic dissidence became its own tradition, up to the minority of students today who, during their college years, opt for a bohemian lifestyle, a community-based house, and the external signs of a largely depoliticized "refusal"—dreadlocks, piercings, tatoos, or the grungy attire of the social deserter. But provocation is not politics. Their older peers in the 1970s, alongside their hippie clothes and tripped-out states of mind, also dreamed above all of professional success, that ethical compromise between the greedy *arrivisme* of the most liberal and the anticapitalism of their predecessors, now deemed obsolete. That is, when they were not fighting against the new specter of unemployment, hoping just to find a decent job and to do a little better than their predecessors, and getting by with odd jobs and government aid after having "wasted" their precious years of study in the activism of their twenties.

Eventually, a gap began to appear between the constraints of the economic order and the looser morals of campus life, and also between the university's mission of general education and that of professional preparation. This gap came to be regulated, in general, and to a greater or lesser degree, by the university institution itself. But it also tended, in certain circumstances or among certain students, to develop into conflictual antagonisms, zones outside the norm, blind spots in the great conformist machine of America: radical political critique as long as the national (civil rights) and international (Vietnam) emergencies caused a diffuse discontent to crystallize; extreme (and exaggerated) forms of liberation (the psychedelic "escape"), or even excesses based on group cohesion (sexual violence against girls in fraternities, or the entirely separate lives of certain groups); and, more generally, under Nixon as well as under George W. Bush, that curious form of passive rebellion without object, most often solitary (through piercing or idleness rather than through mobilization), a refusal of the social order that is less political than silent and anomic, and that characterizes the American "college kid" much more than his or her European counterpart. Alain Touraine glimpsed this when he analyzed the dead end of these "middle-class youths who . . . refuse to play the game, [but] without being able to escape their condition," or the "alienation" of these "virtual rebels" torn between their behavior as "marginals" and the tradition of "non-commitment" from which they were unable to break away.[11] This student anomie, a consequence of the separatism of the university and of its political upheavals, also explains the particular receptivity of students to all the representations of the countercultural world, whether rebellious music or schizo thinkers, a receptivity that is based more on emotion than on politics and is more personal than ideological. It was first of all in order to make the contradictory university of 1975 America more livable—a university that was free *and* repressive, academic *and* full of refusal—that they would read William Burroughs, Allen Ginsberg, Kathy Acker, or Michel Foucault and Gilles Deleuze—the latter thanks to the alternative journals that sprouted up in the literature departments.

Eclectic Journals

During this period of renewed calm, the new theoretical virus first emerged in the United States within the pages of a few para-academic journals, simple mimeographed typescripts in which a first contingent of French texts appeared in translation. The mystique of French theory begins here, with these texts that often appeared in awkward translations, typed out on a typewriter and stapled together, passed from hand to hand in classes or at social gatherings. This mystique began with an underground, artisanal, and passionate labor carried out by certain young academics who were brought together by these foreign voices, and who translated, introduced, or edited the first texts—Allan Bass, Tom Conley, James Creech, Janet Horn, John Rajchman, Mark Seem, and many others. It began with these segments of texts, major fragments or simply press interviews that were chosen somewhat by chance, without requesting publication rights, and were taught in conjunction with their first publication in English—but still only within French departments, where most of these mediators were active. The initial amateur style of these journals, today mostly devoted to literary studies, distinguished them from the journals that proliferated in France during the preceding decade when structuralism reigned. These more established French journals, such as *Communications* (created in 1961), *Langages* (1966), *Poétique* (1970), *Littérature* (1971), and especially *Tel Quel* (1960), were privileged sites for the articulation of the new concepts of the "science" of texts, or of the social structures, and the imperatives of revolt. "According to the jargon of the period, we wanted to join theory with practice," recalled Jean-Claude Chevalier, founder of *Langue française*.[12] These journals, with *Tel Quel* most prominent among them, would justify the "hard" Maoist turn of the years 1970–74 with the idea that "writing had to be shaken up" as only a "precondition for the realization of the revolution."[13] Their younger American counterparts, however, born on the demobilized but more festive campuses, will explore with Derrida and Deleuze the paths of a thought they often considered "postpolitical," an intellectual alternative to the Marxist heritage rather than its intensive continuation. But not all the journals of the time shared this vision. The journals of the American intellectual Left, for example, such as *Partisan Review* and especially *Telos*—more comparable to *Lettres françaises* or to *La nouvelle critique* than to *Tel Quel*—presented these new authors as a group of particularly unorthodox French Marxists, dissident continuations of the project of Marxist critique: they described Baudrillard as the iconoclastic heir to the Frankfurt School, interrogated Foucault on the prison in Attica (which he had visited) and on the crisis of the American penal system, and presented Lyotard as a "libidinal" critic of Adorno.[14]

And yet it was less the political model of the *Partisan Review* than the experimental literary tradition of alternative journals of the 1950s, gravitating around the beat movement in San Francisco or the New York School of poets, that inspired these new campus "intellozines." They looked less to the model of the "forum for debate"—the politically engaged intellectual periodical in its classical form—than to those journals of formal poetry or of *textes bruts* that during the two previous decades had invented a new literary language, new forms of typography, a properly creative approach to publishing a journal: their nostalgia inclined rather in the direction of *Semina, Beatitude,* or the *Black Mountain Review* of the poet Robert Creeley, these autonomous machines of literary expression that were created by the marginal figures of the American literary and artistic scene, from the experimental group L=A=N=G=U=A=G=E to the practitioners of "concrete poetry." But with two major differences: a new cult of the theoretical text and, despite everything, an academic base. These journals were created at the initiative of young professors, supported by their departments, produced on a volunteer basis by a small group of students devoted to the cause, and, although they were distributed in the semiclandestine impromptu manner of a campus samizdat, they were fully attached to the university.

Aside from the first texts on deconstruction or micropolitics, these journals imported from Europe another significant innovation: the review essay, long articles that take as their starting point the book they are reviewing, on the model of the French journal *Critique.* As the historian Dominick LaCapra suggests, the adoption of this textual genre reveals an "understanding of research as a conversation with the past" and a "recognition that critical discourse is dialogical, in that it attempts to address itself simultaneously to problems . . . and the words of others addressing these problems."[15] It thus takes on an ethic of discussion that was more academic than rebellious, a fidelity to the debate form that was less anarchist than democratic, and this is the form largely privileged in these journals. One reason for this is that these readers, dispersed, depoliticized, often unlocatable, far from making up an organized clique, constituted the kind of invisible community described by Georges Bataille as a community of those who have no community, one that is united, without their knowledge, only by the fact that they hold the same cover in their hands, whether of a book or a journal. These readers, in a word, had to be sought out and brought together.

Some sixteen journals appeared over a period of about twelve years in the United States, including *Glyph, Disapora, Semiotext(e),* and *Boundary 2;* their objective, often stated on the title page, was to introduce across the Atlantic the new paradigms coming from Europe. The themes put forth, whether in the choice of the excerpts translated or in the commentaries presented on them, all referred to the critique of the subject in its various modalities: the "end of man" and the "dislocation" of writing in (and around) Derrida, the death of the author and societies of control in Foucault, *dispositifs pulsionnels* encompassing individualities in Lyotard, and the first celebrations of "lines of flight" and the "schizo" subject in Deleuze and Guattari. And yet, what these journals had in common was less a set of themes than an enunciative, or even tonal, style. Acronyms and wordplay, together with a ludic relation to the translated concepts, reduced their cultural distance. A similar allusive or parodic relation to one's own erudition signaled a self-critique of academic procedures. And a discourse tending more toward injunction than description—even if it was in "reporting" the injunction of the quoted author—responded to the exigency of another register, far from both academic objectivism and the naïvetés of narration. With the exception of *Semiotext(e),* whose initiatory role we will see in a moment, the two pioneering journals for the introduction of French theory began in a French department—*Diacritics* at Cornell and *SubStance* at the University of Wisconsin.

Diacritics was created in 1971 by professors David Grossvogel and Robert Matthews. It became widely known already with its first issues, thanks to the lively exchange that it published between Foucault and George Steiner, following a *New York Times* article by the latter in which Steiner described the author of *The Order of Things* (which had just appeared in English) as "the mandarin of the hour."[16] But it also published the future heralds of deconstruction, Harold Bloom and Paul de Man, articles on Artaud and Lacan, a review of Derrida's *Of Grammatology,* but also of Barthes's *Sade Fourier Loyola . . .* and even of a complete edition of the *Superman* comics. Following the example of other journals, and of the professors who ran them, *Diacritics* gradually evolved from a Lacanian-Derridean position, which authorized every sort of play on the *text* alone, to a Deleuzean-Lyotardian mode of subversion *outside the text,* by comparing *Anti-Oedipus* to Nietzsche's *Antichrist* (in 1974), by publishing a comparison between Marx's significance for the Frankfurt School, on the one hand, and for poststructuralism, on the other (in 1976), or by returning to Derrida, but this time for a review of his obscure *Glas* (in 1977)—the first sentence of which declares that Derrida's book can be "read . . . as an ancestral rite."[17] As a sign of an affective rapport with this new corpus—more playful than argumentative—in 1973 the journal printed on the back cover this parodic poem by a professor in Boston:

> Before you let that patient in, please tell us, Doc Lacan,
> The latest dope from Lévi-Strauss, Derrida and de Man . . .
> Can dialectic referents be structured after Hegel?
> Will nominal concretions truly supersede the bagel?
> And does the signifier really mean the signified?
> O merde, Lacan, your patient just committed suicide![18]

SubStance, also founded in 1971, presented itself as a vehicle for French avant-garde thought. In fact, one finds here the same shift (though even more pronounced) from an early period of new material by Saussure, Kristeva, and Derrida and articles in French on structuralism (from 1971 to 1973), to later issues that featured typographical experimentation by poets and discussions of Deleuze's and Guattari's ideas on "schizo-analysis" and the "oedipalized" earth (in 1974–76). Other motifs that were even less textualist in orientation followed: a critique of Freud (in 1976), a return to Artaud (in 1977), and an emphasis on "the margins" in an issue on Deleuze and Foucault (in 1978)—including the first English excerpt of the latter's *History of Sexuality.* Somewhat more conventional in its presentation, the journal *Glyph,* founded in 1976 at Johns Hopkins by Samuel Weber and Henry Sussman, presented itself on the title page as a site for the questioning "of representation and textuality" and for the "confrontation between American and Continental critical science." This journal underwent a more discreet shift from articles on Derrida (in 1976–77) to less densely argued texts that "applied" deconstruction to the novels of Melville or Goethe (in 1978–79). *Social Text,* the future target of Sokal's hoax, was founded at Duke University in 1979 by Stanley Aronowitz and Fredric Jameson. With greater resources at its disposal, and more explicit in positioning itself on the cultural left, the journal published several of the major texts of French theory and of minoritarian thought, including texts by Michel de Certeau, Edward Said, Michel Foucault, and Cornel West.

Then came a number of journals, whether more academic or more openly political, that maintained a certain distance from this first wave, but that nonetheless provided sites for debate and diffusion that were crucial for French theory. This is the case for *Critical Inquiry,* founded in 1974 at the University of Chicago. It published pathbreaking texts by Stanley Fish and Paul de Man, engaged in a debate on Foucault and on the very question of theory, but always maintained a more dialogical perspective, more historicist, less politically engaged—addressing an unpredictable mix of writers and issues such as Camus, Borges, or feminism in art. The journals that thus took into account this French rejuvenation of "theory," rather than directly espousing its propositions, were more numerous: one can cite *Raritan, Representations, Public Culture,* the feminist journal *Signs* (which published the first translations of Luce Irigaray and Hélène Cixous, between 1975 and 1980), or *Contention.* Special mention should be made of *October,* founded in 1976 by Rosalind Krauss and Annette Michelson, who justified its title with a liminal homage to "that moment in our century when revolutionary practice, theoretical inquiry and artistic innovation were joined in a manner exemplary and unique."[19] The journal positioned itself at the intersection of aesthetic theory and political philosophy; it covered the major artistic experiments of the time (including those of Trisha Brown, Richard Serra, and Laurie Anderson), claiming a filiation with Georg Lukács and Walter Benjamin rather than with Foucault or Derrida; it found itself associated with the *Tel Quel* group and later with *L'Infini*—particularly through the intermediary of Denis Hollier. At the same time, with essays by Lyotard on Daniel Buren, by Derrida on painting, and by Hubert Damisch on photography, *October* was the only journal at the time that seriously explored the issues of French theory in relation to art and artistic practice. Finally, the nonacademic leftist journals complete the picture, providing its oldest element and an invaluable intersection with the public space. *Partisan Review, New Left Review, Dissent, Public Interest,* and the *Nation* began to find resonances with the new intellectual vogue, whose political exploits within the French context they usefully recalled, but not without railing, in a more ideological tone, against a "petty-bourgeois textualism."

In the pages of these prestigious journals, as well as in those of new ones such as *Diacritics* or *October,* the 1970s were for French theory the age of a new and electrified discursive object that remained largely unconstrained by any established norms and expectations. This new object provided an opportunity for experiments in graphic or poetic variations and for more or less fortunate intersections thought to be the only approach to its radical novelty. The journal form was used for what it is, or should be—a cultural technology, a conceptual laboratory. But this proliferation of journals quickly evolved and would soon become more restrained. A sign of the times, the most handsome bookstore success for a journal associated with French theory will be, fifteen years later, the very elegant *Zone* (twelve thousand to fourteen thousand copies of each issue sold), founded by Michel Feher and designed by Bruce Mau: this stylish-looking journal brought together references to Foucault and discreet homages to Deleuze in a more sustained, and more didactic, narrative of intellectual history, with a particular focus on the history of bodies and the theories of urban space. This was a far cry from the stapled typescripts of 1975, the initiates' codes of recognition, and the opaque lyricism of the first French theorists. What happened in the meantime was that French theory had entered the realm of established practices—and had entered the classrooms as well.

Counterculture: A Missed Encounter?

If the university has an *other,* it is indeed the problematic concept of "counterculture." This is a deceptive word, no doubt, marked by an adversative prefix that hides the formidable ability of the American culture industry to continually assimilate its margins, to intensify the rage expressed in these margins in order to celebrate, for profit, the fine ideal of American egalitarianism. It is nonetheless true that around the middle of the twentieth century, at the moment when Burroughs, Kerouac, and Ginsberg met at Columbia, and when Jewish writers (such as Norman Mailer) and black writers (such as Richard Wright) suddenly changed the literary landscape, an irreversible displacement occurred: American cultural innovation, its exportable avant-garde, shifted gradually from the agrarian and Jeffersonian tradition, that of the novelists of the South and of New England, to an urban subculture of pariahs and deviants—and its artistic creativity, in everything from jazz to poetry, was quickly transformed into a model to be emulated. Then, in the 1960s, a "cultural" rebellion was invented (rock 'n' roll and beat poetry against the established order), one that brought together, especially in New York and San Francisco, a close-knit countercultural network, giving rise to spontaneous and unpredictable periodicals created in alternative spaces. Then, in denouncing some of the latter in favor of a more inoffensive youth culture, the counterrevolution of the 1970s caused them to slip into a semi-clandestinity—which led to the emergence of an "underground" scene. But the alternative journals appearing on the campuses and the first importers of French texts often found themselves, because of their age and way of life, at the intersection of the academic institution and its parallel circuits, which themselves depended primarily on a student clientele. Thus the diffusion of what was not yet called French theory occurred on the edges of the countercultural space, on the still blurry dividing line between the campuses and sites of dissidence.

Some of the new journals sought out readers by publishing tracts sprinkled with theoretical slogans that were distributed in artists' squats, concert halls, and militant leftist meetings. Whenever the opportunity arose, collaborations were formed with anarchist editors, such as Black and Red Press in Detroit and Something Else Press in New York. The personal networks on both sides led to specific connections with certain countercultural figures, such as the filmmaker John Waters or the musician Laurie Anderson. In New York, word began to spread, as did the well-thumbed copies of certain journals, in places frequented by the young intellectuals of Columbia, at improvised art galleries in small storefront spaces in the East Village, or at the hip Manhattan clubs where the new musical trends were emerging, especially Punk and New Wave—Max's Kansas City, Danceteria, Mudd Club, Beat Lounge, and the legendary CBGB's. Whether one mentioned the names of Foucault and Deleuze in the back of a concert hall or in the latest pages of an alternative magazine (*Bomb, Impulse, East Village Eye*), French theory, diffuse and still undefined, thus circulated in the margins of the margin, at times invisible to the invisible themselves. A few chroniclers of this countercultural scene, after developing a passion for an author or at the instigation of a professor friend, made a place for these new ideas in the columns of the mainstream newspapers where they exercised greater influence, as was the case with the music critic at the *New York Times*, Adam Schatz, and the very "'68" Richard Goldstein at the *Village Voice*. But beyond these parallel circuits, the 1970s were above all a time of possible direct encounters between French authors and their American readers.

We are familiar with the keen interest that both Foucault and Deleuze had in the American counterculture. While Foucault referred to it only in interviews, Deleuze evoked Ginsberg, discreetly named in a footnote, in order to praise the "psychopathology" of the poet,[20] and he alluded more than once to his passion for the repetitive music of John Cage and Steve Reich. Aside from the faithful friendship that bound the two together up to the end,[21] strong affinities existed between Foucault's panopticon and Burroughs's "Novas," machines of a total and mobile mistrust, figures of a cold posttotalitarian control. Richard Goldstein insisted on this community of spirit, making connections between philosophy and science fiction with a political bent: the author of *Junkie*, he says, shares with European youth and its intellectuals—and above all with Foucault—"a desire to break with all the forces of thought control, with the State, with the past, and with the ultimate 'maya' in late 70s semiotics—the integrated self."[22] It must be said that a certain French intellectual avant-garde had already been working for a long time (at least since the beats passed through Paris in 1958) to link these two poles, by making the artistic and political provocations of both the Beatniks and the new formalism better known in France. One need only cite *Tel Quel*, which interviewed Ginsberg in 1974, presented Brion Gysin's "cutups" and Richard Foreman's production notes in 1976, and contrasted the "postmodernism" of Burroughs, Richard Brautigan, and William Gass with the more narrative "modernism" of Flaubert and Joyce.[23] And yet, the actual encounters were much rarer than the interconnections among the texts. Foucault crossed paths with John Cage, Kathy Acker met Félix Guattari, who himself later saw Ginsberg in Paris for a few analytic sessions, and Baudrillard began a correspondence with the novelist J. G. Ballard after meeting him in California. But there was nothing very durable and lasting in any of this—which can also be said of the two major countercultural events of the period with which French theory was associated, both of which were initiated by a young professor at Columbia, Sylvère Lotringer.

While preparing the first eponymous issue of his journal *Semiotext(e)*, Lotringer organized in November 1975 the conference "Schizo-Culture," which brought into the giant lecture hall of Teacher's College hundreds of listeners from every direction, reaching far beyond academia. Deleuze, for whom this was the one and only trip across the Atlantic, was interrupted in his debate with Ronald Laing by a far Left militant feminist, Ti-Grace Atkinson, who worked her way to the front and began to insult them, calling them "phallocrats" and preventing them from continuing. Foucault, for his part, was interrupted in the middle of his presentation on the "new forms of fascism" by a member of Lyndon Larouche's National Caucus of Labor Committees, who accused him of being paid by the CIA—and received the retort that he himself must be working for the KGB. Somewhat stunned, and furious with Lotringer, the three French thinkers, joined by Lyotard, took refuge in the Chelsea Hotel where they were staying, and refused to play any more part in this "last countercultural event of the 60s," as Foucault angrily put it.[24] The artist and activist Jean-Jacques Lebel, who imported "happenings" and beat poetry into France and who was well connected in the alternative circles in New York, decided to show them around. He took them to see Ginsberg at his apartment on Tenth Street and then to a concert in Massachusetts, where Deleuze and Guattari met Bob Dylan and Joan Baez backstage—but the latter hadn't read *Anti-Oedipus,* and the former weren't all that into smoking pot. Lebel continued the journey all the way to San Francisco, where Deleuze and Guattari met Lawrence Ferlinghetti and went to see Patti Smith, then to Los Angeles where they visited the Watts neighborhood and spoke to some members of the Black Panthers, comparing their respective experiences of "active defense" and "local resistance." The four Frenchmen, however, turned down Lotringer's invitation three years later, when he organized the Nova Convention, which was meant to provoke a fruitful confrontation between French theory and Burroughs's work. What happened instead was that the poet John Giorno enlisted several figures from the pop music scene to join the event, including Patti Smith, Frank Zappa, and the B-52's. Even Sid Vicious and Keith Richards made an appearance. During this first week of December 1978, the improvised concerts of these pop stars drew huge crowds of young people to Irving Plaza—to which the event had been moved—going far beyond what the organizers could handle and almost entirely eclipsing the theoretical pretext and the political dialogue that had first motivated Lotringer's project.[25]

One can always imagine the encounters that might have taken place between Foucault, Lyotard, or Deleuze and the Americans present at the event, who included the guru of hallucinogens and professor at Harvard, Timothy Leary, and the musician Philip Glass. Likewise, though perhaps even more pointlessly, one can dream of the dialogues that did not take place with such singular figures of American culture as the filmmaker

David Lynch, the novelist Thomas Pynchon, or the director Robert Wilson. And the California rock group Anti-Oedipus would surely have liked to meet the authors of the book. But in the end the works of these French authors had little more than a brush with the countercultural scene, without really taking hold in it—but not without a few sparks flaring out of these high-speed encounters. The fact is that the university was never far away, waiting for the seeds to sprout. If New York dominatrixes like Terence Sellars and Madame Victoire became interested in a few French texts, even reading passages from Deleuze's essay on Sacher-Masoch during their sessions, this was largely owing to the mediation of certain Francophile professors, and no doubt mostly for the latter's enjoyment. And if Julia Kristeva managed to discover a certain underground space and then recounted having "the impression of being in the catacombs of the early Christians,"[26] it was during a semester spent mostly on the Columbia campus. At the limit, the experience that came the closest to the countercultural fever of the 1970s was no doubt that of a number of French thinkers—Lyotard, Baudrillard, Derrida, Bruno Latour, Louis Marin, Michel de Certeau—who went to teach at the mythical campus of the University of California located in La Jolla, by the San Diego Bay. Between the tutelary figure of Herbert Marcuse, the skirmishes with Marxist or gay activists, the omnipresence of the beach and its bonfires, the fashionable nightclubs (the Jesuit de Certeau is said to have visited "as an anthropologist" the famous Barbaricos),[27] the campus in La Jolla was at the time a hot spot of political contestation and liberated lifestyles—while remaining a campus nonetheless, largely isolated from the rest of the world.

But it is not a question here of opposing point by point the "authentic" life of the counterculture and the privileged droning of the academy. If only because students and even teachers, beyond the particular paths they take, are only the temporary occupants, as it were, of a borrowed knowledge (whether the goal is to deaden it or to electrify it), whereas certain canny marginals tried to make themselves the sole owners of this brand name—*the* margins—"from which they no longer utter anything but the micro-fascist speech of their dependency and their giddiness: 'We are the avant-garde,' 'We are the marginals.'"[28] And the two worlds are not so strictly impermeable to one another—far from it. French theory intervened precisely on the border separating the counterculture from the university, at the point where their propositions become indiscernible, and where their mediators are often the same, whether they are anti-conformist teachers or party-loving poets who still show up in campus lecture halls. French theory delimited a zone in which artistic experimentation and innovative courses on theory began to resonate with one another. Above all, it emerged in an American cultural field in which the elitist austerity of "modernism," accused of having frozen life in museums and libraries, was being confronted with the liberatory experiences of what was not yet called "postmodernism," a deeply experimental culture with no assigned territory or disciplinary compartmentalization. It was the innovative and spontaneously political culture of figures like John Cage and William Burroughs, already in a way a postcultural culture, irreducible to conventional cultural hierarchies, a culture in which the outcasts as well as the restless souls in the university were recognized as an integral part of the campus—and for which the French authors thus played the role of theoretical counterpart to the "Duchamp–Cage–Warhol axis," the official avant-garde.[29]

In the meantime, the period from 1974 to 1978 was a chaotic and idyllic interlude—all the more precious for being brief—between the world of freedom-seeking experimentation, deviant paths, or crisscrossing lines, and that of a focused, intensive thinking. It was a time when, in certain life trajectories, theoretical reading became intertwined with bodily experimentation, the effects of LSD with the effects of Foucault, the memory of Jimi Hendrix with phrases from Deleuze—a singular contiguity of proper names in each itinerary, bio/bibliographic crossings that form each individual's scrapbook, a repository of memories and a repertory of existence. And yet it may not be possible to infer the somewhat general conclusions drawn by a writer such as Greil Marcus concerning the (improbable) marriage between punk music and Situationist refrains.[30] Only during such a strange period as this—not so long ago, after all, and yet still very difficult for cultural historians to retrace—could a journal have published an issue that was so audacious, so joyous in its very limitations, as the issue of *Semiotext(e)* on Nietzsche from 1978. Its justification is clear: "We have decided that Fred should come back (this time) as the clarion of counter-culture." Everything is set up to make the German philosopher the one who announces, celebrates, makes possible the 1970s: his mustache decorates every page; John Cage and Merce Cunningham explain how they put him into "practice"; his floating texts open onto a "certain right to misinterpretation"; articles by Foucault, Deleuze, and Derrida clarify his political value *today;* and a comic strip at the end confirms him as the superhero for a world in need of liberation.[31]

The Adventure of *Semiotext(e)*

Positioned along this porous border between the university and the countercultural networks, the group, the journal, and then the publisher called Semiotext(e) played a pathbreaking role in the early diffusion of French theory. Its participants were even among the very first to use this expression, whose ambiguity they never ceased exploring, while also deliberately foregrounding its American paradoxes, both out of playfulness and as a form of provocation. A first paradox: this national label gives a very inaccurate description of the product. Sylvère Lotringer would repeat many times—in a decisive intuition—that the term French theory was an "American invention . . . no doubt belonging to the continuity of American reception of all sorts of European imports,"[32] and that it became the site of an American *practice* for artists and activists who had no place of their own—painters and militants, musicians and poets, who had all become once again the "white niggers of this earth," as Kathy Acker put it, referring to Patti Smith and Rimbaud.[33] These figures were committed to shaking up American neuroses and conventions from within by intensifying them in experimental forms: John Cage by undoing music from melody, Merce Cunningham by inventing powerful, almost telluric choreographies, and Kathy Acker by improvising a polyphonic autofiction, a mixture of plagiarism and errant movement around a schizo, multiple writing subject, an "I" more polemical than ego-centered. In this sense, Lotringer says, "the first book of French theory published in America . . . was a book by John Cage,"[34] who was, in a way, doing French theory without knowing it, or without giving it this French name, which only came later. A similar anteriority of the *experience* of theory in relation to its fixation as a text is at the core of Lotringer's itinerary. After studying at the Sorbonne, during a period when he also worked for Olivier Burgelin's Maison des lettres and for *Lettres françaises*—which allowed him to meet Roland Barthes, Philippe Sollers, and Alain Robbe-Grillet—he left for the United States in 1970, then in 1972 found himself tenured in Columbia's French department, chaired by Michel Riffatterre. While giving courses at Reid Hall, Columbia's study abroad program in

Paris, he met, most notably, Félix Guattari, Gérard Genette, and Lacan and invited them to speak there. His dialogues with them, together with the openness and availability of an expatriate life, led him in 1973 to create the journal *Semiotext(e),* with his colleagues and students Wlad Godzich, Denis Hollier, Peter Caws, and John Rajchman. He based the journal at Columbia, a fact that only helped to serve the purpose of mocking the academic institution. Likewise, he devoted its first issue to Saussure's work, which, however, focused on the latter's obscure "anagrams" (a manuscript discovered by Lotringer in the library of Geneva) and thus revealed that in reality there were "two Saussures," the master of language but also the playful thinker who invites us to be "suspicious of the linguistic sign": for Jean Starobinski, this discovery announced a "second Saussurian revolution."[35] He gave it the name *Semiotext(e),* the better to subvert or retool semiology, relaying Lyotard's call for a "de-semiology" and publishing a text on "l'en-signement de la sémiotique" by Guattari—thanks to whom he arranged the collaboration of the CERFI (Centre d'Études, de Recherches et de Formation Institutionnelles) and its journal *Recherches.*[36]

After an issue on Bataille in 1976—which printed the article from the journal *L'Arc* in which Derrida says of Hegelian discourse that "a certain burst of laughter [from Bataille] exceeds it and destroys its sense"[37]—the issues on *Anti-Oedipus* (1977), on Nietzsche, then on "schizo-culture" (1978) mark a more sustained, and more joyously subversive, turn toward Deleuze and Guattari than the one found in *Diacritics* or *SubStance.* Translations appeared of programmatic texts by Deleuze (on nomadology) and Lyotard (from *Dispositifs pulsionnels*) that were being published at the time in Christian Bourgois's 10/18 series. Texts by alternative therapists like François Peraldi soon appeared, also by activist artists (the Ramones and the theater group Mabou Mines), but also by schizophrenic creators (Louis Wolfson, Jean-Jacques Abrahams) and by notorious terrorists (Ulrike Meinhof). The use of a direct style constituted a de facto invalidation of scholastic argumentation, and humor and incongruity replaced the old stance of critical distance, whereas, in the manner of a *détournement,* the tactics of "ransacking" texts and the inversion of symbols became a generalized approach. The pages are invaded by fake advertisements—for sedatives, female circumcision, and an electric chair—and by an ingenious archival arsenal (blurry photos and "detourned" or freely appropriated comic strips), all part of a deliberate visual scrambling of codes—or even derive from the "principle of offsetting" once envisioned by Mallarmé, "a surface on which every level of language is crushed together, crisscrossed, and interwoven."[38] The issue on Italian *autonomia* marks a kind of stopping point in this development: the rhetoric is more directly political, even in defining *autonomia* as "the body without organs of politics,"[39] and the issue as a whole is more austere, more elegant, presenting a historical testimony to the present. But because of technical delays, the issue did not appear until 1980, after the brutal repression of the Italian movement, and without the participation of the university Marxists (particularly the journal *Telos*) whom Lotringer approached in vain. After this political failure, a certain ludic excess returned with a vengeance: from the large-format newspaper issue on "Loving Boys" (1980), as audacious as it was humorous, to the issues on polysexuality (1981), Germany (1982), and later on the United States (1987), there was a gradual movement toward a regime of punctual intervention, and toward the eclecticism of a periodical published by a different group each time, which thus began to slip away from its founders. This same logic of overflow, if not dispossession, was at work, as we saw, in the two events organized at the time by Lotringer and his group, Schizo-Culture and the Nova Convention—to which was added, in a defiant gesture of nostalgia, the symposium titled "Chance," which in 1995 brought together poets, DJs, and stockbrokers in a desert casino, a "theoretical rave" whose participants saw a "nonchalant" Baudrillard slowly dispensing his texts on stage dressed in a rhinestone jacket and dubbed the true "sultan of simulation."[40]

A turning point came in 1983. Drawing some lessons from the journal's experience and from its temporal instability, Lotringer diversified his publishing activities. Together with the leftist editor Jim Fleming and the distribution network the latter had already established with his Autonomedia publications, Lotringer proposed to bring out a series under the label "Foreign Agents" to be produced in the same format as the "little black books" of the Berlin publisher Merve Verlag (a German forerunner in the publication of French theory). The first three titles of this series unexpectedly became very successful in the bookstores: *Simulations*, a text by Baudrillard taken from his *Simulacres et Simulations* (more than twenty thousand copies sold), *Pure War*, a long interview with Paul Virilio, and *On the Line*, a compilation of excerpts from Deleuze and Guattari's writings. Later came titles by Lyotard, Guattari, Pierre

Clastres, and Toni Negri, freely edited collections of texts by Foucault (*Remarks on Marx* and *Foucault Live,* and even, in 2000, his mythic lecture in Berkeley on *parrhesia,* unpublished in French, published in English as *Fearless Speech*), but also the prison writings of three black militants (including the soon to be famous Mumia Abu-Jamal) and, in the "Native Agents" series edited by Lotringer's companion Chris Kraus, political autofictions and collections of lesbian short stories. Just as the journal was described as "a weighty journal that appeals to punks, artists and eggheads alike,"[41] these inexpensive volumes reached a variety of readers, as the publishers attempted to insert their production of a new genre in between the two zones that bordered it, mainstream publishing and the university. It was through these small "portable" theory books, and thanks to their unconventional layout and their joyously irreverent tone, that a large number of young Americans became familiar with French theory—or perhaps read the texts firsthand there and only there. But the limits of Semiotext(e)'s approach, which this time were also political limits, had to do precisely with this constantly elusive movement, a refusal to be stably situated, and this affinity for the interstices or intermediate spaces, all set against the social rootedness of reading. Hence the failure, in the end, of the alliance between Semiotext(e) and the Autonomedia collective, a more grassroots anarchist publisher connected with militants around the country and with the network of labor unions and activists of the Brooklyn neighborhood where it is located. Foreshadowed by the growing disagreements between Fleming and Lotringer, later made official by the latter's decision in 2000 to transfer the reprinting of the press's publications to the MIT Press, this rupture indicated an incompatibility between what might be called a political logic of anchoring and the theoretical principle, dear to Lotringer, of aleatory dissemination and of the "one-shot" gesture.

Similarly, the gradual departure of his first collaborators has made Lotringer's wider network something of an anticommunity, a group in a state of permanent disaffiliation, caught up in political misunderstandings and betrayals among friends. Misapprehending texts, attenuating connections, letting go of the self—these could be the three unstated mottoes of this collective without a subject, and perhaps its own Foucauldian-Deleuzean justification. Lotringer's interest in Baudrillard's theme of a "disappearance of theory in the production of its effects,"[42] but also in the self-effacement required of a mediator, both have their source in his personal itinerary, that of an escape artist, and of an experimental relation with exile: as a Jew condemned by history to a long silence on the Shoah; as an intellectual who missed May 1968 (he was in Australia at the time) but was later haunted by the enigma of the self-dissolution of the avant-gardes; as a voluntary exile in another language who made himself a ventriloquist in order to speak the language of French theory to Americans; as a writer by vocation, who has nevertheless left unwritten works by the wayside as he devoted himself to making known those of his favorite authors.

Sylvère Lotringer thus embodies, perhaps more than anyone else, the radically singular figure, always threatened with invisibility, of these transmitters of French theory, caught between adhesion and irony and escaping the bulldozer of its institutionalization in two complementary directions—toward the living world of a rich American itinerary, in which theoretical motifs and life experiences constantly resonate, and toward the lightness of the player and the gambler, the furtive intuition that the whole thing was an intense but impossible task. Nothing better summarizes the contradictory stakes of this category of French theory than Lotringer's ambivalence toward the university, a double game that became for him a veritable ethics of ubiquity. He teaches in the university and has participated in many conferences, but he continues to rail against its "men of *ressentiment*." Between 1973 and 1978, he went from the conventional professor's suit to the attire of the New York punk scene, and yet he did not leave Columbia. He was the first to diffuse certain French texts, but is quick to condemn the "extermination of ideas through a saturation of commentary."[43] For while he worked ceaselessly to forge links between art and theory, percepts and concepts, he nevertheless became certain—in the distress of a dawning realization—and before anyone else, that French theory will be academic, or it will not be.

4

LITERATURE AND THEORY

> My opinion is that theories are themselves narratives, but
> hidden; that one must not let oneself be deceived by their
> pretention to omnitemporality.
>
> JEAN-FRANÇOIS LYOTARD, *Instructions païennes*

DECONTEXTUALIZATION is first of all a matter of disciplinary territories:
French theory entered the United States through the literature departments. The authors concerned were certainly read in courses of literary
theory in France as well. But literary theory there, after the vogue of
the 1970s, was quickly "domesticated [and] await[ed] students at the
appointed hour," and was limited in its effects by traditions that were
"solidly incorporated into the . . . national education," such as *explication de texte* or the *dissertation*[1]—whereas still today it dominates the
American field of the humanities. Moreover, Derrida, Foucault, Deleuze,
and Lyotard were not only philosophers by training, they also advocated
for philosophy as a discipline—as attested by their tenacious opposition
to the Haby reform of 1975 and their role in the creation of the GREPH
[Groupe de recherche sur l'enseignement philosophique—Research
group on the teaching of philosophy] and the Collège International de
Philosophie. Across the Atlantic, however, their writings, grouped together under the label of French theory, would be considered above all
from the perspective of literary studies and sifted through the literary
filter. On the statistical level, the turning point occurred between 1975
and 1980. In comparing the texts on and by Derrida published in France
and in the United States over a period of fifteen years, the sociologist
Michèle Lamont was able to discern a clear inverse relation in the curves

in 1975: the rise of Derrida in the field of literary studies in the United States, and an overall decrease in references to him in France.[2] In addition, limiting herself to the quartet Barthes-Lacan-Foucault-Althusser, she demonstrated that beginning in 1980, the date of their definitive disciplinary "fixing," more than 50 percent of the articles on them in the United States were published in journals devoted to literary studies.[3] The texts of all the authors in question were gradually translated, commented upon, and placed on the reading lists of literature courses, first in French departments and then in English and comparative literature departments. To many, these texts gave the impression of an unprecedented upheaval: "How liberating to encounter the daring epistemological sweep of Foucault's linguistic, economic and biological descriptions," as Edward Said recalled.[4]

Its success would quickly transform French theory into a major ideological and institutional force. And, in the context of increasing competition between campuses in terms of conferences and invited stars, it would become the object of an unprecedented one-upmanship between universities. The battle over the privilege of "showcasing" on their territory such thinkers as Derrida or Foucault at conferences created oppositions between, for example, Berkeley, Buffalo, and New York University (for Foucault) or Yale, Cornell, and Irvine (for Derrida). Even certain less renowned campuses managed to make themselves known as a hot spot for the interpretation of the French thinkers—for example, Miami University, in Oxford, Ohio, where the Francophile feminists Jane Gallop and Peggy Kamuf were teaching. As with sports teams, each university created a specialty that it wanted to broaden into the national market: Yale deconstructionists versus literary epistemologists at Cornell, Harvard psychocritics versus the postcolonials at CUNY, New Historicists at Berkeley versus Irvine Derrideans, Chicago neo-Aristotelians versus Stanford moralists, and so on. But, to get to this point, it was necessary for French theory, first imported and then reinvented, gradually to propel the rejuvenated and sometimes even highly galvanized literature departments to the most prominent position within the old field of the humanities.

Conflict of the Faculties: The Triumph of Narrative

The absence of a single dominant discipline, a crisis of paradigms, the protectionist retreat of certain disciplines, increasing budgetary competition between programs of study, the professionalization and exodus of students into the sciences and business: in the middle of the 1970s all the ingredients were in place for the outbreak of this ecological struggle between the various fields of knowledge in the American university, that structural *conflict of the faculties* (to use Kant's expression from 1798 to designate the relations between philosophy and the other disciplines) that had been calmed in the United States by the postwar boom. By brandishing a few operative concepts and a few names of newly translated authors, the literary field would emerge victorious from this conflict. Its weapon: a narrative (rather than normative) relativism that made it possible to reread the discourses of philosophy, the novel, sociology, or history as so many narratives, embedded in a yet vaster narrative structure. Its tactic: the use of such a perspective as a way to modify the cartography of knowledge, to extend its disciplinary power to adjacent fields, and, more broadly, to activate "*border* disputes" and "make *borders* into topics" of debate—since it is in theorizing the borders, as the sociologist Randall Collins has shown, that an intellectual current "keeps [itself] alive."[5] Three phenomena assured this victory: a literary interpretation of mostly philosophical French texts, an institutional offensive designed to impose this new discourse, and (a key factor) the extension of the new narrative paradigm to subfields more or less connected to literary studies—as was the case with film studies, critical legal studies, and, somewhat paradoxically, even theology.

Everything begins, then, within the French departments, which nonetheless remained quite conventional and would continue to remain so. For French theory only marginally altered their conventional approaches, which relied primarily on literary history and cultural context. Simply put, a handful of North American French professors, themselves from very disparate horizons (Fredric Jameson, Michel Pierssens, Jeffrey Mehlman, Leo Bersani, Mark Poster, to mention only a few), did at the time, in the midst of a crisis in literary studies, only what their predecessors had done with Surrealism or existentialism: they promoted on the other side of the Atlantic the objects of debates taking place in Paris, making resonate across this distance the most brilliant French products of the moment. Very quickly, as soon as a few translations were available, these texts emigrated toward the more noble department of English. Then they integrated the brand-new departments of comparative literature, the first of which began at Yale in 1973: successors to the old departments of "world literature" (*Weltliteratur*), they distinguished themselves from the latter through an approach that is more self-reflective, as well as more transversal, by interrogating literature and its cultural relativity—which is why they became the natural homes for the first interdepartmental programs, in ethnic studies or psychoanalysis. As they strayed away from the French departments, the texts by Foucault, Derrida, Deleuze, and Lacan that had first been encountered underwent a disciplinary recentering that consisted in drawing (not to say stretching) them toward literary studies, foregrounding and prioritizing their analyses of texts (or of textuality), and even casting their philosophical propositions as inherently literary.

The case of Foucault is particularly illuminating. After a limited turn to literary examples, thought of as a "rest, a stopover, a poetic statement," he said that he had "passed from a relatively cautious position (which consisted in signaling literature within its own space, without indicating its relations to the rest of discourse) to a position that is frankly negative, by trying to make all the nonliterary or paraliterary discourses reappear in a positive way . . . and by excluding literature": he was seeking less the "discourses internal to literature [than] discourses external to philosophy."[6] But the American use of Foucault became, on the contrary, more and more literary. Published in English for the first time in 1979, his 1969 lecture "What Is an Author?" is one of Foucault's most widely circulated texts—particularly its famous statement, borrowed from Samuel Beckett: "What matter who speaks?" Much attention was also given to his early texts, little known in France, on Maurice Blanchot or on the critic Jean-Pierre Richard.[7] The comparison was made—considering the two as exemplary figures of the genre of the *récit* or tale—between chivalry according to Don Quixote and madness according to Foucault.[8] Virginia Woolf was reread in the light of Foucauldian concepts as a veritable case history of the sexual frameworks analyzed by Foucault.[9] D. A. Miller's study *The Novel and the Police,* one of the most well known essays of the new American literary studies—because it manages to *sexualize* and to *politicize* an object of literary history, the novel as a genre—even presents itself as a direct application of the concept of the "disciplinary society" to that other great institution of the nineteenth century, the novel.[10] But a certain textualist illusion is at work behind this continuity posited (but left uninterrogated) between the prison or the hospital and the novelistic text. Articles and works abound that present to students an account of the relations between Foucault and literature, or a list of the most operative Foucauldian concepts in literary criticism—such as the classic study by Simon During.[11] Lyotard, and then Deleuze and Guattari, also encountered a similar fate.

Because he distinguished between minor narratives and grand narratives, between paralogical games and totalizing myths, Jean-François Lyotard made it possible, in literary studies, to generalize the notion of postmodernity and to bring together the theoretical and literary genres. Every discourse, including discourse on narrative, is brought back to the status of narrative: "The metalanguage which speaks of narrative," and which sees narratives everywhere—as though in an attempt to subject the literary field to its own power—"must be reminded that it is itself a narrative," states Bill Readings.[12] Nothing, henceforth, can escape it. Recognized more belatedly in literary studies, Deleuze and Guattari, for their part, first served as a support in the new Americanist discourse on "minority" literatures. Which is to say: through a slippage in the concept of *minor* literatures, introduced in the major essay on Kafka,[13] to that of a *minority* corpus, in which the authors of *Anti-Oedipus* would no doubt have seen the resurgence of a rather Oedipal regionalism. A conference on "The Nature and Context of Minority Discourse," held at Berkeley in 1986 by two Americanists, Abdul Jan Mohamed and David Lloyd, inaugurated a critical current devoted to minority literatures in the Americas—African American, Irish, Amerindian. Analyzing minority "stylistics" and "oppositional" writing, certain scholars were inspired by this development, such as the nineteenth-century French scholar Ross Chambers and the critic Louis Renza, but they adopted an approach that was very un-Deleuzo-Guattarian: Renza, referring to a single story by the Boston novelist Sarah Orne Jewett, calls for "a minor criticism of minor literature," but makes himself the sole judge of these categories (while also warning that some might see the discussions resulting from this "minor criticism" as "egregious overreadings"), whereas Chambers applied the conceptual tools of narratology to a description of the political risks taken in nineteenth-century literature.[14] As for authors who were even more closely associated with literary studies in France, such as Barthes and Kristeva, they were themselves the object of a literary overinvestment through the "tonal" or stylistic readings of their work that were offered. In an essay on postmodern thought, the critic Allan Megill even interrogates Derrida's work (as he does Heidegger's) in terms of its "stylistic" figures, the motif of "nostalgia" or the references to Edgar Allan Poe, in order to foreground a "radicality" that is more aesthetic, or apocalyptic, than political.[15] The reference to Nietzsche, which is central to Allan Megill's study, is itself often treated in a literary mode, presenting the phantom figure of the *Twilight of the Idols* as the one who provides poststructuralist theories and the langu-gage of their commentators with a tonality, a lexical field, and a *motif* in the pictorial sense of the term.

If philosophy is thus *made literary,* literature for its part becomes a mere region of theory. For these tactics of *literarization* attach the liter-ary text to theoretical discourse, which frames it and seems to justify it: through a "reversal of the hierarchy," literature henceforth, as An-toine Compagnon observes with regret, "is finding its legitimization in criticism and theory."[16] Yet, in order to impose new French references and to further the new political ambitions of literary studies, this slow process of indistinction between the literary and philosophical corpora would not be sufficient; it would be necessary to have an armed institu-tional branch. This role was filled by the first interdepartmental research institutes, or by programs that bring together scholars from numerous universities, such as the influential "School of Criticism and Theory": based first at Irvine and later at Cornell, this Areopagus of literary theo-rists organizes summer seminars initiating scholars to new theories; the programs are nicknamed "theory camps" in reference to the "summer camps" of American youth. But here too it is only a matter of preaching to the (nearly) converted. In order really to place a rapidly transforming literary field at center stage, the major institutional role will be played by the august Modern Language Association (MLA), founded in 1883. A massive professional organization for literary scholars, the MLA is the primary official body in the United States representing teachers and researchers in the field, of which some thirty thousand to fifty thousand are therefore members. Until the 1960s, the association was seen as a bastion of conservatism. But already, its very well attended annual con-vention made and unmade polemics and reputations: in 1948, the in-augural speech of the president of the MLA, presented by one Douglas Bush, lashed out at New Criticism, denouncing its "aloof intellectual-ity," its "avoidance of moral values," and its treatment of commentary as an "end in itself."[17] Even as late as 1980, and without anyone seeing it coming, the MLA president Helen Vendler praised, in a rather nine-teenth-century mode, "the taste on the tongue . . . of an individual style" and the "early attitude of entire receptivity and plasticity and innocence before the text," over and against the "interdisciplinary" deviations of literary studies.[18]

But within a few years, the MLA would become a crucible for the boldest (and in some cases the most ridiculous) innovations in literary studies; it was also a target for reactionaries who were beside themselves over its provocative politics—an homage to Ginsberg, honors paid to Castro's Cuba, and an invitation to host teaching delegations from the Soviet bloc. Nothing indicates more clearly the evolution of the field from the early 1980s on than the themes announced for the two thousand or so panels and roundtables organized for each MLA convention. The conventional discussions of scholars studying the sixteenth century or of Spanish professors on baroque poetry or Calderón's theater were gradually joined—to give only a very arbitrary selection—by themes as unthinkable before 1980 as "Deconstruction and the Death of God," "Obstetrics, Gynecology, and Venereal Disease in the Eighteenth Century," or "The Future of Marxist Feminism" in 1983, "Clitoral Imagery and Masturbation in Emily Dickinson" or "Coming Out as an Obese Woman" in 1989—and then, in 1990, "The Sodomite Tourist," "Irigaray and the Critique of Western Logocentrism," or "T. S. Eliot and Ethnicity," and, more recently, in 2002, discussions of the "Suburban Dikeaspora" (for lesbians moving out of inner cities), of "Guns and Barbies," or else of "Derrida's Islam" in the post-9/11 context. Each year, between Christmas and New Year's, this eccentric gathering of polished and proper academics has everyone talking. It was by way of this curious barometer of literary studies, and the rather unflattering accounts given of it in the press, that the larger public came to discover these new orientations—deconstruction, gay studies and then queer studies, Marxist and post-Marxist studies, postcolonial studies, black studies, and Chicano studies. Such a development in the MLA can be accounted for with reference both to its members, which it faithfully represents, and to the influence of its successive presidents, whether one thinks of the Derridean J. Hillis Miller, the feminist Catharine Stimpson, the historian of Surrealism Mary-Ann Caws, or the African Americanist Houston Baker.

Literary readings of philosophers and regularly scheduled institutional provocations are still a part of disciplinary strategies. Beyond that, and more profoundly, it was the entire literary episteme at work in the university that the suspicion instilled by means of French theory—or through its American reading—aimed to overturn. This suspicion can take a *pan-textualist* form, when one proposes to explain *all* cultural phenomena entirely from within and solely in terms of the (dys)functions of language. Or else *pan-narrative,* if one flattens *all* forms of discourse, from science to psychoanalysis, into so many narratives. The result is an enlargement ad infinitum of the very category of literature, which remains deliberately and consciously undefined, becoming nothing other than a synonym for such a suspicion without limits. The fluctuation in its definition guarantees its porosity in relation to all adjacent fields and, more tactically, the success of its inchoate wishes to encroach upon these fields. In other words, if everything is literature, who can resist it? This is another difference in comparison to France. Whereas there this "age of suspicion" had provoked for a few years a centrifugal movement of self-reflection, of retreat into the question of definition—it was the age's obsession for the "criteria of literariness" and the limits of "literary space"—the same theoretical influx gave rise in the United States to a centripetal movement of territorial expansion, by absorption or by contamination—by leaving the definition of literature (or of narrative) wide open, as though to better include its disciplinary *others*. A methodical and scientific suspicion, on one side, the better to catch in its nets an object that tended to escape it; a political and pragmatic suspicion on the other side, in the hopes that a field of study in crisis would emerge from it reinvigorated. For it is useful here, without slipping into a psychology of the vendetta, to recall the inferiority complex of a majority of literary scholars in the traditional American university, despite Matthew Arnold and despite the New Criticism: looked down upon by their colleagues in related fields, they were still seen as pleasant companions who were far removed from the true questions, and this is what is meant by the condescending term "belletristic." This time, on the contrary, it was from them that the serious questions came—or at least the questions that aroused anger. By suspecting that logocentrism determined philosophy, that colonialism was the subtext of the literary canon, that the social sciences were guilty of cultural imperialism, and even that the untouchable exact sciences (because of their purely internal legitimation)[19] suffered from autism, literary scholars became the champions of subversion. And their discipline became the sharpest *critical* weapon of the moment. The English department became a new Rome from which prodigious conquests were launched, crusades to evangelize distant territories—as is illustrated by three examples of unexpected literary subfields: film studies, legal studies, and theological studies.

American film studies is peculiar in two ways: because of a distinction between film schools and discourses *about* film, it began as a field attached to the humanities, and in its first phase it had a strong French influence, as evidenced by the success of Jean Mitry's work and the writings of the French New Wave. But the use of new French texts will transform these largely empirical courses (focusing, for example, on the adaptation of novels or the rules of Aristotle's *Poetics*) into veritable theoretical laboratories. The American reception of the writings of Lacan beginning in 1975–76, and especially of the Lacanian film theorist Christian Metz, particularly on visual perception or filmic oneirism, gave film studies a certain disciplinary identity within the literary field. In French-inspired Freudo-Marxist articles—also published in Britain in the journal *Screen*—the emphasis fell on the "machinations" of producers, the "unconscious ideology" of spectators, or the "authorial function" of the director.[20] Indeed, film studies and literature courses spoke the same language. The new journals that were coming into fashion, from *Diacritics* to *October,* published more and more articles on film, and the term most often used by these film theorists is the "reading" of films, as in the title of a textbook published in 1977, *How to Read a Film*—in which nothing is said, however, about the new era then beginning in the American cinema, with *Jaws* (1975) and *Rocky* (1976). However, during a second phase of film studies, as with cultural studies in the literary field, there was an evolution toward problems of identity (in terms of ethnic identity or feminism) and questions of mass culture and cross-cultural relations, an abrupt shift explained by Dudley Andrew in terms of the sheer imperative of academic innovation: "If the cinema studies edifice of semiotics, Marxism, and psychoanalysis was abandoned while its mortar was still wet, . . . look first to a university system that encourages scholars to expand into new subdivisions rather than repair, fortify, or remodel the field's city center."[21] Finally, in a more recent period, film studies became separated some years ago from literary studies, denouncing, in the name of a "posttheoretical age," the theoretical reduction of the filmic object, an anti-intellectualist backlash as excessive as the "hard" Lacanianism of 1975.[22] These were three phases during which film studies in the French university remained largely unchanged, organized around a double approach, both historical and aesthetic, as far from Lacan as it was from Deleuze: history of cinema and of its producers, aesthetics of the image and techniques of shooting and editing, and the complete *filière cinématographique* describing a film's path through the structure of the film industry, from script to distribution. At most, one interrogated in passing the validity of the semiological approach, or the usefulness of theories of literary genre to delimit the unlikely notion of filmic genres.

Still more significant were the incursions of the literary theorists into the territory of law, or rather—far from the segmented programs administered by law schools—into the territory of commentaries on law, without of course having any effects on the law itself. The critic Peter Brooks thus explored the place of confession in Western culture through a double reading of literary classics and jurisprudence—in a book that novelists recommend to lawyers, and vice versa.[23] More corrosive is the work of Stanley Fish (who teaches *both* in a department of English and in a law school), which consists in submitting legal principles to the double test of logical and rhetorical coherence. Gayatri Spivak, a postcolonial theorist and a specialist in Derrida's work, critiqued the "phonocentrism" of the law which, from interrogation to testimony, postulates that a punctual, fragmentary speech, often extracted under pressure, can be taken as the full and complete expression of a subject.[24] The impact of Derrida's work, especially "Force of Law," on this "literary" critique of the foundations of law, in fact led to a collaboration between Derrida and the Cardozo School of Law in New York, where in 1989 he presented a series of lectures on "Deconstruction and the Possibility of Justice." Located at the conjunction between this logical deconstruction and a political critique of American law, the field of "critical legal studies" emerged between 1978 and 1985 around the work of Richard Delgado and Roberto Ungar (at Harvard). It is a continuation both of John Dewey's critique of legal abstraction and of its "objectivity," and of the movement referred to as "legal realism" from the 1930s, according to which the legal vocabulary wrongly excludes from its field of action certain human realities (passion, conflict, event). It adds to these concepts other more recent ones from literary theory in order better to invalidate the law's pretention to "universal" justice, and to critique in particular its false "ideology of neutrality" in racial matters.[25]

Finally, the case of theology offers a still more convincing example of the new theoretical discourse's capacities of interdisciplinary circulation, or even of viral infection, one could say, so counterintuitive is its operation here. With the exception of Michel de Certeau, none of the authors of the corpus had directly addressed the themes of religious practice and discourse—neither Derrida's work on Levinas nor, a fortiori, Lyotard's musings on Jesus as a "calculating prostitute" fit within this framework. And yet, faced with the disaffection of the students and the disarray of the religious figures in confronting the conditions of their age (an age marked by depoliticization and new technologies), academic studies in theology took hold of French theory in their turn, and began to explore the paths of a "postmodern Christianity." Led by Mark Taylor, the "Derridean Christians" at first proposed a "deconstructive theology" linked to the doctrine of "error" and to the virtues of doubt.[26] Then, in the 1990s, a systematic rereading of the Bible in the light of French "antirationalism" made it possible to revalorize the Bible's "counterideological" and "antitotalizing" dimensions, over and against abstract ethics and "objectifying" scientism.[27] Various innovations followed, promoted by new "postevangelical" series from religious presses (such as Intervarsity Press), but there were also some scandals, when teachers strayed too far from dogma.[28] If the same concepts that were decentered by French theory—concepts whose false obviousness it problematized (reason, identity, science, individual)—have been used by these theologians to explain the decline of faith, the target community is no less indirect for all that: at stake in the critique of reason undertaken by French theory was not really a final Revelation. Biblical postmodernism has not in the end slowed the decline of enrollments, nor that of vocations; but it holds out perhaps one last hope of being saved.

In the end, the French theoretical detour has permitted this double tour de force: to place squarely within literary studies the most urgent political and philosophical issues of the age, and to justify the investigation (which literary scholars soon began) of the ellipses, analepses, and metonymies hidden behind the supposedly "neutral" language of philosophy and the social sciences. The victory of literature, and of its new theoretical arsenal, is not only the victory of suspicion, but of a general critical method, as gratifying as it is flexible.

The Politics of Quotation

Before looking at the fortresses that resisted the conquest of narrative, we must examine for a moment the publishing procedures (the production of texts) and the lexical procedures (the establishment of a common language) without which the *invention* of this theoretical discourse would not have taken place. These procedures had to carry out the double task of *uprooting* and *reassembling*. For in order to appropriate the foreign texts, it was necessary to displace their themes and their rhemes, to separate them from their memory and from the context in which they were first elaborated, since every "art of doing [is] also an art of forgetting," to use Michel de Certeau's formulation.[29] And in order to assemble a new society of discourse around these unmoored texts—the second stage of the *invention* in question—it was necessary to deploy the elements of a new community of language, of a veritable *modus loquendi* that would give to the readers encountering it the initiative of enunciation. It is here that the highly coded character of the new discourse comes into play—less as a career strategy or a strategy of exclusion than as a way to organize repetition, to make a language appropriable and "scriptable," to make topoi rhyme among themselves so that they will create relations among their users. Without it being possible, however, to distinguish in these diverse procedures between what was a deliberate tactic from the aleatory destinies of the texts.

The procedures of publishing helped to create an impression of intellectual promiscuity between the texts and authors that were brought together in the same series or in the same collection—a promiscuity that provided the deformed but efficaciously unifying figure of an intertextual space suddenly (and literally) bound more closely together. French theory was first to be found there, in the intermingled contents of an edited collection or of a publisher's catalogs. Such a close grouping can, however, imply amputation, as when in 1967 Pantheon Books chose, for commercial reasons, to publish the much abridged version of Foucault's *Histoire de la folie,* or when in 1984 Columbia University Press published Julia Kristeva's *Révolution du langage poétique* as a treatise on literary theory, excising its last part on Mallarmé, Lautréamont, and revolution.[30] But it meant above all the invention of a label, the sui generis creation of an intellectual family, by setting up circulations and connections among proper names, as occurred with all of the most well known series devoted, completely or in part, to French theory: "Theory and History of Literature" at the University of Minnesota Press, "Post-Contemporary Interventions" at Duke University Press, "Foreign Agents" from Semiotext(e), and, to a lesser extent, "European Perspectives" from

Columbia University Press and the "French Modernist Library" from the University of Nebraska Press. Their editors can thus reinforce this effect of promiscuity by publishing two-sided volumes, editorial Janus faces. Zone, for example, published Foucault's article on Blanchot (cited above) together with the latter's text titled "Michel Foucault as I Imagine Him"[31]—thus staging a dialogue between two authors within whose extensive corpora these are virtually the only references they ever made to each other. And when Deleuze and Guattari, in solidarity with Foucault, threatened to break with Semiotext(e) if it published a translation of the text by Baudrillard titled "Forget Foucault," Lotringer had the idea of adding a text that began on the flip side of the book, a long interview conducted with Baudrillard and given the title "Forget Baudrillard."[32] More generally, editors and mediators privileged coauthored texts, reciprocal articles, and mutual gazes, all of which were more effective than any editorial artifacts for producing the image of a common corpus. It was thus—to take only the example of Deleuze and Foucault—that the texts they wrote together or about each other, reprinted many times in the United States, came to be among their most famous there. This is the case with "Theatrum Philosophicum," Foucault's essay on *Logic of Sense* and *Difference and Repetition,* published in *Critique,* as with "A New Cartographer," Deleuze's review of *Discipline and Punish,* written also for *Critique;* but it also applies to Deleuze's book *Foucault,* first published in London and, with regard to their texts in common, the innovative preface they wrote together for the French edition of Nietzsche's complete works published by Gallimard and, of course, the interview for *L'Arc* that brought them together in 1972 titled "Intellectuals and Power." This text was first published in English in *Telos* and then in *Semiotext(e),* and finally in a collection of essays by Foucault.[33] It was soon criticized by Gayatri Spivak, for the interlocutors' insistence on "proving that intellectual labor is like manual labor" and for the way in which, "in the name of desire, they reintroduce the undivided subject into the discourse of power."[34] It has nonetheless remained, across the Atlantic, the text of reference on the question of the *uses* of theory, partly because of the definition of theory proposed by Deleuze and Foucault as a political "toolbox," called upon in the United States to serve its purpose in a dynamic future full of change.

In another order of ideas, the "readers" on offer for students produce the same effect of naturalizing a corpus through the promiscuity of proper names. These didactic anthology-type volumes cover a theme (postmodernity or homosexual literature, for example) or the work of one thinker—each of the French authors has his or her own, while Foucault and Derrida even have several readers that vary the angle of attack. To these are often added the more commercial argument of a miniaturization of the writer's thought: the "Great Philosophers" collection from Routledge claims to introduce the itinerary of Derrida or Foucault in sixty-four pages, and "Postmodern Encounters" from Totem Books summarizes an oeuvre by associating it with a commonplace of the postmodern vulgate, including volumes such as "Derrida and the End of History" or "Baudrillard and the Millennium." But the editorial tactic is still the same. It consists in substituting for the argumentative logic of each oeuvre the magic of a newly enchanting crisscrossing of names: "when famous names come together, rival sacred objects embodied in actual persons," observes Randall Collins in a commentary on thirty centuries of intellectual history, one sees them "bathing their audience in the clash of their auras."[35] Another form of *editorial* production of the new theoretical discourse is the addition of an abundant peritext—preface, afterword, footnotes, section headings, and the American tradition of the blurb on the back cover. Unless, that is, one of the authors is asked for a new preface, which will infuse the translated work with the prestige of its preface writer. This was the case when Mark Seem requested from Foucault an introductory text for Seem's translation of *Anti-Oedipus,* and when Foucault, with great awareness of the displacements involved, chose a programmatic tone and the imperative mood in order to invite the Americans to use this "great book" as a "guide to everyday life."[36] In the end, these editorial procedures decided, from year to year, the American destiny of the French texts, whose hierarchy they recomposed. Finding specific nodal points in the new corpus, they juxtaposed cross-referenced texts, excerpts that responded to each other, and certain fetishized formulas taken out of their contexts and discussed in turn by the various commentators. Thus it was that after being repeated, paraphrased, allusively evoked, cited as a prefatory guarantee, or even turned into a slogan on a book jacket, the famous formula of Foucault on Deleuze—which, however, cuts both ways—became one of the most often heard refrains about French theory in the United States: "Perhaps one day, this century will be known as Deleuzian."[37]

Lexical and syntactic procedures, for their part, are the operators of a complicity among readers. On the one hand, they theatricalize the text, whether primary or secondary, by deploying what Michel de Certeau called a "dramatics of allocution."[38] On the other hand, through the tone of the footnotes and the recurrence of certain obligatory motifs, they serve as indices of classification allowing one to distinguish immediately between ordinary texts and innovative texts, where the latter could be called *theori-morphic*—in the sense in which certain criteria would designate them at first glance as falling within the new theoretical discourse. One extreme, explained perhaps by a too obvious concern with originality, consists in the recourse to a regime of the unreadable, or to a sexualized jargon more confusing to its author even than its readers: "The anal penis . . . function(s) within a devalued metonymic continuity whereas the notion of the phallomorphic turd functions within the realm of metaphorical substitution," writes, for example, one Calvin Thomas in his *Male Matters* (1995), in a chapter on "the excrementalization of alterity."[39] More commonly, the use of neologisms replaces accurate paraphrase with the initiative exercised by the creator of concepts, who may even cross two authors in a new composite term, as Ian Douglas does by mixing together Foucauldian biopower and Virilio's theses on speed as part of what Douglas calls a "bio-dromology."[40] The flexibility of English allows even more often for abbreviations and acronyms whose dimension of orality and ludic motivations contribute to desacralizing the French texts, making them something that can be imparted in the informal mode of conversation, or even as a slogan: "decon" for deconstruction, "Derridoodle" for its inspirer, "DWEM" for the honored literary canon (Dead White European Males), "we-men" to underline the ambivalence of the feminist vindication, or "pomo lingo" for postmodern jargon, and so on. Finally, and more broadly, translation, because it is itself a transferral and appropriation, participates in its turn—and perhaps more powerfully than all the other procedures—in these modes of production of the theoretical discourse. Indeed, it is this production's liminal stage.

The first reason for this is that the endless difficulties of translation (to render *aveu* [avowal, confession] or *dispositif* [apparatus, arrangement] in Foucault, *jeu* [play, game, gamble] or *hors-texte* [outside-the-text] in Derrida, and *jouissance* or *objet partiel* in Lacan) force the translator into a metadiscourse of justification, whether self-critical or accomplished by omission, that places him from the beginning beyond his

prerogatives—he changes from a transmitter of language into a hermeneut. And in designating the lacuna, he invites his readers to overcome
a loss. Thus the constellation of signifieds hidden in the monosyllable
Sa in Derrida's *Glas* imposes on his translator a welcome explanatory
detour in order to bring together Hegelian absolute Knowledge ("savoir
absolu"), the abbreviation of the signifier, the Lacanian *ça* (it, id), and
the feminine possessive adjective in French, *sa;* likewise, the therapeutic
implications of *panser* (to stanch) in the verb *penser* (to think), on which
Derrida himself plays, provide the occasion for a useful digression.[41] In
their search for viable solutions for circumventing the untranslatable,
the translators are the ones who carry out the first gesture that will allow
readers in turn to *inhabit the gap,* to repeat, in the process of reading,
a bricolage that joins together two language cultures and that was first
carried out by the translator. For it is indeed a question of the "bricolage of contextual adjustments" (to use Jean-René Ladmiral's formula)
in these tactics of circumvention: "synonymic paraphrase," "calque,"
"theorem of minimal misinterpretation," a concern to "resocialize the
connotations"[42]—by assuming the inevitable change of register, or the
muting effects of a word cut off from its allusions. The translator always
encounters the experience of a limit—and a primary negativity—of language. The ruse that he must carry out is also a way of replacing the
impossible neutrality of a mere semantic transmission by the more voluntary, more affirmative gesture of an appropriation. In short, he must
speak, instead of simply reporting. And this was done all the more freely
by the American exegetes of the French corpus when, instead of trying to
render the balance of the arguments in a work, they impose a selection
and grasp onto a single motif, a formula, an entire theme—the death
of the subject, the fable of the map and the territory, the dissemination
of power, desire as flow: they test them and unfold them, turning—or
detouring—them to their advantage, playing with them to the point of
making them slip from symbols to indices, henceforth isolable, manipu-
lable, critiquable, in a word, inhabitable.

The work of quotation is at the center of these procedures. It acts as
a microcosm, suffices to transmit a complex argument, an entire oeuvre,
and is able literally to *present* them: not to summarize them or re-present
them, but to make them present—or at least to call forth their phantoms.
Quotation provides, in the end, the primary material of this intellectual
composite called French theory, which is itself contained entirely in a

handful of these quotations. It might be the false epigraph from Ecclesiastes, "the simulacrum is true," that Baudrillard placed at the beginning of *Simulacres et simulation* and concerning which its American readers no longer know whether it is itself authentic; it might be this encapsulation of Lyotard as he summarizes postmodernity in terms of an "incredulity regarding metanarratives"; it might be Derrida's assertion, translated in many ways, so often repeated outside *its* text, which says that "there is no outside-the-text." Even Deleuze's formula suggesting that the "history of philosophy [is] a sort of buggery" in which one "takes an author from behind and gives him a child that would be his own offspring, yet monstrous," or Foucault's image, at the end of *The Order of Things*, of man being erased "like a face drawn in the sand at the edge of the sea," were themselves repeated and deformed so often that their original texts have practically disappeared.[43] Quotation thus enters into a floating space, a transdiscursive zone traversed by proper names and passing concepts, in which quotation can escape from both the quoted and the quoter, and in which the French loan loses its distinction from the American addendum. Through quotation, what becomes possible is not so much a "possession" of the theoretical referent, which would suppose "closure" and rootedness, as a more furtive appropriation, a "capture": because it "speaks otherwise the discourse of the other," because it is brandished finally "in the name of no one," quotation, as Antoine Compagnon argues, makes possible less a "taking possession of the other than of oneself."[44] It also produces that "distancing of the proper name" analyzed by Bourdieu in another context,[45] when by dint of being quoted, the "empirical individual" who is subject of his discourse *hic et nunc* gradually gives way to the "doxic individual," the name of an oeuvre that divides up opinions, then to the more abstract "epistemic individual," without a face or a proper name, the index of a classification of knowledges, and the almost anonymous source of a chain of conceptual innovation.

Inventing French theory thus signifies nothing other than becoming able, through rhetorical turns and lexical ruses, to make Foucault or Derrida not so much into references as into common nouns, a form of discourse's very breath. Quotations constitute the endlessly reusable material of a changing construction that can always be put together and taken apart. The young undergraduate student who encounters them in a course, the humanist teacher who shouts them down in the name of

Pure Literature, and even the young dilettante who assimilates them in order to complete his general cultivation with a touch of "radical chic"[46] have all come into contact with these fragments of *French Theory*, detachable units of a discourse with variable contours. The internal order of such a discourse has more to do with rhythm than with linear argument, and with the charisma of a name-of-the-concept than with its explication. It is in this sense that the syntactic analysis of French theory I have sketched out here is indissociable from its sociological description as a new academic ethos—whose major features are its ludic approach, its logic of the unjustifiable, an imperative of originality, and a productive heterodoxy, but also a strategic conformity to certain communitarian allegiances. And, of course, a maximum gap—ensuring a certain element of surprise—between a featureless personage, a teacher without histories, and his trenchant discourse. These are so many aspects that will contribute more than a little to the alliance in which philosophy and the social sciences pitted themselves against French theory.

Resistances: From History to Philosophy

The irreverent vitality of this new form of literary studies has in fact given rise, internally and in related fields, to a strong resistance to French theory, and beyond that to the entire new region of knowledge that came to be delimited by this term "theory." Paul de Man, in a famous paradox, claimed that such a resistance is inherent to theory itself, because it is a "resistance to the use of language about language" and therefore "speaks . . . the language of self-resistance," and because it takes up the contents of knowledge that preexisted it by submitting these contents, against their will, as it were, to the suspicion of an autonomous functioning of language.[47] But, for their part, the principal *resisters* in the humanities—historians, sociologists, and particularly philosophers—would especially not have wanted to be connected with French theory in terms of their resistance to it, which would be the very type of paradox they find outrageous.

History as a discipline, already shaken up twenty years earlier by the impact of the *Annales* school, developed ambivalent relations with the new influx of French theory. The rise of social history and intellectual history encouraged borrowings from the French authors, especially Foucault and de Certeau. Then, as Dominick LaCapra put it, "the rethinking of intellectual history by way of the text-context problem raises the issue of language";[48] the linguistic turn thus did not spare the venerable history of ideas, which soon began to question its own methods and the status of the texts whose emergence it recounts, and to reexamine itself *in the mirror* of French theory, as attested by the conference on history and the "linguistic turn" organized at Cornell in 1980 by LaCapra and Steven Kaplan.[49] More broadly, the epistemological crisis that history had been undergoing since the end of the 1960s led to a more or less salutary phase of self-reflection, because, although conservative historiography refused the debate, a number of reputable voices were raised in the opposite direction—Hayden White, for example, who called for an "opening" of historical approaches, and Peter Novick, who directly posed the question of "objectivity" in history.[50] But the limits of such a dialogue between history and literary poststructuralism involve, precisely, the status of texts. For, at a time when the literary theoreticians were reducing history to a distant (and ideologically suspect) context in their field, the historians would have little to do with the equivocalities or the unsaid of the text, or with the misreadings to which it would give rise—concerned above all with replacing documents that were no longer considered trustworthy with others that were. Moreover, to interrogate the two disciplines in the same terms amounts to assuming a certain *continuity* between texts and historical facts. But we saw that such a continuity could hardly be taken for granted (when the prison and the novel are placed on the same level), and the historian Lynn Hunt has even shown that this continuity often led to simplistic causalities—to the detriment, according to her, both of the "complexity" of the literary determinants and of the "scandalous" dimension of the pure historical *event*.[51] In fact, if the historians mistrusted the textualists and the devotees of deconstruction, they nonetheless engaged in a more open but no less problematic dialogue with the other "camp" of the new literary field, those interested in identity politics—who, for their part, cannot do without history, even if this means presenting a political critique of it.

The very diversity of the social sciences makes their case more complex. On the one hand, French theory is at the origin of a major turning point in two ways: in cultural anthropology, with the influence of Foucault and Lévi-Strauss and complemented by the work of Clifford Geertz and his theory of culture as a "mobility of meanings," and in the sociology of science that arose around the research of Bruno Latour, which had been preceded by the epistemological "revolution" of Thomas Kuhn. But, from another perspective, functionalist sociology and field ethnology quite logically closed themselves off to it. A mode of thinking that leads one to consider "society" as a political fiction and to remove the "agent" for the sake of a critique of the *subject* of action could not expect a warm welcome in the United States, where the tradition in the social sciences—since the first American department of sociology was opened at the University of Chicago in 1892—has been based on an inductive approach, quantitative data, life histories, and the social applications of research. And yet, at the beginning of the twentieth century, the initial influence on American sociology of the *qualitative* anthropologies of Gabriel Tarde and Georg Simmel, precursors in their time of social interactionism, might have favored such a dialogue; and the one that actually took place between certain French philosophers from the 1960s and the researchers of the interactionist school of Talcott Parsons, then those of the "invisible college" of Palo Alto (in which the work of Gregory Bateson, for example, interested Foucault and Deleuze), also should have facilitated this exchange. But here too the disciplinary barriers played their role as a sorting mechanism, closing most of these disciplines to the French contributions, which were perceived as threats or unsubstantiated generalizations. The positivist heritage in the social sciences had too much weight in the American university not to incite figures like Peter Gay and even Clifford Geertz to condemn Foucault for a lack of empirical research and for his "evasive" formulas: at the moment of his American triumph, "they made every effort to hold back the Foucauldian wave."[52]

The epistemological disagreement was compounded by an ethical mistrust, not to mention a political rejection. The point of view of the sociologist Janet Wolff clearly summarizes that of the majority of her colleagues: "Poststructuralist theory and discourse theory, in demonstrating the discursive nature of the social, operate as license to deny the social."[53] However, C. Wright Mills, who politicized sociology, and Clifford Geertz, whose 1973 classic *The Interpretation of Cultures* led to a "cultural" turn in the social sciences, did, in their own ways, prepare the ground for a fruitful debate with French theory. But it was precisely in the name of a politically engaged sociology, which they both embodied and which their followers opposed to the presumed theoretical "relativism" of the French, that this debate never took place. On a few occasions, and in terms that were themselves somewhat caricatural, Foucault or Derrida would be applied to the sociology of culture, or of health.[54] But, beyond that, the impact of French theory on the social sciences was limited to certain partial borrowings: an operative concept here and there, or a final suggestive statement, but without ever abandoning the methods of the archivist and the statistician, and only on the condition of "downplaying the most disembodied aspects of French theory," as Michèle Lamont and Marsha Witten have noted.[55]

The case of philosophy is crucial in other ways. Deleuze, who felt it important to define himself as a philosopher in the most classic sense of the term, nonetheless made a call "to get out of philosophy, to do never mind what so as to be able to produce it from outside";[56] the least one can say is that the Cerberuses of the philosophical kingdom in America, jealously guarding a strictly delimited territory, didn't exactly share his opinion. There are, of course, notable exceptions to the stubborn resistance of philosophy: the rare departments of philosophy that teach "Continental" philosophy, including DePaul in Chicago, Stony Brook on Long Island, the New School in New York, and certain Catholic universities such as Loyola and Notre Dame. As for the rest, however, nothing—beginning with the absence of philosophy in high schools—predisposed the American philosophers to cast more than an amused glance, or an irritated glare, at the enthusiasms of their literary colleagues. Not that there is an insurmountable gulf between American analytic philosophy—that of the logical positivists and the experts of "ordinary language" (around Morton White and J. L. Austin)—and the Continental metaphysics that makes up "our" history of philosophy: it is here less a question of a breach, itself philosophical, between two incompatible conceptions of the activity of thought, as certain extremists of both camps would have us believe, than of a historical phenomenon that is both recent and, in its origins, ideologically motivated, in this case by the exile in the United States of the members of the Vienna circle and their deep anticommunism (which also meant for them a fervent anti-Hegelianism), aggravated further by the atmosphere of the cold war.

The logical positivists who came from Europe in fact took up for their own purposes, within a different historical context and ideological framework, the mistrust that the American pragmatist tradition of William James and John Dewey had developed, in the preceding century, toward the moral and political ambitions of European philosophy and the grand explanatory systems of Kant and Hegel. In the 1890s, James inaugurated a century of distrust toward Continental idealism and the Hegelian "dead end" by turning away from the Continental philosophical corpus, and even by exclaiming, as a famous anecdote from Harvard reports: "Damn the Absolute!" Pragmatism and analytic philosophy were thus seen by American philosophy departments as so many antidotes against Hegel—against his German lyricism and his totalizing "violence." At first cultural and historical rather than *epistemic,* this distinction between American and Continental traditions in philosophy is thus an opposition less between two definitions of philosophy than between two types of ethos, two ways of practicing the same activity, two "dispositions," as Pascal Engel put it:[57] on one side are the specialists of the inquiry into truth, all the more austere in that "in order to be deep, it is necessary to be dull," as Charles Sanders Peirce said,[58] and on the other side are generalists invested with a mission, and, from Nietzsche to Sartre, ceaselessly opening a space in which their relation to truth is mediated by style, or by writing. There is plenty here to fuel the conflicts between the philosopher-engineers, sober technicians of "ordinary language," and less restrained literary types suddenly taking up for their own advantage the grand philosophical gesture in the Continental style. On one side, there is the logico-mathematician tradition of Bertrand Russell and Rudolf Carnap, inherited by the "cognitive functionalism" of Hilary Putnam and then by the new research in neurophilosophy and the theories of artificial intelligence: from the first academic cloisters made up of American logicians in the 1930s to the austere colloquiums of today, the American tradition maintains that philosophical questions can only bear on the nature and content of *science,* which is itself the model and horizon of every search for knowledge. While, on the other side, literary scholars versed in French theory and atypical sociologists share certain suspicions regarding the ideological motives and disciplinary separatism among the philosophers, as well as the model of obligatory scientificity and the general postulate of a "neutrality" of ordinary language. We recognize here, between the sciences and letters, an ancient dialogue of the deaf.

The history of American philosophy is also the history of a professionalization of the philosophical field. It has evolved, in effect, toward what John Rajchman calls "a sort of generalized legalistic expertise," a specific competency "with cases, claims, and arguments," and a rejection of the entirety of Continental thought since Kant as "fuzzy thinking, a false historicism, an irrationalism."[59] But the new *theorists* of the literary field who appeared at the end of the 1970s did not hesitate, for their part, to intervene in the philosophical field, citing Derrida on the impossible univocity of philosophical language, recalling with Lyotard that one is always in the grip of a narrative—while they themselves developed a "narrative" rereading of the history of philosophy, which for them meant Continental philosophy. For example, in her first book Judith Butler approaches philosophy as a "story" endowed with "tropes," for which the "narrative" is Hegel's *Phenomenology of Spirit*, which she compares to a bildungsroman or even to a German version of the *Wizard of Oz*.[60] The philosophers reacted with various arguments to this new agitation of the literary field. The most common is the argument calling for clarity, or for rationality: the French texts, like those inspired by them, lack "clarity," contain no "arguments," and break the golden rule according to which one must say only what one can say clearly.

One also encounters from time to time the (less simplistic) idea that a *horizontal* inquiry into truth (the task of the literary thinkers), on the basis of texts and their interconnections, and a *vertical* inquiry interrogating the relation between language and the real, could not truly be compatible. For the attitude of all the philosophers is not the pure and simple rejection of what would be *merely literature*, or that "French fog" denounced by generations of Americans working within a scientistic framework. They also express their perplexity concerning "a conception of philosophy itself as a kind of writing or literature."[61] Most of them are vigorously opposed to the "antireferentialism" of French theory—that is, the idea, considered unacceptable by the logicians, that texts or discourses refer only to other texts and other discourses, and not to the real world. But the unusual commotion produced on the edges of their disciplinary territory by the theoretical vogue also left traces in the philosophical field—by aggravating an internal crisis linked to the problem of the social role of philosophy, by encouraging ethical and aesthetic reflections (which were introduced at the same time in works by John Rawls on the theory of justice and by Nelson Goodman on "worldmaking"), and even by inciting a few rare philosophers (as we will see with Richard Rorty) to build a bridge between American pragmatism and French theory.

Theory, a Critical Education

Finally, a deep mystery, skillfully maintained, surrounds the term "theory," this new transdisciplinary object fashioned by literary scholars from French poststructuralism. This mystery distinguishes it, in any case, from the previous uses of the term, all more or less linked to science: the new American theory is neither the theory of the pragmatists (an investigation of the procedures of cognition that must, however, serve the common good), nor the *Theorie* of the Germans (seen as the rational grasp of an object in the metaphysical tradition, from Kant to Husserl), nor theory as the Marxist science (and demystification) of ideology in Althusser, nor even the more restricted theory of the precursors of American generational grammar in the 1950s, from the linguist Zellig Harris to his disciple Noam Chomsky. Moving against the grain of these more precise definitions, the new theory of which it is everywhere a question for the last thirty years in literature departments, whether it is designated as French or simply as literary, remains mysteriously intransitive, with no other object than its own enigma: it is above all a discourse on itself, and on the conditions of its production—and therefore on the university. It is in a way the institutional effect of a disappearance of literature as a clearly delimited category, of an extension of its territory as well as its indefiniteness. As Gerald Graff comments: "Theory is what is generated when some aspect of literature, its nature, its history, its place in society, its conditions of production and reception, its meaning in general, or the meanings of particular works, ceases to be given and becomes a question to be argued in a generalized way."[62] The context of its sudden emergence in the American university played a role in this orientation, pointing the critical activity toward a situation of crisis (and thus to its etymological origin) and condemning theory to ceaselessly interrogate its own legitimacy: in the age of "excellence," of rampant unemployment, and of the imperative to make knowledge "relevant," theory had to justify to students, and indeed to America, its utility *as an intransitive activity*. For it had to remain itself, without object, since to aim at a more particular or transitive utility it would quickly lose ground in comparison to approaches that were less innovative but otherwise useful outside the campus, from semiotics to literary history. In vindicating the generality of an intransitive procedure, it became linked again with the heuristic value long attributed, in the United States, to the English literature course as an interrogation on pedagogy, a debate on proper method. Already in the nineteenth century, the English department was the central reference point for all pedagogical discussions: "Textbooks on the English language abound . . . , methods [for the approach to texts] are discussed *ad nauseum* . . . , and the opinions of prominent educators are solicited by journals of education, as to the best thing to be done for the study of English," wrote the critic Hiram Corson in 1895.[63] To this tradition, the malaise of the 1970s added a proliferation of reports, pamphlets, and more theoretical essays on the best education to offer in these times of crisis, including *The Idea of a Modern University* by Sydney Hook (1974) and the classic by David Riesman, *The Academic Revolution* (1977). The impact of French theory would, in a way, double this phenomenon: it is precisely because it poses a problem to American higher education, and a fortiori to the age of utilitarianism, that French theory will claim to be useful—or all the more stimulating for being embarrassing—and will declare itself best suited to reflect it, to interrogate it, to hold a faithful mirror to it.

In fact, at the end of the 1970s its success will give rise to an incredible plethora of colloquiums and works on the "crisis of the humanities" or "pedagogy and theory." The conceptual tools of theory, even when used in a partial way, thus renewed the debate on a number of old ideas in higher education. Academics interrogated the forms by which knowledge is transmitted, the "phonocentrism" of the professorial monologue, the "democratic illusions" of the dialogue with the student, the "Eurocentrism" of this anthology-oriented culture that dominated the literary field, or even the "epistemic imperialism" that was promoted by the ordinary methods of evaluation—since a *grade* sanctions the knowledge gained in a course as much as the logical modalities of its presentation. All of these debates were in the end similar to those that agitated the French university after 1968. But the American context was very different from the one in which Lyotard and Deleuze were writing: it was thus necessary to pull, not to say stretch, the French authors in the direction of the American academic crisis, in a *détournement* toward pedagogical debates of which they were unaware, and to read them from a certain angle in order to emphasize the paths that could be opened at a practical level in the humanities. Some of the most astonishing readings of the French authors were perhaps located here: for example, in the attempt to make liberal education the primary issue of the Foucauldian concept of "knowledge/power" (whereas one of the only institutions of knowledge/power that Foucault did *not* interrogate was doubtless the university . . .), to see in the critical aptitudes of the student the most valuable effect of Derridean deconstruction, or to read Deleuze and Guattari in order to ferret out "a useful tool with which to intervene in 'the politics of American education.'"[64]

Even Lyotard was called upon to make a contribution. Pradeep Dhillon, who teaches in education policy studies, and Paul Standish, a critic, thus brought together a dozen thinkers in the domain of literary studies in order to draw from their work the foundations of a "just education." Lyotard was thus read in a pedagogical, or rather an anti-pedagogical, perspective: one writer examines the role of the "sublime" in a just education; another makes the "paralogies" the source of a new "politics of knowledge"; yet another depicts Lyotard, not without irony, as a "moral educator," and the collection draws from his work more generally the first elements of a "libidinal education" or even of an "a-pedagogy" that would lead to a recognition of the Other.[65] Lyotard's effective engagements in this area, when he opposed the education ministry's reforms at Nanterre and later at Vincennes, are cited in support of his critique of the "mercantilization of knowledge" and of its "class monopolization."[66] The ideal type of "Lyotardian teacher" becomes the emblematic figure of "a last and essentially uncooperative line of resistance to the hegemony of capital and of universalist ideas"; he is the one who will know how to set up the "University of the Sublime," whose objective is nothing less than the "production of intellectual and emotional intensity."[67] If *The Postmodern Condition* was originally a "Report on Knowledge" in the university, its author no doubt did not expect things to go quite this far.

Motivated perhaps by the magnitude of his success in the United States (and therefore of the expectations to which this success gave rise), Jacques Derrida was the only one of the authors of the corpus to have directly played this role of the theoretician of education. He did so at the invitation of his American hosts, as with his recent reflections on the "humanist" aporia of the humanities ("The Future of the Profession . . . ," reworked in French under the title *L'Université sans condition*),[68] or on his own initiative in a conference paper—in order to note, for example, that deconstruction is "increasingly a discourse and a practice *on the subject of* the academic institution."[69] As someone familiar with the

American university system, which he began to visit in 1956 (when he participated in an exchange program between the École Normale Supérieure and Harvard), Derrida was able to give an account of American traditions—whether it had to do with the chronic crisis of the humanities beginning a century ago or with the older practices of theory in literary criticism. For it seems that, since the end of the nineteenth century, each generation of American literary scholars reproached the preceding one, to a greater or lesser degree, with its *lack* of theory. But French theory, by calling into question the subject of knowledge, the autonomy of reason, and the logic of representation, suddenly intensified this familiar debate, dramatized it far enough to create points of rupture. The suspicion it expresses insinuated itself like a time bomb between the antagonistic poles of the American field of the humanities, stretching them to their critical limits, by accentuating their historical contradictions: between the moral and cognitive dimensions of the teaching of the humanities; between the scientific (German) and liberal (English) modalities of their development; between its more contemporary temptations toward minoritarian politics, on one side, and toward the maximal indetermination of a theory conceived as pure paradoxical logic, on the other. Indeed, the entire efficacity of theory, as an epistemic virus but also as a "new career path," as David Kaufmann puts it, consists in underscoring these tensions, opposing the old ones to new ones in order to show all the richness of the literary field, and, by the same token, to draw from this situation its own legitimacy: the "vital" function of theory, he concludes, is to "serve [both] the demons of arid professionalization and the gods of general value," to have "militated against the tendencies of specialization at the same time as it has acted as their agent,"[70] floating thus from one extreme to another precisely because only it can connect them.

There is nothing surprising, then, in the fact that theory, despite (or perhaps by means of) its indefiniteness, became the object of academic debates as unthinkable in France as the one that raged in 1982–83 in the pages of *Critical Inquiry,* under the title "Against Theory." This is the unambiguous title of an article by Steven Knapp and Walter Benn Michaels, two professors of literature who reproach theory for being an "attempt to govern interpretations of particular texts by appealing to an account of interpretation in general."[71] The ensuing debate, as described by E. D. Hirsch, set the partisans of a "local hermeneutics"—cobbled together on a case-by-case basis and as the texts would warrant (victory of literature)—against the defenders of a "general hermeneutics" and its principles (or counterprinciples) of reading—that is, the superiority, in this case, of theory. Under the pretext of mediating the debate, Stanley Fish wonders how theory can elicit fear since it has, he says, "no consequences" and is bound up with a project that is aware of its own impossibility, and with the rules that would be dictated by its other, namely, practice.[72]

What is illustrated by this type of exchange, so frequent in the United States, and what it also helps to make possible, is the absorption of contrary opinions (empiricist or humanist) into the very field of theory, which thus becomes a space of discourse rather than a position within this space. "The anti-theoretical polemic is one of the characteristic genres of theoretical discourse," as the editor of the volume himself admits.[73] It matters little, at the limit, what position one holds at the moment when one *occupies* the space in question. In sum, theory is to the American literary field at the end of the twentieth century what "woman" was to Baroque poetry—a source of inspiration, a site for the invention of a language, and a license for expression. Hence the variety and richness of its formulas and definitions. It is thus a "utopian perspective" whose nature is "ocular, spatial, and graphocentric," which "places itself at the beginning or the end of thought," for it is not content with "the middle realm of history, practical conduct,"[74] once again in the terms of the volume's editor. And it becomes, in a more lyrical mode, a "practice of dissidence and of echoing the cry," itself located "at the intersection of the cry and of the System," as Wlad Godzich puts it.[75] The fact that it could inspire such flights, whether sincere or tactical, presents less of a problem than the sheer inflation of its discourse, its excessive chatter, which can often overwhelm the literary text. And that is the entire *ethical* problem of theory: thanks to the innumerable concepts that populate it, whether Foucauldian apparatuses of control, Deleuzean minorities, or a Derridean dispersal of traces, it never ceases to know more than the text that justifies its existence. As Peter Brooks notes in the terms of literary history, it seems always to "know better—better than the deluded discourses we are unmasking, better than the poor old Renaissance, better, especially, than the benighted, repressed, neurotic, oppressive nineteenth century."[76]

But this elusive object called theory cannot be reduced to the folklore surrounding the jousting matches between American literary scholars. It engages larger questions concerning the grasp of the real and the power of discourse, questions that for millennia have haunted the philosophical tradition—such as the pre-Cartesian question, reformulated by Martin Heidegger on the basis of the etymology of the word *theory,* concerning the primary relation of the gaze to that which offers itself to this gaze. At the risk of an association that might be frowned upon by intellectual history, one could indeed connect these two "theories"—over and above the rational theory of Western science—that is, this American theory conceived as a practice of the indefinite, as a blurring of borders, and the pre-Socratic *theoria* celebrated by the German philosopher.[77] The Greek word *theorein,* which combines the words designating vision (*horao*) and outward appearance (*thean*), is a gaze resting on that which comes to presence, a gaze onto the very unity of this presence at the moment when it advenes, a gaze that has no object but only finds itself solicited by this presence; that is, before the moment when its Latin translation into *contemplari* and then *meditatio*—by cutting out (*templum*) this same unity—announces already, according to Heidegger, the modern derouting of theory, which rationalizes and "enframes" the real, enumerates it, compartmentalizes it into objects. In American theory, it is of course a question, if we pursue this comparison, only of the coming to presence of a "text," the plenitude it has before its exegetes cut it into significations, of the irruption of its language against the improbable "mastery" of this language by its readers or its author. Its "clearings" or "paths" do not refer to Heidegger's ontological grounding, to what technical reason has not yet rationalized; they tie together only phrases, shreds of texts. And yet, theory, as it is celebrated by these avant-gardist literary scholars, brings with it an ontological dimension: one that has less to do with a nostalgia for the pure "presence" of the world (to which the Americans have been immunized by reading Derrida) than with a prerational withdrawal toward the "being" of the text—a return to the text as an autarchic life, an event of language, *causa sui.* They are, at least in this sense, rather heirs to the worshippers of the Text, exiled theologians and religious dissidents, or a continuation of the romantic antimodernism and the apoliticism of the New Critics, than the faithful literary disciples of Foucault, Deleuze, or even Derrida. What is most important to them, like Heidegger before the fire described by Heraclitus, is to maintain a capacity for fascination before this miracle—that the text (or the fire) *is.* And at the limit, the true fundamentalists of textual theory regard it as illegitimate to circumscribe its approach, to fix its objects in advance, to produce a reasoned argument: sociocritics or psychocritics, mythocritics or literary historians are thus guilty of decomposing the text, reducing it, enumerating it, somewhat as Descartes was guilty of having mathematized nature.

To delineate more precisely the enigma of "theory," it is better in the end to substitute the Heideggerian specter, to which the American context does not readily lend itself, with a more recent reference, a more political treatment of the theoretical equation, but one that is just as respectful of its fine intransitivity—namely, Roland Barthes's remarks from a 1970 interview. There he evokes, in effect, the slippage from modern scientific *theories* (abstract and transitive) to the singular designation of a "revolutionary" metadiscourse: *theory* thus refers to "a certain discontinuity, a fragmentary nature of exposition, almost analogous to an aphoristic or poetic style of enunciation, and therefore a struggle to fissure the symbolic order of the West," for theory as the "reign of the signifier ceaselessly dissolves the signified," and excludes it as a "representative of monology, of the origin, of determination, of all that does not take multiplicity into account."[78] These few formulas delineate a phenomenon of the times that one might think was buried under the dust of the 1970s. Against the naive sacralization of Works, but also against the dialectical opposition between discourse and praxis, these formulas present theory as the possibility of a discourse liberated from the rational order: a fragmentary enunciation that would rise up against linear argument, a writing of the world that withdraws the world from the great institutions of meaning—Truth, Justice, Power. Here theory is a thinking of struggle, a resource of opposition, all the more operative in that it is fixed by no prior definition—we hear in this the entire tonality of an age, now somewhat forgotten. My hypothesis is that such a logic persisted in the United States within the bounds of literary studies, and behind the walls of the university, whereas the supposedly "pro-totalitarian" exploits of this same theory, that of the Marxists or of the civil libertarians, would soon banish this logic from France. It is also because, within the confined space of academic discourses, bodies and streets tend to disappear, even to have never been, and because this campus-bound theory will at times lose all relation to the object—to the point of no longer designating anything but its own aptitude for dissemination, its sheer power of contamination. Theory is all of this at once, a mode of circulation of ideas, a primary astonishment before the text, and, more trivially, a criterion of promotion in the university. As the antitheory critic Camille Paglia expressed it in her own fashion, that is, in her febrile and spiteful terms, "Lacan, Derrida, and Foucault are the academic equivalents of BMW, Rolex, and Cuisinart," and "French theory is like those how-to tapes guaranteed to make you a real estate millionaire overnight. Gain power by attacking power! Make a killing! Be a master of the universe! Call this number in Paris *now*!"[79] The entire difficulty consists in holding together, as two halves of the same mystery, this theoretical careerism—which is indeed a major force behind French theory—and the intrinsic qualities of the theoretical posture: wily, mobile, corrosive, an enemy of first truths and of all dualisms. Theory: the most valuable commodity on the academic market, or the only approach that breaks down the walls of the humanities; recruitment strategy or science of the text; sectarian seal worn on the lapel, or critical force without equal; or all of this at once.

5

DECONSTRUCTION SITES

Here was a professor of religion . . . babbling on about Derrida
as if he were a combination of Augustine and Aquinas . . . God
was indeed dead, and maybe literature was too, and for [this]
professor and his fellow panelists Derrida had taken their place.

HILTON KRAMER, *The New Criterion*

THERE IS a Derrida mystery. I am referring less to the mystery of his
work, which is indeed not lacking in opacity, than to his canonization,
first in the United States, then globally. How is it that a thought so difficult to categorize and to transmit, a thought that is impossible to situate precisely, one that hovers somewhere between a negative ontothe-
ology and a poetic exploration of the ineffable, a thought that in any
case (and in every sense of the term) remains at a distance—how is it
that this thought was able to become the most bankable product ever
to emerge on the market of academic discourses? How did this obscure
trajectory find itself taken hold of, domesticated, digested, and served
in individual doses in an American literary field that, from this moment
on, began to spread its wings and, not content to have packaged this demanding thought in freshman textbooks, transformed it into an unprecedented program of epistemo-political conquest? How is that for every
French reader of a book by Derrida in the land of obligatory high school
philosophy courses, ten Americans have already looked it over, despite
their meager philosophical formation? And how is it, finally, that this
word *deconstruction,* which Derrida took from Heidegger's *Being and
Time* (as a translation of the word *Destruktion*) in order to sketch a
general theory of philosophical discourse, passed so far into the current

language of the United States that one finds it in advertising slogans, in the mouths of TV journalists, or as part of the title of a successful film by Woody Allen, *Deconstructing Harry* (1997)?[1] These questions present a great many challenges to the historian of cultural transferences—and an ideal case study for a "geopolitics of translation" that still needs to be mapped out.[2]

Reading: Derrida's Stakes

One thing is certain: the answer to these questions does *not* have to do with any personal strategy on Derrida's part. America is certainly central to Derrida's trajectory; it "produces my work," as he put it himself. It was there, during his first stay, that he was married and worked on his first book, a translation of and commentary on Husserl's *Origin of Geometry*. He made important friendships that lasted for decades, and even strengthened family ties—when his cousin Annie Cohen-Solal was the cultural counselor at the French embassy in the United States. He taught in the United States every year after the symposium at Johns Hopkins in 1966, at first taking turns at Yale, Cornell, and Johns Hopkins, and then for fifteen years dividing his time on both coasts, in the fall at New York University and in the spring at the University of California at Irvine (where he established his archives). Since the end of the 1980s, he even lectured and presented papers in English, having his notes translated from French beforehand. His seminars on Plato, Mallarmé, and Rousseau, and the long-standing dialogues with his most faithful interlocutors, played a primary role in the evolution of his work. And having received so many honors, inspired so many new schools of thought and so many works, whether mimetic or abusive, caricatural paraphrases or innovative extensions, seems to have developed for him a double relation to America. These two indissociable registers are those of intimacy, on the one hand, in relation to familiar campuses and networks of friends, and, on the other, the strange objectifying distance of that "America" which he allusively names in the course of his lectures, a conceptual figure on which his arguments sometimes play, and which one might occasionally suspect him of evoking in ways that deliberately counter conventional wisdom, the better to disconcert his listeners. That was the case when, at a conference at the University of Virginia, he proposed to *deconstruct* the Declaration of Independence. It was the case especially with his famous formula from 1985 according to which "America *is* de-construction, . . . its family name, its toponymy," which immediately set off a myriad of commentaries, feverish or perplexed, whereas its author abandoned the hypothesis fifteen lines later, preferring the conclusion that "deconstruction is not a proper name, nor is America the proper name of deconstruction."[3]

The fact remains that his American success—and the fortunes of de-construction—have a much broader scope than any biographical frame-work. It will be necessary, then, for us first to look back at the modalities by which a certain Derrida was first *constructed* in the United States, modalities that themselves involved many unforeseen twists and turns. Indeed, between his first fragmentary American translations, which were not yet framed by a local discourse, and the systematization of decon-struction as a mode of reading, which occurred at Yale around the be-ginning of the 1980s, it was the intervention of a young and brilliant teacher who immigrated from India to the United States that would serve as the catalyst. In 1973, Gayatri Spivak, barely thirty years old at the time, ordered a book whose author was unfamiliar to her but whose description aroused her curiosity—she spotted it in one of those cata-logs of foreign books that she signed up for in order to break her iso-lation, confined as she had been at the University of Iowa already for eight years. This book, *De la grammatologie* [*Of Grammatology*], was a revelation. Convinced of its importance, she took on the difficult job of translating it, and persuaded the Johns Hopkins University Press to publish it, in 1976, with a long translator's preface of a hundred pages which she considered indispensable: it was this publication, quite diffi-cult but still frequently ordered today by students and bookstores (more than eighty thousand copies have been sold) that would launch Derrida's work in the United States. In her preface, Spivak first defines the sign as the impossible adequation of the word to the thing, the very "structure of difference," hence truth's status as "metaphor."[4] She then clarifies the book's philosophical references, its double horizon: to surpass a Heideg-gerian "metaphysics of presence" and to carry out a Nietzschean "undo-ing of opposites." She also adds, in order to complete the filiation, the resonance of Freud, the diffuse "shadow of Hegel," and the Husserlian question of reason, and the five Germans of the book are presented as "proto-grammatologues,"[5] the first phase of a major shift: the Ameri-cans will henceforth see Derrida less as the heterodox continuation of the philosophical tradition, or even the one who dissolves its text, than as its sublime end point, a sort of empyrean of critical thought for which these German precursors would have merely prepared the way.

In her preface, Gayatri Spivak gives a special place to the concept of deconstruction, to which her long prefatory remarks lead as though to a reward, whereas this concept is not the key to Derrida's book—even if it does have a strategic place in it. The first appearance of the word, which is also one of its very first occurrences in the English language, augured its American destinies. A mixture of irony and obstinacy, *deconstruction* designates here first of all the insistence with which Derrida questions Heidegger's indifference, in his commentary on Nietzsche, regarding a curious formula in Nietzsche that Heidegger did not even refer to: "The idea . . . *becomes a woman*" (*sie wird Weib*).[6] What has been omitted as the key to what is present, the inversion of what is important, and what appears to be secondary, the sexualization of a signifier that presents itself as neuter—all the ingredients are already there. By placing the emphasis on "writing" as "différance," in the sense of a deferral and a self-differing, and on the threat that would thereby weigh on the very possibility of a general law,[7] Spivak not only sketches out the major stakes of deconstruction but completes the work begun by Derrida in 1966: if the law is always disrupted from within by writing, if objective description is only an effect of this "différance," if the subject of knowledge cannot be maintained in its integrity when faced with the evidence of these displacements, and, finally, if structure itself is a "simulacrum," this is because "ordinary structuralism" and its "unified-unifying" approach have reached the end of their life span, and must be deconstructed—which is the very task of *poststructuralism*. This is a task at once ambitious, because fundamentally philosophical, and more precise than the very vague literary-institutional definition that will be given to deconstruction in the United States: "the term . . . denotes a style of analytical reading suspicious of the manifest content of texts,"[8] as a recent dictionary of American thought proposes, in terms that limit deconstruction to the *reading* of texts, but that include in it all readings that aim to bring polysemy into play, which amounts to saying *all* critical readings.

Beginning in 1976, what was as yet only a theoretical program will find itself read, studied, and soon set to work in certain graduate literature courses, especially at Yale and Cornell. One began gradually to *apply* deconstruction, to draw from it the modalities of a new "close reading" of the literary classics, and to find in the latter, as though through a magnifying glass, the mechanisms by which the referent is dissipated, the content ceaselessly differed/deferred by writing itself. And this conforms to the image of the French master who, in his American seminars from the end of the 1970s, was himself able to pause at great length on the last sentence of Melville's "Bartleby," or on a page of *In Search of Lost Time* where Proust curiously accumulates verbs ending in *-prendre*. To see a working example of this hypothesis concerning the construction of a text around its voids, one can cite this "deconstructionist" reading of a poem by Wordsworth, related as an example by the philosopher Arthur Danto:

> Small clouds are sailing,
> Blue skies prevailing,
> The rain is over and done.

The reading is organized around an absence. This poem on the passage of spring could therefore be seen to develop as the erasure of the sign "winter," a key term that is absent from the poem but which thus serves as its "matrix" and as that which haunts every element of springtime. Wordsworth, then, would not be depicting a natural reality but would be inscribing "a negative version of a latent text on the opposite of Spring."[9] If it happens that the significant absence in question is no longer a season (or its sign) but a beloved being, a forgotten word, or—even better—a repressed concept that has conditioned the entire argument, deconstruction then demonstrates that no discourse is foreign to it, and that there is no question of remaining limited to British poetry. Such ambitions were inspired by the atmosphere of solemnity and the initiate's enthusiasm that enveloped the first years of deconstruction, as well as the fervor of a discovery that distinguishes its pioneers from the run of the mill of literary history—namely, the discovery of the authors and the major concepts of Continental philosophy, which were unknown to the latter. For someone who has never heard anyone speak about Nietzsche or Husserl, the symbolic gain derived from such an approach is immeasurable, even if the question of its *cognitive* gain remains unresolved: one evokes, one detours, one deconstructs the philosophers, but one does not *study* them properly speaking. In the midst of a conflict of the faculties, deconstruction and its concept of writing are a godsend. The approach of the early

Derrida, which consists in dismantling the "phonocentric" prejudice at work in the subordination of writing to speech, amounts to conferring a brand-new role—liminary, maieutic, and major—on this notion of *writing*. And, after removing writing from the power of speech, to associate it with "supplementarity" as its origin, and to a primary excess of the signifier, then liberates it at the same time from the empire of reason. Whereas the kind of writing considered to be phonocentric, referential, or rationally decomposable always pointed toward history, philosophy, or the social sciences, writing as *différance*, finally detached from its exogenic orders, is the sole privilege of the literary field. Not to mention that the new paradigm is able to clarify the question of the university, feeding in turn into the educational metadiscourse. As I pointed out earlier, essays on Derrida and education abound, and the critic Robert Young even proposed, in arguing against the capitalist and specialist university, that it should rather "function as a surplus that the economy cannot comprehend," and that by being "neither simply useful nor simply useless" it would "deconstruct" the binary terms that haunt it.[10] In any case, this rhetoric, for its part, proclaims loudly and clearly the *utility* of deconstruction.

By the middle of the 1980s, the issues and stakes associated with deconstruction became so enormous—they included rethinking the university, denouncing all dualisms, reinterrogating all texts, arming readers against the domination of Reason—that publishers vastly accelerated their production of books on deconstruction, leading to its prodigious rise as one of the most visible niches in academic publishing. There are innumerable primary texts (by Derrida and the major Derrideans), together with secondary texts (applying deconstruction) and even tertiary ones (proposing some kind of assessment). And yet, among this plethora, one can discern two types of concerns and two types of works. The first, which applies to the majority of these books, involves an endless regression of deconstruction into its own procedures, a circular and paraphrastic metadiscourse, and the offensive strategies of "decon": against psychologism or sociocriticism, against colleagues and competitors, and soon enough, when Derridean critics and identity theoreticians make common cause, against the White Western Oppressor. It was in these at times jargon-ridden essays that the lack of philosophical culture and the intellectual arrogance of certain devotees of deconstruction became manifest. Less numerous and yet less uniform, using a more demanding but less coded language, the second category left behind a few major

works in the American intellectual field. These include all the medita-
tions on *reading*—which is the properly American inflection of Derrida's
project—the essays that denounce the literary ideology of "transparency" and explore, rather, the intrinsic opacity of writing. This orientation, it must be noted, connects with Derrida rather than extending
his thought, to the extent that it was elaborated before he became an
American import.

In Paul de Man or the early Harold Bloom, the famous "critique
of the Enlightenment" did not play out on the superficial terrain of the
history of ideas, but at the heart of this enigma of reading. It does not
yet have recourse to a tactical gesticulation against rationalism and progressivism, but rather to a detailed rejection of the prejudice of *clarity*, of the postulate of a *light* of sense, of the articulation (guarantor of
the established order) between a verbal repertory and the world that it
evokes—an homage above all to the autarchic obscurity of language. In
the land of the transparent sign and of transitive science, a small crew of
desperate men and women of letters thus dared to indulge very textually,
and very obstinately, in the shadowy pleasures of opacity.

This version of "deconstructionism," necessarily in the minority, had
nothing to do with this suffix that turned it into a school of thought, nor
even with the prestige of the new current of thought. Still imbued with
the tragic and haughty ethos of high literary modernism, that of the New
Critics and of the novel-on-nothing, it sought less to shake up the order
of the world, as their younger counterparts very rhetorically did, than to
accede to the disorder of the text, its primary instability, the impossibility from which it arises. It had no need to derive a battle plan from this
new elasticity of meaning, to call for an upheaval of the world based on
the incoherencies of the text—in order to appease the academic's guilt
over his or her disconnection from the "real world." Fewer in number,
these subtle theoreticians of reading did not make as much noise as the
strategists of decentering, the bards of the new crusade against "logocentrism." But they left a more lasting mark in the history of criticism.
Deconstruction, before being the watchword of American postmodernity, designated two castes of literary scholars who in the end were quite
distinct within the university: those who, to echo Marx's eleventh thesis
on Feuerbach, have the naïveté to believe that they will transform the
world *through* interpretation, and those who, more discreetly and with
a greater exigency, had the impudence to want to transform the world of
interpretation itself.

The Yale Quartet

Among these latter, a quartet of major critics teaching in the English department at Yale will make of this department, at the end of the 1970s, the point of entry for Derridean deconstruction, the official temple of its American cult—so that there is indeed reason to credit the idea of a "Yale School," despite the protestations of those included within it. Thus, as the Derridean critical program finds itself preempted and co-opted by the most brilliant professors of their generation, the phrase "gang of four" no longer designates the group in power in Beijing at the time, but the four new (and much more harmless) heroes of literary studies: Paul de Man, Harold Bloom, Geoffrey Hartman, and J. Hillis Miller—a quartet full of ambivalence, an antischool and a group of friends who were iconoclastic yet apolitical, textual materialists and cultural conservatives. Every emerging group has its detractors, and in 1975 there was in fact a critic ready to denounce the "hermeneutical mafia" of Yale.[11] But at the time it was impossible to cast a shadow over this English department which, ensconced in Linsly-Chittenden Hall at Yale, offered the most innovative courses on theory and literary criticism in the country—soon grouped together under the "literature major" program, designed for graduate students. In conferences and essays alike, the atmosphere was one of experimentation, in which each participant tried to bring out the most ambiguous figures and metalinguistic pearls of one canonical classic after another, from Dante to Marlowe, Goethe, and Shakespeare.

And yet, the names of the four pioneers of deconstruction were only rarely associated: for a few years at the time of the well-attended weekly course they took turns giving on "reading and rhetorical structure" and as part of one collection of essays, *Deconstruction and Criticism* (1979), which was treated by the press as a manifesto—despite the manifest polyphony of the volume, in which de Man and Bloom diverge in their readings of Shelley, whereas the other contributions varied in their approaches and references. The reputation of the book was based on a few gestures of bravura, such as the clever phonetic play on "meaning" and "moaning" with which Bloom begins his essay, Hillis Miller's defense of the critic's aptitude for reception over and against his demonization as a "parasite," and Derrida's own contribution (on Maurice Blanchot's *Death Sentence*), which is distinguished by a single footnote of more than a hundred pages—the most famous footnote in French theory.[12] But it remains difficult to bring together under a single banner the four sharpshooters of literary theory, despite analogous references, a common friendship with Derrida, and the same tone of erudite irony and disenchanted humor shared by all four. J. Hillis Miller, who had arrived from Johns Hopkins in 1973, is the only one to have suggested the existence of a critical school, mostly for polemical reasons. But in fact, every argument goes against it: the precocious development of Hartman in an area far removed from deconstruction; the unclassifiable itinerary of the agoraphobic Bloom; the solitary path of Paul de Man, who always preferred the term "rhetorical reading" to the word *deconstruction* (too widely disseminated for his taste); and the proselytizing zeal of a few brilliant critics, a zeal more intense than their own but which required that they too be counted among the leaders of the unlikely school—including Shoshana Felman, who was teaching at Yale at the time, Barbara Johnson, who challenged the hypotheses of her master de Man, Neil Hertz, who explored the psychoanalytic aspects of deconstruction, and Cynthia Chase, who reexamined Romantic poetry. Nonetheless, at the heart of this flourishing activity, the major critical oeuvre is that of Paul de Man.

"Once upon a time, we all thought we knew how to read, and then came de Man . . ."[13] Thus begins Wlad Godzich in his preface to de Man's first collection of essays, *Blindness and Insight* (1971), which would be followed by only two more titles during his lifetime, then three posthumous volumes. This book already presents the two major features of the de Manian approach, namely, an almost mathematical precision of interpretation and a Benjaminian melancholy in the style of thinking. It brings together recent studies on Lukács, Blanchot, and Derrida's reading of Rousseau, and two older articles, one on the dead end of "formalist criticism" and another on Heidegger's exegesis of Hölderlin—written in French (de Man was Belgian by birth, having arrived in the United States in 1947) and first published in *Critique*. Its title, explicated in a brief foreword, refers to the encounter of two parallel dialectics between vision and blindness, one designating a "blind spot" of the text that would organize its linguistic space, distributing it into visible zones and blind zones, and the other linked with each reading as a singular mode of exclusion of certain aspects of the text, whose "blind vision" it thus determines. De Man also cleared a few paths that will remain at the center of literary debates throughout the following decades: a critique of the "rational" distinction between aesthetic (literary) texts and argumentative (critical) texts as one that in fact postulates the "superfluity" of the former, on the pretext of privileging a literary *truth;* a preference, in describing the function of language, for the concept of *allegory* (which will be something like his trademark, thanks to the success of his collection *Allegories of Reading*), read as irreducibly distant from its own origin, over and against that of *symbol* which would bear the nostalgia of self-coincidence and identity; and the sketch of a theory of *figural* language, the other major de Manian concept: a formal language displaying its limits and narrating the void from which it arises, at the expense of the *referential* and *grammatical* languages of classical criticism.

His reading of the episode of the stolen ribbon in Rousseau's *Confessions* is not only a figural reading but also a "machinic" one: we regard as human sentiments—those of the author or of his characters—functions that are purely internal to the textual system, explains de Man, who thus dissociates an autonomous linguistic *machine,* an uncontrolled circulation of tropes and figures, from the ordinary world of intention and representation. The autonomy in question is precisely what requires theory, according to de Man: the latter has become the only recourse when "referentiality" (the fact of referring, of designating a referent) has ceased being an "intuition," a human activity linked to the "world of logic and understanding," but is regarded rather as a "function of language"—in other words, when Saussurean linguistics was applied to literary texts, relegating the question of their "meanings" to the background.[14] All the uses of language are performative, de Man thinks, to the extent that they all set off endogenous mechanisms in language, an underground tectonic of figures. The horizon of his project is a veritable textual, or linguistic, *materialism.* He recommends what he calls a "rhetorical" reading of literary texts, as the only one capable of revealing the properly inhuman character of language, its material dimension, in the sense in which it is as foreign and alienating for us as the world of things—in terms sometimes recalling those of Sartre, whose work had a great influence on the young Paul de Man, and whose descriptions of "bad faith" recall those given by de Man of the deliberate hermeneutic "illusions" of traditional criticism. For every text develops out of a failure of expression, and the role of the critic is to bring to light the dialectic productivity of this "errancy," of the "displacement" of language, as illustrated in his analyses of the impossible "promise of truth" in Rilke's poetry, or of "disjunction" as the specific task of the translator.[15] In the end, beyond de Man's obsessive mistrust of the order of representation and the facile nature of referential readings, the question posed by Wlad Godzich remains open: can it be said that de Man's version of deconstruction merely "tamed" or "domesticated" Derrida's approach, such that it "lost its virulence," or, on the contrary, did it refine it, by bringing it into a more rigorous confrontation with the literary text?[16] The only thing that is certain is that it continued its tendencies in the direction of reading, and against the false obviousness of the latter—to the great advantage of literary criticism.

Although they are no less innovative in their approach, the works of the other critics of the "gang of four" remain less troubling, less meticulously austere than that of Paul de Man. Whereas Geoffrey Hartman moved from a provocative use of deconstruction to a virulent denunciation of it in the name of phenomenology and a critique of the imaginary (similar to those of Georges Poulet or Jean Starobinski, to which he is gradually returning), his colleague Hillis Miller has remained in the end its most loyal practitioner—in his analyses of the Victorian novel's textual impasses or of the unspoken elements of English poetry, and in his defense of deconstruction and its supporters within the framework of his institutional responsibilities at Yale and later at Irvine, and also as the president of the MLA for a time. The work and the itinerary of the other solitary figure of the group, Harold Bloom, are more singular. He became known in 1973 for his book *The Anxiety of Influence*. A prescient radicalization of certain hypotheses of deconstruction, but also of arguments made by Gérard Genette and Michel Riffaterre on the notion of the *intertext*, this brief but difficult essay remains one of the masterpieces of American literary criticism.[17] Its thesis seems classically structuralist: "There are no poems, only relations between poems." But its development is unlike anything that came before it. Exploring both classical and contemporary poets, from Virgil to Milton, Dante, and John Ashbery, and adding to the sorts of references made by Paul de Man a wide-ranging use of Freud and Nietzsche, Bloom renews the theme of literary innovation, which he redefines as "achieved anxiety" before the canonized text, a "forced break" from its repetition, and, more broadly, "creative misreading." The latter proceeds by modifying the previous text (which is also an internal text, refracted within the reading) according to seven rhetorical modes, including *clinamen, kenosis,* and *askesis* or self-purgation, which are all tactics for clearing the imaginative space of its sources, and of its repressed.

But this theory of the rupture of influence, far from psychological in its orientation, is precisely a linguistic argument, for it evokes more the death of the author or the (de Manian) materiality of the text than the banal obligation of a "murder of the fathers" in literature. Bloom takes the opportunity to question generic boundaries, even declaring that "all criticism is prose poetry." Above all, the fundamentally textual function of these procedures of "poetic misprision" (a curious term mixing the necessity of misapprehension and the prison of influence) makes the book an unmatched illustration of the yawning gaps of language and the autonomous ruses of writing. And yet, after a limited flirtation with deconstruction, Bloom gradually evolved toward the irascible elitism of the solitary pessimist, more interested in Judaism than in Derrida, more of an Emersonian than a Francophile, reproaching Paul de Man for his "serene linguistic nihilism," becoming fiercely anti-Marxist, the last defender of a Western canon besieged on all sides, and seeing the innovations of the 1980s as nothing more than a "school of Resentment": "Finding myself now surrounded by professors of hip-hop; by clones of Gallo-Germanic theory; by ideologues of gender and various sexual persuasions, . . . I realize that the Balkanization of literary studies is irreversible"[18]—going so far as to publish in 1999 a thick but successful humanist reading of Shakespeare, which gives no close attention either to language or to construction, but rather only to the dramatic characters, and the "essence" of their personality.[19] The struggle against "phonocentrism" never really concerned him: "as a rabbi, as a prophet, he will not allow himself to be intimidated under the pretext that his language is that of the self, of presence, of the voice," says the conservative critic Denis Donoghue, who argues that what attracted thinkers such as Harold Bloom and Paul de Man to deconstruction was (to use a phrase from Shelley) its "serious folly."[20]

Strategies and Breakaways

Whereas the work of the Yale quartet explored above all the self-devouring nature of the literary text, the hundreds of epigones that followed them thus turned their sights on targets more and more distant from this counter-world of the text—political, historical, and cultural targets that had little relation to de Man's textual materialism. In order to do this, it was necessary to exploit the dramatic, emotional, and affinity-generating potential of deconstruction. Young disciples, simultaneously bewitched and opportunistic, thus came to universalize the hypotheses of "creative *misreading*" and "productive error": they declared that all readings are *misreadings,* that every literary text is an allegory of its illegibility, and soon, as the long reactionary night of the Reagan–Thatcher era fell upon the Anglo-Saxon world, they affirmed that these hidden forces at work in every text are primarily of a *political* nature, and that the entire Western logic of representation is intrinsically imperialist, unbeknownst to itself, at the very level of the text. But to substitute Derrida's patient philological deconstruction with this bellicose drama, in which the villains are concepts armed with capital letters, also leads to the shortcuts of the scriptwriter who has fallen under the spell of his plot: "Derrida wasn't there when Jesus raised the dead," states one R. V. Young, for example, "so he has made a career of killing the Logos and burning down the house of Reason."[21] The exaggeration is not merely melodramatic, it is also philosophical. For, in order to shine the interrogator's lamp on the elements of a rather abstract jigsaw puzzle, and one whose elements (dialectic, reason, *logos*) have been poorly mastered, the "antilogocentric" discourse must twist in its own direction the more poised, and always careful, argumentation of its fetish author. One promises to bring down Hegel and his dialectic, whereas Derrida underscored the obligation borne by contemporary thought to "explicate oneself indefinitely vis-à-vis Hegel."[22] One promises to deconstruct metaphysics, with which Derrida, however, did not cease to affirm a necessary "complicity," without which it would be necessary "also to give up the critical work we are directing against it."[23] Along the way, by fixing Derridean deconstruction into a body of general injunctions, one loses the strategic sinuosity and suppleness of Derrida's trajectory, with its play of aporias whose function is also never to *anchor* thought. The distortion here is literal, and originates first of all in the curious relation of American readers to Derrida's texts: the latter are in the end very rarely read directly, or in their entirety; and, among these works, those of the first period, and their ontophenomenological critique of logocentrism, are more operative than those of the last fifteen years, which are more elliptical and more preoccupied with ethics, democracy, or philosophical homage (to Blanchot or Levinas)—with the exception of the three later texts that have become classics in the United States: *Specters of Marx,* "Force of Law," and *Archive Fever.*[24]

The central question that one often encounters concerns the *utility* of this "hypercritique," as Derrida has sometimes called deconstruction. On the one hand, in a country where the only thing that counts is the "application to education" in order always "to substitute, insofar as possible, doing for learning" (as Hannah Arendt observed),[25] the question becomes whether deconstruction can be taken up for practical purposes, whether it is usable and capable of multiple applications—be it for reading a single poem or for a political rereading of intellectual history as a whole. The slippage toward identity-based discourses has its source in fact in this utilitarian precept rather than in any ideological program that might have preceded it. And its more pointed applications, transitive and almost mechanical, to issues that deconstruction began by displacing and reformulating, sometimes verge on blatant misinterpretation, if not caricature. Aside from courses in management or cooking that teach one how to "deconstruct" the corporate structure or the three-course meal, one can also pour Richard Wagner or ecology through the Derridean sieve: Mary Cicora explains the "romantic irony" by which Wagner's operas would "deconstruct" their mythological sources (an "operatic deconstruction" that makes of *Parsifal* a work in which "metaphor [is] redeemed"),[26] whereas Robert Mugerauer invites us to deconstruct the landscape, and to interrogate the pyramid, for example (from the Egyptians to Las Vegas), as a "posture and strategy" and an "eternal presence."[27] By adopting a more didactic and transversal theme, and a less jargon-ridden language, David Wood's book *The Deconstruction of Time,* which calls for a thinking of time "outside metaphysics" and philosophy "as pure event and performativity," even met with a certain success.[28] But alongside the often dubious attempts to make deconstruction practical, its most rigorous adherents jealously defend its intransmissible difficulty, its irreducible rigor, less out of an elitist reflex than in fidelity to the ontological concern that inspires it. It must be said that its recurrent elements—aporias, *mises en abyme,* negative figures, signifiers in excess—aren't easily accessible conceptually or clearly locatable in the literary or theoretical texts they are supposed to corrode. That is why this celebrated approach will only be evoked, never studied and even less applied, in the context of undergraduate courses. And that is why it will be difficult, in graduate courses, to make of it the unstoppable method that the utilitarianism of American education would have liked to make of it. Moreover, at the end of the 1970s, a time when deconstruction had barely taken root across the Atlantic, it began to drift outside the university in two different directions, and it thus escaped in two directions from the pedagogical mastery of its practitioners—and a fortiori from the rigorous proselytism of its faithful.

On the one hand, it became the object of a continuous series of ideological attacks, beginning in 1977 with a call, coming from the critic Meyer Abrams, to eclipse deconstruction and its moral relativism.[29] Diatribes from both the Right and the Left brandished the public good and collective values against Derridean "textualism," evoking its harmful effects not only on the university but also on American society as a whole. On the other hand, in a more gradual but also more spectacular fashion, the word *deconstruction* slowly entered common parlance, where it served to evoke every form of subversion harbored within the university, and (even more vaguely) an attitude of incredulity, an aptitude for demystification, the vigilant reaction of anyone who refuses to be "taken in": in the mainstream press and even on television, the word *deconstruction,* entirely dissociated from its academic contexts, appears here and there as a synonym for critical insight or individual lucidity in the face of an official message. In the unbridled race to power and success that suddenly accelerated in the 1980s, involving both economic recovery and massive deregulation, one must be able to deconstruct an advertising claim, an electoral promise, or a social game—one must be able to penetrate them and see through them. A sign of the times: home-improvement magazines, advising against the kind of veranda that "dad would build," invite their readers to "deconstruct the concept of the garden," while a comic-book superhero confronts a new kind of villan, "Doctor Deconstructo." An ersatz academic jargon is even used for a sales pitch when a clothing company chose to present, for its campaign in the magazine *Crew,* the "Derrida Jacket" and the "Deconstruction Suit," providing "a style that's emphatically uncanonical." One item, titled *Life's Little Deconstruction Book,* a random and cheerfully satirical collection of vaguely Derridean aphorisms, is even proudly displayed at the checkout counter in bookstores.[30] A phenomenon of symbolic borrowing, a pure surface effect in the social realm, this extra-academic dispersion of a more and more vague reference will help to accelerate the splitting of the Derridean camp: between a conservative minority, concerned with protecting it from its popular deviations, and a more strategic majority that wanted to bring this strong theoretical base, now commonly cited in the media, onto the battleground of identitarian discourses—which were being honed in the new interdepartmental programs of sexuality studies, ethnic studies, and postcolonial studies. Among the former camp, "reality" is a construction of logocentrism, a deceptive effect of figural language; among the latter, it is an ideological construction designed to mask power relations and segregation. The gap between them will only grow larger with time.

If we set aside the former camp—a quasi-monastic minority interested above all in a new epistemology of literary language—the question posed by the latter, in the end, ought to be examined more precisely, for it is not so simple: if one takes Derrida far from his explicit subjects, does this necessarily invalidate him? Because they are in agreement with Derrida's approach on at least one crucial point, namely, their common mistrust of totalizing thought and closed systems, such local, partial, mobile, or operational uses of a particular Derridean concept do not necessarily become caricatures or betrayals, and at times even do reveal the formidable energy and the practical fecundity of Derrida's arguments. Alongside the caricatural uses, there are indeed, in a word, fruitful uses; alongside heavy-handed sweeping paraphrases, there are opportune references that function according to the ruses of time and the proper occasion—alongside a horizonless *utilization,* naively confounding theoretical and prescriptive registers, there is a specific *utility,* by which the work, in Michel de Certeau's formula, suddenly "makes it possible for the construction of a future to replace respect for tradition."[31]

Supplement: The Derrida Effect

The astonishing synergy that, as the issues developed, was thus able to bring American feminist thought together with Derrida's work offers a first set of examples of such a strategy. For the question of the feminine in Derrida is not only the question of "phallogocentrism," as certain epigones hastily generalized it to be, calling for death to the paternal Logos, and down with macho Reason! This question has always been for him an opportunity for suggestions that are more localized and more open-ended, but whose female readers saw as more functional. In the 1963 article "Violence and Metaphysics," Derrida thus interrogates, in a note, not the masculine essence of metaphysics but the "essential *virility* of metaphysical language." "Plato's Pharmacy" from 1968, reprinted in *Dissemination,* is not only the text in which the logos takes the form of the father, but also the occasion for a less often cited suggestion, according to which the excessive signifier, the irreversible dissemination of traces, would also refer to that of sperm, to the scandalous motif of "wasted seed." Even the much-vaunted antihumanism of *On Grammatology* is already an exploration, in the guise of an ally, of the famous "name of the woman." In 1970, in his article "The Double Session" on Mallarmé, Derrida spoke of the "hymen" as an unstable and uncertain membrane: because it "separates without separating" the inside from the outside, it opens already onto a nonidentitarian thought of the sexual, whether it's a question of the possibility of "invagination" or of that strange "third gender" evoked by Derrida as "gender beyond gender." His contribution to the 1972 colloquium at Cerisy on Nietzsche, printed in *Glas,* is the first text explicitly devoted to "woman," whom he identifies with "truth" insofar as she would be "undecidable," while also referring to a space of displacement, of *différance,* over and against the dual opposition of the sexes—twenty years before queer studies. In *Spurs,* he introduces—almost in passing—another distinction that became decisive for American feminist debates between the masculine gesture of "taking" or "taking possession" and the feminine strategy of "giving" in the sense of "giving oneself *as* [se donner *comme*]," a play of roles through which precisely she *keeps herself.* Finally, "The Law of Genre" from 1980 (reprinted in *Parages*) invites us to deconstruct the sign *man* in the metaphysical tradition, and specifies that this task can "produce . . . an element *woman*" that does not signify woman as "person"—that is, the formulation of a femininity without essence, which is neither a principle nor a human incarnation.[32] There are thus many passing remarks and furtive paragraphs in the work of Derrida in which the "antiessentialist" reflection (against the eternal feminine) of second-wave American feminism will find support, and which it will brandish here and there against what it sees as the "dead ends" of woman as identity and of a mere reversal toward a maternal counterpower.

One successful operation carried out by this second wave of feminism was even to play Derrida off, so to speak, against Lacan. The latter owed his impact on the feminist debate to a first movement of *deessentialization.* He made it possible to substitute, in the formation of gender, the autonomous and intrinsically unstable forces of language and fantasy for the idea of a fixed biological nature and its necessary sublimation, inherited from a certain Freudian sexual essentialism. But in doing this he ended up, from the American point of view, promoting a pessimism of sexual roles, if not even a certain conservatism: if "woman does not exist," this is also because the phantasmal instability of sexual roles is without resolution, such that in the absence of a possible gender *strategy,* the figure of the Phallus and the subterranean power of the Law and of the linguistic unconscious can only perpetuate the hierarchies of gender, taking away any recourse for someone who finds herself (or himself) dominated, since there is *no* fixed gender. On the contrary, Derrida would reintroduce some movement, a margin of maneuverability, by insisting on the constant slippages of the linguistic code, on the performative potential of "playing" with the Law and with language—leading even to a possible deconstruction of the hierarchy of gender. If the unconscious is structured like a language, this would not prevent those who are marginalized by this language from finding the productive gaps of its enunciation, and thus the very initiative of its reinterpretation. Thus, it is claimed, Derrida would replace a sexual order frozen in the marble of the Lacanian Law with "a new choreography of sexual difference": it is "against Lacan," says Drucilla Cornell, for example, that Derrida "shows us that what shifts in language, including the definition of gender identity . . . , cannot definitively be stabilized."[33] The Derridean operation therefore reintroduces a certain margin here, some play or leeway, and thus the hope, in short, for effective action against the oppression of gender—a hope on which all feminism vitally depends. Within the framework of feminist debate, the reference to Derrida also has a semantic utility: as Judith Butler proposes, to use the category "women," as Derrida does, without referring to any referent (or to its ordinary signifieds), gives it "a chance of being opened up, indeed, of coming to signify in ways that none of us can predict in advance."[34] Another indication of the great productivity of the reference to Derrida can be seen in Butler's claim that it was from Derrida's reading of Kafka, and not from Foucault or J. L. Austin, that she derived the concept of "gender performativity"[35]—a concept that will have a central role in her work and in the development of queer theory in the 1990s.

In a completely different domain, we have seen the importance, for the field of "critical legal studies," of Derrida's lectures on "deconstruction and the law" at the Cardozo Law School in New York in 1990–91. As for postcolonial studies, more naturally inspired by Foucault (but also more directly critical of him), specific references to Derrida are also able to play this role of unblocking, partly by conferring on the latter this same status as a providential outsider. Such a reference makes it possible for the critic Homi Bhabha, for example, to forge the curious portmanteau word "Dissemi-Nation," in order to think a possible "nation" of the dominated on the basis of a *détournement* of the dominant language and of its migratory dispersion.[36] It also becomes possible to engage this intermediate space between domination and tribalism—the language of the stronger and the orality of the weaker, the historical subject and the chaotic multitude—a space that postcolonial theory takes as its specific focus, a space of *negotiation* to which certain Derridean concepts lent themselves perfectly: the "remainder" or the "traces" that cannot be reduced to their sender or to their context; the fusion of the Other and of the interval proposed by the notion of *antre* [cave; a homonym of *entre*, between—*Trans.*] in Derrida; the search less for a "production of the other" (still an imperialist gesture) than for all the "voice[s] of the other in us,"[37] according to Gayatri Spivak's political reading. Spivak goes further, in fact. She calls for deconstruction to reach out to these *others* (women, non-Westerners, victims of capitalism), and to include, finally, a consideration of political economy, in order to direct the theory of the text toward a *practice* of struggle, and even to connect with Marx by rereading him also as a "deconstructor *avant la lettre*," as Nancy Fraser puts it in her summary of Spivak's evolution in relation to Derrida.[38] But this already goes beyond a partial use, a fragmentary application, in order to pose *the* question that still today divides the field of the humanities in the United States: that of a possible "Derridean politics," its orientations, and its eminently problematic relation to the Marxist heritage.

For the turbulent American destiny of the word *deconstruction* returns constantly to an ambivalence with regard to the political in Derrida's thought itself. Vincent Descombes, while he judges the latter, without indulgence, by the measure of logical and rational criteria that Derrida aimed precisely to call into question, nonetheless has the merit of emphasizing (and he was one of the very first to do so) the political malleability of a thought that is developed in a way that is explicitly *prior* to the notions of true and false, and regardless of their polarity: "Is Derridean deconstruction a tyrannicide . . . or is it a game?" he asks, before concluding that it is precisely this question that is "undecidable."[39] And that explains the distance Derrida maintains from the political question in his early work. Hence, in France, the rarity of political reflections inspired exclusively by Derrida, the negative formulation of themes (avoidance, impossibility) in the political seminar of the first major conference at Cerisy devoted to his work ("Les fins de l'homme" [The ends of man] in 1980), and the uncertainties that confronted the Centre de recherche philosophique sur le politique (Center for Philosophical Research on the Political) that opened at the École Normale Supérieure in 1981 on the initiative of Jean-Luc Nancy and Philippe Lacoue-Labarthe. For deconstruction problematizes normative polarities (progressive/reactionary, reformist/radical) *as* polarities, and invites us to rethink every structure of opposition (between two terms) as irreducible to the referents that it points to—except perhaps as a strategic opposition, or even a reversible one. Deconstruction thus contains within itself the risk of a withdrawal from the political, a neutralization of positions, or even an endless metatheoretical regression that can no longer be brought to a stop by any practical decision or effective political engagement. In order to use it as a basis for a program of subversion or a discourse of conflict, the American solution was thus to "detourn" or divert it, to fragment it, to split it off from itself in order to break out of this paralyzing epistemic balancing act. It is thus that the new thinkers of identity chose, as we will see, to politicize deconstruction, against its reactionary exegetes, who preferred, for their part, to deconstruct politics. In order to formulate within the academic context a deconstruction designed for combat, a Derridean *politics,* feminists and thinkers of postcolonialism forced deconstruction *against itself* to produce a political "supplement"—which led to the ironic paradox that the least directly political author in the corpus of French theory (compared to Deleuze, Lyotard, Foucault) was the most politicized in the United States. Or perhaps it is precisely because he skirted the political exigency (beyond his actions in favor of Czech dissidents, and an engagement with other cultural figures against apartheid) that Derrida contributed, without knowing it, to disinhibiting, liberating, even galvanizing his readers in relation to the political, readers who had at first been rather disconcerted. But this schema itself—the pointed political efficacy of a thought that had remained reticent regarding practical politics, and that was therefore diverted all the more easily—becomes complicated at the beginning of the 1990s, when Derrida addressed himself directly to Marx and the various Marxisms, historical and theoretical—with the event titled *Specters of Marx*.

Not long after the fall of Soviet Communism, Derrida's conversations with the professors Bernd Magnus and Stephen Cullenberg in 1991—but also his rereading of *Hamlet* (in which he was obsessed by the enigmatic line, "The time is out of joint") and the project of a conference in California titled "Whither Marxism"—eventually gave rise in 1993 to this text of multiple intersections, first in the form of a lecture and then as a book.[40] The avenues explored there by Derrida (all connected in some way to Marx), including "the state of the debt" (to Marx?), "the work of mourning" (of the Marxists?), and "the new International" (post-Marxist?), all refer to a rereading of Marx as a *specter*, in the sense of a ghost, a phantasm, and an agent of contamination. With the term "hauntology," Derrida lays out the first indications of a thinking of *spectrality* that would be neither a residual presence of spirit nor the absence of the thing, but a mode of persistence irreducible to the sensible–intelligible dualism, and that would also be the mode of capital at the end of the twentieth century as well as of the political horizon as messianic promise—the commodity and its overcoming. In a decisive affirmation, less a turning point than the end point of a gradual inflection, Derrida relates all his work to a primary *ethics* that would precede all else: henceforth, "what deconstruction sets into motion . . . [is] the undeconstructable injunction of *justice*"—a regrounding of ethics that will be a priority (over and against the first wave of Derrideans) for the American commentators of the later Derrida, somewhat less numerous than before, including Drucilla Cornell and Ashok Kam. And yet this somewhat belated confrontation with Marx (but "I believe in the virtue of the contretemps," says Derrida)[41] did not settle the serious disagreement between the principal figure of deconstruction and the orthodox Marxists of anglophone academia, such as Terry Eagleton, Perry Anderson, or even Noam Chomsky—all of whom had fulminated for two decades against what they perceived as Derrida's "textualism," "antihistoricism," and political "vagueness." Thus they seized the opportunity to respond to *Specters of Marx* with a conference, then a collection of essays, titled *Ghostly Demarcations,* in which, except for the more sympathetic papers by Fredric Jameson and Toni Negri, all were united in their reproaches. Derrida's critics stigmatized a "literary depoliticization" of Marx, the practical inertia to which this discussion of spectrality would lead, the limits of what Pierre Macherey (the only French participant) called a "dematerialized Marx,"[42] or the facilities of a "Marxism without Marxism."[43] This last expression was one that the writer in question, for his part, vindicated with force (adding that it "was first of all that of Marx himself") in his own reply, "Marx & Sons," a long ironic and self-justifying note on the sectarian reflexes of the Marxist "family" and its persistent misreading, he says, of Marx's work as a whole.

But beyond this international settling of scores, the debate thus engaged between deconstruction and the various Marxisms—among which certain overtures to Derrida did take place, some long before, including those of Gayatri Spivak, Fredric Jameson, or Slavoj Žižek—is far from the least interesting consequence of this *Derrida effect* in United States. It was at an equal distance from the two movements of thought, Marxism and deconstruction, that an encounter took place in the 1980s between identity politics and the American university, an encounter that would forever change the American intellectual field. French theory would no longer be merely an innovative discourse, a fashionable corpus, or a magic tool in literary studies, but a more direct target of ideological crossfire—and the theater of new *political uses* of discourse.

PART II

The Uses of Theory

6

THE POLITICS OF IDENTITY

It is sometimes necessary to remind ourselves of the distance
from the classroom to the streets . . . We pay homage to the
marginalized and demonized, and it feels almost as if we've
righted an actual injustice . . . [But] I always think of the folk
tale about the fellow who killed seven with one blow: flies,
not giants.

HENRY LOUIS GATES JR., "Whose Canon Is It Anyway?"

WHETHER ONE IS SPEAKING the Derridean patois or the Foucauldian
dialect, one thing is clear, perhaps clearer than it has ever been in France:
as of now, there is no longer a discourse of truth; there are only *apparatuses* [*dispositifs*] of truth—transient, tactical, and political. But instead
of joining forces with the general battle against domination, this beneficial discovery was to pave the way in the United States for minority theories. In other words, if Derrida or Foucault deconstructed the concept of
objectivity, the Americans would draw on those theories not for a reflection on the figural power of language or on discursive constructions, but
for a more concrete political conclusion: *objectivity* is synonymous with
"subjectivity of the white male." What they developed was an entirely
unexpected link between literary theory and the political Left. Following
the carefree anarcho-poetic textualism of the seventies, and alongside the
literary purism of Derrida's Yale followers, the conservative revolution
of the Reagan years provoked the return of the repressed: the notorious
referent, evacuated by these formalistic versions of French theory, made
a sudden comeback under the name of *identity politics.* This was heart-
warming news for all those who had given up hope of penetrating the
black box—French theory had a focus after all, and it was none other

than unearthing minority identities, and the lot of subjugated groups, whose very existence was being threatened by a reactionary hydra. It became a vital theoretical support in the new *culture wars* that were to divide America.

Indeed, the sense of identity-based membership, the perception of oneself first and foremost as a member of a minority, is far from being a purely verbal invention of idle academics. These sentiments had spread throughout all levels of American society in the course of the preceding decade, as a result of complex historical factors: cultural repercussions of the struggle for civil rights, the decline of the democratic Left, identity-based withdrawal from an increasingly competitive economic climate, and a new segmentation of American consumers into like-minded identity groups. Todd Gitlin cites some startling statistics on this subject about the most underrepresented of minorities: between 1980 and 1990, the number of Americans who officially declared themselves "Native Americans" increased by 255 percent; in the same decade, twenty times more called themselves "Cajun," and three times more Canadians laid claim to their francophone heritage.[1] But this shift, which outside the university manifests itself only in community rituals or in census statistics, becomes, within the university walls, a central focus to the point that *minorities* are encouraged to affirm themselves as such by diverse means, and to piously cultivate what Freud called "the narcissism of minor differences." From "white" people of mixed race to the hard of hearing, the puzzle becomes singularly hard to piece together—a trend that remains very apparent on American campuses. Thus, the latest subfield of study, which made its appearance at the 2002 MLA convention, brought together "disability studies," whose focuses range from the amputated stump motif in medieval poetry to the lack of wheelchair ramps at classroom doors. The advent of American cultural studies at the beginning of the 1990s was a cause as much as an effect of this far-reaching evolution at work within the academic world, and it is the major phenomenon at work here. It has as much bearing on French theory as it does on the significance of these new proclamations of identity. Despite the occasional criticism of what has been termed an academic gimmick, the emergence of cultural studies nonetheless marks a historical turning point in the United States. According to Bill Readings, it heralds "the end of 'culture' as a regulative ideal," or, put differently, it was the advent of what might be called an omniculture, the emergence of a world in which "there is no longer any culture to be excluded from,"[2] no longer any exteriority—real or fantastical—to serve as a battle line.

The Rise of Cult. Studs.

Darling of the bookstores, cultural studies, which was quickly nick-named Cult. Studs., in mockery of its cultlike academic following, has nonetheless had far more success than an insignificant religious group. And yet it does not carry the same academic weight as other identity-based fields of research: while there is a plethora of programs dedicated to ethnic or gender studies, hardly any are explicitly devoted to cultural studies. And so the field of cultural studies is everywhere and yet no-where, drifting without taking root, turning up in whichever department happens to have a specialist in the field, in the choice of a study topic, in a theoretical approach, or in keywords of a new lexicon. Cultural stud-ies has an interdisciplinary influence on all the humanities, even though no one class is devoted to its study, and no clear definition has been laid out. Naturally, this led to a rise in the number of essays questioning the field's focus and limits. To paraphrase the Surrealists' formula, cultural studies could be defined as the chance encounter between a recent Brit-ish Marxist apparatus and a French theoretical umbrella, in the arena of American leisure culture—though on a less than sterilized operating table. Indeed, cultural studies initially came from Great Britain and the Centre for Contemporary Cultural Studies, founded in Birmingham in 1964, inspired by the works of Raymond Williams (*The Long Revolution*) and Richard Hoggart (*The Uses of Literacy*),[3] which both dealt with the traditions and cultural resistance of the British proletariat. The research of this group, which was to influence the works of Althusser, Barthes, and later Bourdieu, contradicted the orthodox Marxist ap-proach, stating that culture is not a superstructural veneer but an entire field of specific battles for *hegemony* (hence the frequent references to Gramsci); the social class system itself is not a simple historic fact, but a symbolic (and therefore cultural) construct, and cultural hierarchy goes in both directions, because it is complicated by a new form of mass cul-ture (thanks to commercial television) and the ways in which it has been appropriated by the lower and middle classes. As for the American form of cultural studies, this appeared at the beginning of the 1980s, first at the University of Illinois (through the work of James Carey) and at the University of Iowa, but there was a general reluctance to rally under the term.[4] It must not be forgotten that several major research fields differentiate the American form of cultural studies from the British school of thought.

In the United States, where social class is much less of a determining factor, a more mobile segmentation of society into "communities" and "microgroups" replaced the English system of polarized social classes. The first American champions of Cult. Studs., spurred by new diatribes against Western "imperialism," attacked the British school for its "ethnocentrism" and "sexism"—although the British proletariat studied by Hoggart and E. P. Thompson was lacking in neither women nor members of the former colonies. In fact, the main shift has more to do with the analysis itself. Whereas the British consider one or several cultures as an extension of a social battlefield, their American counterparts—who are more often trained in literary fields than in sociological or historical ones—attach greater importance to the rise of pop culture and its mass appeal as a new entity, whose social implications interest them less than the invention of specific codes and the "creativity" of its recipients. A new generation of intellectuals had taken over in the United States. With the emergence in the 1960s of a large-scale and mass culture, stimulated by an increase in leisure time and new strategies developed by the culture industry, the decade also saw a changing of the guard in universities. As Andrew Ross summarizes, researchers who had adhered to "the heroic mythologies of the unattached, dissident intellectual" made way for those who accepted "the contradictions of living within a capitalist culture" and were even prepared to "use their involvement with popular culture as a site of contestation in itself."[5] This would explain a certain neutralization of the object: taking an interest in pop culture was not so much a political gesture as a way to exercise a full participation in one's own historical moment. To be considered innovative, one needed to analyze not the persistence of a canonic high culture or the potentially subversive power of truly dissident cultures, but the mysterious and neglected subgenres of pop culture, each of which was thought to conceal its own social *narrative:* B movies, sitcoms, comics, paraliteratures (thrillers and science fiction), pop-star confessions, and best-selling biographies would introduce the consumer into the secret, shifting mosaic of fan clubs and casual social groups, in opposition to the more rigid divisions of sociology. These codified genres would reveal the collective fantasies and real cultural practices of American society.

The dramatic expansion of cultural studies and research on pop culture in the American humanities took place in the second half of the 1980s, peaking in 1991, as shown by results from two large university databases.[6] In 1992, the success of the now indispensable retrospective work directed by Lawrence Grossberg solidified the recognition of the new approach.[7] But the groundbreaking study appeared in 1979: *Subculture* by Dick Hebdige. This study gives a detailed analysis of the young British punk movement's various forms of expression, and it introduced the idea of applying avant-garde European theory—in this case a mixture of Marxist semiology and sociology of deviance—to the United States, and the country's own phenomena of urban countercultures, neglected by the social sciences.[8] The double novelty of both the subject matter and the theoretical parameters was soon to start quite a trend. The most sophisticated tools of textual analysis and the new university penchant for metadiscourse were thus applied to subjects as wide-ranging as gangsta rap, "Harlequin" romance readers, *Star Trek* fans, and even the supposed philosophical "subtext" of the *Seinfeld* series. The list also included the sports industry, fast-food culture, the craze for tattoos, and the resistance of a given culture against economic globalization. The obsession with semiology and the accompanying political overinvestment of notions of "style" and "subtext" made some new experts in Cult. Studs. lose sight of the larger picture of the cultural industry and commercial power. They replaced the old critical paradigm of the British Marxist theorists with stylistic microdescription, whether it be in the spirit of irony or complicity. This would explain how a study on "Madonna politics," renamed *Meta-textual Girl* (in reference to her eponymous song "Material Girl"), can tackle such subjects as perversion, miscegenation, and a postmodern matriarchal system, without ever making reference to what lies beneath this political sphere—for example, the highly profitable Madonna industry and the way her image is marketed.[9] In *Rocking around the Clock*, the critic E. Ann Kaplan goes one step further and graces the singer with the title of "the new postmodern feminist heroine"—once again failing to distinguish between strategy and representation.[10]

Practitioners of cultural studies are on a similarly slippery slope and in fact greatly needed the support of the French theory movement. Now and then they quoted Lyotard or Derrida, and, in their introductions, presented their works as following in the tradition of Barthes or Foucault. More sophisticated analyses, filled with theoretical jargon, were developed around the works of a particular French author. Consider just one example, the rather rare one, in this field, of Gilles Deleuze: his work helped generate analyses of transsexual shows and alternative videos, which referred to them as "bodily flows" and a "performative theater";[11] his writings were also used to justify anorexia as a new postfeminist approach in the name of "nonreactive ethics" of "permanent negotiation";[12] an even broader effect was the reinforcement of cultural studies itself, "enabling the subject to particularize the universal" and "[create] pluralism where homogeneity had previously reigned."[13] In comparison to cultural critics, who are wont to overburden their analyses with theoretical references, Michel de Certeau remains the French author most directly engaged in the field of cultural studies in the strictest sense. This is because he is able to reinvest with meaning not only a TV viewer's or rap fan's modes of perception, but also the "agent," in the functional sense of the word as it is used in American sociology, if not the *subject* itself, which had already been de-composed by French theory. For cultural studies to be possible, a space must be made between the regimes of control and the imperialism of representation, for a modicum of initiative and inventiveness—even localized and limited—from the cultural participant. Thus, de Certeau substitutes what he calls "réseaux d'antidiscipline" and "ruses traversières" for the pessimism of Foucault's panopticon and the Marxist predictions of inevitable domination. This would explain the indisputable success of his book *The Practice of Everyday Life* when it appeared in translation, selling more than three thousand copies in the months following its release.[14] Furthermore, as François Dosse points out, de Certeau's attentive analysis of "operations of transit and exchange" is particularly well suited for this "society based entirely on immigration" found in the United States.[15]

Looking beyond the works of de Certeau, cultural studies was to gradually split and form two distinct fields of research: on one side, reception studies, that is, analysis of effects of the media, and forms of resistance in the spectator (from authors like Elihu Katz and David Morley)—a branch more closely related to American sociology and its epistemological realism than to literary theory; and, on the other side, the entire body of stylistic and textual analysis of pop culture—more closely linked to literary studies and French theory. It is the latter branch, stronghold of semiologists of the cultural *text*, dubbed "semiotic guerrillas" by the critic John Fiske, that is generally more visible in universities, more appealing to students, and more riddled with jargon. This branch was to find itself subjected to an increasingly biting tirade of criticism from a literary offshoot of cultural studies, which cited an excessive influence of French theory in its development—something that the authors, however, could do nothing about. This offshoot could not be ignored. All cultural activities were reduced to texts in need of decoding, rather than social phenomena. The tendency to resort to elliptical quotations, and in particular to metaphors, to not only describe but also to explain these social phenomena (reducing them to little more than acts of *metaphorization*), contributed to this group's artistic vagueness and argumentative weakness. And let us not forget their relativistic irony and the same narcissistic fascination as other literary disciplines with their own expansion—the disciplinary autofiction of cultural studies was sometimes given more space than the cultural objects being studied themselves. But these flaws, commonly found in literary fields with strong desires for expansion, pose, after reflection, less of a threat to cultural studies than their intrinsically ambiguous political nature.

If cultural studies has lauded the transgressive talents of rock stars, and celebrated users' resistant misreadings, they have, on the other hand, almost entirely forgotten the real political factors at stake in those topics. By refusing to question cultural marketing practices, at the very moment when the large corporations of the entertainment world were building their financial strength (notably Disney, Viacom, and Time Warner), cultural studies depoliticized an area of study that was, in fact, politically red hot. By defending popular success as the criterion of quality, in the name of the pleasure principle and a tactical antielitism, cultural studies played into the hands of cultural capitalism—whereas the latter was precisely what their libertarian credentials, authenticated by references to Marcuse and Foucault, had supposedly discredited. With the commercial order accomplished, a tactic of forging ahead regardless—both in work and in play—became the name of the game: because consumer culture is already ubiquitous, you might as well amuse yourself. So it is hardly surprising that the journal *Social Text*, a publication of reference for cultural studies (as its title suggests), justified a special edition on corporate cultures in 1995 with the claim that they make up the final "contested terrain" that had escaped analysis, and that they formed "scenes of ongoing struggle" and an arena of "ideological struggle" that finally needed to be addressed. "Maybe it's time we looked in the mirror of corporate culture and recognized ourselves,"[16] concludes the editor of the edition in his introduction, in what resonates like a slip of the pen that might be valid for the entire field of cultural studies.

Ethnicity, Postcoloniality, Subalterity

Following the investigation into cultural studies, we must consider what lies at the heart of the new community-centered discourses in American universities: ethnic and postcolonial studies. It is here that the old concept of identity is called into question, or at the very least divided into two main components: first, the role of *cratology* is considered, where identity plays a central role in determining international relationships of power, revealing complex layers of historical battles; second, pluralization is examined, along with the increasing complexity of identity that it entails, with so many composite narratives and interwoven journeys, and large numbers of diaspora identities and migrant descendants. This combination can be said to have sprung up from a Foucauldian line of thought—where the subject is constructed first through subjugation by institutions of control and their dominant discourse, and from the Deleuzean motif of a subject that has been de-composed over the course of passages of nomadic flight.

At the heart of this body of thought lies the pivotal African American issue, *the* motivation for examining segregation, but it is also a unique case, an older one, more pressing, loaded with a somber history. Thus, the development of this field was less the result of universities' efforts than were Chicano, Asian American, Native American, or even women's and gay studies. *Black studies* (a term that would soon be banned from the politically correct lexicon), unlike the other minority studies, did not emerge from a desire to affirm a group's minority identity, preparing for its first appearance in the public eye. This is a community that does not so much assert its existence as cope with it—since its formation during the slave-trade era—but this field of studies is a necessity in universities, bringing their important historical heritage to the field of humanities. This also offered a more immediate literary and cultural response to the 1960s struggle for human rights. One consequence of yesterday's battles and today's discourses is that an ancient conflict is being continued, although with perhaps less serious, or vital, stakes, the issue at hand now being a choice between the literary canon and the historical slave narrative. In the 1960s, the black minority already viewed universities as a highly symbolic battleground, when students Clement King and James Meredith attempted, without success (in 1958 and 1961), to enroll in Ph.D. programs in segregated Southern universities. Universities gradually became the new front line in the fight for equality: if certain socioeconomic discriminations have indeed been reduced in the last couple of decades (for example, in access to jobs, bank loans, and mortgages), the black community's attempts to penetrate higher education remained disastrous during the Reagan years.

More eighteen-to-twenty-five-year-old black people were in prison than in college, and 44 percent were illiterate; most of the rare black students could be found on less reputable, marginalized campuses, and only 2 percent of teaching staff (and 2.8 percent of Ph.D. students) were black, for a total of 13 percent of the population.[17] Clearly, before even inquiring into the problem of identity, the first dilemma was getting greater numbers of black students and professors into the academic world, and turning more attention to the historic and literary heritage of this community. And that is the task that important black intellectuals set themselves—Henry Louis Gates, Cornel West, V. Y. Mudimbe, Houston Baker, Manta Diawara—and they only occasionally drew upon French theory to do so. The key figure here was not Foucault or Derrida, but Frantz Fanon, whose widely cited work *The Wretched of the Earth* tackles similar problems of white oppression and means of resistance, and brings some African support to the movement—albeit from the North. Besides a few well-known authors, such as Richard Wright and James Baldwin, the black literary canon also had to be renewed and promoted, by making concrete advances (such as adding an African American literary anthology to the famous Norton collection), a move that allowed for a minimum form of cultural recognition. But this countercanon had to be appreciated as containing a mixture of influences, and representing a complex mesh of assimilated writers, dissident authors, and appropriated white references. In fact, black identity itself is viewed as constituting a "narrative" of an individual's always multiple sense of self. The terms used by black critic Patricia Williams in the following comment exemplify this literary paradigm: "While being black has been the most powerful social attribution in my life, it is only one of a number of governing narratives or presiding fictions by which I am constantly reconfiguring myself in the world."[18]

The controversy was to come from elsewhere. Excessive revisions of African American history led to an exhumation, less scientific than strategic, of the African origins of the West. In 1987, following in the footsteps of the Senegalese master of Afrocentrism, Cheikh Anta Diop, Martin Bernal asserted in his work *Black Athena* that the Greek foundations of Europe were a "mythological fabrication," born of a nineteenth-century Anglo-German "Hellenomania"; he stated that Platonism had Egyptian origins, and dismissed the historical narrative initiated by the "colonists" Herodotus and Thucydides as "distorted" from its beginnings; he even attributes all of Aristotelianism to the resources of Alexandria's library—which, however, did not open until twenty-five years after Aristotle's death.[19] And because man originated from Africa, argues Bernal, so did all the major sources of civilization. The book forced more moderate black intellectuals to dissociate themselves from the movement—in 1992, in the *New York Times,* Henry Louis Gates denounced "black demagogues and pseudo-scholars"[20]—and it notably provoked a conservative backlash, the appearance of damning articles in the *New Republic* and counterrevisionist books like the highly moralizing *Not Out of Africa.*[21] The fact remains that in this hotly disputed battle over the real "sources" of Western civilization, the opposing sides did not have much need for the works of French theory.

In Chicano studies, on the other hand, which is devoted to different forms (migrant and sedentary) of Latin American identity, French theory was somewhat more useful. Not for studying issues of colonial history or migratory economies, but for tackling more literary matters, such as the uncertainty of identity and diaspora testimonies—writings that fall under the emblematic heading of the Chicano *story* or *narration.*[22] In arenas ranging from cinema to autobiography, from union struggles to new cybercommunities, from the literary feminism of Sandra Cisneros to the social history of George Sanchez, and from the famous Chicano studies department at the University of Santa Barbara to the highly reputed one in Colorado, it was the reappearance of themes such as borders and transactions of identity that brought thinking back to French scholars. The work edited by Alfred Arteaga, *An Other Tongue,* is a good example, with contributions from Jean-Luc Nancy and Tzvetan Todorov, and texts dealing with the bilingual migrant's resistant "heteroglossia," or the use of "*différance*" as a "discourse by and about the other."[23] This type of approach distances itself from the kind of historical affirmation of identity that ocurred with black studies, in order to come to terms with the problematic nature of identity and the many possible ways of articulating it—which leads us to the field of postcolonial studies, a direct avatar of French theory.

Unlike the questions raised by black identity and the Hispanic community, postcolonial studies—a field that normally encompasses the other two—represents a second analytic dimension, questioning mixed and uncertain identities, the heritage of a postcolonial world. Postcoloniality is linked to notions of transnational racial miscegenation and to hybridity as both a stigma and a strategy, but it is also a space in which the lines between dominated and dominant cultures become blurred, where the first can nourish the second but can also turn the dominant culture's own weapons against it. As with cultural studies (which could choose to focus on the question of identity rather than pop culture, as black, Chicano, or even French cultural studies do), the field of postcolonial studies perceives itself as representing a crossroads, with no predefined domain and no limits to its scope. In reviews like *Diaspora* and *Transition,* postcolonial studies examines zone-crossing and hybrid cultures, redrawing the world map to show areas of extended "transculturation": from El Paso to Tijuana, the American continent has been crisscrossed by the red line tracing these migratory dramas, and the ocean that joins Harlem, Dakar, and Salvador de Bahia to Brazil has been renamed in the words of Paul Gilroy, "the black Atlantic."

Postcolonialism is first and foremost a literary concept, because, at the heart of its genealogy lie relationships of minority and speech, power and language. Black novels and Native American poetry are not "postcolonial" because of a direct link to slavery or genocide, but because these genres, which appear in English, give rise to a linguistic duality, and the historical tension—whether sublimated or, on the contrary, stirred up—is palpable in the texts themselves. Deleuze, when describing contemporary American English, remarked characteristically that it was "worked upon by a Black English, and also a Yellow English, a Red English, a broken English, each of which is like a language shot with a spray-gun of colors."[24] This leads to the major critical factor of *francophone* literature—so badly named: the word was created in 1878 by the geographer Onésime Reclus "to bring together the colonies"—which many French departments in America study better than French universities themselves, looking at topics such as Édouard Glissant's "poetics of relation," Aimé Césaire's "negritude," and the Algerian novelist Assia Djebar's language in mourning.

The theme of literary *minorities* made Ireland the textbook case for the postcolonial field. Indeed, Ireland was the first country in the twentieth century (and the only country in Europe) to win independence, and its literary renaissance from 1900 to 1920 (George Bernard Shaw, O'Casey, and later Joyce) played a part in undermining the order of the dominant culture. Ireland is famously home to the poet William Butler Yeats, praised by the most high-profile thinkers of the postcolonial movement, from Gayatri Spivak to Edward Said—the latter considers that he follows in the tradition of the great "poets of anti-imperialism," such as Pablo Neruda, Aimé Césaire, and Mahmoud Darwish.[25] But it is also the literary angle, this "contrapuntal" approach (of reversing the narrative lens) used by Edward Said himself, that led to a postcolonial rereading of all the Western classics, including, of course, those that contributed to the creation of the nineteenth-century Anglo–French discourse on "orientalism,"[26] but also those—apparently more neutral—that had nonetheless been "infected" with a sort of unconscious colonialism, such as Charlotte Brontë's *Jane Eyre*. Even Shakespeare is not above suspicion, with his *Tempest*, in which the impossible alliance and founding disagreement between the conquering Prospero and the indigenous Caliban is recounted. But postcolonial literature can also reveal more contemporary tensions: a current exploration of hybrid stances and mixed identities has been used both to criticize the submission of certain assimilated Latin American writers and authors like V. S. Naipaul in using dominant literary forms and Western "mythology," and, conversely, to celebrate aesthetic revolt against the empire. This movement of resistance was first typified by the Cuban writer Alejo Carpentier and his works of "magical realism"; today it has led to the appearance of intermediary novels and narratives from a third realm between domination and identity-based reaction—found in particular in the works of the Indian writers Salman Rushdie and Arundhati Roy, Africans Wole Soyinka and J. M. Coetzee, and Caribbeans Derek Walcott and Patrick Chamoiseau.

French theory is constantly cited, and frequent references are given—as if to provide biographical justification—to the pro-Algerian commitment and the *Manifeste des 121*, to Jean Genet's support of the

Black Panthers, and to Lyotard's bold attitude while leading the Algerian section of Socialisme ou Barbarie. Foucault's and Deleuze's comments on the abstract "universalism" of colonizers, or on Western culture as a conquering one, are often brought in for backup to an argument, as often as Derrida's formula on "what is called Western thought, the thought whose destiny is to extend its domains while the boundaries of the West are drawn back."[27] The more specific impact of Michel de Certeau is also worth noting: if we look at its core values, postcolonial theory matches his own reflections on the necessary reversal of traditional history, as well as his thinking on "heterology" (the title of several "Certalian" collections published in the United States) as the "act of seeing ourselves as others see us."[28] De Certeau's critiques of the notion of one-way history, and Foucault's analyses of historic continuity as a discursive narrative, have allowed postcolonial thinkers to extract a narrative for the colonized people from the dominant historical framework, a Western "myth," and to create the starting point for *another* conception of history, a counterhistory. But it is precisely when people turned from pulling apart accepted theories to considering what possible alternatives exist, from criticizing history to making critical history, that a fertile debate between authors emerged in the postcolonial field, at the limits of French theory.

Typical of this oscillation is the example of the great postcolonial critic Homi Bhabha. In his most frequently studied essays, *Nation and Narration* and *The Location of Culture*, he continuously draws a usable distinction, albeit inevitably shifting, between theory that inflicted violence on colonized peoples and theory that could be used to negotiate improvement of their situation—in other words, a "Eurocentric theoreticism," elitist and reaffirming (he includes Montesquieu's Persia but also Barthes's Japan), and a nonobjectivizing theory as a "revisionary force" in tension with its "institutional containment" (he quotes Foucault and Derrida)—the latter alone capable of illuminating the "contradictory and ambivalent space of enunciation," a space for translation and hybrid forms of expression, inside which the divided subject of the postcolonial world strives for existence.[29] Gayatri Spivak, once again, goes a step further. If she was grateful to the French for having shown the "affinity between the imperialist subject and the subject of humanism,"[30] thus allowing a link to be established between criticism of the subject and struggles for freedom, she also asks whether a simple cultural distance did not prevent Foucault and Deleuze from "[imagining] the kind of Power and Desire that would inhabit the unnamed subject of the Other of Europe"—criticizing their "micrological" approach as a luxury in the face of more pressing "macrological struggles" at play within postcolonialism, aftereffects of the cold war and other American foreign policies.[31] The real problem—one that all intellectuals from the third world have faced since the end of the decolonizing process—is a battle that cannot be fought but with the arms of the adversary itself, a program of postcolonial emancipation whose terms had been directly taken from the Enlightenment and rational progressivism: democracy, citizenship, constitution, nation, socialism, and even culturalism. Spivak concluded that the task at hand, for which French theory (which remained Western) would hardly be useful, was "to wrench these regulative political signifiers out of their represented field of reference."[32] In other words, the large concepts of political change needed to be *de-Westernized*—a vast project that in more concrete terms came to inspire subaltern studies.

What is "subalterity"? It is a condition whereby the dominated subject is placed in a position of boundless alienation, a cognitive—as well as social—objectification, because it represents a breakdown in one's knowledge of self and one's role in political conflict. The subaltern is the blind spot of the historical process. The subaltern is reduced to silence by the forces of power, whether they be religious, colonial, or economic, but also by those who claim to "represent" militants and their Western, juridical-political model of *liberation*. Both the latter and the former ensure that that which is eternally forgotten in great historical narratives remains invisible, when in fact it should be the true focus of history. This was the starting point for subaltern studies, begun in 1982 in Delhi, with the creation of the review of the same name,[33] by the Indian Marxist historians Ranajit Guha and Partha Chatterjee—the latter providing an analysis of Gandhi as a "political signifier" who "appropriated" a people by leading them. And that was before Gayatri Spivak joined the group: in 1983 she gave credibility to the group with her famous article about the subaltern's enforced submission to the Western discourse of emancipation,[34] and in 1988 she joined forces with Guha to put together an initial appraisal of subaltern studies.[35] The primary focus for subaltern studies was the historiography of the decolonization of India; a rewriting that the Marxist historians performed in radical style, based on the Gramscian concepts of "subaltern" and "elaboration," and on

Foucault's comments regarding historical discontinuity. They wanted to break the socioeconomic signifying chain and to rehabilitate the role of grassroots movements and noncoordinated insurrections, in opposition to the backward-looking and all-encompassing image of a consummated, homogeneous program. As a countermovement to history as written by the Westernized elite, the real issue was not just coming up with a version of history that took working-class people into account, but, in a more forward-looking spirit, aspiring toward an antiempirical battle whose terms and objectives are not Western at all. However, as early on as the movement's second meeting, in Calcutta in 1986, differences of opinion became apparent between the Marxist historical branch and a more literary branch, which was more focused on subaltern *stories* and *narrations*. Yet the movement gradually spread to Africa and Latin America, where researchers such as Patricia Seed and Florencia Mallon began to explore traces of the local subaltern's existence. Twenty years on, promises of what insight into the *subaltern* might reveal have been neglected, only picked up now and then by intellectuals from the third world and by certain Westerners trying to understand the wave of post-September 11 America-phobia; this field of research remains one of the few recent political ideas, along with the concept of "multitudes," which was capable of leaving behind prevailing moralism in order to tackle other forms of domination—ethnic, religious, cultural, and sexual.

Gender in Question

From the beginning of the 1980s, this final arena, and its accompanying questions regarding sexual identity, were to give rise to the most fertile of ground for new ideas from the literary field, a ground where the seeds of French theory were to prove most fruitful. But in order to set the scene, one must first go back and examine American feminist academics—though a few lines here can hardly do justice to their rich and diverse work.

It was in the 1960s that an organized feminist movement first began, marked by the creation in 1966 of the National Organization for Women (NOW), and by the immense success, three years earlier, of a humanist critique of *femininity*, casting it as a "mystification" created by men and imposed on women—*The Feminine Mystique* by Betty Friedan. But following this initial unified feminist front, the 1970s saw the first signs of division between universities and civil society. This second group began integrating the first feminist words into the mechanisms of marketing, as demonstrated by the first large-circulation women's magazines—especially *Ms.,* launched in 1972—and the widespread success of poet Adrienne Rich—who recounted the traumatic experience of her pregnancy and denounced the "patriarchal institution" of maternity.[36] In the meantime, universities favored the growth of a separatist form of feminism, isolated on campus both from militant community movements on the outside and from the majority of students and teaching staff inside. This form first emerged in the literary field of studies with the creation of an interdepartmental program of women's studies at the State University of San Diego at the end of the 1960s—followed by the introduction of more than three hundred similar programs across the country from 1970 to 1980—but it remained isolated from the mainstream curriculum, which it did not effectively penetrate until the beginning of the 1990s, in order to combat its declining enrollment numbers. In 1970, Kate Millett's groundbreaking work *Sexual Politics* assigned "feminist politics" a dual mission: to rehabilitate the counterhistory chronicling the oppression of women—something that her book does by analyzing the period from 1930 to 1960 as one of a "sexual counterrevolution" throughout the entire Western world—and to hunt down any examples of misogyny in the literary classics (in favor of a corpus of women writers), such as those cases denounced by Millett herself in the works of Henry Miller, Norman Mailer, and even Jean Genet.[37] Academic programs in the same vein, and the creation of a nucleus of engaged editors (Feminist Press, Daughters Inc.) and reviews (*Signs* and *Sex Roles*) played their part in making the movement more radical—by distancing it from a run-of-the-mill university crowd now made up mostly of students, who, during the recession of the seventies, were more inclined to ask for the same job opportunities as men than an end to patriarchal power. This initial wave of radical feminism on campuses took its inspiration both from the anti-imperialism of SDS and from a mistrust of "masculine" political institutions. Indeed, the movement's leaders had, a few years earlier, encountered a student movement that they deemed "phallocratic," because it neither broached the question of male–female inequality nor gave positions of responsibility to female militants; Casey Hayden is a prime example—she was the wife of the SDS leader but called for female dissidence within the movement in 1965.

Radical academic feminism, however, was to split into two branches. Sometime between the group's initial research work and early publications, a divergence became apparent between those known as "difference feminists," who focused on the otherness of the biological and historical fates reserved for men and women—and who used this as a motivation to call for a feminist *separatism,* whether this be linked to lesbianism or not—and "sameness feminists," who were in favor of working toward similar conditions for men and women, or at least a demystification of overemphasized differences. This shifting and sinuous boundary line would remain, to a greater or lesser degree, the same regardless of evolutions within feminism. Thus, at the beginning of the 1980s, a comparable debate took place between *essentialist* feminists, advocates and historians of a female *essence,* and *constructionist* feminists, who wanted to unveil the social mechanisms behind the making of this false "essence"—the latter were avid supporters of French theory. A similar polarity can be found in the 1980s between theorists who believed in a sexual *fate,* and those who championed a sexual *usage.* The "sex wars" pitted a prohibitionist, antipornography group, centered on Andrea Dworkin and jurist Catharine MacKinnon, against a liberationist, anticensure group (Sex-Positive Feminism), whose figurehead was the critic Gayle Rubin. In order to give a potential sense of political focus, if not an *ecstatic* aspect, to sexual practices, this last movement advocated emancipation through the control of sexuality, and adopted a more sympathetic political position toward gay men and lesbians. Under the title "Pleasure and Danger," a 1982 conference at Barnard College and its eponymous collection of publications promoted the position of a second group, an "uprooted" feminism that examined gender endangering rather than looking to create a supportive feminine community. This conference clearly delineated the new dividing line in academic feminism—with one side focusing on oppressive "dangers," and the other on experimental "pleasures." The feminists of the first group introduced a predefined identity-bearing subject, one in need of protection, according to their defensive perspective, or, for radical separatist feminists, a revolutionary subject; the second group, bolstered by the theoretical contributions of French antiessentialism, preferred to examine relationships, alliances, and unexpected junctions of/areas of common ground for different modes of sexual subjectivization, from a tactical feminist stance that was not so much exclusively *feminine* as micropolitical, because it included gays, lesbians, transgendered people, and sexual deviants. In her contribution to *Pleasure and Danger,* Meryl Altman draws on Foucault to construct a criticism of various forms of sexual therapy and the stimuli of conjugal pleasures, which, under the pretext of "liberating" one's body, instead perpetuate a "regime of power" and regulation of the sexes.[38] Gayle Rubin, meanwhile, used the publication to defend "the constructivist alternative" of a feminism free of all essence, able to reconcile the Foucauldian "radical critique of sexual arrangements" with a vigilance—inspired more by Wilhelm Reich—in the face of collective methods of sexual repression; she concludes that even if Foucault was able to pull apart the "repressive hypothesis," repression remains ubiquitous, and must be intimately resisted.[39]

In both of the aforementioned texts, the target is the same—a feminism based on the female political *subject,* which naturalizes women while claiming to "liberate" them. However, this feminist critique of the subject also comes up against the need to constitute women as *subjects* of the law—whether tactically or juridically: the majority of feminist triumphs can be deemed "humanistic" or "conformist," yet the fact remains that they were a concrete necessity and represented a political victory. This contradiction is reminiscent of those encountered in subaltern studies, and similarly asks, "What are the implications of using 'theory' for feminist analysis, considering that some of what appears under the sign of 'theory' has marked masculinist and Eurocentric roots?"[40] Confronted with this fetish known as "theory," whether or not it was associated with masculine power, radical American feminism was divided over adopting a mimetic reflex or an attitude of political defiance. The literal use of theoretical references betrayed an increasingly reductive and rhetorical form of feminism, whose diatribes tended to tarnish precious critical resources. It was a feminism of "sexed" knowledge, and one that, according to Sandra Harding's lexicon for the philosophy of the sciences, reduced all rationalism to a dogma of the phallus, disciplines such as philosophy and even geography to a macho, heterosexist discourse, and the discoveries of Galileo and Newton to a reinforcement of a scientific "androcentrism" and its political role in serving the "male rapist."[41] The more reasonable approach would be, instead, to distance oneself somewhat from the theoretical referent, only using it occasionally, without falling subservient to it, in order to produce what the critic Naomi Schor calls "a tone of controlled rage,"[42] and a form of feminism that focuses more on the problems surrounding sexual identities. This more stimulating branch of feminism was also to place emphasis on the *"real* body," *"real* struggle," and a *"real* gender," keen as it was to reduce the rift separating it from the off-campus activist community. Because rape is "real" and "not a text," some criticized poststructuralism, claiming that it "forbids recourse to a 'real body,' or a 'real sex,' and that such recourse is necessary to articulate moral and political opposition" to oppression.[43]

Finally, to better comprehend the ambiguous relationship between feminism and French theory, we should examine its relations with each author of the new corpus. Naturally, the introductory figure for transatlantic feminism is Simone de Beauvoir, adulated after the war but subsequently treated with excessive severity by the second wave of American feminism. This movement positioned itself in opposition to the theses of *The Second Sex,* and against the "patriarchal humanism" of the mother figure posited there as an "existentialist subject," as Gayatri Spivak summarizes—before calling for a positive reevaluation of de Beauvoir by reading her work "against the grain of the text."[44] This second feminist movement was to widely use what it named "the new French feminisms,"[45] notably the psychoanalytic approach of Julia Kristeva, Sarah Kofman's rereading of Freud, Derridean Hélène Cixous's texts on forms of expression capable of bursting through the "phallocentric regime" (her 1975 article, "The Laugh of the Medusa,"[46] which introduced the notion of *écriture féminine,* became a classic in American women's studies), and finally, the theses of Luce Irigaray. Irigaray, in works such as *Speculum of the Other Woman* (1974; translation 1985) and *An Ethics of Sexual Difference* (1984; translation 1993), suggests that we consider the figure of the subject as being "always already masculine," and posits, on the other hand, the feminine point of view as a refusal of totality, an affirmation of the indistinct, and a criticism of identity and symmetry—all themes dear to antiessentialist American feminists. The importance of Derrida's deconstruction in this context has already been mentioned, but Lacan's writings also played a decisive role, which emerged thanks to a fruitful misunderstanding that occurred when the text was imported—in this case, it was the identification of the *penis,* and thus of patriarchal power, with the more neutral term *phallus,* which Lacan nonetheless considered to be the lost symbiotic link lying at the source of *all* desire, whether it be masculine or feminine.

Significantly, American feminists adopted this imprecise notion of the *phallus* so that they could deconstruct, along with Lacan, the idea of masculine "superiority," but abandoned it when it meant having to wage less Lacanian attacks against generalized *phallocentrism*. Other French authors, quoted almost everywhere, found themselves used as foils: this was especially true for Jean Baudrillard, whose reflections on women as "appearance" in *On Seduction,* as well as his more controversial attacks on "shortsighted" feminism, transformed him into the French scapegoat for American feminism.

The reception given to Deleuze and Guattari was more complex, marked in this arena by twenty years of misunderstandings. One recalls the violent reaction of one feminist activist when she came to interrupt them at the Schizo-Culture conference in 1975. She perceived the "schizo subjects" as a pretext for silencing the feminist struggle, just as many female academics saw the Guattarian notion of "becoming woman" as a way of espousing what Elizabeth Grosz calls "the subordination, or possibly even the obliteration, of women's struggles for autonomy, identity, and self-determination."[47] Until the middle of the 1990s, there was a feeling of instinctive mistrust for the way that Deleuze and Guattari "molecularized" the feminist issue, and it came to dominate the relationship of American feminism with their work: the "molecular" scale of their analyses—on the micro-intensities of becoming woman and the flow of a desire without subject—wandered dangerously far from the larger ("molar") scale of oppression and effective ways to combat it. It was not until a more tactical, and vehemently antiessentialist, feminism took the upper hand that Deleuze and Guattari's opposition of the great "molar" dualisms (man–woman, homo–hetero) and their energetics of desire could at last play a key role in the feminist movement—a movement that, in 1994, officially declared, in two articles within the same work, its reconciliation with the *Anti-Oedipus* authors.[48] Their call for a sexual *disidentification* of texts was even to prove itself potent in the field of literature—as Deleuze put it: "Woman is not necessarily the writer, but the minority-becoming of her writing, whether it be man or woman,"[49] and, as Guattari added, one should "rather look for what is homosexual in a great writer, even if he does happen to be heterosexual,"[50] pushing principles of sexual indetermination and its molecular mobility in the constant fluctuations of writing to the forefront of discussion—undoing the biographical approach of the first wave of feminists, championing *women* writers and their *separate* corpus.

And yet, the French figure who retained the most influence on the diverse branches of American feminism, and on gay and lesbian studies—to whom they became intellectually allied—was Michel Foucault. However, from his practically legendary misogyny, to *The History of Sexuality*'s indifference to the question of sexual difference, the relationship between Foucault and feminism did not seem destined to go very far. The terms in which one book dedicated to this problem discussed their "convergences" betray difficulties in reconciling Foucault's approach with feminism: apart from a "friendship grounded in political and ethical commitment," this work includes essays suggesting, for example, that Foucault and the feminists share a "theology of liberation," a notion quite uncharacteristic of Foucault, as well as a "poetics of revolution" and an "aesthetics of daily life" that are even further from Foucault's usual style.[51] Yet Foucault's works nonetheless had an impact on the profound evolution that was taking place in the arena of American feminism, shifting from essentialist humanism to radical constructionism; his influence is confirmed by the omnipresence of his work in the research of Joan Scott, Gayle Rubin, and Judith Butler. The English translation of *La Volonté de savoir* (*The Will to Knowledge*) was published in 1978 as "An Introduction," and in this first volume of *The History of Sexuality* the work's general direction is laid out, and it can even be considered the invisible key to American feminism of the 1980s. By pulling apart the "repressive hypothesis" of a sexuality allegedly in need of liberation, and instead analyzing sexuality as a discursive formation and apparatus of subjectification—with the historic period of "liberation" being none other than "a tactical shift and reversal"[52]—the book completed the task of marginalizing "progressive" feminism, paving the way for criticism of *all* forms of sexual discourse. Foucault explained the nineteenth-century creation of the modern system of sexuality through its "four great strategies," namely, "the sexualization of children, the hysterization of women, the specification of the perverted, and the regulation of populations,"[53] thus helping to open up feminist thought by connecting the field to the domains of homosexuality and criminalization of the body. Above all, he managed to situate sexuality and its implications in a political history: sexuality organizes the core elements of the family unit, the economic system, and the political management of society and is thus able to set the norms of monogamy, heterocentrism, and inheritance of wealth, and is intrinsically linked to these larger arenas. The term "biopolitics," used to denote the administrative regulation of life, more specifically refers to the process by which power creates subjects through a system of classification and management, infiltrates and inhabits the body, electrifying it, and is, thus, never fully exterior to them.

On the other side of the Atlantic, Foucault's work not only stirred up lively debates in response to his reevaluation of sexual practices in the classical world, it also altered the conception of sexuality itself, which was no longer one of dominated or repressed sexual subjects but a matter of gendered identity (man or woman) and of sexual practices (homo or hetero) that had become unavoidably problematic. With the common aim of thinking through sexual *subjectivation* instead of pointing to an enemy defined in terms of gender, feminists and homosexuals were able to join in a new type of collaboration. In other words, the success of Foucault's later works meant that the previous prescriptive approach, which characterized both feminism and traditional gay studies—pitting an oppressed identity against a dominant one—was replaced by a *postidentity* archaeology whose aim was to uncover the mechanisms of gender norms analyzed as being a specific political and historical construction. This inquiry into split subjectivities and undefined sexual identities sometimes made use of the entire body of French theory—as does critic Kaja Silverman, by situating her study of modern "deviant masculinities" under a quadruple lens, using not only a Foucauldian genealogy of norms, but also a Lacanian "acephalous unconscious," a distinctly Lyotardesque "politics of the libido," and Deleuze's dissassembly of the reductive binomial "sado-masochism."[54] In most cases, however, it was Foucault's work alone that created the possibility of these kinds of evolution, which also took place during a period marked by many new attempts to theorize homosexuality in the early 1990s.

Thus, in addition to the older field of gay studies, which were often essentialist and oppositional (with gay and straight clearly differentiated), the new movement of queer studies appeared, bearing an ever-present mark of Foucault's influence. The new, more "infectious" approach examined all the intermediary zones of sexual identity, any place where it became blurred. The adoption of the word *queer* (a reappropriation of the homophobic slur) can be traced back to an article in 1991, in which feminist critic Teresa de Lauretis called for a rethinking of sexual identity, based on its constantly shifting forms.[55] It was also a consequence of the essentialist/antiessentialist feminist debates of the 1980s, and of the rereading of Foucault, as well as Derrida (who made possible a repoliticization of the "undecidable"), put forward by Eve Kosofsky Sedgwick and Judith Butler, two of the movement's most crucial figures.

In a groundbreaking work, *Epistemology of the Closet*, which soon acquired cult status, Eve Kosofsky Sedgwick, English literature professor at Duke, asks why a man who has sexual relations with another man should be called "gay." Drawing on Nietzsche and Proust, and examining the norm of monogamy, and the AIDS crisis, she uncovers the fragility and instability of gender, combats the categorizations of sexuality with the "pleasures of the body" using a very Foucauldian viewpoint—and criticizes the separatism of the previous decade's identity politics.[56] Sedgwick proposes that we unearth the sexual disorders and conflicting inclinations within identity (masked by compulsory dualisms) with the ultimate objective of exposing an entire episteme: "many of the major nodes of thought and knowledge in twentieth-century Western culture as a whole are structured—indeed, fractured—by a chronic, now endemic crisis of homo/heterosexual definition, indicatively male, dating from the end of the nineteenth century,"[57] she begins, referring to modern homosexuality's "date of birth," as proposed by Foucault: 1870.[58] This objective would be taken up—sometimes rather literally—by the many authors who, in the following years, proposed that we subject all possible social and cultural objects to this "perverse" reading of sexual indetermination, in other words, a process of "queerification"—the range of subjects included the epistolary novel, oral poetry, Schubert's music, Michelangelo's sculpture, and even the IMF and Zen Buddhism. The other pivotal reference for queer theory was Judith Butler, whose *Gender Trouble* and *Bodies That Matter* gave sophisticated analyses of the performative and dialogic elements of sexual gender as a continuous construction—femininity and virility are shown to be "compulsory citations," mere control examples, whose basis in artifice is demonstrated by drag queens, who make a public parody of them.

The queer movement and its innovative theorists were, like radical university feminism before them, responsible for revealing a growing divergence between, on the one hand, campus-based sexual activism, oratorical and self-contemplating (and closely linked to the careers of a few literature divas), and, on the other, the real, community-based struggle of sexual minorities. This division occurred despite the personal involvement of certain academics, particularly in the fight against AIDS, and despite the notable exception of the extensive interviews given by Foucault to mainstream gay publications such as *Christopher Street* and the *Advocate*. Dialogue between the socially isolated intellectual clique, on the cutting edge of radical new theories, and community activists whose organizations and demands had remained largely the same for twenty-five years, was difficult, disparate, and structurally discordant. Thoroughly convinced of society's backwardness in relation to the university, David Halperin, a historian of homosexuality, went so far as to contrast a real America which, since 1980, "seems to have sunk into a reactionary torpor" and its universities in full "intellectual ferment," whose research "[makes] great strides . . . under the impetus provided by Foucault" and a few others.[59] Halperin even seems to lament the fact that not all the country was as bold as certain academics. It was the return of the old problem of a temporal gap between intellectual innovation and social struggles, between academic departments and the streets, a problem previously raised by Marx and Engels—the latter suggesting that we apply the model of the class struggle to the marital unit, in which the husband plays the bourgeois and the wife plays the proletariat.

Politics and Theory: An Uneasy Alliance

During the 1980s, there was a steadily widening gap between an increasingly sophisticated theoretical justification of the minority struggle and its less spectacular social manifestations, which were hindered by the Reagan counterrevolution—divided into an academic multiculturalism and concrete minority movements. This rift was taken up as a prime argument in the Marxist camp, still strong in the universities, who accused identity politics—and the French theory that inspired it—of having given up the "real" conflict. The dialectical-materialist branch of theory, which posits itself as a revelation of underlying social relationships, is opposed to "postmodernist" theory, which shifts the focus into a purely symbolic sphere, and replaces class struggle with textual conflict: it started in 1979, when Dick Hebdige described the punk movement as a class war fought in an arena of style, but the issues at stake became cultural, stylistic, and, finally, textual—this phenomenon became the much-maligned "textualism" that threatened to deny the relevance of even a work's social context. Alex Callinicos has written a book aiming to assess these trends, in which he summarizes the Marxists' grievances with French theory, which they find guilty of providing this textual battle with weapons: jargon, idealism, pantextualism, nihilism, passive conservatism, and Nietzschean aporias.[60] Terry Eagleton, in one of the Anglo-Saxon humanities field's best sellers, criticizes what he sees as the political defeatism of deconstruction, and the new theorists' headlong dash into wars of words, their passion for the unique theme of self-destruction of texts.[61] According to the Marxists, the very idea of conflict became metaphorical, a mere stylistic figure. In Todd Gitlin's view, it was these postmodernist university cliques who elevated the practice of "dressing like Madonna to an act of 'resistance,' comparable to going out and protesting for the right to abortion,"[62] without drawing any distinction between the social struggle and anticonformist merchandising. The element responsible for blurring the distinction between action and discourse, or politically committed activism and paper activism—a distinction that is essential to the Marxist perspective—was none other than the *hypersemiologization* introduced by cultural studies and continued by minority studies. If signs are all that remain, and social problems can be resolved in text, then the only possible political gesture is one of reappropriation, shifting meaning, and innovatively combining existing signs—which takes us far from the concrete historical forces on which Marxism is based. Thus, we have *post*structuralism, *post*modernism, and *post*humanism, which seems to reveal that those who made a habit of appending "post" to the new "isms" were placing their faith in narrative itself, tolling the death knell of action, ushering in the fin de siècle disillusionment of those who arrived too late, and could only comment sardonically on missed opportunities.

One could make two objections to this Marxist perspective on theory's political impotence. The first is a sociological one. Because it is strictly academic, "accommodated to . . . the norms of academic respectability" and forced to "reformulate its positions according to the codes of the dominant paradigm" (in the terms of two critics),[63] this American Marxism is itself subject to the criticisms it offered: its cardinal motivations are, like those of its poststructuralist or multiculturalist foes, loyalty to one school of thought, argumentative prowess, and the importance of dominating the marketplace of discourses. This version of Marxism is, in a word, as impotent and rhetorical as the other enclaves of the academic world, and far more so, in fact, than its European counterparts, who have the support of political parties, as well as their union background. None of Terry Eagleton's or Michael Ryan's work was capable of *directly* furthering the cause of off-campus social struggles.

The second argument is more theoretical. It is tied to the recurring issue of *enunciation,* and its linguistic uses and sociopolitical conditions—and the links between these two factors—as a central question, if not for French theory, at least for its American adaptations. Taken as an act, enunciation is what turns an expression—as inconsequential as a style of dressing or a song, or as important as the declaration of a collective subject—into a social statement, a collective operation of subjectification, a connection to be made between a vision of the world and intervention in the world. This notion is supported, in different theoretical spheres, by Deleuze's and Guattari's "collective assemblages of enunciation" (which are certainly less territorially oriented than any actual community), by Foucault's project to pin down "the mode of existence of discursive events in a culture," or even by the act of enunciation that, in Michel de Certeau's work, leads to a "historicity of experience." This issue of enunciation is, in fact, the blind spot of the American Marxist perspective. This political dogma, which dismisses French theoretical texts, identity-based university programs, and the more ambiguous, interdisciplinary cultural studies with the same scorn, never took into account the question of enunciation. The Marxists not only made a *political* error in treating the question of social enunciation as a minor concern (if not going so far as to consider it entirely vague and useless), but they might also have profited from considering its applicability to their own practices, to explain their spontaneous appropriation of certain terms in the fight against textualist "treason." Some examples were "reality," "subject," "ethics," "action," and "politics": to examine these concepts—in the name of which the Marxists constructed a sensible form of criticism—would not have been just a ploy to sidestep the debate for the sake of endless philological speculation, but rather an important inquiry into the links between social groups and intellectual discourses, between actions and signifiers—and also into whether political norms dating from the nineteenth century remained valid or had become obsolete in this context.

According to Judith Butler and Joan Scott, it is imperative to "expose the silent violence of these concepts as they have operated not merely to marginalize certain groups but to erase and exclude them from the notion of 'community' altogether"—something that could only be achieved through French theory ("poststructuralism"), because the latter "is not, strictly speaking, *a position,* but rather a critical interrogation of the exclusionary operations by which 'positions' are established."[64] In other words, only theoretical tools would enable a more nuanced perspective to replace the premature distinction between a formerly unified political society, which the Marxists' perspective seems to look back on wistfully, and the balkanized domain of identity politics, revealing the *excluding* methods of the discourse urging for "unity," as well as, conversely, the possibilities of alliance among the various minority cliques. This is, in fact, the crux of the problem: to consider the question of enunciation as clearly as possible is not, in itself, a performative act, the sufficient condition for producing political change—particularly when the rigor and clarity of the question are lost in the course of a very loosely linked chain of discourse conveying French theoretical texts to American activists and other readers, through the vicissitudes of translation, reappropriation, university pedagogy, and the readers' own interests. Those who raised the question of enunciation were not necessarily its potential political beneficiaries, and they had less at stake than the latter in creating social change. Referring to Michael Bérubé, Stanley Fish summed it up perfectly, with the cunning of one who seems to enjoy the "uselessness" of academics: "Although the 'textual' or the 'discursive' is . . . a crucial site of social contestation, the people who *study* that site are not crucial players in the contest."[65] Fish's remark reminds us of the structural separation between academics whose task (and priority) it is to continually analyze, reconsider, and mistrust the question at hand, and minority communities whose whole problem is gaining access to enunciation, as a means to effect change. In other words, it was a separation between academics questioning the very methods of questioning, and minority social groups unable to assert their most urgent demands. The separation was, furthermore, between the methodological quibbling of a veritable ethical position and the cruder problems of certain demographics whose politics were often far less progressive. To put it briefly, a black lesbian who proclaims her "antiestablishmentism" and "deconstructive politics" remains, nevertheless, closer to the academic, discourse-based community than to the political community—in contrast to one whose direct environment, less tolerant than the one on campus, constantly ostracizes her for the color of her skin and her sexual preferences. The symbolic capital of the theoretical approach not only compensates for the meager political capital of isolated academics, but sometimes also enables them to justify their chosen sphere by pointing out the lack of self-awareness of those taking concrete action.

The separation was, ultimately, a pedagogical one. Whereas Marx's *Manifesto* was accessible to German unionists when it was published, theoretical essays discussing race as the "split signifier" or gender norms as linked "metonymically" to sexual identity are simply not readable for the actual victims of sexual or ethnic oppression. We might say that the Tower of Babel of humanities that aimed to be a meeting place of different minorities was succeeded by a tower of babble created by a metadiscourse that grew increasingly impenetrable to its unlikely benefi- ciaries. It was this dynamic that Eve Sedgwick, mother superior of queer studies, astutely points out when she warns of the danger that an overly refined concept of "difference" no longer communicates anything of the social experience of difference: theory, conceived "as a very science of *différ(e/a)nce,* has both so fetishized the idea of difference and so vapor- ized its possible embodiments that its most thoroughgoing practitioners are the last people to whom one would now look for help in thinking about particular differences."[66] This alienation *through theory* cannot, however, be entirely imputed to the long-winded theoretical nitpicking of a few critics, or to their slightly ostentatious ethical-discursive vigi- lance (e.g., from what standpoint, in what way, on what grounds, and in whose name may we speak of *difference?*)—except through the old anti-intellectualism that reappeared in certain minority group leaders' responses to the verbosity of these *academic* positions. The gap we have been discussing is, in a more banal sense, sociological. It brings us back to a familiar misunderstanding: an optical illusion that causes campus ora- tors to mistake their *partial* academic sphere for the social *whole.* It takes only a conference, an article, or a successful debate to make them forget the peripheral and politically ambivalent nature of their chosen field, and take the autarkic logic of academic discourse to be a general rule: if the marginal position of academics contributes to their enunciative produc- tion and intellectual visibility, marginality is precisely what hinders those whose plights are at issue—minorities outside the university who would often like to integrate moderate political-social groups—and keeps them imprisoned in a inexorable spiral of silence. This same separation can also obscure the other crucial factor: the "culture" (popular, mass-mar- ket, commercial, and antiestablishment all at once) that enthusiastic aca- demics took a vulgar pleasure in analyzing, much the way an ethnologist lays claim to his subject, was no longer a clearly delineated sphere, an *object* of study, but became inextricably muddled with the sociopolitical whole. It no longer had limits outside of which one could gain any perspective, and no longer resembled a repertoire of forms of expression so much as an overall view on which subjectivities were founded. The gradual disappearance of the silent minority along with the omniculture formed by the industry of symbols became a twofold area of blindness and denial, to which even the most astute semiologists of identity and the most sophisticated theorists of enunciation fell prey, a dual, repressed reality that can be traced back to their fundamental ambivalence toward capitalism.

Indeed, only an overall critique of capital would have provided proponents of the various voices of resistance, based on identity or postidentity, with the tools to form a political community. Even if cultural studies and identity politics were both eager to tear down cultural hierarchies, to elevate MTV in favor of Shakespeare, or the African American stars of blacksploitation B movies over the white stars of films that garnered awards and recognition, the notion of commodity only comes up in these fields as a secondary concern, sometimes as metaphor, and sometimes as fatality. The most surprising aspect of this unprecedented blossoming of minority-group theories was not that Reagan's America and its universities grounded in a humanist tradition were in favor of the symbolic death sentence of heterosexism, the white pioneer figure, or even the Western world, but that those entrusted with the execution did not notice their minority totems whisked away into the service of symbol mongers, the highly paid experts of cultural reappropriation. This was because the latter, as "guru" consultants or cunning ad executives, sprang on the opportunity to turn a profit on the new trends, to harness the minority-affirming social upheaval of the Reagan years and the identity theories stirring up the universities in order to construct new market niches—they loudly embraced the now unavoidable diversity as a sales booster, through music labels like EMI and retail fashion groups like Benetton, dividing their clientele into as many ranges of expression and individual communities as there were subfields in humanities studies in the 1980s, ranging from straight white rappers to lesbian Hispanic opera aficionados. To put it simply, the academics failed to recognize the commercial possibilities of enunciation: to represent marginal cultures, to tell the story of their collective subjectification through enunciation, is also to make them visible, recognizable, and even legitimate, on the powerful broadcast screens of cultural industries. At the start of this decade, universities, which enjoyed some shelter from the Reaganite reaction, brought out a general declaration of war against all forms of oppression and segregation, but by the end of the 1980s, the minority phenomenon gave rise to marketing campaigns in twenty different languages promoting the industry of rebellion. Specialized advertising strategies aimed at black or Hispanic communities, the new gay tourism offered by shrewd travel agents, the commercial hijacking of the bellicose mythologies of rap and reggae, or custom telephone rates offered by the many long-distance operators (which came into being through the breakup of the AT&T corporation during Reagan's first term) catered to each ethnic group and were all products of the 1980s—along with the intellectual productions that flourished in universities, which provided the commercial ventures with their watchwords.

Thus, what minority enunciation lacked, in order to produce more than just multicultural marketing, was an overall notion—if not a critique—of capital itself. Here we find the most lamentable aspect of the *decontextualization* of French theory: the fact that no one recognized the political implications of the various French theories of "postmodern" capitalism, because the latter were read hastily, with an eye for the flash of a few sharp phrases as ideological weapons, secure in the belief that dialectical exteriority had become obsolete (which explains the almost intrauterine themes of participation, mimesis, and fusion with capital), failing to see its combative dimension as a resource for struggle. French theory also made it possible to cut straight into the heart of the American capitalist machine and carve out a political space. Baudrillard's definition of capitalism as "the extermination of difference" can, thus, also be read as foreshadowing the obliterating absorption of difference by cultural industries. When Deleuze and Guattari characterized the workings of capital as "the transcendence of the despotic signifier," it did not prevent the latter from taking on a libidinal or libertarian disguise—such as Madonna's boldness or MTV's burning trends, or even the provocative gestures of gay pride. When Lyotard addressed Parisian intellectuals, calling them "privileged smooth-skin types," and criticizing them for failing to see "our servile intensities," and for not understanding "that one can enjoy swallowing the shit of capital,"[67] his critique was valid not only in reference to the Marxist intellectuals of that period, theorizing about the proletariat, but was also relevant, in another sense, to the American guerrillas of semiotics who came afterwards, textual warriors, capable of analyzing the role of a cultural apparatus in the formation of a marginal subjectivity, but incapable of understanding how the latter imposes the apparatus on the market, as an object of desire that also represents a victory for industry.

In the end, we arrive back where we started—at the structural isolation of the American intellectual domain, with scant bridges of communication between the university and the outside world (the few potential ones being easily regulated by the "watchers" of cultural innovation). Deleuze's and Guattari's notion, formulated in opposition to orthodox Marxism, which stated that capitalism is more revolutionary than communism—because it replaced belief with desire—proved less relevant in the quasi-autonomous world of university cliques. Unless one counts the way in which the notion was depoliticized and dehistoricized across the Atlantic by an American "ideology that doubly excludes history and the dialectic," as linguist Amiel Van Teslaar emphasized in 1980 to explain why North America presented the "best terrain for a reception of structuralism."[68] Deleuze's and Guattari's suggestion, as we will see, may also have been superfluous and thus inaudible in a land characterized by shifts, segments, arrangements, and a thriving libidinal market. The fact remains that French theory was read by the new proponents of minority discourses only after it had been translated into the distinct, rarefied language of the university. The French critique of authority was only peripherally applied to the current political and economic powers, and was instead reduced to a critique of the professor's authority, of the canonical author, or the academic institution. The question of this theory's use was finally received less in the transitive sense, in which certain passages are used in *combat,* than in a strictly academic setting, in the sense of certain discourses' effectiveness in the discourse market: theory employed in this way is less like the revolutionary theorist's toolbox (or that of the committed intellectual) than like isolable arguments, separable from their textual source and perfectly designed for the format of articles in academic journals that will be discussed and restated during some roundtable or conference. For students and young teachers, reference texts must first and foremost be "user-friendly," a typically American term of praise for a computer program or food processor that suggests a gratifying ease of operation and comprehension, and tellingly personifies the object at hand (in this case, the text) in terms of its "friendliness" toward the user.

New Historicism: The Limits of a Compromise

Within this context of an ever-widening gap between strictly academic practice and broader political implications, between the notion of enunciation and its reappropriation in the commercial world, and between the intransitive nature of theory and the transitive nature of identity (and of different communities), only one new movement within the field of literature attempted a reaction: New Historicism. It expressed a rather uncommon effort to look for a third path, one that would not be a compromise between the radicalism of textual politics and the conventional humanism of traditionalist academics. Keen to reemphasize contextual factors in the practice of reading texts and, more generally, to rehistoricize the field of literature, this loosely defined wave of thinking appeared at U. C. Berkeley at the beginning of the 1980s, thanks to the work of Stephen Greenblatt. This father of New Historicism, also an expert on Shakespeare and the Renaissance, taught at Berkeley after defending his doctoral thesis there in 1969—leaving only in 1996 to become head of the English department at Harvard. Greenblatt went against the grain of new literary and identity theories when, in 1982, taking indirect inspiration from Foucault—whose U.S. stronghold was Berkeley—he and his colleague Svetlana Alpers founded the review *Representations,* which was devoted to analyzing the links between aesthetics and ideology, before going on to create the "New Historicism" collection with the University of California Press. Greenblatt surpassed even the contributions made by Paul de Man to the "Yale School" or by Gayatri Spivak to the field of postcolonialism, as he was the sole founder of this movement—its leader, its strategist, and its inexhaustible unifier. He was able to patiently weave together an impressive network, first at Berkeley and then at Harvard, one that included figures such as Catherine Gallagher, Walter Benn Michaels, Michael Rogin, and Eric Sundquist.

New Historicism was born from a combination of rather unorthodox historical materialism and liberal sociology of art and it developed into an arsenal of attack against two different trends within literary theory—one edging toward critical formalism and the other embracing the illusion of the inherent political nature of all discourse. Greenblatt's movement called for a return to what seemed to be simpler subject matter, but which he nonetheless considered to be more enlightening: the social and historical conditions behind the acts of reading and writing.

Under the title "poetics of culture," he refined the old sociocriticism of the 1960s by analyzing the complex procedures of "negotiation" (a key notion in his thinking) between social factors, knowledge already formed, the creator's "freedom," and the reader's expectations. According to whether this "negotiation" concludes in favor of the popular beliefs of an era, an antiestablishment movement, or the author's project of aesthetic subversion within the established order, the work can produce varied responses in the reader—and can assume a different place in the long and muddled process of innovation and repetition that constitutes cultural history. To place each work in perspective individually in this way, taking account of its sources and the ideological context behind its conception makes it impossible to use a hermeneutic approach as the starting point for analysis, and favors instead an approach that shifts between different scopes, periods, and registers, between the text itself and the subtext. Unlike the textualism employed by some Derrida followers, this technique is more focused on describing the connections between different aspects of a text, not in terms of a self-generating text, but from a desire to attain a point of balance and to maximize the interests involved, using words that are not borrowed by coincidence from the economic lexicon, for example: "circulation," "exchange," "trade," and above all, "negotiation." Thus, by substituting one metaphorical field for another, economics replaces the physical imagery used by Derrida and de Man—the "slippages" and other *mises en abyme* of texts—and emphasis is placed on the role of economic factors in cultural history.

Nonetheless, Greenblatt and his followers constantly warn against the dangers of a return to traditional historicism. In contrast to a totalizing and seamless version of history, they put forward "counterhistories that make apparent the slippages, cracks, fault lines, and surprising absences in the monumental structures that dominated a more traditional historicism": it is the sphere of "representations" which is all-important, and it can be reached through the analysis of *parallel* histories, "the history of the human body and the human subject," and of forms of discourse—even the "attraction to the anecdote" and a ceaseless "commitment to particularity" find a defense in this approach.[69] At the core of New Historicism's open methodology is a new, and indirectly Foucauldian, focus on written works as a means of classification, tools for marking the distinction between legitimate and marginal productions, the latter being useful to the extent that what is excluded can reveal, *a contrario,* the prescriptive principles governing a work's prospects for survival. It is for this reason, and this reason alone, that marginal and therefore subversive countercanons (including Jewish, black, Hispanic, and gay literatures) are brought in as subjects of this approach.[70] Indeed, the majority of the movement's works deal with the English Renaissance and its key authors, rather than with the African American novel or beat poetry, and Greenblatt's most influential essays have focused on the works of Shakespeare. Yet Greenblatt introduced a repoliticized reading of Shakespeare, and a more subtle one than those offered by the identity theorists who were suspicious of the white playwright or the homosexual creator of the Sonnets. This politicization can be seen in a reading of *Hamlet* focused exclusively on the theme of purgatory, in order to demonstrate the role of the wars of religion and virulent anti-Catholicism in Shakespearean theater.[71] Another example is the exploration of Shakespeare's ambiguous stance regarding Elizabethan imperialism, and the role of *anxiety* in his vision of politics, as Greenblatt shows in the work that brought him wide recognition: *Shakespearean Negotiations.*[72] This approach can even be noted in a collective work on *The Tempest,* where Greenblatt urges that the political uncertainties experienced by Shakespeare and his era be taken into account in order to keep the literary canon alive, because "the best way to kill our literary inheritance is to turn it into a decorous celebration of the new world order"[73]—referring to today's changing landscape, as well as the one that was emerging in Elizabethan England. Finally, looking beyond Shakespeare and into the heart of colonial issues, Greenblatt's analysis of the New World explorers' narratives of exploration highlights the decisive interaction between astonishment and conquest that was at work in the Western consciousness. In recognition of the release of Greenblatt's only work to be translated into French, *Marvelous Possessions: The Wonder of the New World* (translated as *Ces merveilleuses possessions*), Roger Chartier summarizes Greenblatt's analysis, revealing the way in which, "by and large, for Western man, the marveling gaze can only lead to a desire for possession."[74]

The approach employed by New Historicism was more inductive, less verbose, more insightful regarding political implications, and less reliant on the mirages of semiology—all of which gave it an undeniable heuristic value. However, it was not able to provide a solution for the aporias of the field of literary studies in the United States: first, because the movement itself held a strategic position within the field, and a particularly bellicose one at that, when it came to attacking the failings of its postcolonial and deconstructionist counterparts; second, because New Historicism's almost exclusive focus on the Renaissance and its caution in relation to more contemporary cultural debates have meant that it hesitated to engage in the "culture wars" that divided American universities; finally, and more broadly, because its disciplinary tactics represent a doubtless justified retreat of literary theory and criticism back into their traditional domain (genetic criticism, the history of texts, and their political context), far from the daring advances that deconstruction and minority studies made into unknown territory, in the direction of philosophy, political science, and even the most fashionable pop culture. One could even interpret the enterprise of Greenblatt and his colleagues, and the success with which it met, as a protectionist withdrawal inside the boundaries of the literary world—a world that the conservative counterattack, in response to the voices championing minority identity, suddenly placed under the media spotlight and, soon afterwards, in the firing range of those in power.

THE IDEOLOGICAL BACKLASH

> One reason why we have theories is in order to stabilize our
> signs. In this sense all theories, even revolutionary ones, have
> something conservative about them.
>
> TERRY EAGLETON, *The Significance of Theory*

THE 1980S IS A MOMENT that calls for a dialectical interpretation: it
was a period of identity-oriented withdrawal and theoretical extremism
in response to American nationalism and a new expansion of the free
market. While Ronald Reagan and his minions insisted that "America is
back," the nation's sociocultural fabric decomposed into as many little
blocks as there were identity-based microgroups. This inspired the rapid
"hyphenization" of America, a proliferation of the dash that was to in-
vade American speech—from Afro-American to Asian American and
Native American. While a policy of unchecked privatization and deregulation triggered a double process that increased both the influence of fi-
nance capital in the economy and the prevalence of temporary, freelance
employment in the job market, the most radical ideas were circulating
on campuses: this period witnessed a dismantling of classical canons,
growing support for liberation movements in third-world countries, and
preferential recruitment of minorities. The distance between classrooms
and stock trading rooms was, at that point, greatest, the atmosphere in
the former engendering all manner of exaggerations, from emancipa-
tory lyricism to a duly dramatized apocalypse. The academic world had
never witnessed such a tempest in a teapot: debates over the canon were
seen as a mortal threat to the Western world; the trend of deconstruction
was thought to mark the end of any consensus on "reality"; affirmative

action in the hiring of university professors was viewed as compromising a thousand years of academic excellence; Derrida and Foucault were accused of corrupting the young generation far more perniciously than the decade of drugs and unbridled sex. In fact, neoconservatives had seized the opportunity to turn an academic dispute into a national debate, and launch an ideological war whose long-term consequences were to prove disastrous.

Canon Battles

The first of these battlefields lends itself to the erudite wordplay that American academics adore. The "canon" became so contentious that it regained its original meaning of artillery. Debate over the canon and its bearing on course reading lists soon propelled universities into a new kind of "class struggle." The new radicals were right to question the classics: one need only split the word *masterpiece* to reveal its imperialist underbelly—the masterpiece of genius becomes the "master's piece," his weapon and commodity. According to the reasoning of certain seditious cliques, the canon of critical works was subject to two separate criticisms. On one hand, its very existence exposes the propagandistic role of the educational system, because Dante, Goethe, and Shakespeare were thought to express the same, unique, "universalistic" and "occidental-centric" perspective on the world. On the other hand, if one were to retain the concept nonetheless, the canon would have to be representative of the different constituent elements of American society, and would therefore include a certain number of women authors and ethnic minorities. It is no coincidence that this question of the canon is at the heart of the battle between radical multiculturalists and the conservatives in power. After all, the canonization of works brings us back both to the historical role of cultural legitimization belonging to educational institutions and, in a more proselytizing sense, to the evangelizing mission that this role of consecration implies: for the university, to distinguish "between what merits being transmitted and what does not," as Pierre Bourdieu suggests, amounts to playing the dual role that Max Weber attributes to the church, namely, "to establish what has and what does not have sacred value and make it penetrate into the faith of the laity."[1] Composing the canon is a practice of exclusion, a way to shut out ideas and unfamiliar forms considered as threats to the established order, and it has been that way since at least the second century BC, when the Romans officially, though unsuccessfully, prohibited Greek works and ideas in Roman schools.

According to the great humanists of Anglo-Saxon literary studies, however, this restricted-intake corpus of masterpieces represented the exact requirement for general knowledge. The role of the university was, in Matthew Arnold's words, to teach "the best that has been thought and said in the world," and in 1930, the president of the University of Chicago, Robert Maynard Hutchins, launched the "Great Books of Western Civilization" program, around which the courses of the entire undergraduate phase were organized. There are two important points differentiating this American doctrine of canonical books from its European counterparts, and which help explain why the American version became the target of the new radicals in the early 1980s—although European young people were going through their most antiestablishment period, they had never made an issue out of the canon, and furthermore, in American secondary education, the history books had been revised ten years earlier to denounce slavery and colonialism, without arousing controversy. The first feature of this American canon is that it is "Western" and not national, grouping together authors whose distance in time and space and whose monumental significance in the history of the Western world (e.g., the Bible, Milton, Homer, and Freud) were also to make them prime targets of the new discourse: the West's role is one of world domination, and America is its iron sword. In addition, general courses studied excerpts rather than books, the history of ideas rather than texts, in a country where, furthermore, college-aged students read less than those in France. It was, therefore, as a response to recent findings in literary theory and identity politics, and from a desire to act upon the inherited dispute over the canon, that some professors and administrators introduced alternative canons, or even syllabi eschewing the canon altogether, to some elite universities, stirring up inordinate levels of controversy over their prudent innovations.

The most celebrated dispute sprang up in March 1988, when Stanford University, presumably in response to the demands of a black student union, replaced its "Western Culture" program of study with a series of courses from whose title all references to the West had been removed: "Culture, Ideas, Values." Nevertheless, seven of the eight courses in the program remained practically unchanged, and on the required reading lists for all of them, non-Western works (from Confucius to African stories, and from the Koran to Indian poetry from South America) were simply *added* and not substituted for the Western classics. The parties involved, however, leaped on this development and each turned it into a symbol of what they deplored. Accompanied by the Reverend Jesse Jackson, minority groups marched across campuses to the sound of a slogan that would make newspaper headlines—"Hey, hey, ho, ho, Western culture's got to go!" While the secretary of education under Ronald Reagan lamented a Western loss against the forces of "ignorance and irrationality," the developments in Stanford quickly spread to many other campuses. Minority groups demanded increased diversity in the canon, or even that it be abandoned in view of its "sexism" and "racism," while conservative professors and teachers organized petitions against the anticipated reforms. As a *New York Times* journalist quipped in the title of a book examining the movement's consequences, the "Book Wars" had begun.[2] Although the press coverage gave a somewhat exaggerated image of the events, highlighting the most absurd stories, both sides were indeed guilty of displays of excessive behavior.

In this way, there was suddenly an abundance of countercorpora, but no end in sight to the minority groups' demands. As in the case of the black female students at University of Michigan who, in 1991, boycotted a women's studies course because "only" a third of the books on the syllabus were written by "nonwhite women," the identity-based groups continued to proliferate and reinforce each other in turning criticism of the canon into a compulsory exercise. The most radical new theorists, for their part, had no qualms about recommending the withdrawal of all reading lists from university courses, because the use of any "specific text" necessarily requires a pedagogical constraint implied in the white, and/or male, university system. Reading lists were acceptable only if they drew from the Western canon to expose its political faults—Shakespeare's ethnocentrism, Balzac's misogyny, and Defoe's colonialism. On the conservative side of the dispute, the defense of great works on the grounds of their intrinsic qualities, an overly restrained argument left to traditional humanists, was often abandoned in favor of more lyrical pleas for "the survival of the Western world" against the barbarians, or of the promotion of "cultural elitism" as the unique principle of education.[3] In this tumult of invectives, more levelheaded, sensible opinions tended to be drowned out. Henry Louis Gates Jr. expressed understandable

shock that the project of constructing a canon of black American literature should be "decried as racist, separatist, nationalist or 'essentialist'"
when, according to Gates, whose opinion is shared by many intellectuals
(though they are less often quoted than the extremists on both sides of
the issue), "to reform core curriculums to account for the comparable
eloquence of the African, the Asian and the Middle Eastern traditions,
is to begin to prepare our students for their roles as citizens of a world
culture, educated through a truly human notion of the humanities."[4] Priority, however, was given to the most virulent perspectives, taken up by
the press and fashionable essayists. On the one hand, retaining a Western canon, even for the sake of comparison, was regarded as an insult
to oppressed groups; on the other, opening the canon up to neglected
cultures, to marginalized groups that nevertheless produced important
works—which amounted to a simple correction of their long-overdue
recognition in universities' programs—amounted, for many, to declaring
war on the West. "I am baffled . . . why we cannot be students of Western
culture and of multiculturalism at the same time, why we cannot show
the historical and present-day relations among many cultures,"[5] commented the president of the MLA, Catherine Stimpson, in her opening
speech at the 1990 convention, which, however, attracted much less attention that year than black historian Leonard Jeffries's declarations of
war on "white culture" or the even simpler choice of conservative Allan
Bloom, "Shakespeare or nothing."

The dispute over the canon also had the effect of widening the gap
separating the two avant-garde movements in American literature, both
inspired by French theory—formalist and deconstructionist critics, and
proponents of cultural studies and minority studies. Whereas the latter
were delighted that countercanons were emerging, or that an elitist canon
was being replaced, in some cases, by products of pop culture as new
objects of study, the former, at Yale and elsewhere, continued to invoke
the same "essential" classics. At the height of the uproar, the Derridean
critic Hillis Miller chose without hesitation to adopt a conservative position that his colleagues are still reluctant to defend: "I believe in the
established canon of English and American literature and in the validity
of the concept of privileged texts."[6] It must be noted that in the flurry of
revised canons and "egalitarian" literary corpora, every author associated with French theory had suddenly fallen under suspicion: Derrida,
because his analyses focus chiefly on Plato, Rousseau, and Heidegger;

Julia Kristeva, for her tributes to Mallarmé and Raymond Roussel; and Deleuze, because of his undisguised preference for Melville and Kafka. Still, underneath the ideological misappropriations for which it had been the impetus, this dispute over the literary canon had the more lasting and salutary consequence of touching off a national debate.[7] Above all, it introduced students, and often professors, to underrecognized traditions, and made them consider, from a theoretical point of view, the cultural relativity of canons, as well as their political dimension of classification and exclusion, and even helped them question the anonymous, disembodied form of culture represented by the lists of classics accepted without question by their predecessors. Relativity, after all, is not equal to relativism, as Edward Said concluded, noting with satisfaction that "for the first time in modern history, the whole imposing edifice of humanistic knowledge resting on the classics of European letters . . . represents only a fraction of the real human relationships and interactions now taking place in the world."[8]

PC Misunderstandings

Following the debate over the canon, experts on minority issues turned their attention to a new task: that of codifying the social interactions on campus between different sexes and races, by regulating behavior and introducing a strict euphemistic lexicon. This was the advent of the "politically correct," or PC, a term already used, significantly, by certain politicized rebels in the 1970s, in reference to the excessive emphasis placed by feminists and cultural theorists on the *signs*, rather than the substance, of oppression. For this was a double-sided phenomenon, whose facade was a caricature, a self-parody that concealed its real political implications. At the beginning of the 1980s, the emergence of multiculturalist perspectives in universities and a more decidedly separatist spirit among minority groups in large cities both contributed to exacerbating historical tensions, and not just minority groups against the majority—the right wing of the former having been galvanized by the Republicans' victory—but between communities themselves, on campuses and beyond. Thus, a certain amount of regulation was doubtless appropriate. Its perverse effects, however, would arise from the movement's excesses, when it became impossible for minority students or professors to exist in the university *outside* of their minority affiliation, or for a gay person not to take note of every homophobic insult, or for a black person not to study Africa. Hence, the PC phenomenon gave rise to exaggerations, and in certain cases—well documented by the press, though unrepresentative of the university as a whole—evolved into a fussy policing of vocabulary and gestures, as Richard Goldstein, columnist for the *Village Voice,* summed up so well in his PC self-portrait: "a short, fat, balding man like me can refer to himself only half-jokingly as a differently statured, follically compromised person of weight."[9] The codification of language was not only the most recognizable aspect of the "politically correct" movement, but also its most important arena. The underlying ethical premise is that ordinary language is insidiously performative (as it produces victims) and unconsciously pejorative, and that it inflicts suffering on minorities of every kind.

In fact, beyond the intended gesture of respect, periphrastic terms, such as "people of color" and "Caucasians," thought to be neutral, play their part in a sort of taxonomic violence, a political procedure of classification, by inscribing each group into the lasting form of an official designation. The PC movement, moreover, like the introduction to a mythological tale, represents a story disconnected from culture. Thus, along with the philologists' debates over the proper term for deaf people, arguing over "hearing impaired" and "audibly challenged," a real combat was taking place to establish the systematic use of the capital first letter in "Deaf," in an attempt to indicate that the group's history and culture needed to be recognized, much as other minorities whose names had already been capitalized. This struggle's goals included gaining recognition for sign language as an official language, lobbying for the requirement that presidents of Gallaudet University (for the hard of hearing) must henceforth be deaf people (an objective which was obtained in 1988), and even, more radically, exposing hearing aids, ear trumpets, and implant aids as threats to deaf culture. We have already seen the case of physically handicapped people who, although they acquired their own field of studies in the 2002 MLA convention (disability studies), had since the 1980s become the subject of a positive reformulation of the notion of being handicapped, namely, "differently abled," a term that tends to mask the suffering involved, to hide the negativity, on the pretext of eliminating all connotative value. Not even the term for a university department head escaped from this general evolution aimed at neutrality: "Madame Chairman," considered to be retrograde, was changed to the

"Chairwoman" of classic feminism, and then to "Chairperson," and finally to "Chair," under the influence of postessentialist feminism. This shift of the political battle into a sole arena—that of language and its use—sometimes verged on the grotesque, but paradoxically drew on the American pragmatist tradition for justification. In universities increasingly disconnected from their towns and struggling to communicate with the outside world, it seemed that the only way to achieve real results was by concentrating their efforts on the symbolic realm of the lexicon—even if it meant emptying the language question of all its extralinguistic implications, of all its real referents, or even of its instrumental role in the debate over ideas, a role that was at times entirely lost. There was a proliferation of conferences in which the only questions that arose were, predictably, concerned with the number of women or blacks scheduled for one roundtable or another.

Another remarkable American tradition is the linguistics-informed behaviorism that considers the physical code of gestures and attitudes as representing a *language* in its own right. This perspective, rather than any real outbreak of criminally insulting gestures or sexual harassment, is the reason that the push for PC language led to a push for PC behavior. In order to handle the profusion of complaints, justified or fraudulent, universities and public administrative offices addressed the issue by releasing flyers and recommendations, which would be quoted out of context by journalists, and were to considerably heighten the controversy. These leaflets described and attempted to prevent what they called aesthetic discrimination, or "lookism," latent racial slurs ("ethnoviolence"), or even sexual harassment within a budding relationship—date rape, in which "date" refers to the already highly codified American practice of gradual, formal steps of increasing intimacy, through dinners and drinks, *before* sexual relations, while "rape" in this case indicates that a mere indiscreet question can be viewed as rape. These doctrines showed up in various places, such as in a working group in New York State's Department of Education, in the preliminary report from Tulane University in Louisiana, in the welcome packets for newly registered students at Smith College, or in the celebrated program, AWARE, launched by the new "Office of Race Relations and Minority Affairs" at Harvard. Because, in this highly charged atmosphere, the threat of a complaint could be used as leverage on superiors in a hierarchy, conservatives touted the rare cases of professors forced to resign by assistant lecturers or "hateful" students, sometimes going so far as to entirely fabricate certain high-pro-file scandals. This was the case in the "Thernstrom affair," named after the Harvard historian supposedly accused of "racial prejudice" by his undergraduate students, and endlessly cited by Republicans like Dinesh D'Souza or Roger Kimball, even though no serious investigation has ever been organized to support their allegations of infringement on freedom of speech.[10] Bristling with references to George Orwell's Newspeak and to nascent campus totalitarianism, these kinds of claims constituted a veritable "PC monster" that appeared poised to devour its next victims, for example, white professors who continued to respect the canon, or all the hardworking students who were still unlucky enough to be reading Milton.

Which still leaves the hotly debated issue of affirmative action, aimed at favoring minorities in student admission and faculty recruitment. This social initiative was to take us back to the theme of "Universal Equal Opportunity," a founding myth of the American work ethic. This myth became, at least partially, a reality, following the advances in social rights with Roosevelt's New Deal, and also through the acceptance of civil rights in the 1960s—it brought changes to the labor code as well as higher paychecks. Nevertheless, the existence of a special committee and a national fund dedicated to increasing the number of minorities being hired, and rare precedents in American jurisprudence, did not prevent the Supreme Court from declaring the practice of quotas and "quanti-fied" diversity unconstitutional in its June 1978 decision in the Allan Bakke case (named after the white student denied admission to the University of California's medical school). These quotas were never *formally* put into practice. In the course of the 1980s, however, internal pressure from minority groups and the exertions of some academic deans brought affirmative action to several universities, often at the price of tending to more urgent problems, such as a rise in tuition costs and a drop in federal aid, and the need to examine each application's content, instead of simply weighing it against the quotas. The case of Loïc Wacquant is a striking example: this young French researcher, after writing a paper on the sociological role of boxing in Chicago ghettos under the supervision of black sociologist William Julius Wilson (he began boxing himself in the name of firsthand experience), was recruited in 1992 by UC Berkeley, at which point campus activists, lobbying for affirmative action, protested his hiring and forced university administrators to reopen the hiring process. Wacquant was hired the following year, but would not forget his bitter discovery, namely, that for new militants, skin color matters more than the nature of research or teaching methods.

More important, conservatives took to reeling off the names of a few "scandalous" cases, both in universities and within the Republican Party, to justify their call for an urgent "remoralization" of America. Contrary to the multicultural model, which had already reshuffled the sociocultural puzzle of the United States before the arrival of the linguistic police in the 1980s, conservatives championed the universalist, integrationist theories of a dominant, hierarchical culture to which one should submit. In their eyes, the excesses of the 1960s and the resulting culture wars twenty years later had shown up the limitations of the old American "melting pot," which now needed a radical reform, using set principles, to salvage and pull together what remained. Hence, not only was the multicultural model soon in a state of crisis in the United States, but the notion of remoralization was presented as the only alternative, whether the issue at hand was defending the imperiled West or, on the contrary, monitoring language and codifying gestures. Another focus, further removed from the conflict over PC issues, was the imposition of new norms of civility—covering topics such as ecology, diet, hygiene, and manners—in order to create "responsible citizens." What with conservative political strategies and the unrest of a divided nation, not to mention the crisis of public primary and secondary education, whose funds dropped during this period, as did the average standard of living—everything conspired to turn a strictly academic debate, linked to minority groups' discourse and radical theories, into one of national importance. We can thus reasonably conclude, as does Eric Fassin in his strong thesis, that beneath the storm of new identity-affirming rhetoric, the "politically correct" movement was, above all, "a construction of the controversy" then raging.[11]

A National Debate

The media backlash against the PC trend was the result of skillful maneuvering by conservatives who, through opinion columns and hints dropped to reporters, grabbed the newspapers' attention. The negative reaction was also tied to the ideological evolution of the media industry, which was undergoing a metamorphosis, having recently seen a capitalist consolidation of the moderate press and decline of the political commentary press, especially in the left wing. The backlash was also, however, a result of sociological factors. The old rivalry between academics and journalists, intensified in America by the social isolation of the former and the career ambitions of the latter, was stirred up again by cases that allowed journalists to suddenly reclaim an intellectual domain (even if their attitude toward the PC movement was sharply critical) from which they had been scornfully excluded by diploma-wearing theory experts. Playing up the amusing effect of enumeration, the newspapers depicted the partisans of PC as one big melee of extremist jargon-slingers, comprising multiculturalists, gay activists, new historicists, Marxist critics, esoteric Derridean theorists, neofeminists, and young proto-Black Panthers. The journalists' tone was often even more caustic than at the height of the cold war. An editorial in the *Chicago Tribune* on January 7, 1991, accused professors of nothing short of "crimes against humanity." The working-class daily *New York Post* followed suit in calling on the public to "rid us of literature's PC police." Already in winter 1990, the *New York Times* had blown the whistle on "the growing hegemony of the politically correct," and *Newsweek*, in its December 24 issue, described this "totalitarian philosophy" and its "thought police" as a form of "leftist McCarthyism," even though, forty years earlier, the very real purges of universities under McCarthy had not earned a single paragraph in this "politically neutral" weekly. As it turned out, the media comparisons to Nazism or the McCarthy purges would be numerous. In *New York* magazine, rather than reference documented proof of his accusations, John Taylor preferred to make an unsubtle reference to the wartime past, using headlines in Gothic lettering and photos of Nazi executions accompanying the article.[12] Certain other stories, without using such explicit analogies and instead employing images of viruses or carnivorous plants (the *New York Times* described deconstruction as "a tropical French colony, a Paris with snakes, [that] sprang up from the turf"), were nonetheless reminiscent of an older kind of rhetoric—the anti-Semitic picture of the Jew, or the cold-war image of communists who, behind their respectable facades, were threatening to strangle innocent citizens in their tentacles. Not all U.S. newspapers spun such dubious metaphors, but the unanimity of the general-interest press, where source cross-checking and even simple groundwork became rare, was nonetheless shocking, and examples can be seen in the *New York Times,* the *Washington Post, Time,* the more satirical *Esquire,* the *Wall Street Journal,* the leftist weekly the *Nation,* and even in publications as diverse as fashion magazines and the financial monthly *Forbes*—the only notable exception being the *Village Voice.*

Only the letters to the editor gave voice to divergent opinions or more moderate perspectives, such as that held by the *New York Times* reader who wrote, in a letter in June 1991, responding to the "infatuated French ideologists" who were vilified in the newspaper, and stating that "people should not feel threatened by French theory, even if it is always tempting to try to eliminate what we don't understand: it isn't a case of either/or, at least it shouldn't be." We should note that the celebrated *Times* had just devoted the front page of its literary supplement to essayist Camille Paglia, who had, using a stream of vitriol worthy of some bygone political tract, ridiculed the French theorists and American experts in the new field of minority-group discourses: she described the former as having "the souls of accountants" and as "eros-killers" that should be "driven from our shores," while the latter, because they had sold themselves abroad, were presented as "pampered American academics down on their knees kissing French egos," and as "lily-livered, trash-talking foreign junk bond dealers"—this article stands out for its exceptional virulence, and also because it revealed to readers that foreign sources were responsible for the rabble fussing over identity—their recent expansion thus appeared more due to French "tyrants" than U.S. academics.[13] In the same year, without taking up these francophobic diatribes, the French press occasionally took part in the new American controversy, to condemn the "new chief censors"[14] of the PC trend in universities, and a new ideological drift taking place on campuses that could mark "the twilight age of Europe."[15] Tzvetan Todorov, who had already won over the conservative camp, even added his voice to the American debate by comparing the multiculturalist critique of "objectivity" to the executioner O'Brien's discourse in Orwell's *1984.*[16] Still, it took a case that brought attention more directly back to anti-Semitism and the Second World War, instead of just the issue of a multicultural "Newspeak," in order for a university dispute, however heated, to stir up such strong feeling even in the most widely circulating American newspapers. It was the scandal over Paul de Man that really captured the national media.

In 1986, the *New York Times* revealed the collaborationist past of the famous Derridean critic, who had written a pro-German, and sometimes anti-Semitic, column in the Belgian daily *Le Soir* until 1942. De Man's article on March 4, 1941, "Les Juifs dans la littérature contemporaine" [Jews in contemporary literature], contained a remark that most disturbed his colleagues: that deporting the European Jews and their "few personalities of mediocre value" [quelques personnalités de médiocre valeur] in the arts world would not have, "for the literary life of the West, any regrettable consequences" [pas, pour la vie littéraire occidentale, de conséquences déplorables].[17] Arriving during the storm of controversy about Martin Heidegger (an essential thinker for deconstructionist theory) and his compromises with the Nazi regime, this exposé touched off a fury of essays and editorials far out of proportion to de Man's past misdeeds, however damning they may have been. The oft-vilified "relativism" of French theory, whose detractors maintained that it led to a blurring between true and false, might draw its historical antecedents from this case. When questioned by the press, professors such as Jeffrey Mehlman decried deconstruction as "a vast amnesty project for the politics of collaboration during World War II" or even, in the words of one professor who preferred to remain anonymous, "the thousand-year Reich that lasted 12 years."[18] In any case, many journalists leaped at the chance to draw a comparison with partisans of the PC movement: they considered the new militant groups in universities only a short step away from Nazi anti-Semitism. These accusations were clearly out of place, because de Man's work cannot be reduced to the reprehensible moments of his youth, and because all his like-minded intellectual peers were Jewish, including Harold Bloom, naturally, but also the Sephardic Derrida (who rather clumsily came to de Man's defense, suggesting that we "deconstruct" the guiding principles of de Man's theory) and the exiled German Jew Geoffrey Hartman, who was cofounder at Yale of the Judaic studies program. Nevertheless, this reverse Dreyfus Affair provided some commentators with biographical elements that they used to justify an apparently factual and historical criticism of the dangers of the new theoretical relativism.

It was not, however, these biographical accusations, or the media campaigns, that turned a campus disagreement into a national debate, but rather the unexpected success of the decade's three major conservative political tracts, which were personal attacks on the new American relativists and their French teachers. Michael Bérubé expresses understandable astonishment, and humor, at what was taking place: "But should you tell the American public that its children are being forcibly indoctrinated by communist fascist feminist deconstructionist multiculturalists, *then* you've got a real bestseller on your hands—and an argument even nonspecialists can follow."[19] The first of these studies was Allan Bloom's *The Closing of the American Mind,* which remained on the best-seller list for more than a year. This work, which championed classical humanities and a unified United States, built on the tried-and-true arguments of Alain Finkielkraut, which appeared that same year in *The Defeat of the Mind* (on "omniculture," the homogenizing effects of TV, and mind-numbing rock music), and gave an apocalyptic vision of American universities overrun by barbarians, where the only set readings would be from black lesbian authors and rock star biographies.[20] This nostalgia-fueled diatribe, however, was less strategic than the period's other two conservative best sellers. The second one was *Illiberal Education,* by the brilliant Dinesh D'Souza, a young, former adviser to Reagan, born in India and educated at Dartmouth. He offered a subtler warning to the United States against the danger posed by the new "Visigoths in tweed," militant multiculturalists "in power" on campus. The author evokes consequences such as the balkanization of the community, loss of freedom of speech, disintegration of merit-based scholarly excellence, and the pernicious effects of programs that could hurt those they were meant to "save."[21] The final essential set of arguments marshaled in support of this perspective was more clearly recognizable in Roger Kimball's moral satire, *Tenured Radicals.* Kimball first presents readers with a specifically French provenance for "totalitarian egalitarianism," starting with the Terror of Robespierre and continuing with the "politicization" of all discourse by Foucault and Derrida, in whose views "All cultural and intellectual life is 'really' a coefficient of power relations."[22] He next points out the American sources of the current situation, because "the radical ethos of the Sixties has been all too successful, achieving indirectly in the classroom, faculty meeting and by administrative decree what they were unable to accomplish on the barricades," thus drawing a parallel between the two generations without much reflection on their significant sociological differences.[23] From time to time, Kimball brings in the psychological argument that many intellectuals throughout history, from Rousseau to Fredric Jameson, have fallen into "utopian Romanticism" because "they hate their own heritage."[24] The book presents us with a constant and intentional jumbling of multiculturalists, textual theorists, and Marxist critics (despite the latter's attacks on French theory), dismissing all the enemies of "democracy" one after another, and even going so far as to compare Frantz Fanon's "incitement to murder" with Göring's Nazism.[25] The conclusion, which bears similarities to Allan Bloom's book, is unequivocal: "The choice facing us today is not between a 'repressive' Western culture and a multicultural paradise, but between culture and barbarism."[26]

While voices supporting the new radicals, or at least denouncing the conservatives' disingenuous tactics, gradually fell silent,[27] the nearly unanimous consolidation of the opposing side reached its peak in May 1991, when the "education president" (as George Bush described himself during the 1988 election) joined in the debate during a speech at University of Michigan. The president lambasted the PC trend "that has ignited controversy across the land" for "[replacing] old prejudices with new ones" and "setting citizens against one another on the basis of their class or race."[28] There were, of course, a few more moderate perspectives to be heard, which criticized the excessive aspects of the PC proponents' evolution without rejecting the movement wholesale. E. D. Hirsch, professor at University of Virginia and author of a book defending the "cultural literacy" of students, stated that "American literate culture" was able to cope with the innovations being so hotly debated because it "has itself assimilated many of the materials that those who favor multiculturalism wish to include."[29] Meanwhile, Christopher Lasch, historian of counterculture, ridiculed the "pseudoradicalism" of offending universities,[30] and critic Russell Jacoby attributed the dialogue of the deaf, which had violently split the United States, to the disappearance over the past twenty years of "leftist intellectuals" as public figures.[31] The celebrated historian Arthur Schlesinger brought his views to the debate as well, looking beyond the flux of intellectual trends to examine what these unprecedented tensions could reveal about the social "disuniting" of the United States.[32] Nevertheless, along with these famous, moderate intellectuals urging for level-headed discussion, conservatives were, instead, trying to further inflame the dispute by heaping the fuel of current scandals on top of it—the "indecency" of photographer Robert Mapplethorpe's male nudes, exhibited using state funding, the "elitism" and "immorality," in the eyes of the populist right wing, of the few public media channels (NPR and PBS), or the "leftist dictatorships" still in power in Cuba or Nicaragua. The debate's expansion onto the national level produced a side effect in universities, exacerbating latent tensions.

Between 1986 and 1988, several universities, including the University of Pennsylvania and the University of Chicago, were struck by racial violence. Financial aid offices were ransacked for having treated non-white students preferentially. Cases of homophobic, and sometimes even anti-Semitic, violence became common. The Southern Confederate flag reappeared in the windows of certain dormitories. In some cases, the media's vivid coverage had the effect of a self-fulfilling prophecy on certain moderate groups, suddenly spurring them to claim some identity they had never before advertised, or even to start behaving in the ways the newspapers claimed they did. At the same time, the conservative camp's attacks had succeeded in galvanizing the most right-wing elements in the student body. Their efforts were, however, only part of a larger ideological campaign, which was tied to the emergence of a new movement on the intellectual and political scene in the United States—the neoconservatives.

The Neoconservative Crusade

In 1984, William Bennett, director of the National Endowment for the Humanities (NEH), published an alarmist report on university literary studies: *To Reclaim a Legacy* declares a cultural state of emergency and calls for a return to "a common culture rooted in civilization's lasting vision, its highest shared ideals and aspirations, and its heritage."[33] A swarm of conservative periodicals took up the matter—including *Commentary, National Interest,* and Hilton Kramer's more recent *New Criterion*—which covered in great detail both the seamy side of the humanities and the annual MLA conference. As the MLA adopted an increasingly radical position, the conservatives offered their support to anyone who broke with its ranks. Midge Decter's Committee for the Free World, an influential group dedicated to the support of a Reaganist foreign policy, was thus to transform an organization of classical humanists—the National Association of Scholars, formed in 1975—into a veritable weapon in the war on the "academic left." With more than five thousand members and chapters in thirty U.S. states, the NAS attempted to seduce away MLA supporters and distributed leaflets on campus "for the sake of civilization"—which eventually led to the creation of an opposition group, Teachers for Democratic Culture, supporting the growth of "radical ideas" in the university.

This campus war, waged with roaring salvos of slogans from rival organizations, may also be explained by feelings of resentment from un-derdog universities, marginalized by the new movements, taken in by the intellectual skill and oratorical talent of the ever more high-profile "radi-cals." The less visible academics had no choice but to graft their own weakness into a moral argument, as is the case with the "conservative populists" so well discussed by Bourdieu: "This internal anti-intellec-tualism is often produced by dominated intellectuals . . . , whose ethical dispositions and lifestyle . . . lead them to feel ill at ease and displaced, as it were, notably in their confrontation with the bourgeois elegance and liberties of born intellectuals."[34] Their righteous criticism met with a mixture of erudite irony and disdain from their most brilliant opponents, such as Stanley Fish, Joan Scott, Fredric Jameson, and Cornel West, which only strengthened their feelings of a "horror . . . which has the vi-olence of disappointed love."[35] This explains why these "downtrodden" academics, drawing on a long-standing, instinctive American distaste for splitting hairs (demonstrated by the pejorative terms for intellectuals like "highbrow" and "egghead"), reappropriated the old utilitarian and puritan anti-intellectual arguments—that is, when they weren't actually signing pacts with the devil, as suggested in a *New York Times* report which revealed that certain highly lucrative debates had been arranged in advance by both sides, like the one between Stanley Fish and Dinesh D'Souza in 1990–91.[36]

Nevertheless, beyond the intellectual inferiority complexes and ami-cable arrangements, there was a veritable ideological crusade at work, with extensive resources and ambitious goals: recover an academic world overrun by "radicals," and promote the development of a con-servative "counter-intelligentsia." They were also, however, employing the tried-and-true strategy of a smokescreen, to provide an ideological justification for the already-scheduled federal budget cuts to state uni-versities. The fact that this was a deliberate tactical move is borne out by the official political positions of the movement's main players. The director of *Commentary* magazine, Norman Podhoretz—whose editori-als urged extreme vigilance in dealing with Gorbachev's alleged opening of the USSR's boundaries—was closely connected to the state depart-ment, which included three of his oldest college friends and his own son-in-law. The magazine's three most virulent writers, when it came to attacking "university leftists," also succeeded one another as direc-tors of the NEH named by the White House: Carol Iannone, William

Bennett, and Lynne Cheney, wife of Secretary of Defense and future Vice President Dick Cheney. When Lynne Cheney, who, like Bennett before her, was seen as a possible secretary of education, was given the strategic position of chairwoman of the National Endowment for the Humanities, the word in Washington was that she was actually "Secretary of Domestic Defense," in charge of defending the timeless values and interests of America.[37] As for young Dinesh D'Souza, appointed adviser to President Reagan in 1981, he had also authored a fawning biography of televangelist Jerry Falwell; similarly, Podhoretz had written in defense of Pat Robertson, founder of the Christian Coalition, when Robertson was accused of anti-Semitism. More important, the heralds of the new moral crusade had the backing of a tightly linked network of ultraconservative foundations, one that bred some important initiatives, and provided de facto funding for the ideological counterattack. The main companies were the American Enterprise Institute, the Rand Corporation, the highly regarded Heritage, Olin, Scaife, and Coors foundations, and even, indirectly, the British Thatcherists' Adam Smith Institute. Using a complex financial distribution system, these organizations gave their support to conservative student groups like Young Conservatives of Texas and Accuracy in Academia, who did their utmost to bar a black student union, and to groups who took their cue from Ralph Nader, champion of "alternative" consumerism; they also kept a watchful eye on left-leaning professors' courses and on the grades their members received from radical theorists. Even neutral organizations like the FIPSE, created to fight illiteracy, were soon receiving subsidies that drew them into the conservative fold.

As Wlad Godzich summarizes, "an administration committed to the redrawing of boundaries between elites and the popular masses (the notorious 'silent majority') trained its guns on the theoretical pursuits harbored by the elite institutions."[38] The objective, however, was not only to eliminate the new wave of "radicalism in writing"; they also had to offer a positive ideological agenda, to convey a clear message about the American system of values and its place in the world, a task that fell to those organizing the campaigns promoting the work of the very same network of organizations. The textbook case was Francis Fukuyama's book *The End of History*,[39] which had the backing of the Rand Corporation and the state department, the two organizations with which Fukuyama was affiliated. Fukuyama's comparison of commercial liberalism's final victory in a postcommunist world to a fulfillment of Hegel's historical dialectic provided the conservative ideological agenda with a claim to the hottest topic in international current events, as well as a philosophical justification. Once again, the real issues went deeper than the general outcry against radical trends in certain universities. This battle was, in a larger sense, an opportunity to establish the political legitimacy and intellectual strength of the neoconservatives, who had arrived on the scene in the late 1970s and were determined to have their ideas accepted by the Republican majority; they even hoped that the party would modify its policy in relation to the rest of the world. Their crucial influence on George W. Bush's administration and post-9/11 American foreign policy proves that they attained their goals.

Most of the neoconservative movement's pioneers were renegades from the postwar noncommunist left, and specifically from the group known as the New York Intellectuals, associated with the *Partisan Review*. A prime example is Norman Podhoretz, whose provocative article from 1963 criticizing the conservative aspects of the civil rights struggle heralded a crucial turning point, or Irving Kristol, whose son, William Kristol, is now one of the most high-profile ideologues of the Republican Party. Some of them had even been (practically orthodox) Marxists, including James Burnham, Sidney Hook, and Eugene Genovese, historian of the working classes, whose articles in the 1980s argued for academic "counterterrorism" and even for introducing "a four-semester sequence in Christian theology or at least in common decency and elementary good sense"[40] in junior high school. As the loyal historian of neoconservatism Mark Gerson claims, this "intellectual movement" has a direct and identifiable ancestor: "The ancestor is liberal anti-Communism."[41] And to illustrate his point, he goes on to claim Hannah Arendt, George Orwell, and Arthur Koestler for the neoconservative camp. The movement was bred of the cultural elitism that characterizes the East Coast powerful bourgeoisie, as well as moral traditionalism and feelings of ambivalence toward the welfare state, which the neoconservatives never attacked as such, but whose prerogatives they wanted to limit at all costs. The neoconservatives' fundamental anticommunism meant that they experienced three successive slaps in the face regarding their core values: the libertarian student movement in the 1960s, the demagogic reaction of the 1970s, with its "Great Society" project, and the emergence of a new class of radicals on campus in the

1980s. Their liberal heritage was, however, what gave the neoconservatives a tactical edge. Instead of a conservative platform characterized
by inertia, they promoted one oriented toward change, taking initiative,
and moving forward.

The second essential influence on the neoconservative movement was
political philosopher Leo Strauss (1899–1973), who came to the United
States from Germany and founded the Committee for Social Thought at
University of Chicago, where his students included Allan Bloom, Irving
Kristol, and future Supreme Court Justice Clarence Thomas. American
editorialists nicknamed Strauss "godfather of the conservative revolution" during the Reagan years. The "Contract with America" that helped
Newt Gingrich and the Republican Party win the legislative elections in
1994 was directly modeled on Strauss's moral and political rationalism.
In opposition to liberalism, which it was thought would bring an end to
capitalism by encouraging the inherent elements of relativism and nihilism, Strauss aimed to wrest the concept of natural law away from the
menace of historical relativism and demonstrate the "primary reality"
of distinctions between good and evil, fact and value. According to his
disciples, this was the only possible response to the dissident mayhem of
the 1960s, and the multiculturalism of the 1980s. According to the thesis
of Canadian political analyst Shadia Drury, Leo Strauss "radicalizes" the
political substantialism of thinkers like Carl Schmitt, adding to the latter's fundamental antimodernism (a political theory whose followers, in
the Romantic tradition, were found in the left wing as well as the right)
the voluntarism of a "monocultural, nationalistic machine" requiring
constant reinforcement in order to stem the postmodern dilution of hierarchies and values.[42]

Situated at the juncture between leftist anticommunism and Straussian political naturalism, the neoconservative trend of the 1980s ultimately set a threefold reactionary creed against the alleged "nihilism" of
French theory. The first point was the existence of a greater Good, which
must be protected by the social elite, but which is not necessarily based
on any theological-political principle; unlike the Christian fundamentalists of the American Right, the Straussian neoconservative perspective
has no difficulty accepting that God is dead, provided that the notion of
natural justice, viewed as "essence," is retained. The second point was
related to the "realism" of a necessary social hierarchy: by the logic of
social Darwinism, the only possible choices are anarchy or plutocracy;

the wealthy class must be responsible for counterbalancing the abstract power of the state and politicians. This mistrust of public authorities goes back to the new movement's libertarian roots. The final point, the neoconservatives' trademark and a strategic consequence of the other two principles, was the idea that maintaining stability and order was a task that could no longer be left to the market's self-regulation or the virtues of the bourgeois oligarchy, but must henceforth be actively imposed: to defend the greater Good required, in the neoconservatives' view, a systematic and preventative implementation of military or police intervention, in contrast with the American traditions of individual freedom and international isolationism. In internal affairs, the neoconservatives developed the famous zero tolerance or "broken windows" police policy, which was first adopted in 1993 by the Republican mayor of New York, Rudolph Giuliani, and then by the police forces of the major powers in Europe, after having each come to observe the American methods in person; the policy dates back to 1982 when neoconservatives James Wilson and George Kelling first articulated the idea in the *Atlantic*.[43] In foreign policy, the new interventionist doctrine of the "Axis of Evil," developed in the aftermath of the September 11 attacks in 2001 to justify the occupations of Afghanistan and Iraq that followed shortly after, was a direct reincarnation of Wilson's and Kelling's ideological precedent: using military force to impose the superior values of commercial democracy constituted a method of protecting U.S. national security, but it was also, as Paul Wolfowitz—assistant secretary of defense and the highest-ranking "Straussian" (and former student of Allan Bloom) in the Bush administration, before leaving to run the World Bank—continually reminded the public, a way to combat the insidious spread of prescriptive relativism.

The neoconservatives' consolidation of ideological power in the 1980s was thus grounded in a dual legacy. In a philosophical and historical sense, the need to unreservedly readopt the Enlightenment's rationalist, civilizing project often won over the same people who had briefly been taken with the Enlightenment's theoretical criticism, and then disturbed by its moral implications. On an institutional level, as Pierre Manent observes, the marginalization (if not outright exclusion) of young, violently anti-PC neoconservatives in radicalized universities in the 1980s may have led them into politics, after forcing them down a one-way track toward think tanks and partisan publications.[44]

Toward a Postpolitical Left?

None of this, however, would have been possible were it not for the Left abandoning the real political arena, which left it wide open for the neoconservatives. For nearly two decades, the "cultural" Left of university radicals and the traditional American political Left had been passing the buck back and forth: the former accused the latter of not adapting its class-oriented, unionist agenda in response to the arguments of the conservative revolution, and in return, the latter criticized the former for having deserted the social arena in favor of a strictly cultural conflict, fought with symbols and rhetoric—or for "Marching on the English Department While the Right Took the White House," as Todd Gitlin aptly puts it.[45] The academics were, moreover, accused of having dissipated their power in isolated communities, without succeeding in building a common platform. Although the dispute is difficult to resolve, one point remains clear: the lack of political *unity* among the various minority groups inspired by French theory allowed the conservatives to take full possession of the public sphere, and to successfully assert their argument against "balkanization." The only joint mobilization of different university radicals during the long Reagan–Thatcher decade came in response to apartheid—the issue gave rise to group cooperation when constructing displays of protest with simulated shantytowns, asking administrators to stop accepting funds from companies that trade with South Africa, and organizing protests at seventy different universities on April 24, 1985.

Apart from this protest, however, no unifying agenda ever took shape. On the contrary, the divergences between postcolonialists, neofeminists, queer activists, and various ethnic minority groups only became sharper. Each community had split off according to the direction of the latest intellectual trend and newest theory, without having come to a real decision between identity-based withdrawal and a more communicative use of these minority stances, or between a defensive discourse that simply aimed to *protect* a culture and a more proselytizing one that emphasized the model qualities of a given group on the front lines of the social struggle. The invisible baseline of habitus and class reflexes that cut across all groups also played its role, for example, in estranging upper-middle-class African Americans, eager for cultural recognition and integration, from activists of more modest birth who called for organized black political resistance, or lawyers litigating for homosexuals' rights to marry and adopt children, whose relations with more radical proponents of poly-sexuality and gay nonconformism remained somewhat strained. These groups' shared political discontent alone did not equate to unity: the fact that black activists and radical feminists both mistrusted left-wing unions' capacity to protect their interests was not enough to bring them together politically. Outside the confines of universities, the sheer radi-calism of the individual movements did not give birth to a community-bridging network. Although the revolutionary, separatist Black Panther movement was emulated by Chicanos, whom Cesar Chavez organized into agricultural work teams, or American Indians, of whom one radi-cal faction even set up a symbolic capture of Alcatraz Island, or by mili-tants advocating for the third world, who organized as many "liberation fronts" as there were countries to be freed, there was never any sugges-tion of cooperative activism, on campus or in the streets. In the explosion of different causes and discourses, the common ferment of social struggle was lost, something that was indispensable if a leftist stronghold was to be created: Todd Gitlin tersely concludes, "If there is no people, but only peoples, there is no Left,"[46] accusing the radicals of having sacrificed the idea of a common good in the name of cultural pluralism. Gitlin's remark, however, explains only part of the problem: the other missing entity (inextricably linked to the first) that was dissolved by the decade of radical *theorizing* was none other than the social adversary itself, power conceived as a homogeneous reality against which political activity may be organized. The culprits, in this case, were Foucault's microphysics of power, the libidinal, wandering drift of capital as conceived by Lyotard or Deleuze and Guattari, and even the recurring notion of dissemina-tion in Derrida's work. "By denying the existence of a directing center, it [the 'conservative doctrine' of 'pluralism'] sought to rob radical politics of its object," writes left-leaning essayist Michael Walzer, claiming that Foucault "desensitizes his readers to the importance of politics," and re-placing the real target of "authoritarian politics" with "'micro-fascism' of everyday life," and for his (Foucault's) own constant hesitation be-tween the "reformist politics" of the microphysician (because, if power is dispersed, its subversion would be as well) and the "utopianism" of the anarchist. "Should we overthrow the panoptic regime?" he asks in conclusion, as a parting shot, using language typical of the American political Left.[47]

The crucial reason for the university radicals' political ineffectualness was, nonetheless, in every case, the pivotal role of emphatic identity affirmation—and of its reactionary constituent elements, as each identity produced, to draw on the notions of Deleuze and Guattari, its own Oedipal stronghold, a constant reassertion of its territory. The cause to be championed, singular, complete, and irreducible, offers the comfort of constant recognition and gratitude, and mutual complicity, and contrasts with the alienation of the social market, foundation of the real-life world. This perspective favored a strictly culturalist reading of social struggles and international conflicts, casting it as a confrontation between essences, ahistorical realities among which cultural differences were seen as insurmountable and incommensurable—a notion that sometimes, paradoxically, came to pave the way for right-wing arguments from writers like Samuel Huntington about the "clash of civilizations," as editor Lindsay Waters suggests.[48] The virulent anti-Americanism of these discourses, which was severely criticized by the traditional Left (who believed that calling for a *real* America, with its ideals of dissidence and social justice, could create the unity that was missing), was not based on political criticism, but on a rigid, identity-based polarization, with its own Oedipal tendencies: a white, or male majority, in one-to-one opposition with a minority. The result was that the anonymous majority flocked to the right wing, which was alone in representing a positive, communal America, in contrast to the nation envisioned by the new radical discourses, which was *by definition* racist and sexist. This tendency was compounded by the institutional inertia of universities: sheltered from theoretical disputes and bibliographical sparring, a minority condition was perpetuated through narrative, isolated in discourse, and dramatized by the very rules of the debate. Initially, however, this condition had arrived on the political scene as a historical *situation,* when its real battles and organizational difficulties continually brought the focus back to its transitory social construction, and to its connection with class injustice—in the sense that a black millionaire is not so much black as a millionaire, and very few company directors are feminist activists. The academic world then extracted this minority question from its social and historical context, as intellectuals who had not experienced the direct confrontations of the 1960s reformulated the issue, which was transferred into an exclusively symbolic arena, after becoming the subject of leftist criticism. Forms of expression substituted conflict, and culture (or rather, minority culture*s*) became a game of surrogate politics, the only political option remaining when the unity of a homogeneous social subject was lost. Gitlin asserts that "the new academic Left tended to mistake strong language for steady, consequential political engagement,"[49] offering an explanation for these paper radicals and this postpolitical Left, in which the social struggle counts less than the mere acquisition of recognition for every group represented, and where political battles count less than the *signs* of affiliation.

Nevertheless, this critique of identity-based campus politics, and of the dilution of the factors at stake in the conflict engendered by French theory, had its own limitations. We might mention three of them: its transfer of responsibility, its predefinition of the political arena, and its ecumenism. First and foremost, the traditional Left, whether Marxist or Democrat, made up of liberals such as Michael Walzer, the rationalistic Noam Chomsky (who flatly accused French "irrationalism" of rendering political action impossible), the journal *Dissent,* and the *Nation* magazine, all wield a double discourse: they assign all responsibility for cultural development to academics, even while recognizing the latter's social isolation and institutional separation. If we are to lay out, in this way, a division between fiction and reality, between a structurally inconsequential academic field and a "real" social sector, it is absurd to criticize those vocationally assigned to the former for not taking charge of the latter. One cannot *at the same time* complain that caged tigers are harmless and that they attack the wrong prey: as Paul de Man observed, "If a cat is called a tiger it can easily be dismissed as a paper tiger; the question remains however why one was so scared of the cat in the first place."[50] There is no question that debates over "phallogocentrism" in the sciences or the capitalization of certain words did not constitute a *political* response to the new conservative creed. The fact is, however, that such a response could only come from the heart of a public space of which the university represents only the border. This public space, however, already staked out by Reagan-following ideologists, was abandoned by its usual players: not one major publisher released a single "political" book, investigative or analytic, about the electoral campaigns of 1988 or 1992, as publisher André Schiffrin notes.[51] The field was deserted, above all, by the political Left, which was increasingly disconnected from its natural constituency after the sixties, and thus unable to propose a solid alternative to the conservative Left, which gained power without difficulty in

1992, with the election of Clinton and Gore. The Left's impotence brings us back to the second limitation of Gitlin's indictment, that is, its definition of the political sphere in terms of a traditionally large scale, that of the major institutions, campaign appearances, and media scheduling, which never see fit to recognize the political implications of sexual identity, atypical domestic situations, postcolonial consciousness, or identity-based groups—the Left was made up of unionist and geopolitical discourses, and it appeared to have spent the previous thirty years waiting for the "personal is political" era, which was never considered worthy of a frontal attack, to come to an end. The third point, finally, is the Left's nostalgia for broad Unitarianism, a socialist version of the old American faith in the virtues of consensus, the strength of gregariousness, if not going so far as to embrace the famous tyranny of the majority. Calling for a reassembly in the interest of greater efficiency was also a way for the Left to try to save face when the crucial and unresolvable problem was precisely that of unity. The success of minority platforms was, after all, a sign that Americanness was in crisis, without content, formally society-based and obligatorily consumer-oriented, and no longer capable of rounding up its flock.

We might even go a step farther, and ask whether such virulent criticism of academic radicalism did not actually play into the hands of the conservatives. When the American Civil Liberties Union (ACLU) and the last remaining public intellectuals of the social Left censured the excessive behavior of the politically correct movement at every opportunity, in the name of preserving freedom of speech, were they perhaps attacking the wrong adversary? Did they commit a tactical error in denouncing identity-based groups that, although they may have often wandered into rhetorical dead ends, nonetheless represented the Left's only potential political allies against the ideology of "civilization" and the free market? Shouldn't they have, instead, seized the opportunity presented by the debate to reformulate its terms, and better acquaint themselves with the participants, instead of ridiculing the very issues involved? This is the position of compromise called "dialectical pluralism," championed, albeit for its pedagogical effectiveness rather than its promotion of political change, by critic Gerald Graff: by trying to preserve the rival positions that divide feminism or postcolonialism, or bring multiculturalists into conflict with unitarian conservatives, without privileging any one group or rejecting the discussion as fruitless, and provided that one bring students in as active participants, it is possible to reinculcate the latter (whom their elders accused of betrayal and disillusionment) with the virtues of discussing ideas, the techniques of successful argument, and the political implications of minority status. To place the dispute and its pedagogical opportunities at the heart of the school system would, according to Graff, restore its role of *political education*.[52] If this defense of the debate itself is somewhat rhetorical, because it assumes a position of exteriority not necessarily feasible in reality, it at least allows us to avoid dismissing wholesale (as left-wing activists critical of French theory have too often done) the theoretical contributions of the brightest figures of this academic hotbed—the intellectual stars of the American scene, who remain practically unknown in France.

ACADEMIC STARS

I have very little taste for the pretentious professions of faith
made by those striving for a place alongside the "founding
fathers"; but I take great delight in those works in which
theory, because it is the air one breathes, is everywhere and
nowhere, in a passing note, in a commentary on an old text, in
the very structure of the interpretive discourse.

PIERRE BOURDIEU, *The Rules of Art*

THEY MAKE for unlikely stars. In a country where the intellectual elite
is sequestered in the academic world, which makes the public space of
general forums and political action hard for them to reach, a few names
nonetheless tower over the intellectual field—of which they are the titled champions, not unlike the Williams sisters in the tennis world, and
Bill Gates and Steve Jobs in the computer industry. They are heroes of
a specific arena, with no ambitions to present an all-encompassing discourse or to be entrusted with a mission from Spirit itself, unlike French
intellectuals who consider their noble mission to answer *all* general inquiries. Nothing really qualifies their American counterparts as experts
on general matters, not even a pedagogical calling: one Jacob Schur-
man, president of Cornell University, remarked, even in 1906, that his
most famous professors, who were rarely known outside their field, had
"chosen their profession not so much from the love of teaching as from
the desire to continue the study of their specialty."[1] Since then, all the
elements of a cutthroat battle for ultimate victory have been added to a
ruthlessly competitive university sector: the youngest faculty members
are pressured into placing themselves in a good position on the (very
strenuous) tenure track; there is a sense of obligation to dominate the

pyramid of publications in a system where the professional imperative is to be published (the notorious "publish-or-perish" dynamic), which makes for a great many pen pushers in proportion to the very few who are truly among the chosen; and once one arrives in the circle of the happy few—those who are cited and revered—a ferocious pace must be maintained in order to remain the most prized product on the market in the bidding wars between elite universities anxious to recruit the most prominent professors. In order to succeed, the only cardinal rule is to be constantly intellectually innovative, showing an originality undefinable according to endogenous criteria (because *new* thought is not always easily recognizable as such), and whose sole yardstick measures one's capacity to walk over the competition, to force a successful colleague's thesis into obsolescence, to alter the previous status of a discipline by showing up, while minimizing risk to oneself, its least successful and least well-used ideas—to become, in a word, one of the "consecrated heretics" that Bourdieu studied in the French *grandes écoles*.[2] Maintaining this capacity for innovation also requires strategic disciplinary positioning, situating oneself at some junction between identity studies, literary theory, and its various offshoots, yet without pledging loyalty to any or finding oneself pinned down to defending the specific interests of one branch; one must always be ready to criticize the simplistic approach of any given discourse or the lack of realism of a certain option—and to create, as we have seen, academic boundaries around which one can constantly create a sense of theoretical distance, and question one's entire method.

It is then, when such a path has been sketched out and one or two suitably controversial works have shaken the most recently embraced certitudes in the field—or one of its subfields—and only then, that the academic concerned achieves the status of university diva. And if an American academic's works do not, as those of their French counterparts do, appear in the columns of important newspapers or as features on mainstream television talk shows, their status nonetheless affords them, in American logic, entry into the hall of fame: then, the press and the society gossip publications, such as the *New York Times Magazine* rather than the cover of *People,* eagerly scrutinize the finery, symbols, and idiosyncrasies that make up the demeanor of the personality in question. The ironic consequence of this phenomenon is that scores of Americans have heard of Stanley Fish's car collection, Cornel West's salary,

Stephen Greenblatt's circle of friends, Donna Haraway's provocative wardrobe, and queer theorist Eve Sedgwick's late conversion to Buddhism before—and, alas, all too often instead of—knowing their academic works. Another difference between the United States and France is the respective roles of reading, and the way it is used to define the public profile of an intellectual figure. Unlike the supposedly sui generis thoughts of French literary intellectuals, who make commentaries on the world rather than focusing on texts they have read, the American theoretical hero owes a good portion of his prestige to the unique way in which he draws on great authors, forming a real trademark, calling upon them in order to associate himself with their works, citing them along the way to back up his own argument. "One reads when one has a market in which . . . discourses on these readings can be situated," as Bourdieu stated, suggesting the idea that a given quotation would have a certain *profitability*.[3] And so it is that the names of Foucault, Derrida, and Lyotard—for in the United States it is this group of "great writers" that, for twenty-five years, has been viewed as embodying French theory, and whose aura of prestige radiates onto those who know how to draw from their work—are invoked as material for discussion and often criticism, and are the figures whom the major works in the intellectual field will choose to make use of. Thus, there is a dynamic, dialogic, and allographic connection, in which an author's work is evoked while its difference is still kept in view, and which, beyond the truncated uses and self-interested simplifications of theory, enriches the interpretation applied to French thinkers. Here, we enter into the realm of "transdiscursivity," as Michel Foucault attempted to define it: just as Marx and Engels were for European thought throughout the twentieth century, these French thinkers became "founders of discursivity" in the United States, elaborating, unbeknownst to them, the rules for the "formation of other texts," coming to represent not so much revered figures as a particular process of "the treatment to which the texts are subjected"; yet this status is achieved only thanks to the "effective and necessary task of transforming the discursive practice itself" that, in return, the most industrious of their readers perform on them, in order to "group together a certain number of texts" and to establish "a relationship among the texts," and so to enter, themselves, into this transdiscursive arena—one in which strategic positions and empirical existences disappear, as though by magic, in favor of the pure mobility of the name.[4] This phenomenon, without which neither French theory nor its great American followers would have gained their status, can be seen operating, briefly, in the works of six important American intellectuals—though it must be emphasized that this is not a complete presentation: the focus is on the French thinkers they have used, and the choice of the members of such a sextet is necessarily somewhat arbitrary.

Judith Butler and the Enigma of Performance

Professor of rhetoric and comparative literature at the University of California, Berkeley, Judith Butler, born in 1955, is the author of demanding theoretical works, written in a sometimes difficult writing style that, much to her displeasure, certain more traditional critics have made fun of at times.[5] Her work is a meeting point for psychoanalysis, feminism, and political theories of sexuality. Beginning with the historical observation that "the subject as a self-identical entity is no more,"[6] Butler's project consists in exploring, within certain classic literary texts and through a free-ranging discussion of philosophers, the tensions that now inhabit the *empty space* left by the subject, namely, those of power, desire, and the multiple ploys of identification. Her first work, *Subjects of Desire*, examines the gradual substitution of *desire* for the old notion of the *subject* in what she calls "French post-Hegelianism," that is, nothing less than the successive works of Kojève, Hyppolite, and Sartre, still faced with their dialectical heritage, Derrida and his "Hegelian irony," Foucault and his postdialectical reinterpretation of the master–slave relationship, Lacan and the notion of desire as an "immanent experience of the Absolute," and finally, the "post-Hegelian erotics" of Deleuze, as inspired by Spinoza.[7] It is in the overall picture given in her subsequent works, more directly influenced by Foucault, that we find Butler's analysis of the fragile subject of enunciation that she views as playing the role of a "gender matrix," this "I" that is always both *subject* (in the sense of submission) *to* gender and subjectivity *through* the experience of gender, subservient to a sexual code at the same time as being produced by the same process of submission—a dialectical and newly affirming variation on the old theme of voluntary servitude.

Judith Butler's major work, a reference for all queer and neofeminist topics, remains the ambitious *Gender Trouble*, which articulates two pivotal moments in her work, one *linguistic* and the other *political: linguistic* because, through new light shed on the concepts of performativity and speech acts, the book helps explain the continuous "production" of sexual gender through "compulsory quotations" and the iterative workings of femininity and masculinity (the period of sexual formation itself governed by two simple performative acts, the "it's a girl/it's a boy" at birth and the "I do" of marriage); and *political* because power, even more diffuse than it appears in Foucault's work, is nonetheless glimpsed at work behind this performative construction of gender identity, a power that is adamant in firmly expressing sexual subjectification and "compulsory heterosexuality," but also gender production and the economic productivity of procreation. Butler often makes attempts, without entirely following through, to question the validity of this general perspective in order to consider other "coercive subjectifications," such as ethnic identity or class. Continuing with the topic of gender, we find in Butler's book that the notion of identity, or fixed subjectivity, disappears in favor of a constant displacement, of a succession of "performed" *acts*. The notion of identity is thus doubly "subverted," first by the imposition of codes of power, which penetrate and split identity, and second by "play," which can pierce through this strict notion of sexuality and gender norms—a play that allows some form of resistance to norms, allowing, for example, the emblematic figure of the drag queen to destabilize these two elements through parody and theatrically expose their artificial dimension.[8] In the depoliticized university arena of the 1990s, all of these angles were used to hone, or simply *deconstruct,* postidentity minority theories of an identity that was simply tactical, disposable, and plural. *The Pyschic Life of Power,* Butler's first work to be translated into French (2002),[9] also reveals the limitations of her project: the double, convergent ambition of politicizing certain Lacanian theses and examining the psychic implications of Foucauldian politics creates, between these two remote poles—the psyche and the polis, the process of subjectification and the modes of power's circulation—a zone of indistinction, neglected and incompletely covered, that the author clearly struggles to bring together theoretically. Unless she reveals the imbalance in her work in order to favor the first pole, an evanescent subjectivity conceived outside of all political and social *terrain*. However, over the course of her work—a constant dialogue with the major figures of French theory, which is at times very enlightening—Butler seems to drift from her own theoretical project, and is instead forced to approach it indirectly, obliquely, and primarily through the intermediate step of "poststructuralist" theses.

Although Butler's preface to the second edition of *Gender Trouble* makes for one of the most stimulating texts on French theory in its new applications in the United States, her work sometimes seems to fall back on the issue of a political recirculation of texts, or a justification in terms of the freedom to draw on key authors: accordingly, she repeatedly stresses that "the unanticipated reappropriations of a given work in areas for which it was never consciously intended are some of the most useful."[10] Analysis of each French author provides her with the opportunity to make a critical shift in perspective and execute a productive theoretical operation. One could say that Butler *delocalizes* the most deep-seated characteristics in these works in order to bring them face-to-face with American academic debates examining the subjectivity of gender and the possibilities of sexual *politics*. Borrowing from Foucault's approach, she suggests applying a genealogical method to the issue of *sexual difference,* which his books do not address, but she remains faithful to his view that, in the emergence of subjectivity, one should never separate *subjection* and *subjectification,* submission and resistance. In a similar vein, Butler analyzes the implications for gender norms in Lacan's principal hypothesis according to which *identification* always precedes the formation of the ego: to understand how a subject is formed by *citing* sexual norms, there is nothing so useful as Lacan's definition of the subject as "that which is subject to the signifier." She is also able to align Althusser's famous "doctrine of interpellation," put forward in "Ideology and State Ideological Apparatuses,"[11] with this same theme of *subjection:* the linguistic production of a subject takes place through the simple act of hailing her, and making her confirm the interpellation ("here I am"), which is also a "demand to align oneself with the law"; does this reveal a "slave morality" or an unshakable "desire to be"?[12] is the question that Butler asks, in an additional variation on the structural, grammatical, and political ambivalence of the *subject,* remaining both submissive and self-perpetuating in its submission. It is a recurrent theme and a rich theoretical project that, despite everything, Butler struggles to transform into a political program beyond the earnest hopes that she expresses here and there, such as her wish to create "a coalition of sexual minorities that will transcend the simple categories of identity."[13]

Gayatri Spivak and the Work of Intotality

Gayatri Chakravorty Spivak, whose work we have already encountered on several occasions, arrived in the United States from Calcutta in 1961.

After a thesis under Paul de Man's supervision, a book published in 1974 on the Irish poet Yeats, which already hinted at the postcolonial approach, and her 1976 translation/introduction to *De la grammatologie* by Derrida—of whom she remains one of the major interpreters, even starting, in 1992 at Columbia, a Sunday reading group on Derrida in America—she taught comparative literature at the University of Iowa, the University of Texas at Austin, Emory University, the University of Pittsburgh, and finally, starting in 1991, at Columbia University. It is difficult to summarize her body of work, positioned at a crossroads between Marxism, feminism, and deconstruction, a work whose common theme—obviously enough, given her background—remains the Western world's *Other*, under all its possible forms, but whose themes can vary from Spivak's *A Critique of Postcolonial Reason: Toward a History of the Vanishing Present* in 1999 to her more recent analysis of the emergence and decline of comparative literature as a "metadiscipline" (*Death of a Discipline*, 2003); it is difficult to summarize her work except perhaps through what I might call *intotality*, a systematic political, strategic, and even autobiographical mistrust of "totalitarian" systems of culture and thought, monism, and the system, which she expresses with a level of mastery rare in American thinkers of her generation. There are at least three leitmotifs in Spivak's work that bear out her vigilant critique of totalizing methods—her *tactical* relationship to concepts, her call for *common ground* between different movements' struggles, and her critique of the university *intellectual*.

This woman, who in the past has mentioned the "*necessary* error of identity" in order to cut short disputes (which were illusory, in her view) between politics of identity and *post*identity, has always shown, in keeping with Marxist praxis, a certain impatience for the great conceptual tabula rasa, whether it represents doing away with rationalism, forgetting History, or erasing the Subject: under the pretext of bringing change, her work itself betrays a fascination for that which she is denouncing in the first place. Spivak considers that the famous *critique of the subject* must not hinder the tactical creation of a subject engaged in struggle, or the consideration of any given dissident group as a historical subject. We may ask, however, whether the critique falls into the excessive *processism* that Spivak criticizes in certain strains of French theory, as it would indicate a move that would reduce power and conflict to shifts and mechanisms to such a point that French theory would run the risk of justifying the self-perpetuation of the established order, or would at least obviate the purpose of any localized strategy of opposition. This is one of the reasons for Spivak's early support for the Subaltern Studies group.[14] Another recurrent theme of Spivak's eclectic body of work is the search for common ground between different struggles—a tactical alliance but also a theoretical interpenetration between feminist, postcolonial, and social struggles, made possible because each forms a different layer of a political *subject* that is always/already multiple. "How does the post-colonial feminist negotiate with the metropolitan feminist?"[15] she asks in her typical manner, because the cause being championed remains un-defined, bringing us back to the North–South dichotomy that has ap-parently played a dangerous role in conflating a subconscious form of universalism found in discourses arguing for "liberation." There is al-ways a blind spot to consider in the fight, a subaltern to the subaltern, emphasizes Spivak, whether it be the ritually circumcised Sudanese stu-dent who fails to speak out among campus feminists or the woman (the "gendered subaltern") found at the core of (post)colonial movements of resistance. In fact, critiques of capitalism through both the sexual subal-tern condition and postcoloniality are, according to Spivak, inseparable; as proof, she draws our attention to women at the forefront of the social movement in India. Finally, and most importantly, this Spivakian attack on the totalizing intellectual method that reifies a subject and robs it of its capacity for enunciation constantly denounces the means of "cultural production" of the Other.

Thus, Spivak criticizes Julia Kristeva, in the latter's work *Des Chinoises*,[16] for a "certain principled 'anti-feminism'" and arguments "symptomatic of a colonialist benevolence," made up of "generaliza-tions" and developments on "the essentially feminine and the essen-tially masculine," as well as for an approach to Chinese *otherness* that remains "obsessively self-centered"—putting herself in the position of "nameless women of the Third World."[17] As Barbara Johnson pointed out, Spivak also warns of the dangers of "the current interest in margins [which] risks either domesticating or romanticizing the heterogeneity of the wholly other."[18] She even reveals, in a more delicate subject area, an "epistemic violence" and "the persistent constitution of the Other as the Self's shadow" in the official historiography of colonial India, which she considered as rather too hasty in thanking the British Empire for having repealed the rite of sacrificing widows under Hindu law.[19] Her critique of intellectual imperialism remains a tireless obsession, one in which traces of the Marxist tendency to self-criticize and the American professor's sentiment of methodological guilt can be detected. Spivak incessantly questions the relationship between "micropolitics," be it that of on-campus activists or the more rhetorical one that she (rather too hastily) accuses Deleuze and Guattari of limiting their arguments to, and the larger-scale apparatuses of postcolonial capitalism—or else, to use her own words, she ceaselessly ponders the fact that "Western intellectual production is, in many ways, complicit with Western international economic interests,"[20] which will always benefit from such an exotic production of the Other, and from the occasional tributes in praise of difference and cultural resistance. Spivak also attributes a specific role to the intellectual, linked to his or her capacity to understand discourses and enunciation, and the ability to decode the power struggles at play, woven into texts and interlinked with linguistic material.

Textuality can prove useful; indeed, it is one of Spivak's major contributions, born of her readings of Derrida as much as from her involvement in Indian political "debates," and is even one of the potential keys to improving the oft-maligned relationship between literary theory and political action. The crucial issue for Spivak, as Colin MacCabe states in his foreword to *In Other Worlds,* is to replace the "text" in textuality, which became coextensive with literature and served as a "fig-leaf behind which one could hide all difficult questions of education and class," with a *political* notion of the "text" as a "concept-metaphor," thanks to which it is possible "to deconstruct both individual and society in order to grasp their complex of contradictory determinations."[21] In other words, the text would function as a political elucidation of the world, in contrast to the textual*ism* resulting from academic reduction of the text. The entirety of Spivak's work encourages such political use of theoretical tools of textuality—this is apparent in the seminar she gave on the concept of indoctrination at the University of Texas at the height of the culture wars, urging students to analyze its manifestations in American universities, and not only in more obvious Soviet or Islamic forms, in her studies of the possible modalities of a "discontinued" and "heterogeneous" discourse on the woman as the only figure capable of appreciating the political nature of this discourse, and even in her criticism of cultural studies' tendency toward Anglo-American "cultural monolinguism." It may be difficult to construct a homogeneous theoretical program out of a work that is, above all, a *discursive critique of discourse,* but rarely have the discursive tools of analysis come so close to capturing certain "off-campus" political realities. And rarely in American academia has a critique of *rational totality* (as a current independent of Western thought, and free of its cultural inspection of the Other) appeared so free of naïveté, simplism, and culturalism, but displaying such high expectations and advanced political strategies. Despite giving such a critique on the limitations of universities, however, the argument, which is itself complex and multifaceted, was not, in fact, accessible beyond the boundaries of the university. But that is another story.

Stanley Fish and the Logic of the Institution

It is precisely with Stanley Fish (born in 1939) that we leave the ethical and political leanings of academia to examine the more cynical mechanisms of its star system, and the academic personality who is perhaps closest—in terms of privileges and provocations—to the idea of academic *glory*. As with the chosen few in Proust who hold invitations to the Duchess of Guermantes's dinner parties and find themselves the center of gossip, it is often what is said about Stanley Fish, even the most trivial things, that carries more weight than what he himself says, which is nonetheless far more theoretical. His personality has been sketched out with a few envious and divertingly superficial strokes, like an ode to a woman in Baroque poetry, or a military shirt front covered in medals—but these are simply the results of a consciously cultivated fame. Stanley Fish is the inspiration behind Morris Zapp, the eccentric and extremely ambitious professor popularized by Fish's friend, British novelist David Lodge, best known for *Small World*.[22] Like Zapp, Fish was one of the first ever literature professors to receive a six-figure annual salary, taking on various positions at Duke, such as chair of the English department, professor of law, assistant dean, and executive director of the University Press. He is a sports-car enthusiast, as is clear enough from the legendary article he wrote, "The Unbearable Ugliness of Volvos." Not content with merely appearing on television shows to defend deconstruction or the PC phenomenon, Fish is the only literary academic to have been (long before Jacques Derrida) the subject of a documentary film (1985). The four universities that were his stomping grounds have all benefited, one after the other, from his growing prestige: Berkeley until 1976, Johns Hopkins until 1985, Duke, of course, until 1999, and currently, the University of Illinois at Chicago.

Trained in seventeenth-century literature, Stanley Fish is one of the most brilliant minds and one of the most unconstrained voices of his generation. If Paul de Man was a textual materialist, Stanley Fish is a *pragmatist* when it comes to reading, he is a logician of interpretation, looking to do away with the *ordinary* rules for reading texts—as analytic philosophers did with *ordinary* language. This was revealed as early as 1972 with the controversial subject of his first book, a study on Milton's *Paradise Lost* that has since become a classic: according to Fish, the premise for this long and often obscure poem is none other than the *fall* of the reader as a symbol for man's own fall—for the "indirection" of Milton's text attempts to disorient the reader, to try to make him lose his hermeneutic "faith," and even fosters appreciation for slippages in meaning, because they offer the literary equivalent of sin.[23] This parable, which presented reading as a paradise lost, brought instant recognition to Fish. It was at this time that he made his first journeys to Paris, where he discovered not only the newest literary theories—by following a seminar at Vincennes, reading Derrida, and meeting Barthes and Todorov—but also synthesized intellectual work and political action, something unknown in the United States. Fish was considered politically conservative, but he was nonetheless innovative, offering the first American classes in narratology, poetics of reading, and even "computational stylistics"—which brought together all the theoretical innovations of the time, from British neo-Freudianism to Californian ethnomethodology. The appearance of "Is There a Text in This Class?"—first as an article in 1987 and then as an essay in 1992—was a milestone for Stanley Fish, because it not only honed his unique didactics (taking a question from a student and approaching it from a purposely uncertain perspective) but also allowed him to introduce the decisive concept of "interpretative communities." These encompass written works, their readers, and the historic institutions that link these two poles, and together they produce the text and its reading in the same movement, before writing and interpretation have even been separated the one from the other. These communities allocate "understood practices and assumptions of the institution," the whole "repertoire for organizing the world and its events," in line with the subtle idea of a "horizon of expectation" as proposed by reception theorist Hans Robert Jauss.[24] Going beyond such an epistemology of reading, Fish redefines the *institution,* broadening and dematerializing its scope, and revealing it as a precisely codified ideological basis for all interpretative activity. The institution is, in this view, the space in which production of meaning takes place; it determines "mis-*pre*-reading"—a misreading that occurs *before* the act of reading itself—and lays the backdrop on which the text itself is created, which is, accordingly, nothing more than "what happens when we read."[25]

The pragmatic manner in which Fish considered a text as being an agreement about norms, and viewed reading as an entanglement of interpretative communities, soon led him closer to embracing a purely logical interpretation—one that certain people deemed dangerously relativist—of political constitutions and judicial texts, a development that was amplified after he was given a position at Duke's law school. This evolution reached its peak in 1994 with the controversy sparked by Fish's written work on the impossibility of free speech, amusingly titled *There's No Such Thing as Free Speech: And It's a Good Thing, Too:*[26] the conditions of possibility for holding a normative discourse (which are predefined by the institution and strictly limiting) and thus reaching an understanding over the issues at stake mean, according to Fish, that there is inevitably a mix of exclusion and selection, a logical succession of *auto-censure,* rendering a political opinion or moral standard incommunicable. The First Amendment thus becomes illusory, because it is in some way the *discourse* itself that prevents the enunciator from speaking. It was ultimately out of a strategic desire for provocation, and as a consequence of his analysis of the "institution"—and not from adhesion to minority movements—that Fish turned into the most well known promoter of the PC movement, of minority-group theorists, and of all those accused of relativism: "Our convictions about truth and factuality have not been imposed on us by the world, or imprinted in our brains, but are derived from the practices of ideologically motivated communities," he observed in 1985.[27]

This was evidence, perhaps, of the pleasure that this ironist takes in thwarting his commentators; this privileged theorist has always been ambivalent toward university radicals. On the one hand, he has always been swift to denounce conservative displays of "racism" or "homophobia," and he masterminded a program of *radicalization* unlike any other at Duke University, during which time, at the beginning of the 1990s, he recruited famous names such as the eccentric Derridean Frank Lentricchia, Marxist critic Fredric Jameson, queer theorist Eve Sedgwick, and black intellectual Henry Louis Gates Jr.—efforts that attracted five times more graduate students to Duke than there had been in 1985 and gave his more staid colleagues the impression that a "cataclysm" had taken place.[28] On the other hand, Fish constantly taunts the ineffectualness and the redundance of radical platforms that are unnecessary to civil society, because they have already been absorbed and integrated into militant outsider groups, and have no need to be excessively theorized. Fish has been inspired by French theory and its lucid approach to politics, rather than becoming (as so many of his contemporaries have) merely a mimetic commentator on it; he knows better than anyone what the limits of the institution are: "The familiar desire of the academic, and especially of the humanist academic, to be something other than what he or she is."[29] For his part, Fish has avoided this feeling so common in academics, this failure to coincide with the reality of oneself, by aiming for honor and controversy rather than *political effects* of one's theory.

Edward Said and the Politics of Criticism

Born in 1935 in Jerusalem to English-speaking Palestinian parents, and educated in Cairo, then in the United States, Edward Said, who taught at Columbia for many years, is somewhat better known in France than the other American literary stars—but almost exclusively because of his sustained support of the Palestinian struggle, his role as a former member of the Palestinian National Council, and his long-standing opposition to Yasir Arafat.[30] However, even beyond postcolonial studies and the impact of French theory, Said's work remains one of the most complete reflections in American academia on the relationship between culture and politics, power and identity. After having written a thesis at Harvard, essays on the function of the "authority" of narration, and a first book on Joseph Conrad in 1966, Said found himself thrust to the forefront of the academic world with the publication in 1978 of his masterful work *Orientalism* (translated into French in 1980),[31] which has remained one of the most important essays in English and American literary studies of the second half of the twentieth century.

Starting from Chateaubriand's comment that the West had a mission of "teaching . . . liberty"[32] to the East, and examining the orientalizing forms of Romanticism that appeared at the end of the century, Said works to demonstrate that, throughout the nineteenth century, in literary and political texts written in both French and English, the West invented a cultural stereotype for the Middle East—an intellectual, colonial construction of its identity as *other*. The book, as with Said's successive works, draws on Foucault's thinking on discursive formations (here, using the Orient as a form of discourse) and the regime of knowledge-power (with the Orient as the knowledge born out of colonial force), and Antonio Gramsci's thoughts on hegemony and the diffusion of *representations* and not truths. In *Orientalism*, Said uses Flaubert's short stories and Richard Burton's adventure tales to define the colonial intellectual not simply as an outsider, freely using cultural material, but as someone whose subservience to power often forces him to join "the consent of the subalterns" with official representations—a criticism of the political world's mistakes as much as an acknowledgment of the superior role played by free intellectuals, which he goes on to elaborate in *Representations of the Intellectual*.[33] However, there are also broader implications to this project, which helped to situate Said's work at the boundary between the academic world and effective political resistance, as well as to explain its influence on all political innovations in the American literary field in the last thirty years: Said managed to tap into the historical unconscious that is present behind works, to a dimension of literature that is not merely contextually or periphically, but *intrinsically* political—which, Said insists, means undergoing a process of rehistoricization and resocialization, and going against the formalist temptations presented by New Criticism and deconstruction. This is one of the aims of Said's immense 1993 work *Culture and Imperialism*. Analyzing the Western notion of empire, from the time of the historically unprecedented Franco-British territorial hold of the nineteenth century, until its lingering desires, which were still detectable in the 1991 Gulf War, Said highlights the insidious and profoundly dialectical forms of imperial domination that can be seen in several masterworks written during Europe's colonial era, including *Heart of Darkness* by Joseph Conrad, *Mansfield Park* by Jane Austen, *The Stranger* by Camus, and even Verdi's *Aida* (Said was also a musical critic for the *Nation*). His objective was to demonstrate both the influence of this new imperial imagination—whether we consider it guilty or triumphant—on all of Western culture, and the reactionary emergence of an "oppositional tension," and of local readings "reappropriating" Western texts and preparing for a "cultural decolonization." This is the nature of sovereignty invented by this "Age of Empire,"[34] and the means of resistance that it provoked in return, spreading beyond economic pillage and political tyranny to aesthetic forms, imaginary representations, and even the "structure of sentiments" felt by both master and subject.[35] This is why, Said concludes (citing Frantz Fanon), the Hegelian dialectic of the master and the slave is necessarily a Western creation, because it posits the simple logical possibility of being able to reverse the two positions.[36]

Said's dialogue with French theory has remained crucial, although less as an explicit engagement than as a constant subtext. For example, he takes issue with Deleuze and Guattari's famous "Treatise on Nomadology,"[37] judging it "strangely evocative" and "mysteriously suggestive" of relation to the "political map of the contemporary world": while Said points out the gulf that divides the "optimistic mobility" and "intellectual liveliness" of such nomadic practices from the "horrors endured in our century's migrations and mutilated lives," he nevertheless uses the Deleuze–Guattari perspective to create the crucial idea that the notions of *resistance* and *liberation,* as parts of an "intellectual mission," have now "shifted from the settled, established, and domesticated dynamics of culture to its unhoused, decentered, and exilic energies"—concepts now embodied by the migrants of globalization, and "whose consciousness is that of the intellectual and artist in exile, the political figure between domains, between forms, between homes, and between languages."[38] Yet this example is rare compared to the sustained relationship, both admiring and critical, that Said maintains with Michel Foucault's work. It is in the name of a tactical politics, and its underlying ethical basis—which he believes the academic ought to take on as his or her own—that Said criticizes the author of *The Order of Things* for his concept of *power,* whose polysemy and quasi-magical functioning would, he says, "obliterate the role of classes . . . and of rebellion" in history;[39] he also finds Foucault's conception of history "ultimately textual, or rather textualized; its mode is one for which Borges would have an affinity,"[40] and, in opposition to the "death of the author," he calls for a recognition of the responsibility of individual authors in the construction of discursive formations such as Orientalism.[41]

Championing a *secular* critical function, one that draws a connection between texts and the outside world, without lapsing into simplification or jargon—or even developing a *third path* between ideological discourse and academic specialization—Said has often pointed to the quibbling of American theorists inspired by French theory as being responsible for certain pernicious political repercussions: because a discourse of power is "monologic" (even more so when it takes place during a conservative revolution), the increasingly technical nature of the intellectual debate—as necessary as it may have been on occasion—may have played into Reagan's hands, according to Said, leaving these complex problems to "experts" and "theoreticians" alone.[42] Choosing a similar tack to that of his colleague Gayatri Spivak, Said is wary of general "methods" and explanatory "systems," which can become "sovereign" and cause their practitioners to "lose touch with the resistance and the heterogeneity of civil society," which could have been more helpful to them in producing a localized criticism, one that is "always situated."[43] Said has never ceased making a plea for such a *situated* critical activity, one that, as Said says (quoting Raymond Williams), "belongs in that potential space of 'alternative acts and alternative intentions which are not yet articulated as a social institution or even as a project'";[44] yet the road is long and holds few rewards, it is as fragile and ephemeral as those moments of spontaneity and social indecision into which the criticism may merge. It is a path that is always strewn with stumbling blocks—whether these be mirages of academic abstraction or, on the contrary, impasses over nationalism and fixed identity, concepts against which, for thirty years (long before the advent of multiculturalism in universities), Said has pitted the intrinsic hybridity of any culture and the historic interdependence of traditions and mythologies. Edward Said has a lucid dream—that literary *criticism,* in the arena of politics and world literature, might be realigned with the method of *critique* defined by Marx and Gramsci.

Richard Rorty and the Ethics of Conversation

Often deemed the greatest living American philosopher, Richard Rorty is the author of boundary-crossing works that are more open to literary theory, and to literature in general, than his colleagues in philosophy. For twenty-five years he has devoted himself to a critique of both rationalism and the objectivism of American analytic philosophy—and these two features of his work have involved him in a continuous dialogue, through articles, books, and even face-to-face, with the great figures of French theory. This is true despite the fact that he has differentiated himself from his literary counterparts by the particular ethos of the philosopher-logician that he has long maintained: more discreet than ostentatious, more argumentative than assertive, and more liberal than radical, his approach is quite unlike that of certain theorists given to avant-garde posturing. Born in 1931 to a family and community of left-leaning anti-communists, Rorty was Rudolph Carnap's student at the University of Chicago before going on to teach philosophy first at Princeton until 1982, then at the University of Virginia until 1998, and currently in Stanford's comparative literature department. After a rather conventional career following the works of American logicians and ordinary theorists of language, Rorty's 1979 work *Philosophy and the Mirror of Nature* brought him immediate recognition—and controversy that still resonates today within the American philosophical institution.

"Philosophy's central concern is to be a general theory of representation" is the immediate stance taken by Rorty.[45] By showing that knowledge is merely a *representation,* an attempt to reflect the outside world in the "mirror" of the mind as precisely as possible, his book manages, through this revelation, to undermine the objective foundations of knowledge—and to sound the knell of the philosophical "foundationalism" that dated back at least as far as Descartes. Rorty demonstrates that knowledge is not based on truth, but is rather condemned to the imperfections of representation and to the social and normative conditions that determine its modalities of existence. Behind the idea that social interests and reciprocal behavior concretely condition knowledge, far more than the elaboration of an improbable fixed referent of knowledge, Rorty defends what he calls an "epistemological *behaviorism"*—claiming to take his inspiration from the general line of thought laid down by John Dewey, father of pragmatism, and a more immediate influence from the logician Donald Davidson. In the central section of his book, Rorty draws attention to the clear distinction between that which is given and that which is created, the objective and the subjective, between appearances and reality, and later, as a consequence, between "facts" and values: according to Rorty, these dichotomies, on which all philosophical examinations have been based, from the Cartesian to those of analytic philosophy, are no longer absolute but always *relative* to the context and the specific objectives of understanding (or representation), or, in a wider sense, relative to the notion elaborated by the philosopher of "conversation"—that is, the play in the position of the speakers, the search for understanding between a speaker and his listener, an ethics based on specific cases and fortuitous opportunities. Accused by his peers of taking a relativist stance and playing into the hands of French theory, Rorty is quick to reply that he considers himself to be more of a "conversational-ist." This became the term of choice.

As early as his first work, Rorty draws the conclusion that such "an-tifoundationalism" has existed in the United States for a century: it is known as pragmatism, and its political tradition is one of American lib-eralism. And thus Rorty speaks of a "neopragmatism" in his following works, one equivalent to "postphilosophy"; he unites elements of the American tradition with the French critique of representation in a con-flation that did away with all invalid elements, eliminating the leftovers of objectivism that continued to blind Dewey's old pragmatism, along with the nihilistic and antisocial temptations that Rorty disapproved of in French theory. In his eyes, this "ironic" pragmatism is a far cry from nihilism and relativism; rather, it embraces the only viable social and moral outlook: a gradual extension of social agreement and forms of solidarity, in a progressive and reformist version of American liberalism, a social volunteerism that he sometimes justifies by referring to Darwin-ian naturalism. This is the train of thought that Rorty upholds in his second work, *Contingency, Irony and Solidarity*. In particular, the book examines Heidegger, opposing his ontological foundations, looks at Der-rida, following him only partly in the direction of the autonomy of lan-guage, applauds George Orwell for having reinforced the pluralist and humanist credo of the Founding Fathers, and finally analyzes Vladimir Nabokov—because literature, like French theory, according to Rorty, reveals the possible "antifoundationalist" and "antirepresentational" uses of language.[46] Rorty's two latest works, *Achieving Our Country* and *Philosophy and Social Hope,* which were written with a wider audi-ence in mind, go beyond such a pragmatist relegitimization of the liberal doctrine: they reinforce the "grandeur" of the American project defined in terms of an availability for the future and an egalitarian evolution toward a classless society—a horizon that certain *objective* factors seem rather to have placed inexorably out of reach since Richard Rorty began writing.

The fact remains that American pragmatism has, since its origins in the nineteenth century, been impossible to dissociate from the politi-cal conservatism of its most illustrious figures, such as Charles Sanders Peirce and Hilary Putnam, and the educational and utilitarian missions that it set itself. However, Rorty's stance as an "ironic liberal," and his occasional defense of Nietzsche, Foucault, and Derrida, have nonetheless led to a significant number of his philosophy colleagues turning against him, particularly more traditional liberals: thus Richard Bernstein pitted an "ethical pragmatism" against Rorty's "ironic pragmatism," one that Bernstein considered to be more faithful to Dewey's line of thinking,[47] and increasing numbers of collective works have appeared discussing the validity of Rorty's "conversationalism," forcing him to issue detailed responses.[48] Nonetheless, it has been in the wake of Rorty's work that a number of communication lines between French theory and American pragmatism have been explored. Indeed, a rational form of antidualism, an instinctive (or tactical) materialism, a fully developed empiricism, and a latent critique of humanist essentialism are all philosophical positions shared by the two schools of thought. After all, did not Deleuze and Guattari claim that "pragmatics . . . is the fundamental element upon which all the rest depends"?[49] And didn't Foucault explain one day, with a few elliptical remarks, that his entire project came down to trying to discover the "analytic philosophy" of power, targeting its "games" and "what happens every day in relations of power," rather than examining its "essence"?[50] Although this dialogue never actually took place, some more recent theoretical experiments have played, as Rorty has, on this possible convergence: for example, Richard Shusterman, a philosopher—who is, incidentally, an expert on Bourdieu—applied Dewey's approach to the most contemporary aesthetic forms, such as rap and video clips,[51] and black critic Cornel West put forward an unusual approach titled "prophetic pragmatism," which is linked to the fate of minorities and the "human powers" of social transformation and spiritual regeneration.[52] With a rare capacity for embracing the most divergent of intellectual heritages, Rorty was the first and most tenacious thinker to bring French and American traditions together—although the link in question may be tenuous, questionable, or even ideologically motivated.

Fredric Jameson and the Postmodern Paradigm

Fredric Jameson, director of Duke's graduate program in literature, is often cited as being the most influential American Marxist intellectual of his time. It must be remembered that he represents a different kind of Marxist intellectual than those we normally come across in Continental Europe: championing no social plight and holding no political membership, he is exclusively academic in his scope of intervention, he is born from literature's inner circle and is devoted to studying the "superstructure" of textual and artistic phenomena, but also, because of this, Jameson has a panoramic view of the entire contemporary cultural sphere. Jameson built his career on his *critical* approach to theoretical and postmodern Anglo-Saxon trends that have developed over the last thirty years—often presenting them before anyone else, following them over time with a rare acuity, and constantly working them back into the larger framework (whose reference points are found in historical materialism) of a political and aesthetic history of the modern Western world. The "hard" Marxism of his early years, however, when he taught at San Diego and united his students against the French "postmodernists" who were invited to the La Jolla campus,[53] had from the beginning been softened, so to speak, by the literary prism of his analyses and by the impact that the existentialist and phenomenologist Sartre had on him (Jameson wrote his doctoral thesis on Sartre's work). Jameson's first works looked at the writer Wyndham Lewis[54] and the idea that structuralism is a *linguistic* reduction of collective historical and social realities[55]—a textualism that he also criticized "poststructuralism" for nurturing, although he did not always make a clear distinction between the two phases of this point of view. His following books interweave two different perspectives of Marxism, first with the history of aesthetic representations,[56] and then with his presentation of a "political unconscious" that he considers unique to literary narrative.[57] However, it was the publication of two works that posited "theory" (both literary and poststructural) as forms of "ideology,"[58] and his famous article that appeared in 1984 in the *New Left Review* (and in 1991 as a long essay)[59] on "postmodernism" as a "cultural" ally of advanced capitalism, that established a Jamesonian position in the anglophone intellectual field, a position that was soon to become highly prominent.

Jameson notes, like others before him, that the cultural sphere has been transformed since World War II, passing from a strictly defined normative zone, as it was during the *modernist* (or industrial) era, founded on bourgeois distinctions between original and copy, or signifier and signified, to embrace the aesthetic populism of *pop culture*, which is characterized by an unlimited extension of what is "cultural," to the point where it is used ironically in the marketing of art and there is no longer any distinction between value and sale—or cited and citing, aesthetics and ideology, or even author and public. According to Jameson, this evolution reveals, at the same time as it encourages—in opposition to the one-way causalism of the economist "reflection" that had already come under attack from his teacher Georg Lukács—the evolution of capitalism as a whole, which was at an advanced, or integrated, stage: by imposing de facto the end of exteriority (in the sense that nothing can be exterior to capital any longer), the end was also nigh for the traditional role of art, and for bi-secular strains of modern philosophy. This is why Jameson groups together what he considers to be two major aspects, under the same "postmodern" label, of this new role played by culture to enhance the market's domination, and which he considers to be not only the most acute symptoms but also the superior forms: pop art, which he examines not only in the works of Warhol but also in postmodern videomakers and architects, and postdialectical theory, in other words, French theory—according to Jameson at least, who was one of the first Americans to read its authors. In other words, it marked the same shift as one that transformed revolution into *writing,* and battle into parody, with Andy Warhol's screen prints of shoes replacing van Gogh's painting of shoes, and with the semiological or ironic rereadings of Marx performed by Baudrillard and Derrida. Jameson's approach involved brilliantly detailing a few examples, creating true analytic vignettes on the "postmodern" hotel Bonaventure in Los Angeles,[60] for example, or on the divergences between Derrida and Paul de Man on the "state of nature" in Rousseau.[61] Rather than present a head-on attack, Jameson works to uncover, in popular novels and Hollywood sagas, a mixture of alienation and imaginary resistance, or, to borrow his own terms, reification and residues of utopia.[62] Yet his concern with showing French theory's participation in the new reifying and fragmentary processes of capital results in his making some hasty generalizations: thus, he presents Deleuze and Baudrillard as standing for a common platform of a "culture of the simulacrum . . . inspired by Plato,"[63] and in a few words he reduces the work of Deleuze and Guattari to an "aesthetic" leading to "the description of and apologia for a new type of discourse: the discontinuous, 'schizophrenic' text."[64]

Jameson's critique of cultural studies is more trenchant than those given by other American Marxists, and it remains largely accurate: in it, he says, "class consciousness" is replaced by a "group libido," and a "doxa" of Style plays the part of critical reason, substituting a "populist carnival" for social struggle.[65] However, bringing together in such a way the fashion for interdisciplinary studies in universities, thirty years of modern art, and texts written by Deleuze, Lyotard, and Derrida (along with the uses made of them) strikes one as a highly questionable condensation. Even Jameson's most rigorous analyses could benefit from a more nuanced recognition not only of the distance that exists between texts and their uses (here we find his sociological lacuna), but also the relationship between Marx and certain authors of the group, which goes far beyond mere aestheticizing misappropriation. It is a simplification that many others besides Jameson have made: American Marxists and non-Marxists prefer to view Deleuze as he is presented in his last works, Foucault as he was in the 1970s, and even Lyotard as he appears in *Libinal Economy* as improbable enemies of Marx, rather than as thinkers of their time attempting to come to terms with the Marxist heritage found in new forms of work and capital. Jameson has nonetheless allowed French theory and critical Marxist theory to be compared and contrasted, and put into perspective, but one wonders whether the limitations of his thinking, which is otherwise highly sophisticated, is not due to Jameson's discreet yet faithful admiration of Sartre and existentialist humanism, which leads him to denounce what he perceives as a dangerous aesthetic antihumanism. An example of this attitude can be seen when Jameson considers that, to illustrate the impossible "plenitude" of presence, Sartre's phenomenology (as with the example of the drink that quenches *only* thirst) should be more highly regarded than the "epistemology" and "aesthetics" of "Derridean ideology"—thus creating a rather strange confrontation between *Of Grammatology* and *Being and Nothingness*.[66] The same person who criticized theory for introducing a dynamic in which it is no longer ideas or social groups, but rather texts, "material texts," as he puts it, that "struggle with one another,"[67] is caught red-handed harboring illusions of *continuity* when it comes to the history of texts and ideas. Could it be that, as with other academic superstars, a more strategic motivation, linked to Jameson's position in his field, inspired him to maintain this dialogue with French theory and its historical significance—a motivation that stemmed from a desire to be recognized as their equal and their only valid interpreter? In any case, it was a desire that was fully satisfied: Jameson is "the only intellectual in the English language who measures up to the French poststructuralists,"[68] according to one American intellectual historian, whose opinion is shared by many of Jameson's colleagues.

Beyond Jameson's work itself, the postmodern issue became *the* major cultural question in America during the 1980s. Integrating new, fun, or lighthearted forms of art into the university just as easily as new theories of identity, postmodernism came to represent an era's zeitgeist, as the *New York Times* affirmed by presenting it as "a new major departure for culture."[69] Despite its usual rigor, the dictionary of American thought cited earlier goes so far as to rate postmodernism as an effective "cultural movement," the latest to occur in the "history of the Western world,"[70] taking note of its plurality and its lack of definition (associating it with figures such as the filmmaker David Lynch, the composer Philip Glass, and the artist Cindy Sherman), but the entry fails to pose any questions regarding its nominalist character or its dimension as a classificatory artifact. It is a conventional employment of postmodernism, paradoxical insofar as it fails to be retrospective, as cultural history would expect it to be, but simultaneous—unless it indicates a final, ironic attempt to cast a serious eye over the opaque, disenchanted *present*. Another possibility is that the movement represents a translation, written in the demiurgic language of words ending in *-ism,* of the typically American obsession with the future and the mythology of the progressive promise that has made American academics for the last three decades add the prefix *post-,* with the same tone of incantation—in the hope that one day there may dawn a world that is *post*humanist, *post*historical, *post*puritan, and even *post*white and *post*male.[71]

The value of this *postmodern axis* as a historic marker and a theoretical division (on which there is no need to insist here) at least explains how it became, beyond Jamesonian Marxism, the main reading perspective for French theory in the United States. Did this approach sound the knell for cultural and philosophical *modernism*? Or did it signal the outright disappearance of the modern *subject* and its *history*? Was it really the theoretical equivalent of pop art and new mysticisms—just a few cases of a postmodern blurring of boundaries? Many questions arise, but they are both too general and too caught up in the present they are trying to illuminate to have as much pertinent value in Europe as they do in the United States; but these questions do at least explain, through a kind of eponymy, the continuous success of the 1984 translation of Jean-François Lyotard's *The Postmodern Condition,*[72] a work that continues to sell nearly four thousand copies across the Atlantic. However, the man that American readers are so quick to hail as the leader of postmodernism and inventor of the very term is in fact far from being its creator, because its use dates back to 1971 at least, when American critic Ihab Hassan first penned the expression.[73] In the United States, an active debate nonetheless remains over whether the big names in French theory themselves are born from *postmodernism,* as the posthumainst and postdialectical reading would have us believe, or from *modernism*'s final death throes, as the distinctly modern(ist) references they make—to Nietzsche and Freud, Flaubert, Bataille, Joyce, and Mallarmé—would indicate. It is an issue that reminds us, if ever there were need of it, that these American interpretations of texts, whether they are carried out by academic superstars or simple students, are, above all, means of reappropriating texts: their first move is a form of reterritorialization, importing texts and using them to shift their own borders and shake up their own categories of thought—sometimes losing sight entirely of the original text in question.

9

STUDENTS AND USERS

As an alienated teenager, you read Sartre. In college, you smoked Gauloises and spouted Derrida. Later, in graduate school, nagged by self-doubt, you found relief in the giddy wanderlust of Baudrillard . . . and the unfettered optimism of Deleuze and Guattari. French philosophers. You grew up with them . . . In retrospect, though, you have to admit it all seems rather preposterous: You and these hopelessly abstruse Gauls—who could have guessed there would be so much chemistry between you?

EMILY EAKIN, *Lingua Franca*

IT IS POSSIBLE to glance through Foucault's books and find lucid descriptions of the regulating authorities one had previously encountered in a less accessible format—in gender studies courses—then, turning the page, to experience the more intimate revelation of coming across a theoretically clear interpretation of how one perceives one's own shameful marginalization. Or one can leaf through Derrida's philosophy to enrich a term paper, or discover an obscure expression that perfectly captures, without pathos, the aesthetic emotion of a more personal repertory, inspired by a film or a concert. Student readings are a mixture of class requirements and personal exploration, diligent underlining and casual skimming over texts before bed. As students were brought into contact with French theory, its works gradually worked their way onto the ever-changing bookshelves of dorm rooms, slipping into the chinks of existential angst and the vocabulary of students' banter, circulating in reading lists and enthusiastic recommendations, and they became familiar points of reference in the United States, living objects of both desire and disapproval—in a word, something quite different from the conceptual material that academic intellectuals skillfully integrated into their theoretical constructions. We must note, however, that French theory's impact on the general student population was relatively limited: as Gerald Graff remarked in 1987, "Thus literary theory has become accepted as a useful option for graduate students and advanced undergraduates, but something to be kept at a distance from the normal run of students."[1] Whether it was French or simply "literary" theory, the higher-level universities, especially the most prestigious ones, were more welcoming than run-of-the-mill colleges. In any schools where theory had some kind of impact, its acceptance by students and famous professors was generally motivated by the same concern for distinction: theory confers an advantage on those who invoke it, an implicit superiority over their younger peers and less well informed students, and sometimes even over the authors they quote. We also ought to remember that for those in this elite clique, who often, after a change of major, take positions at the head of corporations or in upper-level business administration, "only rarely will a course of study [in literature] change a life"[2]—not even a theory class, as David Kaufmann jokes. These students come across a few important names and concepts in the course of their university years, but it would be difficult to say what kind of results, if any, would show in any individual career.

The Play of Parataxis

To a twenty-two-year-old, however, theory is an exciting cerebral revelation, one that endows followers with its elegance and gives the student a freer hand intellectually—as a tool, theory has invigorating and confidence-inspiring effects, sometimes excessively so, leading to naive or caricatured views: "Melville is profoundly suspect, there's not a woman in the book, the plot hinges on unkindness to animals, and the black characters mostly drown by chapter 29," a particularly PC student said of *Moby Dick,* as quoted in the *New York Times.*[3] Leaving aside this extreme example, many students found the theoretical approach easier and more gratifying than traditional written projects like chronological textual analysis or literary history—even when it came to less moralizing projects, ranging, perhaps, from uncovering unspoken sexist and racist subtexts to simply revealing an author's scientistic tendencies or the earmarks of a Parnassian aesthete. Even deconstruction offers a paradoxically easy method: because it seeks to invalidate the principle of the "organic unity" of a text and of "its rhetoric, structure and argument," and reveals, instead, the impasses and gaps that exist between language and its apparent content, even students without any philosophical background or experience in standard semantic criticism "can quite easily produce 'deconstructive readings' that have all the marks of professional accomplishment,"[4] as Peter Brooks observes. In the interest of intellectual performance, in order to maximize personal results with minimal effort, it is best to proceed *directly* to deconstruction—as it is conceived in literature departments—rather than reverting to a contextual, referential, or biographical reading of the text in question.

Beyond the *profitability* offered by theory, and the politically defiant stances of minority students, the language and arguments of the theoretical approach lend themselves much more readily than traditional methods to the development of insiders' codes and playful reappropriation. They are better suited to the empathetic and lighthearted qualities of student conversation and its free use of tactics such as name-dropping and spontaneous association of incompatible concepts, a heady collage of notions in which thinking up the most incongruous combination is a mark of intellectual ease and brilliance. The referential chain was broken, or seriously compromised; it was no longer necessary to present the credentials of works one has mastered or canons one has studied to make an attempt at theorizing oneself. As Edward Said concludes, readers "seized on [certain] words as if they were magic wands by which to transform the humdrum scholastic readings into eye-catching theoretical 'texts.'"[5] In this milieu, the aura of revered figures is often diminished by nicknames (e.g., Deridoodle, or "D&G" for the authors of *Anti-Oedipus*), handy concepts are adjusted at will ("panoptikon" with the visual image of its watchtower conveyed by the "k," or BwO, signifying "Bodies without Organs"), and paralogical or ironic reasoning prevails over the slower and less easily mastered tactics of argumentative rationality. What is unjustifiable becomes a justification in itself: quotations taken out of context or misplaced arguments are legitimate *as such*, in opposition to grand logical constructions, seen as massive, musty, and unfashionable. For those too young to master all the implications of a text, theory provided a great windfall.

It all comes back to the notion of *parataxis*, the literary technique of spasmodic enumeration and elliptical juxtaposition, free of any connector, that formed the common element between the *theorists'* logic and American literature courses—and would explain the fruitfulness of their encounter. In literature courses in the United States, students most often encounter works via the impressionistic format of excerpts and overviews. Reading, moreover, is less concentrated on the literary works themselves (according to Said, students spend less than a fifth of their study time reading them)[6] than on comparing, evaluating, and commenting on the various critical or theoretical approaches—which represents the chief aim of many courses. The way of reading theoretical texts is itself characterized by parataxis and fragmentation: one chapter can sum up an entire work, and often an American commentator's summary discourages readers from consulting the relevant French author's text. In the *Kristeva Reader,* an excerpt dedicated to the theme of the "black sun" replaces Kristeva's long essay on "depression and melancholy"; an American introduction to one of Foucault's works dispenses with reading his main writings; and a structural analysis of Shakespeare could even replace his works themselves. This kind of critical periphery is a pedagogical tradition in the United States, as critic Gustave Lanson found in 1912, when he came to teach at Columbia and was stunned by this "singular ability to do without the texts, . . . to substitute a knowledge of what has been said about authors for that of what the authors said"—and when Lanson told students who asked what they must read, simply "the author's text," he "could see that they were surprised, and found the reading list rather slim."[7] Some eighty years later, an advanced graduate course on "French Theory and Criticism" at Indiana University was structured into ten sessions, in the "digest" format: they covered Russian formalism, Saussure, Jakobson, deconstruction, narratology (Gérard Genette), intertextuality (Michel Riffaterre), Lacanian psychoanalysis, French feminism (Julia Kristeva, Hélène Cixous), and a final catchall meeting on "cultural theory" (Althusser, Bourdieu, and Foucault). In cases like this, parataxic reading is no longer an option, but the only solution. The traditional "reading list" goes beyond the notion of providing an overview and encourages freedom of choice between texts and movements: the resulting perspective is exhaustive but often crudely dissected, and the overall list functions like a menu, from which the students make a selection and behave like customers, confronted with this display of critical and theoretical products, with varying "costs" to the user.

These practices do not allow us to predict the quality of the courses, which depends, as always, on the instructor and his or her pedagogical choices. Nevertheless, this fragmentary teaching approach is not sufficient for students to master concepts and works that they study; to do so requires methods of reappropriation and reactivation of the texts, and the aid of autonomous, nonprofessorial voices. This is where campus activities come in—discussion groups, literary clubs, leaflet writing, and the publication of university fanzines and periodicals started by certain radical students, modeled on *The Missing Link* at Duke. Starting in the mid-1990s, the growth of Internet use and student Web sites created a medium through which students developed alternatives to the linear approach of publications on paper, entirely new ways of using theoretical discourse, stimulated by the possibilities of breaking up the text, following the impulses of Web links, reframing it in a comical sequence or an interactive dialogue, and substituting the modular logic of the network for the argumentative principle of theoretical texts, or even creating visual or audio variations on a concept. All of these were ways of demystifying intimidating texts, appropriating the aura of great authors, and using the means available to hijack the dominant theoretical discourse. Some examples are online e-zines like the cooperative *Rhizome Digest* founded by Alex Galloway in tribute to Deleuze and Guattari,[8] or the more incisive *Hermenaut* started by Joshua Glenn as a parodic criticism of the way commercial interests capitalized on the success of theory[9]—Glenn considers his site to be engaged in "a mortal struggle" against "pseudo-intellectuals who have carried a smattering of theory with them into the entertainment industry," and whose work is "mostly about deconstructing the Smurfs."[10]

The Internet was useful for more than just settling a score with students who had taken their theoretical culture to the bank (via Hollywood or mass-market publishing); it also enabled users to form collaborative constructions, such as the "Baudrillard on the Web" project, whose webmaster, Alan Taylor, states on the home page that the site "will never be completed" but that anyone can "feel free to contribute."[11] It also brings opportunities to subvert, through elliptical judgments or references to technology, the most hermetic works of French theory, as in the "para-site" dedicated to Derrida's *Glas,* on which students state that the "Fleurs du mal of philosophy makes the boundaries between 'coupure' and 'crochet,' philosophy and literature, book and electronic media tremble."[12] On certain sites outside of university networks, a veritable semantic and stylistic frenzy can even render the theoretical argument unrecognizable, as in the tongue-in-cheek online periodical *Ctheory,* which amasses, without punctuation, neologisms and made-up acronyms (the VBRG are Virtual Bodies in Revolt against Globalization), canonizes Saint Foucault and Saint Baudrillard, and calls Descartes's *cogito* the "Ghostly Hangover of Modernity."[13] Ultimately, these student readings of French theory, which began with translations published in paperback, dog-eared and duly annotated by young enthusiasts, and then gave rise to Web sites displaying their playful and cathartic recycling, were linked to what Michel de Certeau calls reader "poaching": these readings, conditioned by a knowledge that is "not known, . . . bear witness to [this knowledge] without being able to appropriate it," and become its "renters and not [its] owners," creating, in its margins, an "art of the in-between," at once complicit and fragmented, semiclandestine and highly stylized.[14] Reading thus becomes a way of turning the theoretical text into a strategic ruse.

Bildungstheorie versus Legitimate Readings

Nonetheless, the texts that students are most likely to hijack or subvert are those brought to their attention by their professors—an ever-narrowing collection of texts determined by a traditional approach designed to provide a broad overview and which is framed in terms of the history of ideas. The most ubiquitous ones were Derrida's 1966 lecture at Johns Hopkins or an excerpt from *Of Grammatology;* a passage from Foucault's *Discipline and Punish* or the conference "What Is an Author?"; Lacan's seminar on "The Purloined Letter"; Hélène Cixous's essay "The Laugh of the Medusa"; the "Treatise on Nomadology" by Deleuze and Guattari, or an excerpt from Deleuze's two-part work on cinema; and the indispensable *Postmodern Condition* by Lyotard. In this context, the professor plays a mediating role between student and theoretical text—even if the mediation remains quite informal. After all, everything in the U.S. academic system, from small workshops to in-class debates on the relevance of readings covered, is designed to create a greater familiarity between students and professors than one finds in France, in keeping with the American egalitarian tradition. As early as in the eighteenth century, Alexis de Tocqueville remarked that this tradition was a key to pedagogy in the United States, and the same observation struck Gustave Lanson, for his part, in the 1900s, who remarked that there was an "academic promiscuity that brings students and professors together: their exchanges are closer and more frequent, and involve considerable exchange of influence."[15]

However, even if professors remain closer to their students, they nonetheless retain a monopoly on legitimate readings, as is the case everywhere. The mission of the scholarly institution is to produce readers that meet certain standards, and, in the name of professorial competence, to impose not only a list of required texts but also the various modes of reading appropriate to them. The professor's authority reintroduces the optics of power. This authority is, however, less focused on the actual semantic or ideological content of readings than in constructing, through exclusion, a list of works to read and questions to consider—in contrast with readings deemed "illegitimate." This authority that intercedes between the student and French theory does not, thus, simply represent propaganda so much as an "agenda-setting function" brought to light by political analysts:[16] it directs students not in *what* or *how* to think, but *about what* (and, in this case, *on what grounds*) to think. This authority dictates the respective importance of different theoretical movements, lays out key predecessors and essential texts, and comes to play the role of symbolic arbiter or gatekeeper between student and text, like the opinion experts for undecided voters. French theory has always had the support of professors, as experts and mediators—despite students' resistance to academic authority, their attempts to create alternatives to the compulsory canon, and loud, constant protests in the form of indifference, parody, or rebellion against the paternal figures that inhabit their university programs, whether they be feminist professors or an abstruse text by Derrida.

Thus, it is generally along the margins of these functions of authority that pivotal encounters between students and theoretical texts take place, through a different relationship with readings that is closer to the mechanism of *enchantment* and the need for *prophecy* (to use two major terms from Max Weber's analyses). There is an abundance of fond memories and campus anecdotes in which certain students, particularly those isolated from their peers and alienated from societal norms, were inspired by a word, a motif, or the existential landscape of a thematic tendency—such as Lyotard's rehabilitation of "little stories," which can be associated with the parallel narratives circulating on campus; Baudrillard's delightful motto of a copy "truer" than the original; Foucault's "care of the self," suddenly applicable to this age of transition in the university; or the "desiring machines" of Deleuze and Guattari, arriving to decipher new, unsuspected libidinal impulses. Conceptual figures and theoretical allegories, encountered during bookish wanderings, become markers, fetishes, or refrains of a countercreed. Even if they do not always fully master these elements of theory, they appropriate them as a form of opposition to the prior world of the family, and to the external world of professionalization, or to fill a melancholic void. This process offers students a sense of initiation, which is strengthened by the rite-of-passage aspects of these few years, during which one can construct oneself on neutral ground. Thus, as the term *Bildungsroman* appeared in the nineteenth century in Germany, referring to a literature of initiation, avidly consumed by adolescents, we might venture to coin the term *Bildungstheorie* for this new theoretical presence, intimately embraced by many students for its familiar otherness, so different from other required readings. In this way, theoretical texts came to guide the student through the confusion of tangled discourse—in the various spheres we might call social, intimate, domestic, cultural, and professorial—into which student life propels young people.

Books, as Bourdieu characterizes them, represent a "depository of magic secrets, . . . like a text from which one wants to learn the art of living,"[17] and in student readers they find a receptive audience keen for semantic values, in need of tools to delineate a private space for ideas, to construct a corpus of unprescribed references in order to mark off one's terrain in the social and generational limbo of university life. It is a period characterized by a certain departure from the dominant priority of work, and formative exploration through play and transgression, and generally the only period of one's life conducive to inconsequential infatuations, without immediate results; thus, this academic detour in American schools lends itself to the existential dimension of French theory. It offers a form of subjectification, reenchantment, and even emancipation from inherited or environmental shackles. We should also note the consolidating effect these exchanges could play, through the codes of certain cliques and friendly proselytizing, in bringing together a community of peers sharing some schoolboy jargon or the veneration of an author. Invented dialects, codes of reappropriation, and shared revelations come together to form a kind of collective reading. Students recommend books to each other, discuss them in groups, exchange literary discoveries, ridicule the unenlightened, compose leaflets or the text of a Web site together—even if in some cases it gives rise to *illegitimate,* entirely unique readings, like the one constructed by students delegated to create a page about Lyotard on the strange Web site called "k.i.s.s. of the panopticon" based at the University of Washington, which presents Lyotard not so much in relation to his works as through the lens of a "parallel universe" that the webmasters view as Lyotardian, and personified by the rock group Talking Heads or the cult film *Blade Runner.*[18] More often, the liberating function of these readings allows students to release themselves from constraints carried over from childhood or adolescence, not only through the texts' actual themes but also through the sheer vigor of the transgressive or defiant gestures formed right on the page, in an abstract register, by Foucault's or Derrida's writings. The lyrical impulses and feelings of gratitude produced by these *ruptures* can, in turn (although less often), give rise to new writings, a sort of textual recycling: one example is an essay by student R. A. Brinckley and young assistant professor Robert Dyer, published in the periodical *Semiotext(e),* a mixture of parodied jargon and shared autobiography, which aims to "deconstruct" their "Oedipal roots"—in Brinckley's case, Ithaca's suburbs, and, for Dyer, the Victorian setting of his native New Zealand—and to tell *through theory,* using ironic notes and allusions for the initiated, the story of each man's journey from the "original vagina" to the "nomadic moment,"[19] and, through this exercise, to tell the story of a submission to free writing.

Growth of the World and the Privatization of Knowledge

Looking beyond the student population, this subjective and, it might be said, atmospheric connection to the works of French theory (in spite of the difficulty of these texts) becomes a general tactic for all those who, without a published work to their name, and without a recognized discourse in which to contextualize theoretical references, never fully mastered them. These groups might typically include teachers engaged in research, assistant professors, young students feeling uncertain after graduation but still hooked on nomadology or French feminism, and all the other "dominated" members of the strict hierarchy of knowledge and publications. Their link to theory is not grounded in the mediating institution, or in a career project, but rather in a fear or sense of mystery, a prerational aura that they attempt to disperse by short-circuiting the overall logic, selecting a fragment from the corpus to employ it in a more familiar context. The use they make of theory in these cases is thus all the more unrestrained precisely because of its fragmented nature. In contrast with the official, diploma-bearing experts of French theory, the objective for these readers is to carve out for themselves a bio/bibliography, a unique connection between text and real life, by releasing a theoretical enigma from its paper prison and trying out its implications in every aspect of existence. Thus, just as Baudrillard considers that the Gulf War, waged through the mediation of television screens, "did not take place,"[20] some feigned doubt as to whether the highly publicized presidential election really occurred; because Deleuze writes that nothing is deeper than the skin and "surface effects," certain readers have defended the sensual play of caresses and unfulfilled acts in preference to sexual athleticism; because, in Foucault's work, the repressive delineation of a category known as "madness" *produces* Reason and reveals an intimate relation between the two poles, the dealer of mind-altering substances becomes, in the eyes of his student customers, a Foucauldian figure who grants access to the other side of normality, a normalized state of hallucination. In certain ways, theory creates a *narrative* from which to glean uses and practices that help tame the reader's world.

More specifically, this fantastical world of Derridean specters and Lyotardian antiheroes, and marginal or transgressive figures taken from Foucault or Deleuze, is an alternative to the conventional world of career-oriented choices and the pursuit of top grades: it *arms* the student, affectively and conceptually, against the prospect of alienation that looms at graduation under the cold and abstract notions of professional ambition and the job market. In some cases, this brush with theory, along with other factors such as positive experiences with volunteer groups or ecological convictions, may inspire students, in contrast with the more radical rebels of the past, to choose the more personal and committed choice of a "calling" instead of a selfish "career," a profession motivated by the heart rather than mere lucrative gain. The latter option, however, which reading Foucault or Derrida might curiously provide with "a meaning," does not truly serve to prolong the theory-oriented community that was formed during the university years, of which the only

means of continuation would be teaching. Although some of Sylvère
Lotringer's students were bold enough to extend into their professional
lives the universe of perspectives he taught them—such as Margaret San-
dell, who started the Bataillian periodical *Documents,* and Tim Grif-
fin, who founded the alternative magazine *Artbyte,* or John Kelsey, who
launched the subversive fashion company Bernadette Corporation—the
vast majority of students who encounter French theory later abandon it
to pursue their "vocation." Projects that entail spreading disorder in the
fashion world, as John Kelsey's magazine *Made in USA* recommends, or
that study the political and anthropological value of excrement, as does
a special issue of *Documents,* take part in projects still directly linked
to French theory; working for an NGO in the name of the "minorities" featured in Deleuze and Guattari's works, or even embracing a law-
yer's career to combat Foucauldian "institutions of control," amounts
to nothing but a questionable, ostentatious, and nostalgic justification.
In these cases, French theory functions above all as a memory, carrying
with it a vague injunction of biographical coherence, but no longer a
living reference, in the present setting of campus life or on the fringe of
cultural industries.

   In order to better understand this living and almost excessively intimate connection between the reader's subjectivity and a theoretical text,
we may apply the notion of a "field reference" offered by Paul Ricoeur.
Using the example of narrative, Ricoeur demonstrates that certain utterances are capable of liberating "on the ruins of the literal meaning" a
"more radical power to refer to aspects of our being-in-the-world that
cannot be said directly."[21] These utterances are precisely the domain of
theoretical terms as they are recomposed by American students—fragments taken from the French corpus and recirculated elsewhere. From
this perspective, the notion of *metaphorization* no longer refers only to
a function of language, in the way that the "bunker" of Virilio's writings or Deleuze's concept of "intensity" could perform as simple metaphors for students in an extratextual existential situation, but they also
contain an ontological dimension: the *world* of the student or activist,
permeated with theoretical references, becomes itself "the ensemble of
references opened by every sort of text [that they have] read, interpreted,
and loved"; it is no longer an "environment" (*Umwelt*) of signs, but a
"world" (*Welt*) of significations, which is not an example of the "see-
ing-as" of mere metaphorical *perception,* but rather the "being-as" of

full participation in the world thus constituted.[22] In other words, when certain American readers identify with Baudrillard's theory of "simulation" or Foucault's "subjugation," and gain a sense of coherence from these theories, it is not through an existential distortion or naive appropriation of the French text, on the premise of a fundamental difference between the text and the world, but a reciprocal permeation of both spheres. Rather, there is a certain naïveté, and a kind of literality, in this kind of relationship to texts, but which contributes to their existential function and empathetic potential.

Thus, each text offers the reader's subjectivity "a world that I could inhabit and in which my ownmost possibilities could unfold."[23] This world is *reconciled,* as it were, through this system enabling one to combine elements taken from both text and life. Whereas Ricoeur argues for a *narrative* increase or growth, and philosopher François Dagognet, through the optical alphabet of painting, for an *iconic* growth, we might, in this case, speak of a veritable *theoretical* growth of the reference world, which, fortified by the text's contributions, becomes more "readable," but also more practicable and more livable. We ought to specify that the increase in question does not refer to the quantitative accumulation of knowledge, or an expansion of light across an opaque world (which are voluntary acts, and are based in the premise of a world *free* of all text), but rather to an aptitude for inhabiting this world without objectifying it, to page through it without mechanically assigning it a meaning, to subjectivize oneself in it but also to *de*subjectivize oneself in it. French theory, in bypassing the accepted discourse of argument, and constantly reaffirming the motifs of dispersion and the multiple subject, encourages its readers "without published works" to lose themselves, to reach a position of quasi fusion with the text. This relationship with knowledge is not unlike Foucault's definition of *curiosity:* "not the curiosity that seeks to assimilate what it is proper for one to know, but that which enables one to get free of oneself," a certain "passion for knowledge" insofar as its objeive is not simply "a certain amount of knowledgeableness," but, "to the extent possible, . . . the knower's straying afield of himself."[24] Although the intimate and radically singular register of such texts prevents them from being grasped using the tools of sociological questioning, these textual means of construction, and also of relinquishing oneself through theoretical reading and knowledge, these unfamiliar ways of inhabiting the text, put to tangible use in American universities, represent perhaps the most striking result of French theory in the United States, but not the most durable or the most cooperative one, because it rarely extends past the confines of the university. A rapid privatization of knowledge, which can clearly be seen in the United States by increasing academic specialization and the gradual disappearance of a public intellectual arena, played its part in preventing the experience that these invigorating readings delivered during students' late-adolescent university years from developing into more than just one additional factor of their education—perhaps the most unusual and least conventional factor, but never the most political one.

10

ART PRACTICES

Every work of art is an uncommitted crime.

THEODOR ADORNO, *Minima Moralia*

TWO CENTURIES AGO, Hegel became the first in a long line of prophets announcing the end of art, stating that it was already "a thing of the past." Since then, art has not ceased to be canceled, wiped out, and vaporized, gradually becoming nonart and losing the autonomy that it enjoyed in its unlikely golden age, and sparking debates everywhere concerning its "corruption" and "obsolescence." It was in the United States that, for the last half century, art's traditional foundations have been the most concretely and permanently shaken—those same foundations that the century of Hegel and Cézanne had in fact reinforced. It was also in the United States, with its continual metamorphoses and new social (and financial) promiscuities, that the ethereal sphere of an art conceived as the domain of the creator was replaced by the decisive concept of *art worlds*—a concept formulated by the philosopher Arthur Danto and theorized by the sociologist Howard Becker. Far from aesthetic thought, art worlds are defined (in the plural) as an "established network of cooperative links among participants"—from creator to curator to critic—the works becoming "joint products of all the people who cooperate" in this process. The very coherence of these worlds is no longer reliant on a predefined notion of art, but precisely on the "problematic character of both 'artness' and 'worldness.'"[1] In other words, when surrounded with the multiplication of social signs and the unlimited extension of the market, a new indistinction has become apparent in art, between practice and discourse, artist and critic, and also between work and product, subversion and promotion, and this indistinction is now firmly planted at the heart of what makes one, or several, art world(s). If, as Jacques Rancière states, "the aesthetic regime of art . . . has introduced into the very life of artworks the infinite task of critique that alters them,"[2] then the question has become whether a shift to a postaesthetic has occurred—in which the very boundary between work and discourse would disappear.

It is here that French theory stepped in from across the Atlantic. Indeed, its most intensive uses and most dazzling successes, but also its crudest distortions, occurred in artistic circles, far from the more recent French debates over the "dead ends" of contemporary art. French theory's impact was unanimously recognized, and was certainly more apparent than that created by French artists: in the thirty-year anniversary edition of *Artpress,* Robert Storr remembers that "at the beginning of the 1980s, . . . American magazines gave little space to French art, but the wave of French theory was inexorably rising," a wave of which Baudrillard "was the foamy crest, whereas in Barthes, Foucault, Kristeva, and others one could hear the rumbling of deeper currents."[3] The French authors all put forward, in various forms, a novel articulation between the practice and discourse of art, affirming the validity of a historical convergence between these two elements, in opposition to their old dialectical hierarchy. They broke away from the two-hundred-year-old practice of theoretically objectivizing art, with *aesthetics* as a separate domain of knowledge: Derrida investigated the notion of "truth" in painting; Foucault detected the modern "self-referential" regime of art found already in Manet's work; Baudrillard described the "simulacra" at work in Andy Warhol's art or in the Beaubourg *effect;* Virilio drew our attention to the "aesthetics of disappearance"; Guattari took the risk of analyzing stage performances and suggested his theory of "process art"; Deleuze studied "rhythm" in Francis Bacon and placed a photograph of the installation *Boy with Machine* by Richard Lindner on the cover page of *Anti-Oedipus;* and finally, Lyotard wrote about Daniel Buren, and in 1985 came up with his "The Immaterials" exhibition for the Centre Pompidou.

From Artwork to Art Market

In the ideological formulations of the great art critics of the time, abstract expressionism was born *in opposition* to the artistic and theoretical avant-gardes of Europe, and the movement was buoyed by aspirations for independence from the Old Continent's artistic models. Nonetheless, in the twenty years that followed the Second World War, tentative links were forged here and there between great American painters and future leaders of French (post)structuralism—as with the example of the meeting between Cy Twombly and Roland Barthes, which led the Frenchman to applaud American art for its "awkwardness [which] does not want to *grasp* anything."[4] Moreover, several strong thematic convergences brought together, over an interval of a few years, the two projects: a focus on rhythm and energy, an elaboration of centerless structures (according to the famous statement made by Jackson Pollock: "my paintings do not have a center"), the "new flatness," as coined by Clement Greenberg in speaking of Mark Rothko and his flat monochromes,[5] and more directly the artistic complicity between Rauschenberg, for example, and Jasper Johns with John Cage and Merce Cunningham, whose "theoretical" complicity with Deleuze and Foucault has already been mentioned.

The American artistic scene was shaken up during the 1960s, as different postwar "vitalisms" were gradually displaced from the forefront of the artistic world to be replaced by a new wave, which had yet to be clearly defined: pop art, whose name itself, as well as certain of its principles (the recuperation and reuse of urban scraps, and an ironic attitude toward merchandise), were imported from Britain—and whose undertow was soon to force the modern (or modernist) figure of the solitary, autonomous, and tragic artist into obsolescence, whether he be *outside* of the world or *against* it. Andy Warhol, an illustrator who had worked in advertising, opened a cooperative studio in Manhattan—the Factory—in 1963, where he perfected his first silkscreen series, hosted poets and musicians (including Lou Reed and other members of the yet-to-be-formed Velvet Underground), and later launched the magazine *Interview*. Claes Oldenburg constructed his first installations, Roy Lichtenstein came up with his first comic-book paintings, and curators Leo Castelli and Ileana Sonnabend exhibited the new maverick artists. Robert Indiana, for his part, maintained strong links with the literary counterculture of Greenwich Village; meanwhile, the first artistic *happenings* were taking place (in which the artwork was shifted from its material domain into the domain of the event), as were performances by the Living Theater—soon to be imported to Paris through the efforts of Jean-Jacques Lebel.

Contrary to the notion that art performs a superior function and is submissive to critical reason, the new implicit precept involved upping the ante in every direction, in relation both to the world of the market and to countercultural provocations—as Baudrillard correctly observed in his comments regarding Warhol, stating that "art should not seek its salvation in a critical disavowal . . . but by outstripping the formal and fetishized abstraction of commodities," by "becoming more commodity than commodities."[6] Yet such an evolution also marked the end to the sharply delineated discourses that appeared after the Second World War regarding the mission of the artist and the difference between "avant-garde and kitsch" (to use one of Greenberg's titles). This evolution thus signaled the end of the more self-reflective and programmatic artistic practices that held sway during the 1950s, which were, as Bernard Blistène summarizes, "engaged in a critical approach to the pictorial medium, concerning both its finality and its use-value," which placed them in polar opposition to the "principle of mechanical reproduction"[7] that pop art later put into practice. The autonomy of a creation that disposed of its own discourse and instances of enunciation (even if they were exogenous, coming from art historians writing for *Partisan Review,* and not directly from the artist himself) was replaced by a heteronomy vindicated by a secular *artistic* practice, traversed by the chaotic statements of the time—and from which it was no longer protected by a legitimate discourse that would assign it a specific value.

A multiplication of new waves and innovations, and a true blossoming of schools and groups, also contributed to this evolution, in the sense that their appearance indicated the production of what Bourdieu calls "classificatory notions," which had a primary function of communicating in the market for the purpose of "identifying groups united in practical terms" and providing "marks of distinction" that struggle for "recognition."[8] Thus, the artistic notion of "minimalism" appeared in 1965, with the advent of the groundbreaking work of Donald Judd and Sol Lewitt. "Conceptual" art itself, whose boundaries were still blurred, arrived in the United States in 1967. And one must not forget the new experiments being carried out in sculpture, graphic design, video (a little later), and the "land art" installed in the desert and agricultural expanses of the continent. In order to make sense of such diverse practices, which were immersed in the new influx of social signs, and to support the proposal to begin a possible subversion of internal signs ("semioclasm"), alternative semiologies arriving from France proved to be far more useful during the 1970s than the Marxist paradigm that dominated art criticism and the most conventional forms of aesthetic theory still being taught in universities. From Soho, which was already on its way to becoming institutionalized, to the improvised galleries and militant bohemian squats in the East Village, a few key texts were being circulated: Barthes's *Mythologies,* for an understanding of how brands and labels functioned as social myths; *The Mirror of Production* (which had a significant impact on the sociofeminist artist Barbara Kruger) and *The Consumer Society* by Baudrillard, to glean the tools provided by a critical semiology; and even Foucault's *Discipline and Punish,* to see oneself reflected in his political theory concerning the margins of society. However, these texts are still not widely read, and to the extent that they are, it is most often by way of the university, from which many budding artists had dropped out, or through up-to-date articles that appeared in alternative publications such as *Bomb* and *East Village Eye.*

The confusion over possible roles reached a critical point in countercultural circles, where everyone could have a turn at being an artist, a curator, a critic, and even a patron, ritually reunited by numerous group exhibitions.[9] As for the best established galleries, the boom enjoyed by the art market at the beginning of the 1980s, caught up in the stockmarket frenzy and real-estate speculation, had the same effect of upsetting all that was familiar, distancing artists from their usual supporters (critics and art historians), and pushing them toward the financial elite and mass media. In this context, where the roles at the heart of the art world were being redefined and a general loss of autonomy within the aesthetic movement was taking place, the arrival of French theory on the scene at the beginning of the 1980s was providential. Although its advent was not without misinterpretations, it breathed new life into a field of practices that found itself adrift and was ready to merge with the flow of the market, and endowed it with a historical and political dimension, and possibly the illusion of a transgressive force. French theory allowed artists, who this time read the texts directly, the opportunity to once more participate in discourse—or in criticism—by revealing the close similarity, or even the interchangeable nature, of discursive and creative poles: the artist *wields* a performative discourse about the world at the same time as the critic, or the theorist, almost fulfills the role of a conceptual artist, an author of language events and textual *happenings.* This new influx of theory was able to reach artists without any suspicious provenance, be it the academic elite or a regressive institution, threatening an a priori invalidation of its arguments; and it allowed artists to interpret their practices through a formalized discourse, bringing together their concepts and their percepts. As artist and novelist Kathy Acker puts it, theory allowed her to "verbalize what I had been doing: . . . And then when I read *Anti-Oedipus* and Foucault's work, suddenly I had this whole language at my disposal."[10]

The generation of "artist-thinkers" of the 1960s, figures such as Donald Judd, Richard Serra, and Joseph Kosuth, was replaced by a band of orphans, without any theoretical reference point or aptitude for self-reflection; they were caught between a caste of moralizing critical ideologues and the destabilizing magic spells of the financial world. Suddenly, French theory appeared as the ideal ally, offering this hybrid generation an accessible alternative—with the top spot occupied by Baudrillard and his work, whose double-edged statements began to sound like the solution to the art world's aporias: "The challenge posed to us by the delirium of capital . . . must be taken up in a way that insanely outstrips it."[11] Sylvère Lotringer states that it was an editorial chance that led him to consider allowing Baudrillard's texts to be made more widely available in the artistic world, because the promotional tour for *Simulations* in 1983 had attracted only a handful of students at universities. Why not then consider targeting curators and artists instead? Within a couple of months, Baudrillard's work was to take on a crucial position: "within two years, everyone had read *Simulations*," a curator confided to Lotringer; one painter also told him that "people knew Baudrillard more than anyone else, . . . everyone was using him in their work."[12] It was the beginning of a misinterpretation that was to leave its mark on the New York art scene—and one that was to remain in the annals of the tormented relationship between artistic practice and theoretical discourse.

Simulations: A Misunderstanding

One of the first openly fought battles marked the election of French theory to its new role of involuntary referee; this was the controversy over neo-Expressionist art. It referred to a group of artists who, without necessarily wishing to create a separate movement, reintroduced a figurative, narrative, transitive art form to the German and Italian scenes of the 1970s. Their work was enriched by the use of video and photography, and by a certain political note of irony; this work included the industrial photographs by Bernd and Hilla Becker, then later photos by Andreas Gursky—their student from Düsseldorf (whose pictures ranged from a stock-market room to a supermarket aisle)—Anselm Kiefer's shocking works which evoked Nazi High Masses, homages made to 1930s Expressionism by the painters Baselitz and Middendorf, and, of course, the work by Italian neofigurative artists Clemente and Cucchi. Two men took it upon themselves to lay siege to the artistic fortress of New York in order to make a place for these artists. The young Berlin museum curator Wolfgang Max Faust, in a controversial article that he turned in to the monthly publication *Art Forum,* backed the aesthetic movement by making continuous references—which varied in degrees of explicitness—to Lyotard, Deleuze, and Guattari: it appealed for desire and anarchy, praised "lines of flight" and "productive intensity," and made allusions to a "becoming revolutionary" of the artist when faced with the overly rational discourse of the social critique.[13] A curator from Milan, Achille Bonito Oliva, called upon Nietzsche, "nomadism," and European punk movements in order to defend this new "trans-avant-garde," which he considered to be characterized by a contagious exaltation and a lyrical emotion.[14]

The defensive machinery of New York critics formed almost immediately in response to the movement's exhibitions and, in a broader sense, to the German–Italian "irrationalism" that they did not hesitate to link to the two countries' political pasts. They raised their voices in the art publications: Thomas Lawson spoke of a "retardataire mimeticism" and "neo-primitivism";[15] Hal Foster mocked a provocation "at once scandalous and servile"; the Marxist Benjamin Buchloh denounced the "morbid symptoms" of neo-Expressionism[16] and its "authoritarian irrationality" or "proto-fascist libertarianism," while Donald Kuspit opposed an "*expressive* will-to-power" to the "social conscience" and the "laconic expression" of American artists.[17] Such a unanimous overreaction from the American Left's authoritative voices in art criticism caused a far greater stir than was anticipated: certain critics (like Donald Kuspit) began to back off, in favor of the neo-Expressionist camp; artists soon called for a "subversive complicity," in the name of "reappropriation," which attacked capitalism through its own means (graffiti, photos, and altered advertisements, as the neo-Expressionists themselves did when they were linked to punk culture and squat movements), in reaction to the illusion of art as autonomous and criticism as exterior to it; and all those involved transformed the controversy into a politically loaded debate regarding the "French Nietzscheanism"—an ideological regression for the Marxist critics and a breath of new life into the political-artistic scene for others.[18]

Aside from this transatlantic debate, New York was also witness to the neoconceptualist movement, which was centered on its constant references to Baudrillard, who had successfully placed French theory at the heart of the American artistic world. Indeed, at the beginning of the 1980s, a mixed group of artists vented their frustration with the inflexible options available to them. On the one hand was a para-Marxist art criticism whose strategies appeared obsolete when faced with the Reagan neoconservative revolution; on the other was the gleefully grasping cynicism of an entirely commercial art form. The sense of dissatisfaction was too widespread to form the foundations of a new movement: with works more often displayed in independent galleries such as Nature Morte, International with Monument, and CASH, as well as in Eileen Weiner's Artist Space and at the Parsons School of Design, the artists themselves formed an eclectic group that included photographers Cindy Sherman, Sherrie Levine, and Richard Prince, painters Archie Pickerton and Robert Longo, and "multimedia innovators" Sarah Charlesworth and Jeff Koons—who had recently reinvented himself, leaving a career as a stockbroker to become an agitator of the artistic world. As sources of inspiration, they tended to draw upon pop art, New Wave music (and groups like Talking Heads), and figures such as Roland Barthes and William Burroughs, rather than using figurative painting, the punk movement, or the Frankfurt School. The artists combined existing materials of conceptual art with the latest technological advances (video, photo, and sound) and were convinced that the latest possible form of artistic subversion consisted in uncovering every aspect of art's complicit relationship with "the system," and pushing the limits of capital excess in order to better expose its true nature: as Richard Prince emphasized, "Advertising is reality, the *only* reality."

In order to accomplish their goals, these artists sought to create a theory and approach based on a *social critique of signs*. Just as the "New Capital" exhibition came out at the end of 1984, organized by the curators Milazzo and Collins—who presented the movement as the advent of *post*conceptualism—a more restrained group took shape, under the banner of "neoconceptualism"; its members included Hyme Steinbach, Jeff Koons, Ross Bleckner, Julie Wachtel, Archie Pickerton, Deleuze scholar Tim Rollins (who promoted the theses of *Capitalism and Schizophrenia* along with his own), and Baudrillard specialist Peter Halley, whose theoretical culture propelled him to the center of the group. Their ongoing projects, which included an "ironic critique" of capital and a "social realism" of abstraction, favored above all what was deemed a *nonhumanist* vision of all the urban, geometric lines whose purpose is to control (the course adopted by roads, administrative hallways, highway off-ramps, etc.) and grouped them under the term "neogeometry" (Neo-Geo). As Peter Halley explains, the issue at hand was leaving a mark on the canvas of "the soft geometries of interstate highways, computers, and electronic entertainment" that was unique to this stage of capital's development.[19] At this point, Baudrillard was at the height of his New York glory. Translations of his books were being reprinted several times a year. He was elected ex officio onto *Art Forum*'s editorial staff. Above all, he was constantly quoted by the *New York Times* and the *Village Voice,* which produced an increasing number of articles on "hyperreality" and the "simulacrum." Baudrillard's concept of simulation—which Americans understood, in a Platonist mode, as the "fake" used by illusionists, and as a mere imitation without original—gradually gave rise to the term "simulationist" as an American school that denoted not only the neoconceptualists but also all those who experimented with social signs.

But then relations turned sour. Baudrillard was invited in March 1987 to the Whitney Museum and to Columbia to give two lectures, and thousands of New York artists were falling over themselves to get tickets—there was such a frenzy that Collins and Milazzo came up with the parodical idea of scheduling at the same time an "Anti-Baudrillard Show." During the lectures, the author of *Simulacres et Simulation* declared in no uncertain terms that "a simulationist school cannot exist because the simulacrum cannot be *represented.*" He refused to acknowledge his role in creating this new movement and even indirectly criticized their liberal use of a concept that is by nature mobile, difficult to grasp, and by definition impossible to apply. This was deemed "a betrayal"; it turned the New York artists who had followed Baudrillard into orphans once again, and made headlines in all the artistic publications. Such a misunderstanding provided many valuable lessons. Within a few years, the word *simulation* had become the secret password of the New York art scene, and one of the keys to American culture, just as *deconstruction* had been earlier. But although Baudrillard predicted that the primacy of the sign would supplant representation, American artists formed a *different* mode of representation, which marked a new step in modern art—allowing them to imitate the world of commerce without becoming subservient to it, to toy with the illusions it creates without succumbing to them—in an ethical and political compromise completely foreign to the fundamentally apolitical thinking of Baudrillard.

On the one hand, simulation exists because art no longer does, which is Baudrillard's theoretical ode; on the other hand, simulation must exist if art is to continue to do so, a reaction to save an artistic scene in turmoil. Françoise Gaillard accurately comments on this paradox: whereas Baudrillard drew up "the death certificate of every critical function in the world of the simulacrum," and saw "in simulation the death of art," Americans looked to it for "a means of continuing to play art against reality, . . . to preserve the critical function, . . . to save art as an institution and as a business."[20] In Baudrillard's thinking, simulation is tied to a certain manner of writing, a theory of seduction, a critique of the symbolic object—not to a moral code of representation. What Baudrillard today considers to be a "deviationism" or a "literalism" on the part of his American (ex-)admirers also reveals, at least in the context of the New York art scene, their own degree of inaptitude when it comes to understanding paradoxical thinking, and the way in which Baudrillard has always practiced it. The discrepancy is all the more striking when we consider that Baudrillard closely studied the works of Warhol and photographer Nan Goldin, although in the end he did not collaborate with either, and that he was also in contact for a time with the artist Barbara Kruger and the painter Edward Ruscha; and yet Baudrillard considered the movements of the 1980s, over the course of which everyone (from Jeff Koons to Peter Halley) extended fruitless offers to work with him, as no more than a "subproduct of pop art"—refusing to interest himself, even declaring outright that "the entire misunderstanding . . . is based on the fact that, at bottom, art is not my problem."[21]

The case of Peter Halley remains emblematic, nonetheless, of a new relationship between art and discourse, in view of what Françoise Gaillard calls his "theoretical good will."[22] Born in 1953, it was during his schooling at Yale that he discovered the works of Foucault and Derrida.

Halley is not only the author of an innovative pictorial work based on simple geometric lines and the use of Day-Glo wall paint, but he was also involved in a truly collaborative project—creating a working group, founding the magazine *Index,* and trying to put in place a theoretical credo. Thus, he drew upon Foucault's thinking to reinterpret Barnett Newman's work, Virilio was used to justify the intriguing idea of the battle that exists between History and abstract art, and, of course, Baudrillard was called upon to explain the role that "nostalgia" played in pop culture and the fascination that Frank Stella's work inspired.[23] If Halley is able to acknowledge with hindsight that he interpreted the simulacrum "literally," in a realist mode, reading Baudrillard "as if it was Warhol himself who had written a book," he nonetheless insists on a certain *need for theory* that arose in a particular historical context: the first generation of American artists brought up with television in middle-class suburbia, who arrived too late to participate in pop art or beat culture, nonetheless felt the need to make a symbolic break from accepted values—Emersonian humanism, the modernist high culture of the mid-century, and what he calls artistic "transcendentalism." They felt driven to create a rupture *through* theory and *in* theory, but it was one that postmodern society and its triumphant middle class—open to anything and free of any utopia—prevented them from executing effectively. Such a notion of a *need for theory* cannot, therefore, be reduced to strategies of distinction or to a value-based necessity. This idea is, in a certain sense, not so far removed from what Adorno said regarding the relationship between art and aesthetics (as a theory of art): "Art cannot search for norms that would be prescribed to it by aesthetics . . . but must develop in aesthetics the force for a reflection that it could not carry out on its own."[24] Put differently, we find ourselves once again in contact with the principle—this time in art—of *theoretical practice.*

In the United States, this idea of theoretical practice exists in every possible form that the fragile, indirect, but obsessional, dialogue between French theory and artistic creation could assume. It exists in the rare cases—as much symptoms as they are *productions* of the link in question—where the theoretical referent has itself been integrated into the artistic work, revealing an unexpected intimacy of register between philosophical texts and artistic production; examples include Mark Tansey's photomontages in which Derrida and Paul de Man play the parts of Sherlock Holmes and Professor Moriarty, Robert Morris's work which "illustrates" on canvas Foucault's prison world, and Rainer Ganahl's experiments which projected Deleuze quotations onto screens on the walls of the Thomas Soloman Garage gallery in California. In such a context, art and theory directly influenced each other, pretending to ignore the differences in their symbolic registers. Their closeness was often revealed by the intervention of an intermediary critic who unearthed traces of French theory and forced them onto a work, with, for example, the *Los Angeles Times* critic who described a video installation by the artist Diana Thater as "boldly illustrat[ing] theorist Gilles Deleuze's argument in *The Logic of Sense.*"[25] Running contrary to this interplay, the living dialogue was also maintained in universities, where art history classes—given by Andrea Fraser, Hal Foster, Rosalind Kraus, and many others—not only brought to light the historical and political implications of French theory in the art world, as would be the approach in literary fields, but also examined its practical effects on techniques of representation and even on artistic *styles of existence.* Unlike other bodies of theory used by discourses of the artistic world, this one, created by figures such as Deleuze, Lyotard, and even Baudrillard, had the ambition—or perhaps the humility—not to interpret art but to experience it, not to semanticize a work but to connect with it. Thus, Lyotard's concepts of the "sublime" and the "figure" do not *express* a work's content, as a text would, but simply present "the intensive space of desire." Along similar lines, Baudrillard creates wordplays, which extend whatever message appears to stem logically or parodically from a work rather than search for its improbable "meaning." And, above all, there is the important work carried out by Deleuze, for whom painting goes "beneath representation" and "beyond representation," to a place where one can grapple with a concept's *gaze,* as he himself attempts to do with Francis Bacon: "in art . . . it is not a matter of reproducing or inventing forms, but of capturing forces"; it is here that the "community of the arts" can be found, which demonstrates "that no art is figurative" but that all forms aim to produce a *force* "closely related to sensation."[26]

Immaterial Architecture

Architecture is a case unto itself—first of all, because of its involvement in several distinct worlds. Caught between the tendencies of functionalism and utopia, it can establish itself as legitimate only through *opposition* to these two impulses: by putting into practice projects whose realization immediately divorces them from the discourses that originally inspired their existence, and at the same time claiming to represent more than mere utilitarianism, because, as Hegel remarked, "architecture refers to all the elements of a building that are not based on utility." A product of both art and technology, of functional concerns and ideological perspectives, it bears many historical and collective implications, because of which its relationship to theoretical (or political) discourse has always appeared as a sine qua non, a necessary alliance, far removed from the dialectical complementarity more recently conceived between fine arts and aesthetic philosophy. Architecture's encounter with French theory was, accordingly, inevitable, especially considering the attention that the principal theorists devoted to the subject—one naturally thinks of all the writings of Paul Virilio, who, in 1963, cofounded the group (and periodical) known as *Architecture Principe,* but also of Baudrillard's work, which developed a theory of Beaubourg, and entered into a dialogue with Jean Nouvel, and one might even consider Foucault's reflections on space and power as relevant to the issue. This encounter was not, however, as clandestine as in France, where both the teaching and the practice of architecture maintained an age-old mistrust of theory, which can be observed in the resolutely antitheoretical professional publication *Le Moniteur,* or even in the frontispiece of the École des Beaux-Arts in Paris, which calls, in no uncertain terms, for the burning of all books. In contrast, however, the extended cooperation, which began in the early 1980s, between American architecture and French theory, and more particularly Derrida's deconstruction, can be differentiated in two important ways from the occasional references to *useful* theories that took place in France: first of all, due to a sophisticated *textual* bias, which resulted in the dematerialization of architecture and even inspired an architectural movement that conceived itself as existing outside of concrete materializations, and second, because of the surprisingly reciprocal permeation of the two forms of expression, with architecture turning toward deconstruction and theory suddenly focusing on the questions of urban centers and space. The explanation behind this is, again, a historical one. French theory took shape, across the Atlantic, in the space left empty by the disappearing critical and political functions of architecture, the same functions that motivated Le Corbusier's utopianism as well as Situationist psychogeography. The texts of French theorists reached American shores just as a depoliticized, "postmodern" architecture was replacing the more political, modernist tradition—which was revived from time to time by debates on current events, as in the recent discussion of the reconstruction of the World Trade Center and Daniel Libeskind's project, which was ultimately selected.

Critic Charles Jencks has even offered a very precise symbolic date for the fall of architectural modernism: July 15, 1972, at 3:32 p.m., which corresponds to the dynamite demolition, in Saint Louis, of a building by architect Minoru Yamasaki, which was typical of the functionalist working design and the industrial rationality of mid-twentieth-century architecture, as exemplified by exiled Germans Gropius and Mies van der Rohe, and also of Frank Lloyd Wright. It was also the year that architect Robert Venturi published *Learning from Las Vegas,* a manifesto to the glories of neon-lit chaos and the kitsch of the sequin-studded gambling capital. Postmodernism, which was inaugurated by the hybrid architecture of the 1970s, as seen in the work of Aldo Rossi, Michael Graves, and Ricardo Bofil, overturned the ideals of the preceding utopian minimalism in favor of irony and ostentation: it ushered in a mixture of historical styles, ranging from rococo to mannerism; a futuristic use of forms and materials, far removed from the modernist glass and cement cube; playful or parodic references to pop culture; and a preference for the arabesque and asymmetry over straight lines.

The resulting new relationship between space and building was literally, this time, *textual* in many respects: architects placed quotations from historical periods directly on building facades, and multiplied the use of different styles so as to raise the question of style itself (the very element that Bauhaus had tried to eliminate in its return to spare, unadorned aesthetics); they employed gaudy colors in formal defiance against the economic principle of using only what is strictly necessary, creating an art of extravagance—which, using an accumulation of aestheticizing detours, aimed to stand, in relation to modernism, as literature does to the phone book, adding a dose of irony. As this new postmodern architecture drew more theoretical attention, it became associated with other academic fields that were also beginning to employ similar theoretical discourses, such as comparative literature and film studies. Furthermore, alongside the run-of-the-mill postmodern crowd, predictable and flashy, the architectural world of the 1980s witnessed the emergence of several unique stylists, distinguished by their conceptual boldness and formal rigor—Dutchman Rem Koolhas, Anglo-Iraqi Zaha Hadid, and American Frank Gehry. This new avant-garde group formed the nucleus around which a *theoretical practice* of architecture took shape, through conferences and cooperative projects, and with extensive reference to French texts, written by Baudrillard, Virilio, and, above all, Derrida. A number of French authors had already served as catalysts for the discourses of the preceding era, during which Henri Lefebvre and Guy Debord were read in architecture schools, and the group who created the publication *Utopie,* inspired by Baudrillard and Hubert Tonka, were invited to an industrial design conference. Only this time, theory was more than just a tool—it came to represent a veritable architectural outlook. Much to the chagrin of the mainstream press, whose architecture critics quickly attacked the power recently acquired by these "intellectual parasites" controlling the "demiurge architects," as Paul Goldberger of the *New Yorker* and Ada Louise Huxtable of the *New York Times* claimed, at times even going so far as to ridicule this "time of supreme silliness which deconstructs and self-destructs," in the words of critic Vincent Scully.

Indeed, in the ferment of theoretical thought that was shaking not only architecture schools but also several firms, Derrida's writings were fast becoming texts of reference. With no set program other than drawing a critique of functionalism and the causalism that were inherent to achitectural activity, through essays and roundtable discussions were elaborated the diffuse principles of a deconstructionist (or *deconstructivist*) architectural approach, which declared itself "nonanthropocentric" and "posthumanist." In light of these new theories, architects aimed to play on the fragmentation of space, and reveal, in each project, the *impossibility* of achieving totality; to emphasize the notions of displacement and contamination; to replace planning with "events" orchestrated by the designer (hardly compatible with the ideal of bringing a project to fruition); to highlight the underlying conflict between various contradictory demands of the structure (particularly by repeating a formal motif from one building, or room, to another); and finally, in more concrete terms, to train the first truly interdisciplinary architects. And so it was that, beginning in this era, newly licensed architects were expected to be theorists *and* technicians, critics *and* performers, in order to overcome the dilemma of a profession, on the one hand, condemned to conservatism, in the sense that architecture has always reflected existing social structures and norms, and, on the other hand, nostalgic for its great post–Second World War social projects, when altering space was considered tantamount to changing the world. The introduction of theory into course reading lists and specialized publications (such as *Abstract*) took place, around 1987–88, at a time when the use of computers and the graphic design palette was becoming widespread, which were sometimes viewed as theoretical testing tools in themselves. The principal proponents of this new architectural *theorism,* who were often both practicing architects and academics, included Peter Eisenman, founder of the Institute of Architecture and Urban Studies of New York and director of the periodical *Oppositions,* the Franco-American Bernard Tschumi (head of Columbia's architecture school), his counterpart at New York's Cooper Union, Anthony Vidler, Derrida scholar Mark Wigley, Sanford Kwinter, cofounder of the publication *Zone,* avant-garde critic Jeffrey Kipnis and his predecessors James Wines and Charles Jencks, and even the old Philip Johnson—the critic and architect who shifted from the modernism that characterized the 1950s to embrace postmodernism, before later taking up the role of patron of the new movement, organizing, in 1988 at the MOMA in New York, the exhibition and series of conferences titled "Deconstructivist Architecture," following which the American press announced the advent of a far more extensive movement than actually emerged.

This movement, moreover, produced few effective materializations, which might better be described as experimental works than living space. Some examples include the "undefined facade" made by the research group SITE, which was exhibited in Houston, and the bizarre column, which does not touch the ground, installed by Peter Eisenman in a building lobby at the Ohio State University. Eisenman joined forces with Derrida, at Bernard Tschumi's encouragement, on a proposed project for the Parc de la Villette that aimed to represent spatially the notion of "Chora" taken by Derrida from Plato's *Timaeus*—a project that was never to be undertaken, but that, significantly, gave birth to a cult book.[27] The chief objective, inspired by Derrida's writings, was to harness the theoretical tools required to approach building, be it potential or existing, *as a language:* literary figures of metalepsis and metonymy and the genres of fable and parable provided material for this new discourse, the intertextual sources of various philosophical and literary references gave it a framework, and the "metaphysical" forms of architecture, the house and centered structures, were dismissed in a para-Derridean jargon. In a more extreme case, critic James Wines even lamented the fact that "rarely have contemporary buildings come close to the kind of sociological and psychological content expressed in, say, a Beckett play, a Magritte painting, or a Chaplin film."[28] Peter Eisenman goes a step further and recommends that "the reader augment a traditional reading of this book by also treating the texts and the book as a whole as objects, and by reading the houses, individually and in ensemble, as texts."[29] It was Mark Wigley, however, who most accurately conceptualized this implicit "contract" between text and building, deconstruction and architecture, that lays out the terms by which the latter provides theory with spatial metaphors and the lexicon of stability, whereas the former, in exchange, offers a philosophical backing and the elements of a "dislocation of space": rereading Derrida's early works, especially those touching on Husserl and geometry, Wigley shows the ways in which deconstruction is intrinsically *architectural*, in its arguments and vocabulary, as well as its original project, even though architecture is also its Achilles' heel, and could bring it to its ruin—thus reversing the simplistic perspective of an architecture that attempted to "apply" the theses of Derrida.[30]

Bernard Tschumi, whose perspective is closer to that of a practitioner, which is not surprising given that he owns an architectural firm based in New York and in view of his completed works at the Parc de la Villette, nevertheless reexamines his own practice through the lens of a diverse theoretical and literary body of work. Beginning with the pivotal concept of "disjunction" as an architectural project in itself, he compares architecture to Foucault's notion of madness, Lacan's theory of "dispersion," or even the concept of "transgression" found in Bataille's work, invoking texts by Blanchot and the young Philippe Sollers for support, integrating concepts of literary theory (such as *defamiliarization* and *destructuralization*), and he even confesses, in an author's note, that "to make buildings that work and make people happy is not the goal of architecture but, of course, a welcome side effect."[31] The series titled ANY (Architecture New York), which started in 1988, consisting of conferences and publications that appeared over a period of ten years, was a perfect example of this kind of evolution: it featured luxury brochures and periodicals, innovative design, international funding, and the involvement of not only Derrida but also Rem Koolhas and Frank Gehry, but its audience and consequences were grounded in the elite classes, and it ultimately had a meager impact on the architectural profession. By *detotalizing* buildings using Derrida's writings, or drawing on Deleuze in order to speak of an architecture based on the "fold" and "flow" inspired by his distinction between "smooth" and "striated" spaces, the trend of theory in the 1990s, which nonetheless left its mark on teaching approaches, did not allow a return to the political implications of modernist architecture, nor a bringing together of figures capable of putting effective projects into practice. This trend, it must be granted, did force architecture, in more textual terms, to test its own limits—to explore impossible forms, unrealized projects, and notions of the building as a historical narrative, and also to pose new questions that emerged with the arrival of new technologies.

11

THEORETICAL MACHINATIONS

> More than twenty years after meeting the ideas of Lacan,
> Foucault, Deleuze, and Guattari, I am meeting them again in
> my new life on the screen. But this time the Gallic abstractions
> are more concrete. In my computer-mediated worlds, the self
> is multiple, fluid, and constituted in interaction with machine
> connections; it is made and transformed by language; sexual
> congress is an exchange of signifiers; and understanding follows
> from navigation and tinkering rather than analysis.
>
> SHERRY TURKLE, *Life on the Screen*

WE MUST STILL ADDRESS the question of technology—including the
technology involved in the modes of circulation and inscription of French
theory. It is an issue that the notions of "apparatus" in Foucault's work,
"machine" in Deleuze's, or *technē* in Derrida's situate as a primary concern for French theorists. Strangely enough, American technorationalists
from every camp, sworn to the unconditional defense of the technological panacea, and the technophobic moralists of the French intellectual
scene, beneath a diametrically opposed conception of technology, con-
curred on one point: their strong aversion to the alleged "irrationalism"
of theorists like Foucault, Deleuze, and Derrida. Everything else seemed
to divide them: the former had for years dismissed the European "intellectual debates" as quibbling between sophists or as a literary hobby; from
the 1920s, the latter had viewed the American adoration of machines
and technology as the source of all evil and, furthermore, as evidence of
a dangerous streak of conformity in American society, which could be
"molded as easily as clay," in the words of André Siegfried.[1] Beyond the
differences between eulogizing the future and gazing wistfully into the

past, the factor that united the two camps was none other than the universalist measure of Man, as master over his tools in the first case, and critical observer of science in the second. In fact, beneath the genealogy (rather than the critique) of the humanism postulated in various forms by French theory, a question was waiting to emerge, one that seemed to antagonize the stalwart defenders of Reason or Conscience and which they even forbade theory to ask: "What if Man had come to an end, henceforth replaced by a nameless entity, a social interface, a genetic singularity, an accumulator of waves, or a tangle of technological connections? What if Man were merely a figure of technology?"

This question, which might itself evoke the realm of science fiction for some readers, has not produced as many academic essays or theoretical trends as the question of textuality or of minorities, because technology-oriented intellectuals in the United States rarely draw their ideas from literary studies. Still, it is a question that haunted the experimental practices of pioneers of the "technological revolution" that took place in the last two decades of the twentieth century. Many among them, whether marginal academics or self-taught technicians, read Deleuze and Guattari for their logic of "flows" and their expanded definition of the "machine," and they studied Paul Virilio for his theory of speed and his essays on the self-destruction of technical society, and they even looked at Baudrillard's work, in spite of his legendary technological incompetence. Strangely enough, Derrida's inclusion here was less conspicuous. Nevertheless, Derrida's grammatology and his critique of logocentrism can be read, according to Bernard Stiegler's convincing argument, as a continuation of the work of Leroi-Gourhan on the process of *hominization,* referring to the way in which *technē* invents man, and not the other way around: "The history of the gramme is that of electronic files and reading machines as well—*a history of technics* . . . both as inventive and as invented," a "hypothesis [that] destroys the traditional thought of technics, from Plato to Heidegger and beyond."[2] Although it was not taken into consideration by ordinary users of French theory, literary critics, or minority community activists, this hypothesis of a primary technical substratum of being, of a mechanical network, constituting the "human" as well as the "social" spheres of reality, nevertheless inspired in other arenas (in the margins of the academic and technological worlds, for example) entirely new uses of French texts—veritable *theoretical machinations.*

A Temporary Autonomous Zone

The first electronic networks were developed during the 1980s, but remained unknown to the general public, and were used only by experts in computer programming and by certain academics. These networks embodied, for some, a space for resistance, a social dead zone, a territory that was still imperceptible, in whose shelter they could build a new community and undermine the ruling powers. It was the era when the first groups of hackers emerged, were pursued by a new section of the FBI, and gave themselves mythological names like Lords of Chaos or Legion of Doom. They launched surprise attacks on major institutions, sabotaging databases and blocking national telephone networks, and formed, in Bruce Sterling's words, a veritable "digital underground."[3] It was also the era during which an atypical California academic, militant anarchist, and friend of Sylvère Lotringer and Jim Fleming, working under the pseudonym of Hakim Bey, introduced his theory of "Temporary Autonomous Zones," or TAZ. This term was destined for great success, because it would soon perfectly sum up this prehistory of the Internet, during which, for several years, without advertising or major commercial sites, still in the blind spot of those in power, a network became the medium for a genuine alternative political culture. Hakim Bey's text, which would soon attain cult status, and of which the first version was published in 1985, made an appeal for "clandestine illegal and rebellious use of the Web," and for the development of "a shadowy sort of *counter-Net*," or "Web," a structure built from horizontal exchanges of information, similar to the samizdat or the black market.[4] This book, which refers not only to Caliban of *The Tempest* and the myth of an uncorrupted colonist, but also to Guy Debord and the libertarians, makes significant use of French theory, from two main angles: on the one hand, it makes use of an eclectic pillaging of its concepts, invoking Baudrillardian perspectives of an "Age of Simulation," or "chaos science," and drawing upon concepts of "revolutionary nomadism," and "empty spaces," in which one hears echoes of Deleuze; on the other hand, there is also a sharp criticism of certain servile uses of French theory in universities, the "S/M intellectuals" of the 1980s, which Bey contrasts with free, playful uses of a theoretical corpus of authors ranging from Virilio to Guattari.[5]

Although this "zone" was soon to lose its autonomy, a certain mystical idea of sheltered utopia and online counterculture lived on, and continued to employ (and sometimes misappropriate) a few choice expressions from French authors. The passage in which Deleuze and Guattari compare the "thinker [to] a sort of surfer who 'slides' into new ways of thinking"[6]—even though they intended an analogy with actual water sports and not online navigation—was used to support the notion of a different mode of thought on the Internet, an alternative to linear reason. This was a digital and modular thinking that the student Web sites evoked above associated precisely with *theory.* The individual works of Félix Guattari had a distinct impact on the early American cybercommunity activists, because of its references to the "autopoietic machine" of biologist Francisco Varela, who uses the term to refer to an *ontogenesis* (the nonsubjective construction of the self) that is achieved through "machinic structures";[7] they also embraced this work for its more utopian discussion of "data banks" and new forms of "interactivity" that would "enable us to leave behind the current oppressive period and bring us into a post-media age defined by a reappropriation and a re-singularization of media use"[8]—in other words, they called for the equivalent of TAZ activists in a France where the Minitel was still king of network devices. But instead of being read as an invitation to *politicize* the network, to conceive of the Internet as a weapon of resistance, French theory became, above all, a pretext for playful self-reflective musing on technical practices. French texts provided a means of illuminating, *through theory,* a tool that had been little analyzed at the time. They were combed through for phrases or concepts that might aid in illustrating the role of the network, describing its mechanisms, and showing that its operation could be compared to that of French theory—this recurring comparison between the Internet and theory, a medium of technical dissemination and a corpus of philosophical texts, can be found across a wide range of Web sites on French theory: one gives a selective transcription of an interview with Baudrillard, turning it into a monologue on new technologies;[9] another offers its readers, under the name of "The Deleuze and Guattari Rhizomat," a bank of "pirated" quotes from the two authors, which is rearranged according to the order of links one clicks, as if the theory itself represented a randomizing machine;[10] yet another calls the themes of infection and dissemination discussed by Derrida a perfect description of the Net itself.[11] These French authors are presented, one after another, as prophets of the Internet—with Deleuze and Guattari as the key voices, because their botanical notion of the *rhizome,* an underground and nonhierarchical network of laterally linked stems, appears to be a precise foreshadowing of the Web.

These mirror effects between theoretical weaponry and uses of the network were reinforced by a mutual sense of novelty, discursive for the former and technical for the latter. Certain discussion forums suggested a rereading of every French text as a *network of concepts* and, conversely, that the Net itself be regarded as a successfully implemented program of French theory. One example is the famous "D&G List," a chat room and meeting place for fans and specialists of Deleuze and Guattari. Members from cities including Montreal, Sydney, Los Angeles, and Warwick (the stronghold of England's Deleuze followers) refer to the Internet as a "BwO zone" (as in "bodies without organs"), or speak of "machinic multiplications" and "conjunctive synthesis," a variation on the "disjunctive syntheses" championed by Deleuze and Guattari.[12] The Web site's users consider the opportunities for anonymity afforded by the Internet, along with all the forms of play made possible by e-mail, as a fulfillment of the wish expressed in *A Thousand Plateaus,* from the first page of the book, to "make ourselves unrecognizable," and to "render imperceptible . . . what makes us act, feel, and think."[13] In the United States, as in Europe, Internet-savvy followers of Deleuze and Guattari grouped these online tactics of invisibility and self-compounding under the general heading of "cybernetic materialism," insisting on the notion of continuity between the Net and the material world, but also between the user's body and the body formed by the Internet, and emphasizing the pleasure of losing oneself in the "rhizosphere"—in the same way that Jaron Lanier, coinventor of the first virtual-reality machine, employed a phrase reminiscent of Barthes to sing the praises of "the erotic body of the Net," the "unforeseeability" of hypertext as a "force of desire."[14] Whether we are considering *desire* as it is manifested in the Net or, instead, examining a theoretical discourse that imitates the Internet's mechanisms, a utopian anarchy, or more textual liberties (whether stylistic, lexical, or referential) embraced by users of theory-oriented e-zines, the Internet clearly gave rise to new forms of subjectification. Thanks to a new language, a veritable self-construction became possible at the junction between the new medium and the theoretical referent. There was a convergence of technical skill and theoretical backing, along with a personalized use of both the machine and the French texts in question, as each user borrowed from both to come up with new approaches—becoming as autonomous as the Web, while remaining just as "affirmitive" as the text, alone at their keyboards, or within the context of one of the countless online microcommunities.

This convergence afforded two main benefits. It provided Internet pioneers with language and concepts with which they could consider their practices, and it offered French theorists a much broader and more affordable channel of distribution than the publishing industry, which helped them gain readers outside the academic sphere. The promising political aspects of the Temporary Autonomous Zone did not, however, survive the rapid expansion of the Internet in the mid-1990s. Of all the alternative cybercultures and political subgroups born during the early days of the Internet, the movement that would emerge victorious, whose arguments had already permeated Hakim Bey's book, was that of the civil libertarians, veritable descendants of the first pioneers, who successfully championed the ideology of "free access": they argued for freedom of expression without regard to content, intransitive to the point of tautology, for the abolition of copyright laws in favor of self-regulating use by communities, and, above all, who brandished the notion of a "Washington conspiracy" and called for general privatization and dismantling of state power, which allegedly policed communication and encrypted its own internal messages. Promoted by John Perry Barlowe (ex-lyric writer for the Grateful Dead) and his Electric Frontier Foundation, along with several other white and regionalist lobby groups, the movement made the sacrosanct freedom of expression into the sole "content" of the Internet, instead of working toward an exogenous political program, some form of collective action *off* of the Internet—because it denied the very notion of public space. Although they may have won the ideological battle of the Internet, the libertarians lost sight of its *other* political interpretation, a more tactical one, less enchanted with technology itself, one that would defend a parallel use of the Net to serve the struggles that preceded it, one that Guattari hoped for in his image of free radio—and which the young Kroker couple, founders of the e-zine *Ctheory*, vainly championed, quoting Virilio and Deleuze, and lamenting, in 1997, the reactionary hedonism of an Internet without limits that had become, in their view, simply an immense amusement park.[15]

Cyborgs, DJ Decks, and Found Objects

The more dreamlike arena of science fiction remained open as a space in which to apply French theory. It provided the possibility of exploring mutations of the *posthuman* in literary imagination and cultural practices, because the apparent political promise of the Internet had not been fulfilled. Thus, it was not unusual for French theory and science fiction to be associated with each other. In some cases, this association provided a theoretical framework for a literary genre experiencing a major metamorphosis, but it also created a kind of fusion of the two discourses—sometimes resulting in a blending of simulation, abstract machines, and the microphysics of power into a fantastic, futuristic world, teeming with living objects, monsters, and concepts but devoid of human beings. This development marked a certain departure from the rigor of the French texts, which users had to some extent lost sight of, and from a sense of familiarity with the theoretical object, assimilated into the imaginary world of a society avid for all things futuristic. It is not so surprising, then, that a science journalist for the *New York Times* compared Foucault to Elastic Man from the Fantastic Four, because of his supple notion of identity, and critic Istvan Csicsery-Ronay went so far as to call theory a "form of SF," a specific register of science fiction.[16] Similarly, Sylvère Lotringer described Baudrillard as a "special agent in the extra-terrestrial space our world was fast becoming,"[17] and critic Erik Davis, writing in the *Village Voice,* calls Deleuze an "SF mutant," a "virtual philosopher" whose philosophy strives to be "science fiction" and whose "strange rhetorics and monster slang . . . allow us to leap into 'untimely' futures."[18]

In a less rhetorical sense, the very genre of science fiction opened avenues for French theory, as it evolved out of themes such as the exploration of distant worlds (across time or space) in the golden age of Ray Bradbury and *Star Trek,* and introduced us to hypotheses of parallel, underground, or invisible worlds; sci-fi literature, having begun as simple entertainment, produced a more critical perspective, allowing us to interpret the present, to examine the real world *hic et nunc,* which American Internet users dubbed RL, for "real life." At the cutting edge of this evolution was "cyberpunk" science fiction, inspired by the stories of early hackers, and the prospect of human mechanization (which it warns against), and which often claimed to be inspired by a French theoretical heritage. Figures such as John Shirley and the introspective Samuel Delany (who considers science fiction to be a "game of disorienting language"), and the pioneer of the genre, William Gibson, who in 1982 invented the term "cyberspace," were among the well-known novelists associated with French theoretical authors. They sometimes quoted Deleuze or Baudrillard in interviews and were read by their critics, or enlightened fans, through the lens of "simulation," or the "body without organs," a metaphor for the Internet. One key publication of the new genre, *Mondo 2000,* a cyberpunk fanzine soon to become science fiction's anthological dictionary, made reference to Deleuze and Guattari as well as to Bataille.[19] Also significant was the title of a recent academic book on Deleuze, which dubs him "the difference engineer,"[20] borrowing the title of the cult novel *The Difference Engine,* written by two masters of the sci-fi genre, Gibson and Bruce Sterling, who describe a vision in which the computer age bursts into the world of Victorian England. There were many echoes to be detected between cyberpunk culture and American appropriations of French theory. It was nonetheless through the figure of the cyborg, with all its theoretical implications, that French philosophers became established as the essential references for a futuristic, "posthumanist," and excessively technology-oriented world. This brings us into the domain of *theoretical science fiction.*

Cyborg theory was pioneered by feminist critic and science historian Donna Haraway, who for years served as chair in the department of history of consciousness at U. C. Santa Cruz. Haraway started out studying crystallography, and then the "construction" of apes used in experiments as a "primate" by nineteenth-century scientists (see *Primate Visions*)—determined to reveal a historical *invention* of nature, which, according to Haraway, includes the gradual naturalization of categories such as sex, race, and even class. Unlike most feminists, she considers biology and sociology of science much more useful for feminism's famous antiessentialist perspective than literature. This would explain Haraway's focus on the theme of cyborgs, defined in 1985 in her most famous work, "A Cyborg Manifesto," as a "cybernetic organism, a hybrid of machine and organism, a creature of social reality as well as a creature of fiction." The task at hand, then, is to embrace our cyborg dimension, linked to new technology and mechanical simulations, in order to move beyond two centuries of false "separations" (between human and animal, machine and organism, and even "science fiction and social reality"), but also to see past the feminist myth of a unified natural matrix, which Haraway opposed with the motto for which she became famous: "I would rather be a cyborg than a goddess," one of the few expressions in the American theoretical field, employing *the first person,* that become a central watchword.[21] Haraway argues in her writing for a veritable "cyborg politics," effecting a reevaluation, in prescriptive terms, of Deleuze's "machinic assemblages" and even of Foucault's "biopolitics," which she considers to be less the contemporary form of power (as it is in Foucault) than a desirable "premonition." Referencing the cybernetic extensions represented by computer technology and microelectronics, Haraway presents a case for transforming oneself into something closer to a machine, in order to discover new personal capabilities and to rid oneself of vestiges of naturalist ontology and illusions. Her writings soon inspired an expansion of the domain called "cyborg studies," which are prescriptive as well as academic, and of which the boldest manifestations were collected in 1995 into a manifesto volume that aimed to promote "machinic experiences" and theoretical practices on the Internet.[22]

One of the most active practitioners of these theories is transsexual academic Allucquere Rosanne (or "Sandy") Stone, former computer technician (born Zelig Ben-Nausaan Cohen) who, after a sex-change operation, became professor of theater and communication at University of Texas. Stone refers to new technology as "apparatuses for the production of community and of body" and defends the "schizo modes" of "collective structures whose informing epistemology is multiplicity and reinvention" of the self, for which she borrows the method found in Deleuze's "disruptive experiential bricolage."[23] Her defense of a multiple and mechanical identity is not, however, focused only on its political and sexual implications, as was the case in her 1995 work, whose title recalls Walter Benjamin: *The War of Desire and Technology at the Close of the Mechanical Age.*[24] She also performs theater herself, in productions that emphasize the amorphous pleasures of an entirely transgendered world, and which she refers to as "theory-performance" (a theoretical practice no longer taking the form of activism or visual representation, but rather, theatrical performance)—in which Stone, singing refrains she composes from theory set to music, or dancing to interactive choreographies, describes the cheerful misunderstandings caused by e-mailing with correspondents she has never met in person after having undergone her sex change. A similar issue also emerges as one of the principal themes of sociologist Sherry Turkle's successful book *Life on the Screen,* about new forms of identity that become possible online, in which she discusses male Internet users who find it easier to be "affirmative" under a woman's name, and women for whom it is often less dangerous to be "aggressive" as a man.[25] Turkle's book also makes frequent reference to French theory, praising the "culture of simulation" and, in the introduction, comparing the device of hyperlinks to Derrida's theory of writing.[26]

Nevertheless, beyond the (anti)feminist theatrical performances and provocations, the perspectives of Haraway, Stone, and their successors remained grounded in the academic sphere, in which they employed French theory as a sort of discursive motor, a machine used to produce a machine's *discourse.* For a more tangible example of "mechanical" applications of theory, we ought to turn our attention to the specific culture of self-taught musicians who, on both sides of the Atlantic, have been developing alternative electronic music since the early 1990s, beginning with the first experimental DJs, who are to jungle and commercial techno roughly what serial composition (which was, incidentally, a favorite of Deleuze's) is to the ballad tradition. Deleuze, in fact, was a major reference for electronic music as it developed its methods. In Europe, for example, the ex-punk anarchist Achim Szepanski founded, in 1991 in Germany, the electronic music label Mille Plateaux, and the Brussels-based label Sub Rosa released, in 1996, a tribute album titled "Folds and Rhizomes for Gilles Deleuze." Many American and English DJs, including Kirk, DJ Shadow, Mouse on Mars, and former philosophy student Paul Miller (aka DJ Spooky)—who included quotations from *Anti-Oedipus* on the covers of his early albums, thus spreading Deleuze and Guattari's thought in record stores' display bins—apparently found a perfect description of their musical approach in the work of these two authors: the system constituted by the DJ, his or her turntables, and the crowd form a "desiring machine"; the musical trance it can produce allows fans to turn into "bodies without organs"; the brief snatches of music ("vinyl fragments") undermined in the mix can be described as "sonorous blocks of affect," whose "molecular flows" come together to form "chance sonic assemblages," following the operations of cutting, scratching, and sampling performed live by the DJ on his decks.[27]

Experimental DJs are on the cutting edge of technoculture, and their still less visible counterparts in the Internet sector are Web designers and programmers; both were crucial figures of postmodern society as it was foreshadowed to American readers by French theory. This shadowy figure of the DJ, mixing music under an artistic pseudonym, heralds the twilight hour for star icons, the death of the author, and the dawn of an ironic recycling of influences, if only by erasing the clear boundary separating the listener from the composer (or musician). The DJ gradually substitutes the art of "sequencing," with all its tricks and trends, for the creation myth, and guides his fans through the maze of a fragmented, molecularized, and generally decentered pop culture. Simply rearranging modernism's "found objects" (by recontextualizing and subverting pop songs or remixing new versions of rock albums) is not enough; these DJs go further and explore the depersonalized world of postindustrial sounds, to experience the madness born out of the quivering waves that surround us, waves of sound, vibrations, and information. DJs in general, however, were in fact also products of a temporary autonomy zone, and were soon to be engulfed by the popularity of commercial "mixing," and in turn reincorporated into purely entertainment-oriented channels, in which mentioning Deleuze or Artaud would only meet with perplexity or yawns.

There is perhaps no clearer embodiment of this ever-shifting counterculture than the eclectic DJ Spooky. This young black New Yorker, who started the SoundLab group and the musical genre known as "illbient," has been performing since 1995 under the nickname "subliminal kid," and also writes for several technotheoretical fanzines he inspired (for example, *Artbyte* and, more recently, *21C*), as well as on the Web sites of his associates, a parallel project of critical thought that he himself conceives as an elliptical "sample" of concepts and references. Spooky brings together Duchamp and Frantz Fanon, Nietzsche and Philip Glass, haiku and jazz, music as an "extension of science fiction," and culture as an "exquisite corpse" of quotations "in ruins," while Andy Warhol and Jimi Hendrix are seen as heralds of "a pataphysical world of disjunctions and fluid transitions."[28] In summary, we see that it was through elements as disparate as jazz and "cutups," theories of excess and creative misreading, artistic reappropriation and DJ Spooky's "data clouds," in a broad continuum of intensity and fragmentation, random citations, and sudden shifts in register that French theory became, in the United States, associated with this culture of subversion—and we should note that this link was born out of the actual practice of rearrangement, or a certain combination producing a real event, and was no longer created in the sheltered surroundings of universities, grounded in legitimate histories and established discourses.

Pop: Haphazard Circulation

It was cinema, however, that would provide certain hypotheses of French theory, duly adapted for the big screen, with their largest American audience. The textbook case is Andy and Larry Wachowski's 1998 film *The Matrix*. The movie depicts a small group of rebels who, with the help of their savior, Neo (Keanu Reeves), continue to fight the absolute control of machines in a world where computers reign; because they require human beings as a source of energy, however, the computers have enslaved them through a program created specifically for human use, the "matrix" (a term borrowed from William Gibson), an exact sensory copy of the vanished late-twentieth-century world—that is, the complete fictional equivalent of the "simulacrum," the "copy without an original," which, according to Baudrillard, is the product of modernity. In the film's opening scenes, endlessly analyzed by fans with a penchant for theory, the hero furtively flashes a copy of *Simulacra and Simulation,* which he opens to the last chapter, "On Nihilism." Although this theoretical calling card, which lasts only a few seconds, may have contributed to the film's cult following, it remains, nevertheless, deceptive: the film's main elements, from the Christlike parable of Neo (an anagram of "One") to the group's heroic resistance against the machines, all of which are depicted using extensive action scenes and special effects, have little to do with Baudrillard's writings. As the *New York Times* concluded, the filmmakers "skillfully retold an archetypal messiah story with a dash of postmodern theory."[29]

When asked by the producers to participate as "theoretical" consultant during the preparations for the two sequels to *The Matrix,* which appeared in 2003, accompanied by major publicity campaigns, Baudrillard declined the offer, later commenting that theory is, for the Wachowski brothers, at most a vague "asymptotic horizon." Baudrillard had similarly refused an offer to contribute to producing the TV series *Wild Palms* in 1993, produced by Oliver Stone, which told the story of a virtual-reality magnate who seized power using "holograms" he controlled. Other examples of French theory's "cameos" in pop culture, generally far less convincing than that of the opening scene of *The Matrix,* constitute a broad, loosely linked network of concepts and theoretical references circulating through certain innovative products of the culture industry, associated together so that inspiration may be drawn from them: taken from fragmented readings of French texts (often by former students who have ended up working for major production studios), they were cycled through the cyberpunk trend and even certain video games, and their echoes can be heard in some mainstream rock groups' songs (U2's *Zooropa* album is one example), and even came to permeate (more or less with the creators' intent) several successful Hollywood films dealing with the theme of a duplicate world, or mechanical simulation. The films of Canadian filmmaker David Cronenberg are one example, starting with *Videodrome* in 1983, in which a man is swallowed by a television set, and particularly *Existenz,* which depicts life as a video-game scenario; other examples include Peter Weir's *The Truman Show* (1998), in which Jim Carey is the victim of reality TV taken to cosmic dimensions; there is also *Minority Report* by Steven Spielberg (2002), which shows us a panoptic regime extended to the level of psychic (and, therefore, self-fulfilling) anticipation of all human crimes.

Nevertheless, French theoretical references (particularly from Baudrillard's work) to which these filmmakers do not explicitly lay claim but which are trumpeted incessantly by fans and critics were miscast in these productions, if not placed in the service of a profound misinterpretation: theories on concepts like simulation, hyperreality, or derealization of the negative have nothing to do with the humanist mythology, a mixture of Christian morality and political liberalism, on view in these stories of humans controlling computers and being pitted against a mechanical apocalypse (e.g., *The Matrix*), or in the condemnations of state demiurges (*Minority Report*), or of TV's illusory world (*The Truman Show*). The fact is that if these French authors, so admired in the university context, can be appropriated in support of the exact ideological message they were writing against, it should indicate that we are dealing with a situation of dispersion, fragmentation, and superficial, random circulation of mere *traces* of French theory; the latter has been exported far from academic institutions, which would ordinarily regulate the use and terms one makes of these theories, and has emerged in the workings of the porous and infinitely malleable machine of the American culture industry. Accordingly, any use becomes permissible, freed from the logic of discursive production that governs the university. Even the mainstream press, which is a mechanism of prescription and legitimation of cultural industries, peppered its articles, according to the terms currently in fashion and the backgrounds of its journalists, with skillfully integrated doses of French theory: an article in the *New York Times* on Los Angeles's parking lots evokes "a city that would have sent Roland Barthes into spasms,"[30] and the rock critic for the *Village Voice* describes the relationship between singer Kathleen Hanna and her audience by quoting Lacan in terms of "ever-proliferating, always-was-there . . . jouissance."[31]

To consider examples in another arena—less elliptical, less subject to the one-dimensional logic of the media, but even more whimsical than the previous ones, playing lightly with their subject matter—certain widely read novels also work French theory into their plots, either through a single quotation or through an evocation of the entire corpus, constituting a *nonacademic* literary use of these theoretical texts. Percival Everett, in his novel *Glyph,* recounts the kidnapping and political negotiations in which Ralph Ellison was involved as a child—he was the eighteen-month-old son of a famous Derrida scholar, but, by magic, could understand and speak the language of poststructuralism better than his father—even if the novel's theoretical methods and epigraphs make this difficult material for uninitiated readers.[32] One young professor, Patricia Duncker, attempted the feat of turning Foucault into a character in her novel, *Hallucinating Foucault,* where she places him in a love triangle that links together the eponymous philosopher, the student narrator, and French novelist Paul Michel, whom the student, out of love for his prose, has sworn to free from the asylum where he has been committed.[33] More akin to the academic satire, to which David Lodge and Malcolm Bradbury had restored its respectability, *Book* by Robert Grudin explains the murder of Adam Snell, a classical humanist who perished on a campus overrun by radicals.[34] Even more recently, and in a more classical vein, there is Saul Bellow's *Ravelstein,* a portrait in novel form of his deceased friend, conservative critic Allan Bloom, and also *The Human Stain* by Philip Roth, which shows the misadventures of black Jewish professor Coleman Silk in the hell of a PC world, both of which display the traditional narrative mainspring that the theoretical controversy came to resemble.[35] We could easily multiply the examples of such indirect traces of theory, more or less diluted, and sometimes scarcely detectable, ranging from articles in the music press to sitcom dialogues, advertising slogans, and romantic comedies depicting educated characters—examples that would, on their own, deserve an entire, exhaustive study, and, furthermore, suggest an examination of contemporary methods of circulating the work of canonical intellectuals.

The fact remains that this haphazard dissemination of the traces of French theory throughout the wide world of American pop culture was produced (as was their more emphatic, sedentary, and reasoned inscription into academic discourse) by a certain cultural mechanism or "machination": not in the sense of a conspiracy, but in terms of the various technologies of cultural distribution—the culture industry, the media system, and writing itself. The difference is that the industrial *dissemination* and the academic *inscription* of these same traces took place according to symmetrically inverse modalities: the latter was vertical, textual, and anthological, employing the institutional violence implicit in closed systems of memorization (such as books, courses, dogmas) that American academics, unable to open them up, have been striving to destabilize since the emergence of theory; the culture industry's use was horizontal, disposable, and forgetful, blithely condemned to an inconsequential succession of publications and events, ceaselessly accumulating them as though the better to forget them. In this sense, we might say that in the United States French theory continually "disappeared" in the production of its effects.

PART III

There and Back

12

THEORY AS NORM: A LASTING INFLUENCE

> In America, the majority draws a formidable circle around the
> activity of thought. Within these limits, the writer is free; but
> woe to him who dares to step outside of them.
>
> TOCQUEVILLE, *Democracy in America*

WHAT IMPACT, in the long run, did French theory have in the United
States? The answer depends entirely on one's perspective: we might as
well ask what tangible effects a discourse, a philosophical proposition,
or even a sequence of phrases have had on humanity or on History—it
is an old line of questioning that has always caused philosophers sleep-
less nights. The question itself is, however, not so much theoretical as
ballistic: how far and how deep did French theory go? And what were
its caliber and aftereffects? That this corpus of French texts has had an
effect in the United States is clearly proven by pointing to several facts,
namely, that American academics do not think in the same terms as they
used to, that from Hollywood mavericks to postmodern essayists these
theoretical texts may be used to justify or to reenchant the current state
of things, or that, inversely, many art galleries or activist groups have
found in French theory arguments for the subversion, if not the outright
refusal, of the new American order. This question as to the *depth* of its
impact lends itself to infinite metaphorical elaborations, which are laid
out in the style held dear by Americans. French Theory: plague or gad-
fly? Ice pick or toothpick? An indecipherable virus or simply a misappropriation? Avid for tangible results and solid proof, some have opted
for the latter series, claiming that it has merely had a benign, amusing

impact, in keeping with the discursive and institutional limits inherent to the American infatuation with French theory.

It is true that the increasingly radical perspectives of minority groups who seize on the key texts of French theory were, as we have seen, first and foremost a rhetorical technique. The issues of writing and textuality were explored from every point of view, more thoroughly than at the height of the literary theory era in France, but with disappointing results outside of the literary domain and, a fortiori, outside of universities. The trend of sprinkling bits of theory into productions of the cultural industry, such as the press and the cinema, for the sake of its subversive sheen or its intellectual backing, generally resulted in completely emptying the theoretical reference of its content—as well as its philosophical implications. Should we therefore conclude that French theory had *no impact* on an American nation more concerned with searching for jobs, embarking on the next global crusade, and as always, "amusing themselves to death,"[1] rather than examining the status of the text or considering the concept of a minority? The main argument advanced by those who, whether for or against theory, are tempted to answer "yes" is to consider French theory's success as nothing more than a passing trend, an infatuation without any lasting effects, simply a particularly active stage in the uninterrupted succession of intellectual products that academics, condemned to coming up with ever-original projects, embrace one after another. This argument constructing French theory as an ephemeral fashion runs contrary to the actual epistemic transitions taking place. The proof was thought to lie in the ongoing decline of French theory that had ostensibly occurred since the early 1990s under the pressure wrought by increasingly virulent attacks. Having reached the turn of the century, however, we find that in looking back over the past twenty-five years, the facts do not really support this hypothesis; at best they lead to an uncertain conclusion in which each point may be viewed in more than one way.

In the first place, the proliferation of different schools of thought, subfields, and metadiscourses makes the situation considerably less clear than it was in the 1980s, when radical muticulturalists and deconstructionists had the field to themselves. Although critic Herman Rapaport views the current situation as an inextricable muddle, or a "theory mess,"[2] we might instead recognize the richness of a composite theoretical field that could never be called sterile. If we consult American intellectuals, another impression that emerges is that French theory has somehow become commonplace, or lost its original aura, falling victim to what Max Weber, writing on the sociology of religions, calls the "routinization" of charisma. Or perhaps it was simply the victim of the aging process that typically befalls all European products exported to the United States—they are considered indispensable for a while, and then, after the fashion has passed, are seen as nothing more than Eurotrash, disposable and depreciated, as they begin to smack of European "bad taste" in Americans' eyes. This back-and-forth treatment of innovations is, in fact, more the result of a general law that is borne out in the history of institutions than of French theory having a superficial impact in the United States. Every intellectual innovation adopted in the academic world by one generation soon becomes absorbed into an "old world, which, however revolutionary its actions may be, is always, from the standpoint of the next generation, superannuated and close to destruction," as Hannah Arendt observes, defending the inherent conservatism of education.[3] In academia, the word *change* itself is deceptive and its implementation takes peculiar forms; even the slightest recognizability requires a kind of durability. One sign of the times was a new seminar on theory taught at Berkeley in 2003 by Foucault scholar Didier Éribon, whose title was "The Seventies Revisited." Is this meant to indicate that an era has come to an end, and that French theory has become an exotic curio from a bygone decade, as a part of "retro" fashion that, as in France, also includes music and clothing styles? It is rather a question of drawing some conclusions about that decade *for today*. And, beyond this one example, we must conclude that French theory has had a lasting effect: the persistent attacks against it, the loss of its aura, the fact that it has become almost commonplace and has been the object of retrospective accounts—all of this indicates that theory has in fact been *normalized,* adopted, and institutionalized, penetrating deep into American intellectual practices, and remaining a fixture on class reading lists.

The Refrain of Decline

Opposition to French theory, therefore, does not indicate its loss of aura; the opposition preceded this loss, and can even be traced back to its moment of arrival. There were, first of all, several efforts of resistance devoted to checking the progress of *theorism:* some had existed for ages, like Boston University's literature department, where another "anti-MLA" was founded—Roger Shattuck and Chrisptopher Hicks's ACLS (Association of Critics and Literary Scholars)—while others were begun during the ideological struggles of the 1980s, when some moderates turned against the popularity of theory, taking their cue from Princeton University Press, or the famous *New York Review of Books*. It was the particular violence of the antitheory diatribes of the 1990s that might serve to support the view that theory was in decline, when in fact the coarseness of the accusations was simply proportionate to the fame of their targets, the price to pay for their success. We must again consider the commentaries of critic Camille Paglia, whose patriotic zeal soon made her caustic arguments known far beyond the academic world: her previously quoted article, appearing in 1991 on the front page of the *New York Times Book Review,* was reprinted by the *San Francisco Examiner,* then again by *Cosmopolitan,* and Paglia later published a longer version in a collection of essays, which became a top seller.[4] Paglia's working-class background and her exploits in the Sikorsky aerospace factories, where she taught English literature to workers, lend an air of moral credibility to her supposedly populist argument. Paglia sets up a direct opposition between the fun, innocent vitality of American pop culture and the moaning of these "pampered American academics on their knees kissing French bums." She boasts of "choosing" rock over Samuel Beckett, and the Marx brothers over Paul de Man, and even dreams of seeing Aretha Franklin whip Lacan and his friends down the Champs-Élysées—"we didn't need Derrida, we had Jimi Hendrix,"[5] she insists, offering a comparison so incongruous that it only reveals the extent of French theory's cultural impact.

Paglia's ire against Foucault is especially virulent: she refers to him as "incompetent," claims that he "made smirky glibness an art form," but also that he was "one of the dullest, most frigid and constipated theorists of sex ever," calling him an "armchair French leftist" and even an "arrogant bastard."[6] Paglia's text is driven onward by a veritable frenzy of Francophobia. The "decentered subject," she says, is "one of the fattest pieces of rotten French cheese" that Americans have ever swallowed, and the concept of decentering is claimed to have been originally inspired by the fact that "France . . . was lying flat on her face under the Nazi boot"; the clichéd image of the French as "cold, elegant, ironic, linear" and as having "affectations [and] pomposity" that conceal a total "intellectual emptiness" leads finally to a rousing revolutionary conclusion, a call for liberation from French "ideology," similar to the one that took place in 1776 under British rule: "Let's dump the French in Boston Harbor and let them swim home."[7] This outburst was, in a sense, a defense of America as a *cultural exception*. In recognition of her unabashed opinions, and for having, in her supporters' view, opened the eyes of her countrymen, who were "fatuously taking as literal truth statements that were merely the malicious boutades of the flâneur,"[8] Paglia became a star, and was named "intellectual pinup of the 90s" by the tabloid *Newsday*.[9] Her name appeared on the cover of *New York* magazine, *Harper's,* and the *Village Voice,* and she made *Rolling Stone*'s end-of-the-year list, and she even reached the pages of the international press in *Der Spiegel* and *Corriere della Sera,* also appearing in publications in Moscow and Barcelona. Nevertheless, as with the neoconservatives' attacks in the preceding decade, including those inspired by the Paul de Man affair, Paglia's provocative claims served to exaggerate, in the mind of the public, the real impact of French theory on American youth. In this case, the criticism turned French theory into a genre of its own in contemporary culture, like free jazz and adventure films, or at least made it appear to be the intellectual worm in the fruit—bursting with juice—represented by American cultural activity. The controversies that followed Paglia's attacks, though less public or less high-profile, had similar effects.

Published the following year, critic James Miller's biography of Michel Foucault drew a parallel between the latter's theories of power and his alleged "passion" for the sadomasochistic practices of San Francisco's back rooms, which he did frequent in the late 1970s: in a reductively biographical interpretation, based on shaky psychoanalytic notions, Miller considers the life and work of Foucault as representative of the same "death instinct"—as shown in both the death of the author and his real death—inspiring many newspapers, following this book, to similarly reduce Foucault's entire career to the same simplistic perspective.[10] The books of political analyst Tony Judt, while based on sounder historical grounds, were just as dubious ideologically, vilifying, in the same breath, the "totalitarian" wanderings and irresponsibility of French avant-garde intellectuals, so as to restore the champions of democratic reformism, or figures of the French intellectual "center," such as Camus or Mendès-France.[11] In other fields, the furor was even more extreme: art critic Robert Hughes used the fluid metaphors of a tsunami and of a putrid swamp, lamenting the impossibility of succeeding in academia unless "you add something to the lake of jargons whose waters (bottled for export to the States) well up between Nanterre and the Sorbonne and to whose marshy verge the bleating flocks of poststructuralists go each night to drink";[12] speaking more laconically, a trio of historians determined to rescue their discipline from a French "relativism" that they referred to as "pure repugnance."[13] It is difficult to know how to make sense of this rich palette of tired insults and mockeries, except by remembering that the fervor of these calls for cultural independence was proportionate to the admiration inspired by the French writers, in what Walter Benjamin calls the "fetishism of the master's name."

In fact, instead of discrediting the theoretical movement, this explosion of diatribes actually set off a retroactive process in which the attacks contributed to maintaining the well-being of their object. Vilifying French theory as a category was also a way of recognizing this group of authors and concepts; it legitimated a premise, and validated through negation a movement that the most enthusiastic proponents of French theory had struggled to present as a homogeneous entity. Such virulent criticism also had the salutary effect, as we have seen, of shifting this specialized, if not abstruse, field of study into the center of American public space. Besides, in order to highlight certain works, at the expense of the category of theory considered as a whole, the storm of controversy inspired some critics to play one author against another, condemning, for example, Baudrillard's theoretical games so as to construct a contrasting eulogy of the more important work of Deleuze and Guattari, or stigmatizing the political ambiguities of deconstruction in order to better praise Lyotard, with his ability to examine the "political pertinence" of a "critical thought."[14] Thus, in addition to the quantitative effect, which provided French theory a general reactivation, we might also add an effect of *selective* reactivation—which functions according to the principle that criticism amounts to granting the object a place in the shared arena of discussion, and conferring on it all the seductive characteristics associated with outcasts—which forces each participant to clarify his or her positions and distinguish between the different French theorists. More important, the simple fact that such debates, whether they were ideological or more specialized, were focused on the theoretical tradition, confirms its role as a guiding principle of the American intellectual scene, according to the logic Bourdieu describes as the translation (in the geometrical sense) of the entire "système de goûts": "To impose a new producer, a new product and a new system of taste on the market at a given moment means to relegate to the past a whole set of producers, products and systems of taste, all hierarchized in relation to their degree of legitimacy."[15] The translation that took place was significant and lasting, and cannot be reduced to an ephemeral fashion trend—thus we find a distinctly different situation *before* and *after* the arrival of theory in the American public sphere. To put it simply, theory did not merely enable a reenchantment of the art scene and the academic world that lasted for only a few years, but rather brought about a long-term change in Americans' relationship to knowledge.

Another factor contributing to the belief that French theory is in decline is that the influence of French culture in general has been steadily and inexorably waning in the United States for the past fifty years, which leads some to conclude that theory is in decline, even while granting that theory has something peculiarly "homegrown" and American about it. The broader decline is undeniable, even when one does not take the mood swings of the aggressive American press into consideration: fewer and fewer students are studying French in school, while Spanish and Chinese increase in popularity; fewer books are being translated from French (in part because of the crisis in university press sales already mentioned); and, following the decline of France's international role, one can observe a decrease in the space devoted to French culture in the mainstream American press. The number of articles on France was seven times lower between 1994 and 1998 than between 1920 and 1924, according to the highly official *Reader's Digest Guide to Periodical Literature*.[16] In this general context of decline, we might hastily assume that certain texts are also experiencing a decline, the very texts that American universities have been reappropriating over the past thirty years, and that there is hardly any French politico-cultural clout to promote in the United States. We might go a step further and suggest, following Derrida's view, that French criticisms of humanism and semanticism have perhaps *always* been viewed by some, ever since their emergence in the United States, as an intellectual movement in decline, conceived in decline, that some prefer to view as a free fall: "From the beginning of the nineteen seventies, . . . they were already beginning the prognosis . . . of the fall [of deconstruction], its decadence and decline. They were already saying that it was damaged, that it was going over the dam," he suggests in an ironic tone, adding that "what is dead is dead. The fall takes place once, and it's over. But when it comes to the end . . . of French theory, the fall lasts, it repeats itself, it keeps insisting, it keeps multiplying . . . this suspended imminence, this . . . desire for the fall."[17] In this sense, decline was not the fate of French theory so much as its very theme, reflecting its foiled ambitions.

As for the 1990s, looking beyond the storm of diatribes, the decade emerges as one during which French theory became institutionalized. Adopted as a standard group of texts, and criticized even by certain minority activists, it became less closely associated with identity-based radicalism than in the preceding decade. Reviled by the press, theory nonetheless lost much of its controversial dimension in the universities, where the texts of Foucault, Derrida, and Deleuze were waiting patiently, less incendiary than in earlier days, in humanities class reading lists for their student readers. The controversy gradually fell silent, and many critics then produced strictly academic overviews of the movement, with less theatrical belligerence than theory had previously inspired. The year 2001 saw the publication of the *Derrida Reader,* a collection devoted to the philosopher's impact on the entire humanities field, which marked the changing tone of commentaries on theory: the table of contents offers an anaphoric series of didactic roles ("Derrida and . . ." according to the range of disciplines, such as literature, aesthetics, ethics, and law); in the guise of an ambitious project (namely, to consider the future of the humanities), the preface writer suggests a view of Derrida that is both more strictly academic and more riddled with jargon than those of his predecessors; deconstruction appears bravely defending itself against accusations of nihilism, but no longer has the same violent effect on its "imperialist" adversaries.[18] The documentary film *Derrida,* by Amy Ziering Kofman and Kirby Dick, was similarly greeted with critical acclaim that included none of the excess that dominated earlier attitudes inspired by French theory. It did not escape without a few typical witticisms about his fame ("Derrida is the Madonna of thought," for example), but the film inspired interpretations of an almost . . . Derridean nature, lamenting the fact that the camera fails to capture the "play" or "Derrida's irony about himself."[19] Apart from the example of Derrida, we should note that, although theory courses may later have been titled "After Theory," or "Post-Theory," they still used the same list of authors, with closely related themes, perhaps with slightly more emphasis on literary texts; they thus offered the same cast, now considered classic, of names and movements, organizing a rotation of certain other isolated figures, such as Walter Benjamin, Ludwig Wittgenstein, or Peter Sloterdijk, around a hub of theorists that remained essentially French.[20]

Vive le Cliché: Culturalist Preconceptions

The explanation of French theory's success, which we have attempted to unfold in the course of this book, has deliberately underplayed the role of cultural representations, concluding, along with many American participants in the phenomenon, that if French theory managed to take root in the United States, it was because there was a fundamental interest in *theory* rather than in France itself. We must now look more closely at this question. The notion of discontinuity, which experts on the transatlantic axis hold so dear, and which attempts to magnify small cultural differences into historical divides and conflicts of values, is ultimately a myth invented by journalists, or at least a distortion created by ethnographers: both the latter and the former are quite naturally interested more in the contrasts, which serve to justify their activities, than in the similarities, which are far less exciting—and which bring up the guilt-inducing image of a homogeneous "first world," stretching clear across the Atlantic. Whether true or false, the deep resonance of this notion of discontinuity in our thinking has given it an important role. First of all, it brought us the idea of a discontinuity between concept and reality: thus, French theory could hardly help winning followers in a country where, in Henry Ford's words, "history is bunk"; in this paradise of social mobility and unrestrained capital, one imagines, Deleuze and Guattari's schizo-theory could not fail to find a home—in one of the endless variations on the theme of a dialectical, complementary Franco–American relationship, in both discourse and practice, vitalism and genealogy, European words and American things. This schema was certainly not invented by the discourse of journalism: well before the arrival of French theory, it was the result of two centuries of exchanged cultural narratives—an exchange that began even earlier, if we count the accounts of the earliest evangelists—creating the idea of a dialectical interlocking between the Old and New Worlds, and the widely accepted image of the United States as a sort of referent of French concepts, with European thought being seen as *always-already-realized.*[21]

Tocqueville himself contributed to this discourse, emphasizing, for example, Americans' "naturally" Cartesian points of view: "America is . . . the one country in the world where the precepts of Descartes are least studied and best followed," because Americans "have not needed to draw their philosophic method from books; they have found it within themselves."[22] Similarly, a century later, André Breton claimed that his remarks on Surrealism in major cities "apply more to New York than they do to Paris."[23] Sartre also described the United States as a fulfillment of the dialectic: he viewed the country as a revelation, where, in the streets of New York, Hegelian intellect is reconciled with matter, "this concrete, daily presence of a flesh and blood Reason, a visible Reason."[24] Philippe Sollers rightly observes that, for Paul Morand as well as all the other French writers faced with the enormity of the United States, writing about America requires that they enter "a mode of superproduction" and place themselves *in writing* "according to the extent of the audiovisual realm surrounding them."[25] The list of such authors is long, and even includes some of those in the theoretical field. Some took up the torch of a tradition of writing that attempted to come to grips with the staggering scale of the country, such as Baudrillard, with *America,* or Lyotard, with his novel *Pacific Wall;* in some cases they can be read as seismographers of the American tectonic situation, or tranquilizers for American anxieties. Everything would lead us to believe that, in writing about "simulacra" or "dissemination," they were bringing to light some mystery of the contemporary United States that its everyday observers had failed to notice—as though French theory and America *resembled each other.* This was the case with Foucault when he found, in the United States, the kinds of "new modes of life" and "construction of the self" whose classical antecedents he had examined in his own work.[26] Julia Kristeva also found that, in teaching theory to American students and young artists, she had the impression "of speaking to people . . . [for whom] it corresponded to something lived, to a pictorial, gestural, or sexual experience."[27] And Baudrillard, of course, found the paradoxes about which he wrote *already* materialized in the existence of Disneyland, a Nevada highway, or the film *Apocalypse Now*—futuristic America thus becoming the original of which out-of-date Europe is only a copy. It became a match between American schizophrenia and European paranoia, vitalism against idealism, discourse against intensity: these pairings naturally serve to prolong the worn-out and often repeated view that America provides entertainment and Europe provides philosophy, but they must nevertheless be recognized as relevant to the objectives of French theory. American readers constantly mention its radical unfamiliarity to their usual ways of thinking, while *at the same time* recognizing theory's radical approach as uniquely capable of laying hold of the madness particular to America.

Theory was thus complementary through its otherness, enlightening because of its radically different approach, and also perhaps simply sought after because it was unavailable locally. Nothing better demonstrates the importance of this old Franco-American discontinuity in the success of French theory than the *a contrario* example of the failure of recent French philosophy—a strain that more closely resembled its American counterparts—to find a foothold in the United States: it seemed invisible because it was redundant, and useless because it was too familiar. In 1994, literature professor Thomas Pavel and his colleague in political science, Mark Lilla, in cooperation with the Fondation Saint-Simon and with French followers of Aron's work, launched a project called New French Thought, or NFT, whose ideological aims were clear: to establish, against the monopoly of French followers of Nietzsche and Heidegger, the works of famous philosophers of democracy, composed of thinkers carrying on the legacies of Tocqueville and Kant, including Pierre Manent, Gilles Lipovetsky, Alain Renaut, and Blandine Kriegel, but also Jacques Bouveresse and Marcel Gauchet. The "New French Thought" series published by Princeton University Press was inaugurated by an eponymous conference and, funded by the cultural service of the French embassy (it, too, determined to find some new successors to Foucault and Derrida), it released English publications of the important works of French liberalism in the 1980s. NFT, which its organizers hoped would become the new reigning acronym and dethrone the master figures of "la pensée 68," quickly showed itself to be a failure: sales were lackluster, press reviews few and far between, and the academic world turned a cold shoulder. "How different in tone, ambitions and claims," remarked Edward Said;[28] and leftist journalist Richard Wolin, one of the last people one would suspect of favoring the French theory movement, remarked that "a new generation of neoliberal thinkers . . . who were politically respectable but intellectually unexceptional" has tried to "reenter the discourse of contemporary democracy" against the current of the previous French "avant-garde."[29] Without entering into the ideological debate, it still emerges clearly that the culturalist argument was at work here: the American intellectual scene had more use for a *critical* system of thought that remained foreign (imported from Germany) or an *intensive* system of thought (imported from France) than for a legalistic one, which its own thinkers, such as William James or Michael Ryan, had already been refining, more capably than anyone else, for the past century. It is not surprising, then, that Gayatri Spivak and Michael Ryan, writing about the emergence of the new philosophers in France—whom they somewhat curiously associate with an "anarchism" inherited from French theory—commented on the redundance of these newer thinkers' contributions, in comparison with the "least-government principle . . . of ordinary American conservatism" and with the "conservative libertarian position" of an "ongoing non-revolutionary revolt."[30] The *difference* that theoretical works presented was thus not only a political theme, but it provided them with an entry visa to the United States.

In summary, French theory did not acquire its crucial dimension of *difference* only through its aesthetic and political radicalism, but also through its ineluctable Frenchness—which, however clichéd this may be, is defined in the American mind-set by the values of seduction and irony. For theory too involves a certain seduction through irony. In the phrase "It's so French," repeated so often by American Francophiles—a zero degree of culturalist expression, but which is used only in reference to the French ("it's so German" or "it's so Italian" come up far less often)—the quantitative adverb "so" points to an excess viewed as a flaw, an insidious form of immoderation, as if Frenchness signified a certain polite form of arrogance, a way of employing courteous verbiage or a sophisticated writing style to draw its interlocutor into doubtful paths and false conclusions, bringing us back to the primary sense of *seducere* in Latin. We might consider that an unstable balance has been struck, one that appears miraculous in American eyes, between formal classicism (as in Foucault's case) and extreme arguments, or between the accessibility and openness of a philosopher in person (for which Derrida was often praised) and the difficulty of the author and his works; it is this sense of balance that gave rise to the notion of a *French seduction* to which these authors owe much of their success in the United States. Feminist Jane Gallop, duly mistrustful of all forms of seduction, nonetheless recognizes "this particular intersection of Seduction and Theory": "A good number of us have, in recent years, been swept away by something both charming and dangerous which, for lack of an honest name, I will call French Theory."[31] Even the strong French accents of Derrida or Baudrillard, when speaking to their audience in English, play a role in this seduction, because, as Erving Goffman remarks, in a public conference, "what is noise from the point of view of the text" can become "music from the point of view of interaction."[32] In this way, certain cultural archetypes based on typical French *seduction* or *chatter* preceded, permeated, and even helped construct, to a large extent, the idea of theory. This is also why, for the past thirty years, American universities, after their extensive use of this small group of theoretical authors, scarcely more than a dozen, have taken an interest in everything they could find that appeared related to French theory and its charms of irony, considering New Wave cinema or the Nouveau Roman as accessories to theory, with Robbe-Grillet often being studied as an illustration of Derrida's thought, or Georges Perec as an extension of Deleuze's work—all pointing to an avant-garde French culture to be reevaluated in light of this same culture's "theory." The latter continues to be seen as polyphonic, coolly critical, obscure, seductive, and crafty: thus defined, French theory has clearly become a cultural norm.

From Foucault to Barthes: The Fine Shades of Paradox

We must now break apart the smooth unity of the theoretical body one last time in order to sketch out, for each of the major authors, a picture of each one's respective *effect* in the United States. In so doing, we will also try to form a notion of the specific fixture that each one came to represent. This brief section is, naturally, not ample enough to paint a complete portrait of the American Foucault, the American Derrida, or the American Lyotard—or to discuss all the authors associated in the United States with the theory movement, including René Girard, who has lived in the States for forty years, Michel Serres, who joined him on the Stanford faculty, Jacques Rancière, Alain Badiou, Paul Virilio, and Jean-Pierre Dupuy, who also teaches in California. The objective will be to focus on the seven authors whose works form the backbone of French theory and provide it with its major conceptual directions as well as its theoretical *style*. The aim will be to give, for each author, not an exhaustive synthesis, but rather an overview of the *contradictions* that arise around his work, and of the way in which they have been imported and reinvented in America, while considering the tensions that arose between the overall logic of the work (which includes its original French context) and the uses or needs it served in the United States—and noting that the precarious solutions to such tensions, whether we call them distortion or deterritorialization, were precisely what enabled these theories to per-petuate and institutionalize each of their respective American "aliases."

The hypothesis proposed here is that the transfer of each of these authors' works to the American context produced a double bind, in the sense given to this term by Gregory Bateson and his colleagues in their 1956 report "Toward a Theory of Schizophrenia": it signifies a con-tradiction between two aspects of a statement, most often between its register and meaningful content (as in the order: "Be spontaneous!"), which renders its meaning almost entirely "undecidable" and prevents "the receiver [of the message] from exiting the framework set up by the [statement]."[33] When a message "confirms something" and at the same time "confirms something regarding its own confirmation," in such a way that the two elements cancel each other out, a pragmatic paradox appears whose solution must necessarily be pragmatic as well: whether by ignoring one element of the statement, by inverting the two levels of the message (for example, treating the "commentary becomes the text and vice versa," as Yves Winkin suggests),[34] or by imposing a renewed link of "metacommunication," which had been interrupted by the ob-stacle—which may, perhaps, explain the explosion of commentaries and metadiscourses surrounding French theory in the United States. The con-tradiction in this case is, of course, implicit. It arises from the fact that the very logic of French theoretical texts prohibits certain uses of them, uses that were often necessary, however, to their American readers in order to *put the texts to work*. It is an example of the recognized interplay between betrayal and reappropriation. To put it more bluntly, Foucault writes about something called "care of the self," and Baudrillard, about "simulation," but the register of these texts, as well as their overall logic, prohibits the reader from drawing out new styles of existence or a simu-lationist school of thought—except precisely by going against the let-ter of the texts. The American "invention" of these French texts, there-fore, designates a skill at *making texts say what one has understood of them* or, at least, what one needs to draw from them. In other words, it served to reconcile the text and the world, to reduce the inevitable gap between the autonomous logic of a work and the requirement to make it useful, and it was this process that was perfected, through many trials and guesses, in versions of Derrida, Deleuze, or Lyotard entirely *unknown* in France.

Foucault's work is an example that stands apart. Even in comparison with Derrida, who became an icon and an institution during his lifetime, Foucault's long-term impact in the United States remains unequaled, both in terms of his books sold in translation (more than three hundred thousand copies of the first volume of *The History of Sexuality*, more than two hundred thousand copies of *Madness and Civilization*, and more than 150,000 copies of *The Order of Things*) and in the range of fields of study he has transformed or brought into existence, as well as in the diversity of his audience: the works in his immense bibliography of readers and collections include one on Foucault for social workers,[35] one in comic-book form for beginners,[36] and even one to remind us that Nelson Mandela's South Africa is not free from apartheid.[37] John Rajchman's book, which calls Foucault the modern *skeptic* and praises his "ethics of freedom,"[38] and the Dreyfus and Rabinow classic study[39] offer interpretations of Foucault of a quality that few similar projects in France have matched. There is, nevertheless, a considerable gap between the American Foucault and the French one, which Vincent Descombes views as "incompatible" with each other in an influential article in which he contrasts the French anarchistic agitator Foucault, reading Surrealist theory, with an American Foucault focused on practices and political morals, who attempts to "redefine *autonomy* in purely human terms."[40] The difference is primarily one of status: in the United States, Foucault represents the *intellectual-oracle*, whose prose unmasks biopower, furnishes weapons to contemporary struggles, and heralds the queer movement, and who is also the figure whose invigorating "philosophical laughter" provides assurance of the critical distance from his own discourses. In the American reading of Foucault, we find that the explosive pairing of "knowledge and power" occupies a much more central position than in Foucault's own perspective, and is seen as the key to his entire work, as well as the basis for an entire intellectual outlook. In the United States, the rallying cry that was developed out of this binomial, power-knowledge, has served many purposes: an impetus for a push to require the ivory tower of academia to carry out its own performative duties, a theoretical proof that universalism and rationalism can be used as discourses of conquest, and a support for the notion that it is exclusion (of the insane, of criminals) that produces the norm (reason, justice). This interpretation of Foucault, taking the aforementioned three main directions, provided his American readers with a veritable *conspiracy theory*, in the name of which they scoured society to uncover its aggressors and victims. American cultural studies or minority studies texts inspired by Foucault consistently focus on the notion of "unmasking" or "delegitimizing" some form of power that is "stifling" or "marginalizing" one oppressed minority group or another—an approach that stands in direct opposition to Foucault's genealogical method.

Foucault's aim, after all, was to create an *analytics* of power, not an axiology of it; as for turning him into the most fervent advocate for those without a voice, this role is conceivable only if we neglect the two limits of Foucault's "politics": first, the difficulty of establishing a coherent notion of the *subject,* of history, or of political struggle, because power itself "is exercised from innumerable points" and "resistance is never in a position of exteriority to power,"[41] and, second, the opposite criticism of which Foucault is often the target, according to which he steals the voice of those without a voice, speaking on behalf of the silent residents of asylums or prisons just for the sake of the sparks this produces on a written page. We might remember that Foucault asked to be spared this "morality of bureaucrats and police" that requires philosophers "to remain the same."[42] This gap continued to grow with the thematic focuses of the following years, centered on the "ethics of the self" and the "truth-telling" elements of his work. Foucault's renown, which began growing in 1977, reached such a peak that his successors wanted to derive a "method" of self-construction from his work, a task for which they solicited Foucault's assistance during a series of lectures he gave at New York University (to which he is said to have responded, "The last thing I want to tell you is how to live!").[43] Their objective was to glean the essential principles of *savoir-vivre,* whether of a gay, stoic, philosophical, or activist variety. In an interview with the periodical *Salmagundi*, Foucault was even compelled to repeat insistently, "I am wary of imposing my own views," and then "I want to avoid imposing my own scheme," and finally, "as for prescribing [a] direction . . . I prefer not to legislate such matters."[44] Certain critics even heard in Foucault the distant strains of a patriotic interpretation: Foucault's lexicon was made to resonate with an "American Aesthetics of Liberty," the idea being that Foucault and the United States share "a tradition of ethics that presents self-stylization as a practice of freedom," in which the self is "assumed to be a work of art" and "the desirability of normalization itself" is ceaselessly questioned[45]—a mostly literary take on the subject amounting overall to a para-Foucauldian ode to pioneering, repressive America and its unexamined myths, one that Foucault the activist would no doubt have found distasteful.

We have already mentioned, on the subject of deconstruction, Derrida's pragmatic paradox: to *construct* a deconstructive approach to any text, as a communicable method of reading, and a body of guidelines, which creates a contradiction, not so much between method and an unmediated surge as between the text's *autonomy* and the reader's *will*. We can never *choose* to deconstruct the essence or the origin, as Derrida, in his characteristic way, emphasizes: "In the deconstruction of the arche, one does not make a choice."[46] This double prohibition brings us back to the problem of taking a criticism of all methods of putting texts to work and trying to put them to work. The aims of deconstruction are also required, as its condition of possibility. As Paul de Man suggests, deconstructing the "illusion of reference," the possibility that a text can relate us to nontextual reality, can only be accomplished in a referential mode, even if once removed; as Derrida reminds us, if metaphysics makes critical thought possible, a critique of metaphysics will necessarily be its accomplice. Thus, the project of deconstruction is constantly slipping away, extending the hope of an escape from metaphysics like a light glimmering on the horizon for its American readers, keen to break from the hold of nostalgia, when in fact these categories of interior and exterior are themselves metaphysical concepts. The evolution of Derrida's works, beginning with a more or less systematic theorization of deconstruction and proceeding toward its textual and intertextual application, employing an experimental style of language and elliptical arguments, only added to this gap by making Derrida's later work much less *literally* usable in the United States—especially because Derrida himself often added fuel to the fire, ridiculing the "didactic" approach of a certain type of deconstruction, repackaged as "practical, in the sense of easy, convenient, and even salable as a commodity," when this theory is really "indissociable from a process and a law of expropriation . . . that resists in the last instance, in order to challenge it, every subjective movement of appropriation of the following sort: I deconstruct . . ."[47] Because this contradiction brings to light the workings of metaphysical philosophy, it is, in fact, a central element of Derrida's work, which explores the smallest shifts in metaphysical perspective. Creating a pedagogical system based in this contradiction, however, was a strategy far removed from Derrida's own approach. It reduced the method's flexibility, ductibility, and meticulousness, for the sake of a counterreading that often took on crudely dialectical forms—in which the deconstructed text is seen as an unveiling, the hidden aspect of the apparent text—whereas, in Derrida's work, it had been only a light shift, or a barely perceptible slippage. The key is that a strong contrast of this kind was much more functionally usable.

The impact of Deleuze, which took place later, particularly through the four books he cowrote with Félix Guattari, was preceded by two decades of misunderstandings. The translations of *Proust et les signes* and *Présentation de Sacher Masoch* made him appear, to a still very small reading audience, as a cross between atypical literary critic and alternative sexologist. The conceptual shortcuts of several American Marxist critics that we have already discussed (including Fredric Jameson) then gave Deleuze the public image of a postmodern aesthete, while the leftist periodical *Telos* viewed *Anti-Oedipus* and schizo-analysis as "an extension of Reich and, to a lesser extent, of Marcuse."[48] The famous beginning of *Anti-Oedipus,* with its themes of desiring machines and the nomadic subject, was quoted during the 1980s often to support a critique of the colonial or heterosexual subject. Apart from the fleeting experimentation of the periodical *Semiotext(e),* and the more personal use that certain analysts made (including Kathy Acker and DJ Spooky), the philosophical implications of this intensive system of thought and its affirmative approach were not to be perceived until much later in the United States, starting in the mid-1990s, when they were immediately reintegrated into the discourse of the academic institution, which appears to have wholeheartedly embraced Deleuze and Guattari's work, to the detriment of their nonacademic uses—although no one has really grasped the real political dimensions of their writings, in which *A Thousand Plateaus* stands as a veritable declaration of war, and micropolitics emerges as a new form of community. The pragmatic paradox arose, in this case, through the simple practice of *commentary,* that obligatory unwrapping of the discursive content, of a theoretical expression that was aimed, instead, at *creating concepts.* The major American interpreters of Deleuze, including Charles Stivale and Brian Massumi, generally produce somewhat mimetic commentaries of his works: they construct a theatrical evocation, within the text, of the suddenness of the "event," they discuss Deleuze's concepts through the magical mode of incantation, or even make a rhetorical challenge to the reader to "become Deleuzian" or to "merge with [Deleuze's] work" and duly carry its set of concepts "along their lines of flight."[49] Certain literal approaches run counter to the project and overall ethic held by Deleuze and Guattari, who viewed such "mimetic procedures" as "technonarcissism."[50] As philosopher Élie During concludes, by adopting "a rather too doctrinaire notion of Deleuzeanism," his American commentators acquired "a very un-Deleuzean idea of philosophy," whereas in fact it would have been impossible to remain "truly faithful to the Master except by betraying him, . . . by applying to Deleuze his own working methods,"[51] by setting into motion his own contradictions, for example, rather than devotedly mimicking his canonical vision.

As for Jean-François Lyotard, his American readers have too often reduced his work to the question of postmodernity. This makes Lyotard a striking example of theory slipping in register, or a sort of *tonal* misunderstanding, which was facilitated in this case by the liberties he took with conventional argumentative writing methods. Lyotard's principal philosophical contribution—the end of grand narrative (along with the alternative of paralogy and the driving intensity of capital)—of which he offered a theoretical genealogy, and which his style sometimes imitates in order to demonstrate his argument, was often read in the United States entirely in the register of prescription: it became a postmodern epiphany in praise of small narrative projects, if not a libidinal injunction or a call to demolish the last remaining notions of totality. Much of the richness of Lyotard's work is derived from a certain distance maintained between the refraction of the present and policies of judgment, between assertions and prescriptions—which Lyotard allows himself to put forward in his shorter writings, as, for example, when he enjoys the notion of a "decadence of truth" in *Rudiments païens* (Pagan rudiments), but he does not, as a rule, include it in his work. This prescriptive American reading also sometimes lapses into misinterpretation. Lyotard has been read by some as a great illuminator of a historical turning point, the advent of postmodernity, although the latter, for him, has always represented an internal component or recurring stage of modernity, without conceiving of these as two separate *phases*. Similarly, Lyotard's political critique of the concept of representation has often been used to justify using his texts as support for feminism and ethnic minority struggles, in the name of a kind of postmodern messianism for the excluded and the subaltern that does not integrate well with the logic of his work and that detracts from Lyotard's significance as a theorist of aesthetics, the Lyotard of *Discours figure* and the "analytic of the sublime," which remains poorly known across the Atlantic.

In Baudrillard's case, the paradox comes principally from the series of "isms" that he has been considered to represent in the United States, all of them ill-fitting. The first was Marxism: his early works, including *The System Objects, Symbolic Exchange and Death,* and, in particular, *The Mirror of Production,* earned him a place in the tradition of Adorno and Lefebvre. Baudrillard's political semiology was read as a critique of commercial signs, a semiotic continuation or symbolic deconstruction of Marx, according to these readings. At the same time, his theoretical extrapolations were being read from a realist perspective; passages that dealt with the emptying of certain paradigms were read as speaking of the real and of certain referents, and his critique of Marxist determin-ism, along with that of the mirages of semiology, were seen by some as heralding "the [end] of the Social and of the Real as essences."[52] Other intepretations, as we have seen, continued along the same lines: Baudril-lard's theory of simulation inspired a "simulationist" movement in art, his remarks on "hyperreality" led journalists and filmmakers to view him as a "hyperrealist," and we can only be thankful that his discussions of the desert and casinos did not serve to launch a school of thought called "chancism." Paradoxical thought, which is for Baudrillard the basis for writing in general as well as theory, and which often confused his followers, became the object of a veritable interpretative obsession for Anglo-Saxon specialists on his work. Critics including Mark Poster and Douglas Kenner produced, in all, around twenty academic mon-ographs, each one thematically organized and meticulously reasoned, whereas there have been none in France, where Baudrillard has never been well received by the press. Americans have continued to read him with more passion than irony, quoting phrases from *The Perfect Crime* or *The Transparency of Evil* like postmodern mantras, all the while vili-fying *America,* which was even burned in public at one university, and, after September 11, calling on the state to refuse entry to the author of *The Spirit of Terrorism,* who had dared to claim that the Twin Towers had "committed suicide." These readers could not follow Baudrillard along the elusive path of a "theory [that] becomes its own object," that "must become simulation if it speaks of simulation, . . . seductive if it speaks of seduction,"[53] except by speaking, in a more tautological mode, of "Baudrillardian" theory whenever his name appears.

Finally, apart from the cases of Jacques Lacan and Julia Kristeva, whose reception was no less paradoxical—they are generally adored in the humanities, whereas the American psychoanalytic field is extremely hostile to their work—there remains the peculiar American avatars of Roland Barthes. "Of all the intellectual notables who have emerged since World War II in France, Roland Barthes is the one whose work I am most certain will endure," wrote Susan Sontag, introducing a text written in tribute to Barthes, with whom she had become friends, and whose work she helped introduce in the United States.[54] Barthes's early books, for example, his structuralist work *Writing Degree Zero,* were received in the Anglo-Saxon world with an overemphasis on their political dimensions, whether by condemning Barthes's "anti-bourgeois grimaces" and a body of work made of "three parts Marxism, two parts psychoanalysis, four parts recycled linguistics" or, on the contrary, to celebrate Barthes's "liberatory criticism" that was able to "find ideology out in the moment that it is produced."[55] After this interpretation, which politicized the semiotician, others followed attempting to sexualize the freethinker: Barthes's numerous later works, including *Incidents* and *Camera Lucida,* experienced an academic rebirth in the United States beginning in the mid-1980s, especially in connection with issues of autobiography, criticism as confession, and homosexual literary *style*—all of these themes being antithetical to Barthes's sense of discretion, his aversion for *doxa,* and his habitually indirect and periphrastic approach to sexual issues. *The Pleasure of the Text,* which was an academic best seller in the United States in the 1970s, was read as a postmodern prophecy, the allegory of a "textualization" of the world, in marked contrast to the "pleasure" in question. Even the persistent notion that Barthes represents a contemporary model of the "complete writer"[56] fails to consider the tensions, turning points, and fissures that separate the many facets of his intellectual career. The problem is that insisting on an author's name, within an already highly diverse list of names, means also assigning a label, reducing an author whose work was plural to a singular character—producing a zero degree of pragmatic paradox.

In most of these cases, the problem that arose was a contradiction between the logic of the use made of theory and the logic of labile, unplaceable texts, resistant to prescriptive applications. After American readers' initial hesitation on encountering these authors, the usual strategy was to force their works into a prescriptive register, whether it be political, ethical, or joyfully textualist, whereas what remained elusive in these texts was precisely the register in which they function. The contradiction also arose through a tension inherent to the theoretical approach, a tension that, through their eagerness to put the texts to work, by putting them into practice and into circulation, American readers also allowed to develop into all its possible dimensions. This tension, which is central to all the works we have discussed—and which these works themselves explicitly problematize—arises from an inability, characteristic of theoretical texts, to oppose reason with anything other than reason itself, to criticize metaphysics without using metaphysical tools, to deconstruct historical continuity without rebuilding, on its ruins, a new form of historical continuity. Americans, it would seem, do not take kindly to things being impossible: there was a need to shift into action, or at least into injunctions to action (crucial to the academic world), to aestheticize the tension in order to reveal its traces in all the "texts" of contemporary culture, or to solemnly dramatize it, so as to produce the impression of a historical moment and an imminent future—these, it seems, were the American methods of dealing with what is *impossible* in theory.

13

WORLDWIDE THEORY: A GLOBAL LEGACY

> I define the intellectual as an exile, someone on the margins, an amateur, and finally the author of a language that attempts to speak truth to power.
>
> EDWARD SAID, *Representations of the Intellectual*

THE AMERICAN INTERPRETATION of French theory is just one of many that have taken shape across the world; French theoretical writings have been scrutinized in cities as diverse as Beijing and Bogotá, by Russian Neolibertarians and Brazilian activists, and have been translated into many different languages, ranging from Korean to Swahili. Avant-garde textualism and minority radicalism are the two principal offshoots that French theory has inspired in American universities, but they are merely examples of local uses, two possible cultural metamorphoses. There are as many different readings and usages of Foucault, Deleuze, and Derrida as there are fields of study and activity drawing upon their work or political contexts and cultural traditions in which they have been integrated or lost. The staggering globalization of French theory, which began—depending on the country in question—between the early 1970s and the late 1980s, also played its part in exacerbating this chiasmus: as France gradually buried the heralds of *intensive thought* (often during their lifetimes) and dismissed the works of Foucault, Deleuze, Lyotard, and even Derrida, in order to fall back onto the more presentable democratic humanism put forward by some of the country's young scholars, it was not only the United States but the entire rest of the world that found, in these authors who had been discredited in their own country, a heuristic, political, and intercultural ferment of ideas—establishing a meeting ground with local authors and discourses that had never before existed. They took from these writings a manner of thinking that was closely tuned in to the new state of disorder of the world, as well as, quite often, the necessary tools to emancipate themselves from the dominant intellectual discourse of locally existing liberation movements, whether Marxist or nationalist. It was a worldwide destiny that proved Baudrillard wrong when, in *America,* he dismissed as an "unfortunate transfer" the "moving attempts to acclimatize" European theoretical thought, which was in fact "like fine wines and fine cooking"—since it "[would] not really cross" the oceans very successfully.[1]

In order to avoid a Benetton-like analogy with the marvel of diversity, in this case with rainbow-colored reading packets and polychromatic uses of texts, this worldwide dissemination of thought deserves an in-depth study, or at least more than the brief overview that follows here. The spread of French thought is, above all, inextricably linked to the unquestionable American domination of cultural industries and academic and publishing institutions. Indeed, the United States also exported its theoretical trends; we have only to look at the global diffusion of its "readers," and the many different local forms of impact brought by cultural studies. In fact, French theory often passed through Stanford and Columbia before reaching the less affluent universities of subaltern countries—which set these universities a twofold challenge of reading French texts that had *passed through* but could also be *turned against* America. The essential point is that critical reappropriation and active hybridization were at work, and that theory can *examine,* without *reproducing,* global relationships of power in precisely the regions of the world where these relationships produce the most extreme economic inequality. All things considered, even if a French avant-garde interpretation of German philosophy does reach Indian or Argentinean readers after a detour through Anglo-American commentary, this process does not represent a distancing from any unlikely "source," because a work's value can be determined only through the uses one makes of it, and, as Deleuze states, all thought begins by deciphering distance: "There is no Logos, only hieroglyphs," is his perspective, because "to think is therefore to interpret, is therefore to translate."[2]

America and Its Others

On several occasions, it has been a question here of an undifferentiated *Anglo-American* academic group, but this does not do justice to a largely independent British intellectual arena. There are several important features that distinguish the latter from its American counterpart when it comes to French theory: a more extensive history of public intellectuals, less of a tendency to innovate for the sake of innovation, a greater measure of clout held by Marxist academics, and, in a broader sense, the same sociopolitical paradigm of social class that exists in France. Nonetheless, when it comes to intellectual politics—in terms of established approaches, high-profile universities, and academic publishers—all the exclusively English-speaking countries are completely submissive to America's authority, its key authors, its pedagogical techniques, and its generously financed international conferences. These countries include Great Britain, despite its divergences; Canada, of course; Australia and New Zealand, where there is a tendency to examine only minority issues (such as the relationship with the British monarchy, or the segregation suffered by the Aborigines and Maoris);[3] South Africa, since the end of apartheid; and even Israel and its Americanized universities—there are also several American economic and military offshoots, where American foundations have financed study programs and set up research exchanges, in countries such as Singapore and Saudi Arabia. When Gayatri Spivak was invited in 1980, along with other academics, to teach deconstruction and structuralism at the (all-male) University of Riyadh, she was struck by the generous welcome and extensive resources she was given; she remarked, however, that "Saudi Arabia, with American help, is in fact slowly fabricating for itself a 'humanist' intellectual elite that will be unable to read the relationship between its own production and the flow of oil, money, and arms"—where "humanist" refers to a technocratic elite that was necessary to the Wahabi dictatorship to affirm its presence on the international scene.[4]

Such a direct domination of these countries' university systems by the American academic machine has meant that French theory was initially introduced in its American, popularized form. Paul de Man's writings were read everywhere from Sydney to Tel Aviv. Foucault, for readers in Montreal or Johannesburg, was viewed as representing, first and foremost, an author whose books expand on Judith Butler's queer theory or Homi Bhabha's postcolonial work. And everywhere from London to Auckland people were reflecting on the dichotomies between modernism and postmodernism and essentialism and constructionism. The United States, however, an object of scorn for Duke University's "radicals," as well as for leftist academics in Quebec or Ireland, did not implement any active *intention* to export its intellectual products, or even acquire hegemony, as was the case for its film studios or weapons industry. It was the emergence of a new, transnational, academic class that enabled pedagogical methods and theoretical discourses in the humanities of *all* English-speaking universities to apply this uniform standard. As early as 1979, sociologist Alvin Gouldner examined this phenomenon from a Marxist perspective: he saw it as part of the emergence of an "international cultural bourgeoisie" made up of multilingual academics born of the scientific and technical intelligentsia as well as the humanities, a new type of cultural bourgeoisie that was allied with the "structure of bureaucratic power" (of universities as well as the broader political society) but designed to defend "its own interests," and which as a whole formed a "flawed universal class" giving rise, in turn, to a veritable "global monopoly" of general knowledge and critical discourse.[5] Gouldner's thesis is at times rather simplistic, particularly when he suggests that an organic submission of these new transnational academics to bureaucratic power has taken place. His work nonetheless recognizes a shift that was occurring on an international scale, as the world moved away from the public intellectuals of the mid-twentieth century—politically engaged writers and bards of decolonization—to the "specific intellectuals" that Michel Foucault evokes. Indeed, within two or three decades, the world had undergone a change of focus, moving from an international group of writers, an oligarchic intelligentsia that addressed public opinion and the powers that be directly (from which today's International Parliament of Writers remains as a reminder of the epoch), to an international network of universities, an organized and professionalized alternative group whose members generally address one another, and whose policies are directly modeled on those of academic globalization—or what Bourdieu calls "the complex network of international exchanges between holders of dominant academic posts."[6] Nevertheless, contrary to what Gouldner and, on occasion, certain Bourdieu scholars suggest, such an evolution, which effectively correlates to a reterritorialization of international academic discussion, as undertaken by the university world, should not obscure the conceptual and political boldness assumed by these new university mavericks, now unhindered by borders.

Today, a true international avant-garde has taken shape, composed of members acting both as leaders *and* as relentless critics of this new academic "class"; they are innovative intellectuals, generally from the humanities (often philosophy scholars), and are more often European than American (although not so French). This group formed as the cumulative result of three different elements: the power wielded by American universities, the newfound mobility of the academic elite, and the living (and constantly disputed) legacy left by French theory. A few important members should be mentioned, although the overview will necessarily remain too brief. There is, for example, the international influence of the Italian philosopher Antonio Negri—who took refuge in Paris following the struggles of the Autonomisti—which carries the weight it does thanks to the support of American universities. Currently, several radical branches of the antiglobalization movement have declared their affiliation to Negri's thinking, including the Italian activists *tute bianche*[7] led by Luca Casarini, the young German anarchists, alternative Latin American unions, and the French group behind the quarterly journal *Multitudes*. This hybrid movement, along with Negri, stands for an ontology of liberation, inspired by Deleuze and Spinoza, linked to an atypical Marxist notion of the fractured political subject (that of "multitudes"), and to a broadened poststructuralist redefinition of imperial power (a microphysical and multipolar "empire"). Once again, this is a by-product of American universities' production, because it was there that the worldwide success of *Empire* began (published in 2000 by Harvard University Press),[8] it was there alone that this unexpected meeting ground between Foucault, Marx, and Derrida—at times tinged with mysticism—could have taken place, and it was also there that, more concretely, the most discreet, but also most effective, of Negri's followers carried out his research—for example, Michael Hardt, a former student of Negri in Paris, coauthor of *Empire,* and literature professor at Duke, to whom we owe a brief political introduction to Deleuze's works as well as the *Reader* devoted to his colleague Fredric Jameson.[9]

Another Italian philosopher, Giorgio Agamben, serves as the primary point of reference for certain dissident extreme-left movements across the world, and also demonstrates the increasing importance assumed by the American theoretical industry. America's most prestigious universities study Agamben, and he is often invited there, where he draws crowds that his seminars in Paris and Venice have been unable to match. From the beginning of the 1980s, his varied writings have relentlessly revealed a political and cultural counterhistory of the West: he has explored the poetic and/or financial implications generated by the notions of fetish and fantasy, formulated a theory of the impossible community as an assemblage of "whatever" singularities (*singolarità qualunque*), and, more recently, examined the "state of exception," from Roman law to post-September 11.[10] Each of his projects has worked in harmony with the three segments of his major work, *Homo sacer,* a historical genealogy of the political as a mechanism of exclusion and power over life. His work can be situated at the conceptual meeting point between Foucault's biopolitics—which Agamben's writings on "sovereignty" and "bare life" elaborate—a French, left-wing version of Heidegger's thought, and Walter Benjamin's hypotheses regarding messianism and history. These are three important sources of inspiration, interwoven and augmented by Agamben's work on the history of religion and the philosophy of law, which constructs a perspective highly attuned to the historical transitions taking place at the dawn of this new millennium.

The verbose work of Slovenian philosopher Slavoj Žižek is preoccupied, rather, with Marx, American pop culture, and French theory. Freely interweaving the works of Marx and Lacan, being one of the first in Eastern Europe to read the latter's writings, and drawing partially on the theories elaborated by Deleuze and Lyotard regarding the libidinal nature of capitalism, Žižek explores the persistent notion of fantasy in commercial society, and in its new, supposedly *post*political "ideology." He brings this off with a consummate talent for theoretical provocation and dizzying shifts in register,[11] whether the purpose is to uncover the "linguistic unconscious" in David Lynch or to bring Heidegger's ontology into uneasy contact with the science-fiction comedy *Men in Black.* Unlike many others, he does not call for a political ontology *without a subject,* but follows Lacan's thinking, and counters postmodern conventions when he suggests maintaining the "ticklish" figure of the subject,[12] provided that it is suitably distanced from the individualist, humanist subject. Žižek's history provides an emblematic example of the globalization of French theory: born in 1949 in Ljubljana, he grew up in Yugoslavia during the Tito regime, before spending time in London and Paris's Latin Quarter; he has had his works translated into more than a dozen languages, but it is only in American universities—where he has penned more than thirty works, and has already become the object of half a dozen critical introductions—that he has been able to fully elaborate his protean theoretical project, drawing upon Judith Butler's use of feminism and poststructuralism, rereading Georg Lukács and Alain Badiou, denouncing in no uncertain terms the "capitalist fundamentalism" that was set in place following September 11,[13] and even playing his part in repoliticizing the overly textual field of cultural studies. So it is that, with the influence of the Italian philosophers, Žižek, American left-wing deconstructionists (like Spivak and Tom Keenan), staunch British Marxists, the unique German scholar Peter Sloterdijk, and new Japanese and Latin American sociologists, a veritable international political-theoretical arena has gradually taken shape, enriched by French theoretical thought and centered in American universities. It is true, however, that recent French academics have played almost no part in this movement—they struggle with foreign languages more than their European counterparts, they are institutionally cut off, owing to the rarity of exchange programs and sabbaticals, sidelined in France by public intellectuals, and they have shifted abruptly from a generally accepted academic agreement on Marxism to a vehement anti-Marxist stance today.

The vitality of this international university network owes much to the animated role played by ex-political exiles and representatives of minority groups, and, moreover, to the veritable international migratory crossroads that, in the space of thirty years, American universities have come to represent. It is in this sense that new arrivals and old dual-nationals alike—who are all exiled academics (in a more or less benign way)—have been able to come together to build a "theory world," drawing on the experiences and perspectives of each. Staying with the writers and movements previously mentioned, a few examples of this international movement can be evoked: in the poscolonial field, two important canonical writers are Indian-born Gayatri Spivak and Anglo-Indian Homi Bhabha; two leaders of critical legal studies are the Latin American scholar Richard Delgado and Japanese thinker Mari Matsuda; Ihab Hassan, the pioneer of postmodernism in literary criticism, was born in Egypt; Edward Said has remained an active pro-Palestinian; the field of ethnic studies has been marked by the great African American figures Cornel West, Henry Louis Gates Jr., and Zairean-born V. Y. Mudimbe; it was an Indian, Ranajit Guha, who formalized subaltern studies; and one must not

forget the European exiles—Paul de Man from Belgium, Geoffrey Hartman from Germany, Wlad Godzich from Switzerland, and Sylvère Lotringer from France, whose partner and peer, Chris Kraus, is originally
from New Zealand. It is also this movement that ushered in the denationalization of the great academic debates and the theorization of exile
and miscegenation as a political condition of the contemporary subject.
These themes first took root in the sometimes rocky path taken by many
individual itineraries before coming to meet under the Gothic bell towers of California's and New England's universities. The questions that
surround Caribbean immigration are emblematic of the well-established
polyculture that exists in American universities and lie at the heart of
the nuanced reflection on power and discourse, and on the "worldwide
theory" that is being played out in North American universities.

Indeed, literary and political figures from the Caribbean who have
been forced to move to the United States by political dictatorships or
the economic recession suffered in their islands have laid bare questions
surrounding the international balance of power. They have been able to
raise such issues because they come from an area that has been devas-
tated by the political and economic interests of their neighboring giant
in the North, because they are situated along a linguistic dividing line
between the French- and English-speaking worlds, because each of these
dominant languages has generated for them an intimate conflict that has
been going on for more than a century, and because they are geographically *and* historically linked to the two major subaltern cultures that exist
in the United States, namely, Latin American and African—which has
even led to the increasingly frequent references to an underlying Afro-
Caribbean political axis. Beyond the specific implications of culture and
Creole language, it is the key notion of *creolization* and the theories it
has generated concerning a primary hybridity and a resistance through
cultural mixing that have had the greatest impact. American universities
form a safe haven, and have played host to middle-class, Cuban anti-
Castro writers, left-wing Jamaican activists, intellectuals from Trinidad
and Santo Domingo, and, above all, many French-speaking writers who
have re-created, in Montreal and New York, Haitian and West Indian literary communities: Guadalupean Maryse Condé at Columbia, Édouard
Glissant at the City University of New York, and Haitians Joël Des
Rosiers and Émile Ollivier in Quebec. Besides bringing a more global
and political perspective to many conventional French departments, this

West Indian presence has also created many interesting interactions with French theory. Indeed, besides his more romantic works, Édouard Glissant's much-read theoretical writings draw on several different points of French theory, using his unique style of writing that blurs the distinction between poetry and criticism.[14] He defends an "orality" that is not submissive to the authority of writing, the act of which he describes as a series of "earthquakes," and a rupture with "linear" narration and its culture of "comprehension" (as he emphasizes, "in comprehending, there is the intention of taking, grasping, apprehending, and subjecting"), using terms reminiscent of Derrida and deconstruction. The elliptical therorizations of the "chaos-world" and the "opacity [of] the existent" that he presents in contrast to European ontology and its weighty "pretention of Being" are ideas that resonate closely with Deleuze and Guattari's work on nomadism and lines of flight, which he cites on occasion. His praise for the "roiling of time" [*barattement du temps*] in Creole literature that contrasts with the linear time of "legitimacy and filiation" also seems to bear traces of Foucault's historical criticism.

Patrick Chamoiseau, a novelist from Martinique, who, since the translation in 1996 of *Texaco,* has enjoyed extensive critical success in the United States, with the *New York Times* heralding him as a "García Márquez of the West Indies," and John Updike, for the *New Yorker,* considering him a "tropical Céline," complete with hints of Lévi-Strauss and Derrida.[15] Academic literary criticism also got in on the act. Françoise Lionnet, for example, of Northwestern University (now at UCLA), presented a study of Caribbean women writers under the lens of a Foucauldian dichotomy between "the continuity of historical discourse" and the inevitable "scattering" in space, time, and language of a "formerly colonized subject," drawing on Foucault to shed light, in this postcolonial context, on sexual differences that had previously gone unnoticed.[16] Michael Dash, a Jamaican studying the history of Haiti, considers "Haiti's *heterocosm,*" downtrodden and then abandoned by the United States, as the "blind spot," ignored by the powerful, on which a strong criticism of Enlightenment values and of a world order centered on America could be based.[17]

India offers another example—extraterritorial in this case—of the cultural and political interactions that have arisen thanks to the American exportation of French theory. Here, the key factor has been the rise in American universities of Indian-born academics, such as Gayatri

Spivak and the anthropologist Arjun Appadurai, who teaches at Yale. From 1965, when Lyndon Johnson relaxed restrictions on Asian immigration, the uprooted first-, and then second-generation Indians gradually came to join the ranks of minorities interested in cultural studies and the new theoretical tools available in American universities—which explains why they have maintained such a strong connection, through conferences and collective publications, with Indian universities. Thus, India gradually became a theoretically privileged terrain, where the limitations of Western political paradigms were brought to light. Edward Said was able to criticize, in Marx's articles on colonial India, the implicit hierarchy assumed to hold between the two worlds;[18] subaltern studies, as we have seen, were founded in Delhi, as an alternative to the Western historiography of decolonialization; Gayatri Spivak, on the other hand, who was quick to criticize the stereotypes of intellectuals living in affluent countries, has found herself the object of sharp criticism from Indian teachers, who attacked her American success and her excessive use of "First World elite theory."[19]

It was perhaps in India, and not in the United States, that scholars most skillfully recognized the interest of taking antirationalist and anti-Western arguments from French theory as it was read by certain American scholars and using them for *political* means. Indeed, these arguments were upheld at the beginning of the 1990s by the ideologues of the Bharatiya Janata Party (BJP), the right-wing religious and nationalistic party, who wanted to use them to justify the "Hinduization" of science and social values, notably by reintroducing Vedic mathematics in schools and establishing the Rashtra (the Hindu nation) as the ultimate moral standard. Assimilating rational science with Western imperialism, these ideologists promoted through force (notably in the 1988 Declaration of Penang) the notion of ethnoscience; their actions were motivated by a desire not so much to spread popular knowledge as to deploy a weapon in the eternal war against the Hindu nation's "hereditary enemies"—the Muslims to the North and the Christians in the East. In any case, it provided the context for a most unusual interaction. According to critic Meera Nanda, these Indian "science wars" gave rise to the formation of an unexpected alliance between Indian nationalists and American postcolonialists, which took place after just a few meetings, and whose key figures included feminist epistemologist Sandra Harding, who was in favor of "multicultural sciences," and critic Ashis

Nandy, who grouped together the notions of scientific rationality and internal colonization.[20] This unsettling example, far from invalidating the spread of radical American theories (particularly toward Europe's ex-colonies), suggests rather that a significant inequality remained at the heart of this international university network. While such dialogues and collaborative projects led both the locals and immigrants to transform the American universities where they met into veritable hubs of activism and alternative political thought, similar links were far weaker with most universities from the Southern Hemisphere—where, at that time, it was mostly members of the local elite who were permitted to control intellectual thought, and who used their status not to generate a subaltern "revolution" but to maintain their monopoly over the academic and political spheres.

Far-Reaching Consequences, Immediate Effects

The international trail left by French theory does not quite cover the globe's hemispheres equally. The American empire seems to have unwittingly promoted the creation of independent and even outright hostile enclaves quite close to home. To put it succinctly, the writings of Foucault and Derrida are read more *directly* in Mexico and São Paulo than in Melbourne, Calcutta, or even London: they have not been refracted through American academic thought in the same way. Indeed, the nature of migration and linguistics means that rich, English-speaking nations, as well as much of the Caribbean, and even countries as far away as India, have proved to be a captive market for American theoretical products. The case of Latin America—which has been so subjected to the financial and military force of the United States that, since the Monroe Doctrine of 1824, it became little more than the backyard to the United States' closed-door policy—is far more ambivalent, even invalidating certain general rules regarding international intellectual domination. Naturally, the new generation has favored the acceptance of cultural studies; while Chileans and Mexicans educated just after the war read French texts and looked to Europe for political thought, the younger generations, quickly made aware of the power of the American economy, learned English, and preferred to follow—albeit from a reasonable distance—the trends of cultural movements on the other side of the Rio Grande. Subaltern studies and Derridean deconstruction have

also had an impact in Latin America, but it has been measured by the extent to which the movements' American academic strongholds have been
able to export the texts to the Southern Hemisphere. Three important elements in Latin America's cultural tradition explain why, even today, its
twenty countries display such resistance to this new American *theoreticism*. First, the scorn felt by Latin Americans toward the migrant workers who have sold their labor power on the American market is also felt,
in an academic context, toward scholars of Chicano studies and other
forms of "border studies," fields that Latin American scholars do not
deem to be worthy of study, preferring to leave them to sociologists in
Tijuana and literary scholars who have exiled themselves in California.
Second, social sciences have always formed the most active academic
field, as much because of intellectual innovation as because of political
pressure—a field in which key French texts have been read from a less
literary angle than when they were in the hands of North American textualists. Although Hillis Miller and Geoffrey Hartman relate how they
were invited, in winter 1985, by the University of Montevideo, to come
and "explain" deconstruction to Uruguayan scholars, the different theories inspired by Derrida's deconstruction have always had a more limited
impact in South and Central America than in the North.

The role played by social sciences as a paradigm of reference also
helps to explain why, in Latin America, cultural studies did not trigger
literary analyses of pop culture, but rather a movement of thinking more
closely related to ethnography—and which was encouraged in France
by anthropologists like Serge Gruzinski—examining notions such as
syncretism, miscegenation, and ethnocultural hybridity. This explains
why the essays by Colombian scholar Jesús Martín-Barbero, which deal
with cultural domination and mass media, and which, in translation,
have become classic reference texts in American cultural studies, actually speak from a more European Marxist perspective in their analysis
of relationships between subjugated nations and examination of global
hegemony.[21] The works of Argentinean Néstor García Canclini, which
are also read in American universities but which are more influenced by
Foucault and Paul Ricoeur (who was his teacher in Paris) than by either
Derrida or de Man, examine the reaction of popular culture when faced
with touristic globalization, interested less in its symbolic regime than
its potential for political resistance—against the folklore surrounding
local crafts and "authentic" products, reinforcing the Western dogma of

individual initiative and harmonious development, as García Canclini shows in the interesting example of Mexico.[22] Third, Latin American mistrust of American textualism can also be explained by the persistence of a revolutionary, Marxist-Leninist militancy found in some social circles, particularly in the university (which for a long time has been a breeding ground for such sympathies), and which takes on a far less abstract form than the written forms of extremism experienced by American "radicals"—and which has been experienced firsthand on a far more dangerous level. This orthodox Marxism explains why, as early as the 1960s, Althusser's writings were well received, although it would also be worth examining the pivotal changes that the Marxist sector underwent as a result of newly translated works of Foucault and Derrida in Andean universities.

Mexico presents a unique example, one that is all the more interesting given that its cultural and geographic proximity to the United States did not necessarily make it likely to define its own version of French theory. In fact, Mexico was the first Spanish-speaking country to begin spreading French structuralism, long before Spain (where Franco was still in power), and even ten years before the United States. On this occasion, the great importer was the publisher Arnaldo Orfila, who was married to a French anthropologist and, as director of the Fondo de Cultura Económica, published the works of Foucault, Althusser, and Lévi-Strauss just one or two years after their release in France. Orfila went on to establish his own publishing house, Siglo 21, and continued to publish translations of Foucault and Althusser, in particular (more than Derrida), and to pursue an interest in French structuralism rather than American poststructuralism. This interest marked the start of a separate local destiny for these authors, which, in the end, was closer to the reception they received in France, no doubt due to a long-standing Mexican interest in French culture, and to a Mexican university system that closely followed the Spanish and French models. The National Autonomous University of Mexico (UNAM), which is the oldest on the American continent, founded in 1551, more than eighty years before Harvard, was the chosen place of study for one Rafael Guillén—who went on to lead the EZLN (Ejército Zapatista de Liberación Nacional) under the name of Subcomandante Marcos—but who, twenty years earlier, wrote a philosophy thesis on Foucault and Althusser. Mexico's intellectual elite has so fully immersed itself in the world of French theory—once again, more in the works of Foucault and Althusser than Baudrillard and Derrida—that the Mexican embassy's cultural attaché in France, writer Jorge Volpi, wrote the first fictional saga dedicated to French theory, published in France in 2003.[23]

Argentina also distinguishes itself, because of its close links with Europe, the vitality and heterodoxy of its psychoanalytic field—which would explain why Lacan's and particularly Guattari's works were so well received—and the country's history of freethinkers. An original philosopher such as Tomás Abraham is a prime example of these hybrid academics who are less subservient to the writings of previous scholars and more tuned in to the playful and ironic writing style used by certain French authors. Abraham was born in Romania, educated in France, and has lived in Buenos Aires for more than twenty years. It is there that he teaches, that he founded the publication *La Caja,* and that, in his various works, he has explored the beauties of the writings of Foucault and Derrida, whom he deems "low thinkers" (*pensadores bajos*), and the powerful grip that economic discourse holds over different forms of life (examining the "enterprise of living"); he also takes up, with a touch of humor, the notion of "illustrious lives," inventing conversations between Sartre and John Huston, or between philosopher Simone Weil and financier George Soros.[24] And, most recently, he has used concepts from Foucault and Deleuze to shed a new light on Argentina's social unrest and grassroots politics of 2000–2001.[25] Argentinean sociologist Martin Hopenhayn, who wrote a philosophy thesis under Deleuze's supervision, adopts a more classical approach, using Deleuze's insights to create a critique concerning the concept of work and Western forms of development—a critique that became very topical given the context in which it appeared, with the long economic crisis of 2001–2 striking concurrently with resurgent expressions of social protest.[26]

Brazil is also an example worth mentioning in its own right, for more obvious reasons: its inhabitants speak a language other than Spanish, which means that the circulation and translation of texts is different. Portuguese culture and history set the country apart from its neighbors, and, unlike Spanish-speaking countries, it has a social system closer to that of the United States, with its federal organization and its official multiculturalism. Whenever Baudrillard visits, he is welcomed by television cameras and has, there too, been asked to participate in a TV series on U.S. history, following the success of his book *America* in

Portuguese. The works of Michel Foucault, and to a lesser extent those of Jacques Derrida, are avidly read by the academic and political left, and one of Foucault's most incisive critics is the great Brazilian sociologist José-Guilhermeoo Merquior.[27] When the Sokal affair reached Brazil's shores in 1996, columnist Olavo de Carvalho took the defense of French theorists, stating that, "Derrida, Foucault, Lyotard . . . are not the cult objects of a provincial fan club, they are the idols of the international intelligentsia."[28] It was Deleuze and Guattari, however, who had the greatest impact in Brazil, as though this country lent itself better than any other to putting their hypotheses into practice. Thanks to the popularity of Deleuze and Guattari throughout Brazil, from Rio de Janeiro to Recife, and from the south to Belo Horizonte (where the Instituto Félix Guattari was founded), and because of the dynamic approach of their translators and commentators (including Suely Rolnik and Peter Pàl Pelbart), local universities and urban activists were able to join in and create veritable institutes of pluridisciplinary social action devoted to schizoanalysis, rhizomatic thought, and institutional therapies—and one must not forget the close friendship that Félix Guattari forged with unionist Luiz "Lula" da Silva, future president of Brazil.

We could continue on this worldwide tour, tracking the spread of French theory, looking at regions where the texts have had a direct impact, being read in full awareness of their French context, but where the unavoidable American hermeneutic influence can also be seen. In Russia, for example, it is claimed by Derrida scholars that the best translation of the word *perestroika* is *deconstruction;* in the European nations bordering France, naturally, French theory was, for several years, less an academic field than an active policy of political resistance (one thinks of Foucault's success with the militant bohemians of Kreuzberg in Berlin, and the rebellious Radio Alice station in Bologna, influenced by Deleuze and Guattari); and even in China, the editor and survivor of the Cultural Revolution Yue Daiyun[29] is now having Jameson and Lyotard translated for the state university press, and deconstruction and poststructuralism are currently meeting with great success, heralded as theorizations of an "exhaustion of Western culture."[30] It is, however, in Japan, that this brief journey must come to an end, so that we can understand the untarnished vitality that French theory retains when in contact with antipodal cultures, but also so that we may fully appreciate the inextricable blend of French texts and American commentary that French theory has come to represent abroad. One must not forget Japan's economic power and sense of cultural initiative—Japan represents American university presses' most important customer for exported works, which means that the country often forms a gateway to Asia through which Western academic imports undergo a Japanese mediation before being passed on to Korea, Taiwan, or Southeast Asia.

In principle, the linguistic and cultural distance is all-important. "Deconstruction," "essentialism," "postmodernity," and even "geometry" are examples of Western words that have been integrated into the Japanese language in the last two or three decades, because no *conceptual* Japanese equivalent existed. Academic exchanges with the West are not so recent. Kitaro Nishida, the great philosopher from the Meiji era, who died in 1945, had already interwoven some of Japanese culture's major motifs, including the *Zen* experience, the light of *satori,* and, as always, the melancholic awareness of the fragility of life (the *mono no aware*), with some of the important themes found in European philosophy—all the while denouncing the same conceptual dualisms criticized by French theory (between belief and knowledge, the self and the world, and nature and culture). It was this gradually built dialogue between the underlying correspondences of Japanese philosophy and the shifting positions of metaphysics, linking Bergson's *durée* with Buddhist time, and Baudelaire's city with the "amorphous" urbanity of Edo (Tokyo), that ensured that, forty years later, French theory would not be received as an exotic import but would be welcomed with an *active* integration. Following the war, the existentialist theses formulated by Sartre and de Beauvoir met with great success among the Japanese bourgeoisie, because their dialectic of a freedom *en situation* and their ethic of responsibility went some way toward soothing the pain of defeat and American occupation. Left-wing and anticapitalist movements became increasingly popular after the war and made extensive use of German philosophy, which was not limited to Hegel and Marx: before long in Japan, people casually spoke of *ka-ni-sho* when referring to the trio Kant, Nietzsche, and Schopenhauer. It was toward the end of the 1960s that French theory reached Japan, initially flying the colors of structuralism at its zenith. There were two distinct periods to its integration, however: first came the pioneering stage of dialogue, when the first translations of Foucault, Deleuze, and Derrida were made by talented scholars, who also wrote excellent introductions to the works (Foucault scholar Moriaki Watanabe and Deleuze disciple

Yujiro Nakamura, for example), which was also a time when several French authors made important trips to the country: Barthes, from 1967 to 1968, Foucault in 1970 and 1978, and Baudrillard in 1973 and 1981, stimulating a period of intense political activity, and testifying to the attempts to bring together left-thinking Japanese and European groups; second was the period of French theory's Americanization, which began in the mid-1980s, thanks to the impact of gender studies and cultural studies, and a new wave of feminist and homosexual activism taking place in Japan. At this time, American versions of French theory and pop culture were being used to reexamine the tradition of manga as a form of simulacrum, and the fantastical monster Godzilla was being cast in the light of a "Deleuzo-Guattarian schizo-science."[31] When people wanted to learn about Foucault, they now turned to David Halperin and Drefyus and Rabinow, and for commentaries on Derrida, they looked to de Man and Gayatri Spivak.

The boldness of contemporary Japanese art and architecture can be traced at once to local political activism, traditional Japanese practice, and the aesthetic theories of Deleuze, Lyotard, and Derrida (the latter being enlisted to boost the public success of art events, such as the antiapartheid exhibition held in Tokyo in 1988–90)—its forms were vast and varied, and included the fantastical urban events organized by the activist curator Fram Kitagawa and the temporary "habitats" installed by architect Shigeru Ban for use in natural disasters (such as the Kobe earthquake) or political catastrophes (like the Rwandan genocide). Indeed, at the turn of the millennium, Japan's *theoretical landscape* is rich and diverse, composed of its ancestral antidualism and the convergence of French theory and American imports. Thus, the series of events at Architecture New York (ANY) came to its close in 1998 in liaison with Japanese architects and art critics, and the great literary critic Karatani Kôjin cited a "will to architecture" as lying at the foundations of Western philosophy, and displaced the initial American project of deconstructivist architecture into the ranks of formalism or else dissecting it through Deleuze's critique of capital.[32] The young philosopher and social critic Hiroki Hazuma, who in 1999 won the famous Suntory prize for the humanities, studied the desubjectification of *otaku* (the anomic fans of manga and video games) while simultaneously working on the "second" Derridean deconstruction, which he called "postal," and put into perspective with the works of Lacan and Slavoj Žižek.[33] Even the Japanese actor from Peter Brooks's Parisian theater troupe, Yoshi Oida, who, with Barthes, wrote for the publication *Théâtre public* in the 1970s, is able to write, today, about his profession by intertwining the traditions of Noh and Kabuki with Artaud's reflections and Deleuze's theme of "becoming invisible."[34] The contributions of philosopher Akira Asada are particularly important: during the 1980s, he wrote several political theory treatises on "structure and power" (*kôzô to chikara*), inspired by the works of Deleuze and Foucault, that were intensively debated in Japan. His work paved the way for a highly contested use of French texts: he chose to use them to attack Japan's "infantile capitalism" and its illusions, rather than keep it within the safer territory of the *dialogue between cultures* that had traditionally been the way to mediate between Western philosophy and Japanese thought.[35] This was a promising possibility, but its future was less dependent on the French, or American, texts themselves than on the effectiveness of the social struggles being undertaken in Japan, between an economic power in crisis and an often flawed system of democracy. The dilemma faced by this potential new path was perceived by Félix Guattari in 1986 when, walking through the streets of Tokyo, he had the foresight to remark on the "vertigo of a different path for Japan: if Tokyo gave up being the capital of the East, of Western capitalism, to become the northern capital of the emancipation of the Third World."[36] This articulates the not entirely imaginary outlook of a veritable international counterpower: an axis between Mexico City, Rio, and Tokyo that would allow French theory, political discontent, effective micropolitical experiments, and the search for alternatives to the Western dogma of "modernization" to combine.

A German Subtext

While French theory's *effects* may extend as far as the plateaus of the Andes or the slopes of Mount Fuji, its cultural genealogy is to be found on territory much closer to home—just across the Rhine—where French "neostructuralism" enjoyed a critical reception that, although it came from a small number of sources, was nonetheless sharper and more in-depth than the one it received in the United States. The global circuits of French thought in the 1970s thus lead us, in the end, to Germany and its philosophical tradition, of which French theory sometimes served as a simple cultural translator—French mediation allowed the heritage of Marx,

Hegel, Nietzsche, and Heidegger to be discussed in Spanish, Japanese, or the many varieties of English spoken on campuses around the world. All of French theory's contributions, after all, from Foucault to Derrida, represented, before anything else, a critical dialogue with the two main branches of the German philosophical tradition (Husserlian, or phenomenological, on the one hand, and Hegelian-Marxist, on the other), which was introduced into French universities by the preceding generation in the period between the two world wars. Although its French detractors in the 1980s tried to demonize the foursome of Nietzsche, Heidegger, Marx, and Freud—supposedly the source of all French theory—simplistically and reductively claiming that "'68 thought" merely "slavishly prolonged" this "German antihumanism,"[37] it would be more accurate to describe French theory, while incorporating highly diverse influences, as a creative rereading of these four German thinkers rather than a continuation of structuralist criticism or French phenomenology.

Its American adversaries were not wrong in comparing French theory to a "selective reading" and an "aggressive rereading" of the four essential German sources.[38] In the United States, therefore, what took place was an American interpretation of French readings of German philosophy. Everything seems to suggest that the free uses of evaluation, reappropriation, reworking, and subversion that Foucault, Deleuze, and Derrida employed in their readings of Nietzsche, Freud, or Heidegger were subsequently extended to the American intellectual scene, and that it then used these techniques on the French authors themselves, in an example of unconscious mimetism that also brings us back to the notion of *transdiscursivity* we have already discussed—and furthermore helps explain why the themes of reading and interpretation became major preoccupations in the American approach to French theory. Indeed, sociologist Louis Pinto's keen observations regarding Foucault's and Deleuze's free readings of Nietzsche, and the "philosophical capital" that these readings provided, are equally applicable to the American interpretations of Foucault and Deleuze: "Nietzsche becomes the mirror in which his interpreters admire a discourse that is at once sophisticated and free, for which they aim to provide a new form of philosophical fulfillment" (or, in the United States, a *theoretical* form), so that Nietzsche's work is, in the end, no more than the "support for the discourses it inspires." It is a French *reworking* of the German text, followed by a secondary, American reworking of French texts, which aimed not so much to "propose hypotheses with contents that can be analyzed and evaluated" as to "locate in the text the singularities, paradoxes, and anomalies that confer on it all its hermeneutic plenitude."[39] The objective was not to construct a synthesis of Nietzsche's work (or, in the United States, of the works of Foucault or Derrida), but rather, through these names, to effect a complete dissociation, a break from all of history, as well as from the contemporary world, from philosophy, and from theory.

We might even discern echoes of the Franco-German philosophical debate of the 1970s and 1980s in certain controversies that arose in the new American intellectual scene. The confrontations between Marxists and poststructuralists, for example, or between modernists and postmodernists, which divided American academia as early as the 1980s, reflected and re-created the lively, and occasionally turbulent, dialogue between French theory and German critical theory. American thinkers, including Richard Rorty and Charles Taylor (the philosopher who theorized notions of individualism and communitarianism), and publications such as *Telos* and *New German Critique,* often attempted to mediate this more fundamental, and much older, dialogue; others tried to actively take part in the debate, including Butler, Spivak, and Stanley Fish, who wrote in defense of theory, and, on the other side, American successors to the Frankfurt School, including Nancy Fraser at the New School in New York, Seyla Benhabib at Yale, and Martin Jay at Berkeley. As with all hotly debated issues, however, this one tended to transform small divergences into sharp disagreements, and turn differences of opinion into oppositions that pitted one group against another, while obscuring the points that these two lines of inquiry had in common. Or, rather, this controversy made certain extreme positions—such as conservative naturalism versus radical relativism in the United States, or, in Germany, an all-out attack by devoted followers of Kant on French "irrationalism" and "neo-vitalism"—representative of the majority perspective. Admittedly, without reviving a debate that has already given birth to a weighty bibliography in France, we must remember that the divergences between French theory and critical theory, or *intensive* critique of reason and a democratic pragmatics of reason, have often appeared to represent a veritable Kulturkampf.

Thus, an appreciation for "surface effects" and "intensive" signs emerged in the works of French theorists like Deleuze and Lyotard, often in opposition to the concepts of metaphysical depth and the German obsession with foundations and absolutes. This Franco-German exchange, which began in the 1970s, later gave rise to several notable debates. The first one took place in 1981 at the Goethe Institute in Paris, between Derrida and Hans-Georg Gadamer: although the deconstructionist and the hermeneut could agree on exposing the transcendental illusion of "external" language, that is, one that we entirely control (because we do not so much speak language as language speaks through us), they disagreed on the very possibility of a discussion, which, in Gadamer's view, is conditioned by the agreement of the participants, whereas for Derrida it is constantly fraught with absence and disjunction.[40] Soon after, there was a similar debate between Lyotard and Jürgen Habermas, in which the positions at stake were Habermas's ethics of discussion, which posits the rational agreement of the interlocutors, and, on the other side, the critique of any "universal" consensus, which instead championed "small narratives" and the singularities of paralogy.[41] Finally, there was the Franco-German debate that sprang up at the time of Foucault's death concerning the philosophical legacy of his critique of Enlightenment thinkers: Manfred Frank made an opposing case for "critical" rationalism, and reproached "the aporias of a social critique that bypasses ethics and thus falls into categories derived from vitalism and social Darwinism,"[42] and Habermas, in one notorious article, also criticized the "reductionist" theories of power in Foucault and the French tradition of "transgressive" thought, while championing the notion of "communicative" rationalism, and even pointing to the icon of transgression, Georges Bataille, as the source for all of Foucault's work.[43] It was Habermas, in fact, who began this general debate: as early as his Frankfurt speech in 1980, given in acceptance of the Adorno Prize, Habermas called for a continuation of the "project of modernity" against postmodern "conservatism," and its "compromises" with late capitalism.

There were, however, many points of convergence between French and German philosophy. Beyond the facile, media-friendly image of philosophical disagreement, it was in fact largely by bringing together French theory and post-Frankfurt critical theory (or Frankfurters and French fries, as critic Rainer Nägele humorously dubbed the two schools of thought)[44] and examining each through the lens of the other that the international academic community, from Tokyo to Mexico, sought to illuminate contemporary mechanisms of power and capital, and the implications of social struggles—and constructed the foundations of a "world of theory." In fact, the historical diagnoses and critical outlooks of both sides of the debate dealt with similar concerns and objectives. French theory's desubstantialized subject, constructed through subjugation, on the one hand, and Habermas's notion of individual identity as "fluidified through communication," on the other, both played important and complementary roles in the famous investigation of the subject: Albrecht Wellmer even goes so far as to place these two concepts under the same heading of a "form of subjectivity that no longer corresponds to the rigid unity of the bourgeois subject."[45] Seyla Benhabib, moreover, evokes a continuity between "suspicion regarding the logic of identity," already found in the work of Adorno, and American feminist theses inspired by Foucault and Derrida (as found in Judith Butler and Joan Scott) concerning "identitarian categories . . . as necessarily leading to exclusion," a continuity—and a tension—that lead to her call to "rethink the project of contemporary critical theory" in order to adapt it to the historical present, which is marked by a "coming together of global integration and cultural fragmentation."[46] Those in favor of such a theoretical *alliance* support their position by delving into Deleuze's and Foucault's intuitions, as well as those found in the works of Adorno's successors, in order to concretely understand the new social forms currently replacing the old, liberal model of the bourgeois public sphere, for which Habermas offered a genealogy forty years earlier. In a similar manner, we might discern common ground between German philosopher Axel Honneth's notion of "contempt" and Lyotard's concept of "wrong" [*tort*], enabling us to consider new forms of social invisibility and humiliation.[47] The future of worldwide theory is therefore *also* contingent on complementary Franco-German thought; it is based on a limited, but crucial, alliance between approaches whose respective ethos, styles of thought, basic thematic preoccupations, and, above all, intellectual followers set them at odds, but whose common objective of forming an active critique of the historical present nonetheless unites them.

14

MEANWHILE, BACK IN FRANCE . . .

> Everything eventually begins to look old, so sooner or later
> we'll start hearing talk about the old *anti-'68* generation.
> PHILIPPE SOLLERS, *Le nihilisme ordinaire*

THIS CHAPTER could be placed under the heading "France; or, The World Inverted." Following the developments in the United States, Lacanian-Derridean and Foucauldian-Deleuzean perspectives gradually began to occupy the intellectual field in many countries. But not only did these discourses gradually subside in France, the mere possibility of discussing theory was virtually banished from the scene. As the authors passed away (Barthes in 1980, Lacan in 1981, Foucault in 1984, Guattari in 1992, Deleuze in 1995, Lyotard in 1998),[1] their presence in the public sphere gradually shrank into obituaries and intellectual nostalgia, and their legacy became the monopoly of a few isolated heirs and the official rights holders of their publications. Henceforth, their only relevance was editorial, historical, or commemorative, in other words, posthumous. Whereas French economic policy between 1981 and 1983 had dared to move against the current followed everywhere else, for more than a quarter century the French intellectual community had practiced its very own exceptionalism, obstinately turning its back on the rest of the world. Intellectual sociodemography may one day shed light on the long-term consequences of the sudden reversal of the turn of the 1980s, a change whose history I will recall here. One day, one might be able to produce a solid explanation of this brutal interruption of growth, this clipping of the blossoms, this sudden withering of young shoots—to use botanical metaphors for a process that prevented French theory from having more than a very few disciples in France itself, and, in the last analysis, any successors. Which may well explain the inexorable decline of French intellectual influence in the world since the high point of French theory—even if we take into account the time needed for cultural exchange (for example, the fifteen years that separated *Anti-Oedipus*'s moment of glory in France from its explosive impact in Argentina)—a decline that the current French intelligentsia hardly seems capable of reversing anytime soon. This unfortunate gap involves an entire history of traditions, grudges, bad faith, and ideology, and is, of course, a tactical and political history as well. Perhaps it is also an effect of France's unjustifiable superiority complex in intellectual matters, which has led to statements about the Americans like the one made in 1909 by a certain Saint-André de Lignereux: "They can try all they like to throw around huge checks and found universities, academies, and museums, it will not do any good; they will have to bow to our intellectual supremacy."[2]

Restoring Humanism, or the Return of Bloated Concepts

The facts are well known. In 1974, the famous Soviet dissident Aleksandr Solzhenitsyn arrived in Paris. His *Gulag Archipelago* was published, sparking acerbic polemics between anti-Marxist intellectuals and the French Communist Party, which dug in its heels, going so far as to suggest that dissidents were either fascists or CIA agents. The leitmotif of *revolution* so pervasive since 1968 was eclipsed and within a few months was pushed from center stage in favor of a different question, more moral than utopian. As Bernard-Henri Lévy summed up in 1977, "the chief question of our time . . . [is] the totalitarian state."[3] Moreover, from 1976 to 1978, an organized opposition to all forms of the revolutionary Left still active in France crystallized around the support of dissidents, anti-Soviet petitions, and the first large-scale humanitarian operations (including the media free-for-all that accompanied Bernard Kouchner's operation "A Boat for Vietnam"). Reversals and defections came one after the other, with former Maoist militants and student leaders joining forces against the Soviet (and Chinese) gulags or taking up the cause of the "boat people," going so far as to develop a systematic moral blackmail aimed at intellectuals. The message: either convert immediately or you will go into the stocks and be displayed in the public square. Because this time, they warned, the die-hard radicals will not pass through the net. It was time to proclaim the end of the great masters and their decrees in the intellectual sphere—a call for expulsion that would resonate, for example, in the inaugural issue of Pierre Nora's journal *Le Débat*, which he founded in 1980 in order to create what he called a "Republic *in* letters"—in other words, to impose a Republican order within the realm of public debate and literary activity.[4]

Thus was launched an offensive against dictatorships, against May 1968, against rebellion in general, *and* against theory. A group of young intellectuals supported by the journal *Les Nouvelles littéraires* and the publisher Grasset constituted the avant-garde of the reaction, dubbing themselves the "nouveaux philosophes." Their leaders, Bernard-Henri Lévy, André Glucksmann, Maurice Clavel, and a few others saw spectacular successes in bookstores with their topical essays denouncing revolutionary thought and placing human rights once again at the center of the "debate." This literary operation was first of all focused on the conquest of the intellectual field. For Lévy seemed more interested in attacking of Deleuze and Guattari's "ideology of desire" than denouncing the Soviet camps, and Glucksmann, quoting Hegel, declared that "to think is to dominate," laying the charge of Nazism and Stalinism on the great German philosophers. The secular Republic found its last idol to smash in thought itself. If the new censors were to be believed, theoretical critique, or even critical theory, led straight to Auschwitz and Kolyma, henceforth interchangeable. As Michael Löwy and Robert Sayre put it, "the '*nouveaux philosophes*' and others are gleefully trampling their ideological idols of yesterday, relegating every notion of social critique to the dustbin of history while they were at it."[5] The publication of the first issue of *Révoltes logiques*—the journal created by Jacques Rancière to rethink the question of the proletariat—was met with general indifference, while the contemporary appearance of *Esprit* and Raymond Aron's journal *Commentaire* caused quite a stir, as did *Le Matin de Paris,* a new daily newspaper close to the Socialist Party. And then there was the newly festive format of the (formerly underground) magazine *Actuel,* whose inaugural editorial column now predicted that "the 1980s will be active, technological, and fun."

These were above all years during which the intellectual field, particularly the French liberal tradition of the nineteenth century, underwent an exhumation, a digging up of graves that also sought to smooth over ideological differences. This process occurred within the concomitant horizon (after a century of French political exceptionalism) of a "republic of the center."[6] Marcel Gauchet and Pierre Rosanvallon led the rediscovery of Tocqueville and Benjamin Constant. Alain Renaut and Gilles Lipovetsky explored the figure of the "individual" as an accomplishment of modernity. Roger Faroux, Alain Minc, and François Furet created the Fondation Saint-Simon, France's elite think tank, and Pierre Nora's *Le Débat* went so far as to relegate the concept of alienation to the Marxian Middle Ages.[7] Similarly, Blandine Kriegel linked every form of political romanticism with totalitarian logic. John Rawls and Friedrich Hayek were finally translated into French. A few months before the bicentennial of the Revolution Mona Ozouf and François Furet asserted that, contrary to Marxian historiography, "the French Revolution [was] over," and that according to Furet's 1978 reinterpretation of the period, it had been invalidated by the Terror already in 1793.[8] Meanwhile, the transition from the 1970s to the 1980s also saw Foucault and Deleuze, seconded by the aging Sartre and Claude Mauriac, come together to fight for the Vietnamese refugees and against the police actions in the Arab-African quarter of Paris known as the Goutte d'Or. Along with others, the same group later threw their weight behind the Solidarity movement in Poland following General Jaruzelski's attempts to repress it. These were specific actions, focused on the site and event in question, and none of these activists participated in the witch hunts that were then brewing.

For their part, the "nouveaux philosophes" saw that they could capture part of the prestige of the very intellectuals they were striving to render irrelevant, discreetly co-opting various themes or concepts precisely to turn them against what in the United States was not yet called "French Theory." Glucksmann, for example, was a student of Foucault. Lévy was a student of Derrida. Similarly, Blandine Kriegel and Pierre Rosanvallon were both mainstays, for a time, in Foucault's seminar at the Collège de France. The tactical *détournement* of the older generation was carried out in the bluntest and most direct manner possible. As early as 1978, Lévy asserted that the events of May 1968 constituted "the first important mass *anticommunist* resistance in the West."[9] He then went on to attack the "barbarism" and "death wish" of Foucault and Deleuze (*Anti-Oedipus,* according to Lévy, was the "master text of the movement"). But in doing this he also appropriated the vocabulary of their opponents, using the Deleuzean concepts of "flows" and hubris to describe capitalism,[10] while Glucksmann, in his *La Cuisinière et le mangeur d'hommes*, employed concepts from Foucault's *Discipline and Punish* in his denunciation of the gulag. If the new movement was not yet ideologically unified—the "Christo-Leftists" Christian Jambet and Guy Lardreau created their own postmodern and vaguely anarchist version of left Hegelianism[11]—it quickly left the "anarchist temptation" and the libertarian accents of the early days behind in favor of moral change and, politically speaking, a tactical centrism that nevertheless suffered from its contacts with "the institutional Left." Lévy had already directed *Barbarism with a Human Face* at the latter, assuring us that it would soon have "our destiny in its hands." Indeed it did.

During François Mitterrand's first term in office as the socialist president of France (from 1981 to 1988), feuding between the Left in power and the intellectual avant-garde of the preceding decade aided the new "centrist" humanists. Concerning the situation in Poland and the harsh criticism voiced by radical left-wing intellectuals against the French Socialists' refusal to react, Jack Lang denounced "a typically structuralist ineffectiveness"[12] in a December 1981 editorial in *Le Matin;* not long after this, editorialist and government spokesperson Max Gallo, in a July 1983 issue of *Le Monde*, expressed his regret at the "silence of left-wing intellectuals" and their lackluster support for the "forces" of the Socialist-Communist coalition in the French government known as the "union of the Left." Some broke ranks, others spouted clichés about the "end of ideology," but the main result was the intellectual disarray that characterized France in the 1980s. The causes and conditions of this situation would require a historical analysis of its own, but even at the time editorialists and magazines were already highlighting certain obvious factors: the social triumph of the individual (rather than the "return of the subject"), the celebration of irony and carefree fun as stopgap values, a new antiutopian realism linked to rising unemployment, and the conversion of the baby boomers (and the activists of 1968) to a professional business culture long held in contempt. The disarray was also linked to a profound reorganization of the French intellectual world, where dominant positions were to an ever greater extent transferred from alternative universities to the official media. This transformation also included a migration from unaffiliated radical Left positions toward new center-left circles. The critique of capital and bourgeois culture was left behind in favor of a new geopolitical and humanitarian outrage. And if we survey

the ruins of third worldism, the vacuum left by a general intellectual de-
mobilization, and the empty forums of an abandoned debate, we see the
empty space that had to be filled. What soon emerged in that space was a
combination of republican neo-Kantianism (in the intellectual field) and
an "ethical" mobilization (in favor of victims of starvation or of racism,
for example) that remained the last political rallying point, focused on
specific issues and highly mediatized—all of which helps to explain the
rise of a new ideology of consensus officially promoted by members of
the government: humanitarian moralism.

The issue here is not the legitimacy of this discourse, or the needs
of its distant "beneficiaries." The question is how it became central to
French intellectual life, restructuring its contours and giving rise to a
medicalization of French political thought. This role was organized
around the community of NGOs, which can be considered as part of the
horizon of a new "humanitarian" biopower. And it emerged just as the
American multiculturalists and British Marxists, galvanized, no doubt,
by the more clearly reactionary agenda of Margaret Thatcher and Ronald Reagan, were stigmatizing the Western "condescension" and bourgeois "good conscience" behind the newly fashionable wave of Western
philanthropy. For French ideologues, humanitarian intervention henceforth became the "Eleventh Commandment."[13] Soon, humanitarian intervention would play the same role for the intellectual community that
revolt had played for the preceding generation. A new "martyrology"
was created, a catalog of victims that not only filled the political vacuum
but, more tactically, branded with moral vacuity the ideological analysis
and the critical discussion that attempted to put it in perspective. Moreover, from Médecins du monde to the Restos du cœur, the shift resulted
in strong public support for the new "postmetaphysical" humanism defended by the young Turks of the transformed intellectual scene. As early
as 1977, Deleuze had attacked this "martyrology" that fed "off cadav-
ers" for its morality of ressentiment and its censorious paternalism, for
its way of imposing itself on the public sphere and defusing the power
of affirmation (vital or even revolutionary) of the "victims" in question.
"The victims had to be people who think and live in a completely different way, only then could they provide a basis for the actions of those who
are now weeping in their name, thinking in their name, and handing out
lessons in their name."[14]

However, there was never a genuine discussion between the new "democrats" of the intellectual scene and the writers, their elders, whom they denounced as perpetrators of a deliberate intellectual muddle—1968 thinking, libertarian barbarism, irrationalism, dictatorship, irresponsibility. As for the targets of these accusations, they were busy with their own work and quite rightly considered that they had better things to do than respond to such attacks. For his part, Lyotard was content to sit back and laugh. In his *Instructions païennes,* the new "game" in Paris was being played by "Clavie" (Clavel) and "Glukie" (Glucksmann) as they tossed the "grand narrative" of "Jessie" (Jesus) back and forth. Deleuze had already said it all in the 1977 article, which went virtually unnoticed: return of the "gross dualisms" and "bloated concepts, all puffed up like an abscess" (*the* law, *the* world, etc.), a "wholesale return to the author, to an empty and vain subject," an annoying "reactionary development," the invention of a kind of "literary or philosophical marketing" that was no more than "journalism [considered as] an autonomous and sufficient thought within itself." In conclusion, Deleuze wrote that "where once a little breeze was blowing, they have closed the window. It's stifling, suffocating. This is the total negation of politics and experiment."[15] The only thing missing from his brief analysis was this two-pronged argument, more sociological than philosophical, which lay behind the movement's strategic goals: the pursuit of a new moralizing "careerism," on the one hand, and, on the other, the supposed anticonformism and freedom of thought now associated with such populist denunciations of older legitimate thinkers. Bourdieu had formulated this last general law, the dynamic that regulates competition within the intellectual field in terms of the field's own logic, creating marvelous opportunities for the new French moralists (from Lévy to Finkielkraut or Bruckner) as well as for their conservative cousins in the United States (the Kimballs, Kramers, or D'Souzas of the anti-PC front): "It is a matter of overturning the dominant representation . . . and of demonstrating that conformity lies on the side of the avant-garde . . . : true daring belongs to those who have the courage to defy the conformity of anticonformity."[16] The new message, in other words, presented itself as ecumenical and straightforward—one reason for its great success. Don't worry, they repeated, the aristocracy of exclusionary jargon and of "radical chic" is over, tossed into the dustbin of history—the field is now clear and good, honest people can finally return.

Less than ten years after the beginning of this offensive, the coup de grâce—which horrified the less prescient disciples of poststructural-ism—was applied by Luc Ferry and Alain Renaut in *La Pensée 68*.[17] Their copious writings denounced Nietzscheanism, and then, in the midst of the uproar created by the 1987 Heidegger affair, Heidegger and French Heideggerianism. Calling for a "return to Kant" and to the ideal of human rights, Ferry and Renaut went on to elevate Man to the status of a divinity while humanizing God, a double project that in a single ges-ture revealed just how far French philosophy had come since the 1970s.[18] Yet *La Pensée 68* had more specific targets. Unsatisfied with condemning Foucault, Derrida, or Lacan for having "gone even further" than Ger-man irrationalism, Ferry and Renaut now leaped upon Marx, exhibit-ing in their book an obsessive anti-Marxism that was enough in itself to demonstrate their total ignorance of the real significance of French theory, insofar as it was above all an alternative and a complement to Marx. The attack was a preamble to an attempt to lay the foundations for a fin de siècle humanism, supposedly less "naive" than those that had arisen before the 1960s, a maturity this humanism also owed to the "aporias . . . of antihumanism."[19] The interlude is over, the two authors concluded, and to the extent that it was able to arm responsible citizens against the illusions of the first humanism, the folklore of the "ideolo-gies of desire" was perhaps not a completely futile adventure. But over-whelmingly, the virtuous argument of moral commitment was the order of the day here, there, and everywhere. Just as Lévy launched his crusade in 1977, concluding that "there remains only ethics and moral duty" to help us avoid "surrender and abandonment before the procession of Evil,"[20] Pierre Nora accused the human sciences of having discarded the "ethical function" and "everyday morality" for twenty years.[21] For their part, Ferry and Renaut went so far as to accuse Foucault and Deleuze for having privileged—as an implication of their work—the "Ego of con-temporary narcissism," its "cool" disintegration and its heteronomy,[22] thus without so much as a wink imputing to them the long egocentric celebration of the 1980s.

Convinced that every one of France's problems, and thus the prob-lems of the rest of the world, were the result of May 1968, of the un-ruly philosophies of the 1970s, and of the new identity-based "relativ-ism"—made in the USA—these moral athletes continue to hold the reins of power in the French intellectual world. Lévy via the press and publish-ing, and through his presence in the hallways of power. Nora as director of *Le Débat* and through his friends at *Esprit* and *Commentaire*, not to mention his links to Aronians and Tocquevillians young and old at the Sorbonne and the EHESS (École des Hautes Études en Sciences Sociales). Rosanvallon and Kriegel exert their influence via the CFDT (Confédération française démocratique du travail, France's leading center-left labor union) and their close ties to various cabinet ministers. Finally, other members of the movement hold or have held actual political posts, Renaut at the Conseil national des programmes, and Luc Ferry, the first minister of education to come from "civil society"—a sermonizing minister who during the debate over his controversial reforms or in his "Letter to all those who love school," officially sent to every French teacher, routinely blamed the "disaster" of the education system on "communitarian tendencies," "demagogic youthism," and the "ideology of spontaneity" inherited from "May 68" and its intellectual leaders.[23]

A Gradual Return of the Repressed

But not all the important actors of this "modernized" French society agree that Foucault, Deleuze, Baudrillard, or even Guy Debord should be consigned to oblivion. Among the readers of these writers were business theoreticians, management strategists, insurers and risk managers, advertising executives and the pioneers of the infomercial, C-level execs of the culture industry, columnists in hip magazines, and all the other enthusiasts of "self-organization conceived of as festive neoconservatism."[24] This readership has discovered unexpected relevance in the writings of the incriminated philosophers of the preceding generation—for the greater benefit of the new "self-organizing" social order they are promoting. First, they appropriated the logic of flux and of dissemination, along with their distinctive vocabulary, and then placed them at the service of vague theories of "streamlined" or "networked" businesses. "Together with the authoritative argument conferred by innumerable references to Derrida, Foucault, and Lyotard," writes Armand Mattelart, "we are given explanations of the birth of the 'postmodern business' as an immaterial entity, . . . an abstract conception, . . . a vaporous world of flows, fluids, and communicating vessels."[25] In pursuit of a fashionable edginess, many in the world of French PR, advertising, and the press brandished slogans taken from Debord's *Society of the Spectacle*, turning them into refrains on the "integrated spectacle" or the "shift from

having to appearing." Generally speaking, all of the canonical thinkers whose work could be made to recite, in the opposite direction of
their own internal logic, the new credo of self-generation and subjectless
organization—the fashionable variant of the invisible hand (and much
less burdened with older connotations)—found themselves parodied in
the press and in the speeches of the new consultants-philosophers of the
1990s. From the Spinozan *conatus* to Deleuzean immanence to Foucauldian microphysics, to the even more mystical theses drawn from karma-
cola Buddhism, suddenly everything could be used to sing the new ode to
the self-regulating market, even if it had to be coated in a new libertarian
lyricism.

More specifically in this context, the work of Michel Foucault became
the object of an ideological appropriation, discreet but persistent, by certain important managerial and government groups—from the scientists
theorizing social engineering and cybernetic control at the École Poly-
technique, to the CFDT, the centrist labor union run by Jacques Julliard
and Nicole Notat that pushed for the final shift from the more utopian
notion of self-management in the 1970s toward new and "empowering"
types of "participatory" management programs, all the way up to government roundtables on unemployment, insurance reform, and social
security.[26] At the initiative of François Ewald, Foucault's former assistant
at the Collège de France, and Denis Kessler, the president of the French
Federation of Insurance Companies (and soon to be the vice president of
the Medef, the French union of employers, and the man behind its project of "social refoundation"), right-leaning and entrepreneurial readings
of Foucault's work began to appear in a more systematic manner, building on the new *assurantielle* or insurance-based conceptions of society.
The new social management theories developed by Ewald and Kessler
were founded on a distinction between "risk-prone" and "risk-averse"
individuals, making the concept of risk the basis of a "morality and an
epistemology," which they argued was the only "way to define the value
of values."[27] Ewald, who would go on to reinterpret the "precautionary
principle" during the clamor over mad cow disease,[28] began to study law
just before the death of Foucault and cultivated contacts in the new networks created by the Fondation Saint-Simon. He wrote the foundation's
first "green paper" in 1982. He quickly subverted the legacy of Foucault,
incited by his former master to "replace" him (but so that he could "develop his own point of view in his place") at a conference on philosophy

and international law in the Hague at the end of 1983, where Ewald described the "crisis" of the Kantian universal in the same way that Foucault had before him, but concluding on a note more legalistic than Foucauldian and asserting that "Foucault's entire oeuvre demands that . . . we examine how the transformations of the international community, power relations, commercial practices, and cultural relations can be and will be the basis for a *new juridical order*."[29]

But it is with *L'État providence*, published in 1986 and dedicated to Foucault, that Ewald laid the theoretical bases of this right-wing neoliberal insurance-inspired Foucauldianism. In this book he cites certain key concepts of the late Foucault to prop up a variously formulated ideological project, which more or less corresponds to "the formulation of a *new political imaginary*"[30] based on the rethinking of the notion of insurance and risk management, an *imaginaire assurantiel*. Beginning from Foucault's archaeology, Ewald goes on to construct a historical fatalism and a prescriptive bias that are strictly his own. Foucault's major historical discovery of a "shift from law to norm" is not used to think the new form of power "whose task is to take charge of life,"[31] but rather is employed in support of a loosening of the law and a "revision of the Civil Code" to cover all possible risks. Further, the category of "abnormals" studied by Foucault in his 1975 seminar now refers more particularly to all those who, "deviating too far from the norm . . . [become] a *risk* for the group, a danger."[32] Justifying his work on the welfare state by the urgency of reflecting on "better ways of managing it," namely, via a "postcritical hypothesis" that he opposes to the "oversensitive denunciations that too frequently characterize the human sciences," Ewald's program here was indeed a genealogy, but also (going beyond the genealogical method) a political justification of the "process by which responsibility comes to be conceived in terms of insurance" and of a society that in his view has historically succeeded the age of the "legal identification of culpability and responsibility."[33] The thrust of this program was to demonstrate that insurance was the last viable form of the social bond at a moment when each individual—whether he be the owner of an oil tanker, a die-hard smoker, or someone lacking job security—is first of all understood as a bearer of a certain fraction of the collective risk. "Through the diversity and the articulation of its *networks*, insurance has become what *practically* links us to one another, outside of the *free* and *voluntary* relationships of the family; it is the social bond itself, its *materiality*."[34] This is very far indeed from the modes of subjection studied by Foucault. Beneath the surface of the only joint essay of Ewald and Kessler, who redefine society as "one vast system of insurance against the risks provoked by its own development,"[35] another program is being launched: a wall-to-wall cybernetic reinterpretation of the Foucauldian theories of "biopower" and "security societies" that is not primarily concerned with historical archaeology, but rather with legitimizing technocracy. For more than twenty years, between postmodern apocalypticism and managerial rationality, a sociology of collective chaos and its management through insurance had been developing around the concept of the "society of risk" (*Risikogesellschaft*) introduced by the German sociologist Ulrich Beck.[36] This society of risk reevaluates the social hierarchy in terms of the "cost" that individuals represent for social security and health care (the oppressed being stigmatized for the "risk" that their insecure position poses to society), and envisages real-time mechanisms of reaction to "accidents" and "inequalities." A spectral form of survival in an aggressively ideological form that Foucault would surely have rejected.

At the moment when the philosophical and political debates spurred by French theory were taking center stage in American academia, in France itself it was thus being doubly mistreated. Evacuated, on the one hand, from the public intellectual scene by the neoliberals or the traditionalists who called on everyone to put May 1968 behind them, it was also, on the other hand, the object of distortions by the new experts attempting to renew an outmoded tradition of managerial and administrative theory. As for the French university, where French theory first blossomed yet where it had always had a more or less marginal status (it was more widely read at the Université de Vincennes than at the Sorbonne, cited in a few literary theory courses, but rarely placed in graduate philosophy programs), it was often presented as a prime example of academia gazing at its own navel, far removed from the debates being pursued in the media and the public sphere and remote from the completely different issues that preoccupied the international academic world at the time. Save for a few atypical and thus duly marginalized institutions, it seemed as though yesterday's pedagogical methods and cognitive "universalism" had not changed for decades. Such developments are symptoms of French academia's obstinacy when confronted with anything that, from interdisciplinary studies to identity studies, might begin to erode its precious ahistorical *autonomy*. Philosophy departments in particular preferred to retain a *prestructuralist* curriculum rather than make a place for the paradigm of *la pensée intensive,* from which, as Foucault warned in 1969, it would be difficult for the history of philosophy as it was then taught to recover: "to think intensity . . . is to reject the negative, . . . to reject, in the same movement, the philosophies of identity and those of contradiction, . . . finally, to reject the great figure of the Same, in whose circle Western philosophy, from Plato to Heidegger, has always been bound."[37] French academia, however, saved its fiercest resistance for Anglo-Saxon thought inspired by intensive philosophy, banning from the institution anything redolent of minority studies, the debate on communitarianism, theories on sexual identity, and even constructionist sociologies of science.

In the French university, philosophy and literature departments, with their uniform methodologies and their unified canon, were quite stubborn in their resistance to the epistemological eclecticism and bibliographical heterogeneity characteristic of the bastardized interdisciplinary programs, such as gender and cultural studies, that had been appearing in the United States for the last twenty-five years. As for the French social sciences, they often touted the fact that they had repelled the wave of American postmodernism, a category into which they tossed the anthropologist Clifford Geertz and studies of postcolonialism or pop culture. So strong was the resistance to these American trends that in certain fields the social sciences remained attached to the anthropological paradigms of the 1950s. Anyone who proposed organizing a seminar on sexual minorities or even on the cultural practices of migrant workers often ran the risk of being branded a dangerous communitarian or a purveyor of superficial postmodern concepts—all defects attributed by hearsay to the American academic. Such criticism was more broadly directed at American society, which French observers had always viewed as a financial and technological monster rotten with cultural ignorance and tribalism: "From Duhamel to Bernanos, from Mounier to Garaudy, the cause seemed clear," notes Philippe Roger, referring to this very French tradition. "No detractor of the American way of life has ever failed to pose as an advocate of downtrodden humanity."[38]

And yet . . . In spite of the resistance of academia, in spite of the demonization of America and its "balkanized" universities, in spite of the occupation of the French public sphere by the pundits of universalist humanism and abstract ideals of the Republic, the door finally opened a crack, after a twenty-year delay, allowing in certain American contributions to theory. Very gradually, very polemically, and with great difficulty, this opening provoked a return of the repressed from the 1970s, this time in the form of a theoretical inquiry into identity and communities. The ongoing controversy over what is referred to as the "Islamic head scarf" [*le foulard islamique*], which first erupted in October 1989 after two junior high school students in the Parisian suburb of Creil refused to "leave God behind at the school gates," has allowed moderate viewpoints to gradually emerge and receive a hearing. The mainstream secular camp could no longer denounce the holders of such opinions as "traitors to the Republic"—unless they simply wanted to forbid any discussion of the issue. The year 1997 saw the first major national conference on gay and lesbian studies, organized at the initiative of Didier Éribon at Beaubourg, as well as the parliament vote on the PACS (Pacte Civil de Solidarité), a civil union bill drawn up by the government of Lionel Jospin and designed to offer a civil status to homosexual couples. At the same time, the laws on "parity" or gender equality in government jobs provided the occasion for a debate on affirmative action, a discussion that had long been considered impossible, limited though it was for the time being to relations between the sexes. But little by little, between the mockery of some and the universalist sermons of others—whose shrill warnings about a slide into "tribalism" or cultural "Leninism" still echoed through the media—issues such as discrimination against minorities, the presence of ethnic groups in the media, same-sex parenting, or even subversive forms of pop culture in certain communities finally became topics of serious and legitimate debate throughout France.

But there is still a long road ahead. French cultural isolation on these issues of communitarian being-together and identity politics is very far from dissipating. For it is not enough merely to concede a formal, or folklorist, type of legitimacy to certain people in the way one might add a new category to a census form. French society has only begun to grope toward the question of the multiple subject and the simultaneous appurtenance to multiple minorities—contrary to the Republican request to kindly leave all such affiliations at the door when entering the neutral space of "common values." This question has yet to be fully integrated into the social sciences, activist organizations, and the major institutions (or their alternative counterparts) in the intellectual field, much less into a long-term historical paradigm. Not to mention the fact that the major

Anglo-American intellectuals in question—widely translated into German, Italian, or Spanish—have yet to be published in French: although key works by Judith Butler, Paul Gilroy, and Fredric Jameson have finally appeared in French since 2002–3, much remains to be done with the likes of Gayatri Spivak, Stanley Fish, or Donna Haraway. And although seminars and roundtables are finally being organized on French campuses in order better to understand the nature of such exotic academic objects as "cultural studies" or the "postcolonial paradigm" (the latter having much to contribute to an understanding of France's current immigration and assimilation crisis), no interdepartmental program or even reading list has been established for them yet. Such a belatedness can only be seen as part of a tenacious tradition of intellectual isolationism, especially if one considers that it took more than twenty years for works as widely recognized as Thomas Kuhn's *The Structure of Scientific Revolutions* or John Rawls's *A Theory of Justice* to be translated into French. Among the major American intellectual currents of the last quarter century, virtually none have been received to any significant degree in France, neither analytic philosophy, nor the convergences of pragmatism and Continental philosophy, nor radical multiculturalism, nor deconstructionist readings of literature, nor postcolonial theory and subaltern studies, nor even the new theories of gender identity—despite a timid, recent emergence, "slowly but surely," of the queer question.[39] Indeed, France changes only slowly, or under duress. In addition to its enduring relevance, Walter Benjamin's observation from the beginning of the 1930s regarding the "left-wing French intellectual," from the "République des professeurs" to the no longer new "nouveaux philosophes" of the following century, seems even more relevant today than it was thirty years ago: "their positive function derives entirely from a feeling of obligation, not to the revolution but to traditional culture," because very often in France the "conformism [of writers] turns a blind eye to the world in which it lives." As an example, he goes on to say that what the "novel of the last decade [i.e., the late 1920s and early 1930s] has achieved for freedom" is more present in Proust's pages on homosexuality than in any "social novel" from the period between the wars.[40]

It is thus that, politically rejected in its own country and rendered largely textual on American campuses, French theory, thirty years after the publication of its major texts, still points toward a collective task left undone, an intellectual potential that remains intact, and to the horizon, specifically its own, of a full and complete theoretical practice, neither demonized by the moralists nor vaporized into rhetorical abstraction or armchair radicalism. An unlikely third way has been suggested by the critic Peter Starr, who dismisses both the moral blackmail of the "nouveaux philosophes" and the invectives of academics "too attached to the sublime body of theory" to confront social struggles or the chaos of the commodity. It is urgently necessary, he concluded in 1995, to invent alternatives to this "overly simple choice between terroristic antiterrorism [in France] and a monarchism driven by the terror of the commodity [in the United States]."[41] Alternatives, in other words, to the choice we have had so far between moralism and sophistry, between the narrow rationality of the French guard dogs and the discussions of the crisis of reason that very often, in the United States, veer into a mere "crisis of verse."[42]

Pure Science and the *Raison d'État*

Alan Sokal set himself up as a critic of French theory using a hoax as his manifesto. Sokal, with whom we began this inquiry, did nothing more than lift the veil of prudery obscuring the veritable theoretical orgy that had shaken American academia for thirty years, thirty years of discursive and conceptual debauchery of which France, on the other side of the Atlantic, had little awareness. All Sokal did was to pluck one loose thread from this veil, but it was enough to unravel the entire cloth. The physicist certainly had his reasons—his ambition was less to make an apology for an ideological program (in spite of his dubious call for a return to "values") than to defend his disciplinary turf, the territory occupied by the hard sciences. For if in this overview it has been less a question of science's territoriality than of the "culture wars," the latter nonetheless set off, as if by ricochet, a genuine *war of the sciences* in the United States, waged with beating drums as the human sciences stormed the impenetrable fortress of the American technoscientific complex. For the pioneers of French theory, there was from the very beginning a great temptation to deploy their new subversive tools against the scientific world and its austere separatism. As early as 1973, the critics Marilyn August and Ann Liddle suggested that "the process which uses science to interrogate literature is reversed, so that works such as those of Artaud and Bataille become the instruments which operate upon and contest the sciences."[43] But it was in 1976 at an interdisciplinary conference held at

Cornell, and with the creation of the Society for Social Studies of Science, that a *constructionist* sociology of the sciences was born. It was derived less from Bataille and his posterity than from the intersection of French theory, the British Marxian anthropology of the sciences of the Edinburgh School, and the American functionalist sociology of institutions launched by Robert Merton in the 1950s. Thus, an epistemological phase of the sociology of sciences, linked to the Anglo-American reception of the work of Thomas Kuhn, was succeeded by a more empirical current originating in the studies of California laboratories undertaken by Bruno Latour and Steve Woolgar, a current that would soon integrate cultural, ethnic, and even sexual factors into its inquiries. Prior to the emergence of the radical identity politics of the 1990s, which turned its weapons on Patriarchal Reason or Imperialist Science, the tide was already rising and triggering a new type of interdepartmental conflict within the university, between the hard sciences and the humanities and literary studies.

But rather than identifying an enemy or designating its victims, the mission that Bruno Latour defined for "science studies," far more rigorous but no less ambitious, was to go beyond the old normative approaches (which distinguished "good" and "bad" science) and historicist approaches (content to trace a simple "progress" of knowledge), in order to "understand how science and technology were providing some of the ingredients necessary to account for the very making and the very stability of society."[44] Science as a rational model, as the ultimate guarantor of the social order: this was an epistemo-political hypothesis that French sociology of science, which had attempted to isolate figures like Latour or Isabelle Stengers and to circumvent their research networks, did not wish to reevaluate, rejecting the idea that science could be understood first of all as a *construct*,[45] that it might exist wholly within the limits of history, and that the French "passion" for science (hand in hand with widespread technophobia) might also be able to shed light on France's political mores. For the old radical-socialist trust in science and research conceals the typically French model of the "rational state," a state whose model is precisely that of scientific rationality, a French Republic historically constituted by science. Science, as the ultimate foundation, here becomes a veritable *"raison d'État"* [literally, "reason of state," or public policy], and the ultimate rampart against every form of relativism, whether cognitive or identitarian. Just as in France the activity of a laboratory or research unit, whether concerned with physics or with history, is called "scientific" prior to (or instead of) specifying the object of that activity—as if the designation "scientific" rendered irrelevant the question of whether the work deals with a specific field or a specific procedure or depends on a specific social or ethnic community—the French conception of the Republic likewise declares to the minorities it includes that it does not regard them as Jews, North Africans, or homosexuals, but *exclusively* as citizens. Citizenship and science function here, if not as ideological fictions, at least as the political incarnations of a unifying rationality whose vocation is to decree generality and ignore the specific conditions that might invalidate it. Thus it is not surprising, in light of this "French exception," that the constructivist theses popularized in the United States by the work of Latour and Ian Hacking, and a fortiori the question of minorities or cultural difference, never succeeded in penetrating the epistemology and the sociology of the sciences in France—and hence the institutional isolation of Bruno Latour, who was shunted into the sociology laboratory of the École des mines, an engineering school. It would seem that neither faith in reason nor even the unity of the Republic could survive in such conditions.

It is not only against the French obsession with rationalism—shared by the transcendental empiricism of Bergson and the epistemology of Bachelard or even of Georges Canguilhem—but also, and inversely, against the textualization of the American human sciences (with cultural studies, for example, so interested in the register of the "symbolic") that Bruno Latour and his colleague Michel Callon deployed all the tools of *constructivist empiricism*. They have engaged the scientific world in a pragmatic mode that examines its objects, its specific instruments, its immaterial flows, its hybrid beings, and its living machines—in other words, everything that escapes the "symbolic" domain. In addition, Latour and Callon confront rationalism by examining science in terms of its geographic sites or by applying quantitative sociology, because the localization of science, its cultural context, and the statistical and budgetary data that belong to it are not vulgar secondary factors of scientific activity, as the French rationalists would have it. Behind this constructivist project that Latour himself later qualified as "compositionist," what is therefore at issue, Latour concludes—careful to ensure that the Derridean textualism still omnipotent in the United States does not in its turn infect science studies—is to illuminate the internal discursive mechanisms of the sciences, but also their ideological function; to dismantle the simplistic dualism, still omnipresent in France, between science as a discourse and science as a practice, or between "word and world," between realism and nominalism, "refusing to leave the field . . . exclusively to naturalists on the one hand and deconstructionists on the other."[46] Thus, what Latour and his colleagues seek to demystify, to empirically invalidate, is the very position Sokal and Bricmont were so obstinately defending against the postmodern "menace" and what they called the "errors" of Thomas Kuhn and Paul Feyerabend (who sought, they say, to "[evade] the problems of truth and objectivity").[47] In fact, what the latter sought to undermine is what Sokal and Bricmont want to save at any price: on the one hand, the *progressivist* continuity, posited by scientism, between "ordinary knowledge" and advanced scientific discourse, as if these were two degrees of the same objective explanation of the real; and, on the other hand, the sharp *discontinuity* that they affirm, conversely, between facts and discourse, between the "truths" of science and the extrapolations of any commentary on these truths—in a word, a double dismantling of unified knowledge and of the unviolated "truth."

In other words, against the progressivism and naturalism still in the ascendant, science studies attempt to reveal the power effects of each discursive formation and the discursive effects at the very heart of scientific practices. Following in the footsteps of many others, they sought to show the way in which this supposedly exterior or referential world is always framed, bound, and traversed by discourse. Beyond the case of the sciences, the French attempt to draw disciplines out of their intellectual enclaves necessarily involves mobilizing this set of *theoretical practices* that refuse to see discourse as a strictly delimited sphere, or the "real" as a primordial given, pure and external. For what all the French rationalists who are sure of their enterprise see here, a bit prematurely, as a tired old structuralist tune, a poorly digested "linguistic turn," or even some sort of Yankee textual relativism, merely corresponds to what was being thought and done, whether well or poorly, in the rest of the global intellectual community for the last quarter century.

Conclusion

DIFFERENCE AND AFFIRMATION

> To be a traitor to one's regime, a traitor to one's sex, to one's
> class, to one's majority—what other reasons are there to write?
> And to be a traitor to writing itself.
>
> GILLES DELEUZE, *Dialogues*

AND SO without a second thought, the new France repudiated the leading French thinkers of the preceding generation. This done, it barred the
way to American-style identity politics and to theories that view society
as an intertwining of different communities. Henceforth, all it could oppose to rising fears of globalization and cultural rootlessness was the
same group of concepts formulated more than two centuries earlier, the
concepts of universalist humanism—*the* Subject, or *the* Debate, or Society—or else the progressivist abstraction of "making another world
possible." Abstract, protocolonial, or neo-Kantian universalism and its
symbolic violence—underpinned by the normative figures of the *Republic* or of *progress*—sometimes sound like the watchwords of a certain
cultural parochialism. For all these reasons, it seems as though France
has deserted the international intellectual discussion. It has not adopted
the international community's new academic forms, and it has not really become part of its international networks, into which, however, it
jettisoned a dozen or so French writers marginalized in their own country (not to mention an entire intellectual and historical *Stimmung*). The
French elite has determined that their analyses would be useless, if not
dangerous, in any attempt to comprehend the present, or to explore
this world that has "become infinite all over again" and is now made
up of "infinite interpretations," as Nietzsche wrote.[1] Thirty years ago,

discussions of ideas vibrated in certain Left Bank streets, in publishers' offices, in the official sites and outlets of discussion, or in the various forums available in the mainstream press—these debates carried, and still carry, a great deal of weight, sometimes far too much (especially in the hothouse atmosphere of academia's minor dramas), from New York to Mexico City, and from Tokyo to San Diego; but the debates now echoing in those same corridors in Paris barely make it to the Right Bank of the Seine, or even hold the interest of their own participants.

The key to such a complete transformation and to the decline into which it has cast French influence across the world may perhaps be sought in the French intellectual scene's relationship to Marx. In a dozen years, theory in France has moved from the Marxist dogmatism of yesterday to the abandonment pure and simple of Marxian critical thought and its relegation to the exegetes or the nostalgic. This occurred without any other transition than the conquest of intellectual power we have chronicled above—and the parallel decline of the Communist vote. In fact, regardless of what the Marxian detractors of French theory may say, its international success was only possible *alongside*—as a complement to, or perhaps as an alternative to—the splintered branches of the Marxian corpus and the adjacent orthodoxies that history has rendered obsolete. Thus, everywhere except in France, Deleuze, Foucault, Lyotard, and even Derridean "hypercriticism" incarnate the possibility of *continuing* a radical social critique beyond Marx, a critique that relative to Marx was finally detotalized, refined, diversified, opened up to the questions of desire and intensity, to flux and signs and the multiple subject—in a word, the tools of a social critique *for today*. From Chicago to São Paulo, even in the short term, even when they were too metaphorical or were the property of activists still confined to the campus or the intellectual caste, contemporary social movements have confronted the crucial question of *difference*. They have made it a part of their programs and their tactical methods, whether it be understood in a sexual, ethnic, cultural, or even ontological context. It is a concept that remains mobile, changing, and available for all practices and at every intersection. It is this decisive question, indissociably epistemological and social, that the philosophical projects of Foucault, Deleuze, and Derrida explored, and that the new masters of the French intellectual scene have gone out of their way to avoid in the name of a fiction of universal Man and bourgeois democracy. However, from unassimilated immigrants to collector subcultures or video artists, from new sexual or ethnic identities to newly important issues of territory, and from the hidden identities of Internet users to the new forms of job insecurity, the question of difference now concerns all of the increasingly numerous situations that no longer fit within the traditional divisions of market democracy, be it republican or federal. It is these invisible remains or supplements that are gradually being produced by the governing signifiers of the traditional political community—professions, classes, districts, faiths, or generations. The question of difference is now the site of the most fertile crossroads. It is the only way to link micropolitics and social struggles, to connect the abstract decrees of the community to the problems of the body and of daily life. The molecular question of difference has today come to traverse all of the vast reified totalities of Marxism, from *surplus value* to *ideology,* kneading them, fissuring them, renewing them. Sexual minorities, neighborhood counterrituals, the opacity of individual obsessions, and all forms of interior exile carry an irreducible difference, "trace out a plane of consistence which undermines the plane of organization of the World and of States."[2] Today it is more important than ever to confront one with the other, and in the same gesture to confront, for example, the categories of *revolution* and of *woman,* of social struggles and what Walter Benjamin called "affective classes," or, similarly, forms of life and activist solidarities across distant borders. Such strategies would provide significant encouragement for those new configurations thanks to which "a new type of revolution is in the process of becoming possible,"[3] this time in the present, stretching across the planes of certain strata, in vivo, through various modes of desertion or, more tactically, of sabotage, but in any case far from the substantialist myth of the revolutionary *Grand soir* when all would suddenly change, an inaccessible horizon that has always been more fundamentally monotheistic than communist.

Every minority must confront the problems of organization and enunciation in its attempt to form a group, however disparate. In this respect, difference represents the decisive challenge to *community* in everyday life, its historical transformations and its political aporias—this old concept of community whose bloody schisms were revealed in the twentieth century, along with its indispensable "principle of incompletion." For it is difference and its tactics of sublimated affinities, continually placed in question but continually returning, that today offer the experience of the "unavowable" community Maurice Blanchot spoke of—this community that "comes to an end as randomly as it began," that unmasks the illusions of "communion," yet also sets itself against the collective abstractions imposed by the social order and the mythologies of work. This particular notion of community is tied to a fundamental *désœuvrement,* an idleness or "unworking" that "denies itself the possibility of producing a work and does not set up any value of production as its end," precisely thereby linking itself to something not contained within any border, because community is "what . . . includes the exteriority of being that excludes it."[4]

Experiments following this very logic have just begun to appear, fanzines addressing loosely knit communities, group actions organized around a specific event rather than a program, or activist associations confronted with the question of inclusion and its limits (bring *who* together, address *whom,* attack *whom,* and for what reasons?). These experiments, however, remain largely unconceptualized by French intellectual culture. This unique, fragile form of community, continually confronted by the impossible reduction of difference, is not a middle way or a myth of the golden mean between "individual" and "society." Its projects, its failures, its ongoing experimentation constitute the only way to repopulate the cold, anomic space that has gradually opened between abandoned ideals (the general will, the sovereign nation) and aggressive, identity-based reterritorializations, or between the abstractions of the collective (Society, or *the* world) and individualist or familial withdrawal, salutary but also exclusionary, which recalls Tocqueville's famous definition of a secluded community life—according to which each citizen tends "to isolate himself from the mass of those like him and to withdraw to one side with his family and his friends, so that after having thus created a little society for his own use, he willingly abandons the society at large to itself."[5] An amniotic, separatist kind of fusion that works precisely to preclude difference—the very opposite of community.

Finally, and above all, difference is a political and philosophical question too urgent to be left to those who manage it, organize it, and knowingly redistribute it across various segments of the market. For, during the period when it was treated like an illegal alien in the French intellectual community and was simultaneously nourishing theoretical debate in American academia, difference became the providential ally of advanced capitalism, one of the very components, in fact, of the "new spirit of capitalism"[6] then emerging and consolidating itself through the co-optation of its critics and the alternatives to its logic. Debated by the theorists of minorities in the 1980s, theorized by the radical philosophers of the 1970s, emerging from the communitarian avatars of the great social protest movement of the 1960s, difference has more than anything else ended up authorizing a more fine-grained segmentation of the marketplace, an extension of capital into the spheres of affinity and the clandestine intimacy of small or invisible differences. Instead of toppling the homogenizing forces of Western capital, "difference . . . has meanwhile become the principal instrument for the management of biopower,"[7] the instrument of a personalization of "demand," of a partitioning of bodies, of a renaturalization of social types, as the French collective Tiqqun observed—a radical group itself emblematic of the new activist forms that could comprise a postidentitarian critique of the universal, its theory of contemporary "disaster" having been inspired as much by Marx as by the new errant subjectivities, as much by revolutionary messianism as by the more recent contributions of Deleuze and Foucault.

It is in this direction that theory can and ought to direct its attention, as the sole form of political vigilance capable of addressing the historical transition in which we find ourselves on both sides of the Atlantic. It is in this sense, perhaps, that the discussions of theory that have preoccupied certain fringes of academia in the United States and around the world for the last quarter century have not been ineffective, or purely rhetorical. For, regardless of the cant and the campus rituals surrounding them, they have been more in touch with the world and the ongoing processes of pluralization and absorption (or of exclusion and integration) than the French debates during the same period. At a time when thousands of young Europeans inspired by communism were abandoning *the* Theory (with its fervent capital "T" and its presumptuous definite article)—that is to say, the old Marxist "science" of ideological demystification—to take up their studies once again or to embark on careers, it happened that across the Atlantic, behind the political agendas of the multiculturalists and the scholastic blinders of the textualists, a *composite* theory, exploratory and relevant to practice, was developing. It was an enterprise consistent with Deleuze and Foucault's search for a *theory* that broke with metaphysical idealism, a theory that would constitute neither a rational law nor a morality, nor a textual history, nor merely a metaphilosophy, but one that would in the end consist in *producing hypotheses* in a completely different sense from those of the scientistic tradition—namely, *intensive* hypotheses, general and specific at the same time, hypotheses on communitarian apparatuses, discursive regimes, or the machinery of capitalist desire.

Finally, if there is one lesson to be learned from the American reinvention of French theory, its abandonment in France, and its global avatars, it is that a certain continuity must at any cost be reestablished in opposition to the polarized representations and binary discourses that we have heard so often: German Marxism against French Nietzscheanism (whereas micropolitics is in fact the prolongation, and not the negation, of the idea of revolution); French phenomenology against poststructuralist "perspectivism" and its multiplication of points of view, its pluralization of the subject (whereas the latter is perhaps only a radicalization, and a politicization, of the former, as Vincent Descombes has suggested);[8] or American communitarianism versus French universalism, both of which conceal, beneath divergent approaches and contexts, the profound convergence of two closely associated powers; or the disputes that Bourdieu found to exist between "two imperialisms of the universal," two competing but complementary positions.[9] Thus, much work remains to be done to join, to hook together, to pursue the connections between apparently disparate camps—to link Marx, for example, to nondialectical theories of difference, struggles for civil rights to academic identity politics, revolutionary romanticism to more tactical micropolitics, gender or race to social class, and American theoretical radicalism to the new forms of social dissidence in France. Whether in the classroom or among small political groups, there are innumerable continuities to be established in opposition to the fashionable fatalisms of the postmodern age—about the end of history, for example, and of the lost generation, and their powerlessness. As an intellectual tradition, materialism is first of all that joyous distrust before all the ideologies of discontinuity and their false distinctions. It is a practice of making connections, in other words, a practice directed against the myth of isolation, the fantasy of dislocation and disconnection from historical, material, or other contexts.

There is doubtless nothing surprising in the fact that these inquiries into difference and community, this obligation to reestablish continuities, this old problem of discourse in its relation to action and to power, should have been pursued with a greater intensity in the United States than elsewhere. There, and not elsewhere, for many reasons that were peculiar to America at the end of the twentieth century: a university apparatus set up for a certain conceptual production, the experimental ease with which a young, pluralist country is always ready to "move on to something else," the historical triumph of the American empire during this same period, the new ideological polarity that developed among America's intellectual elite at the end of the century (the West versus its minorities), right up to the terrifying ability of its free market to ceaselessly appropriate for its own purposes any negativity that seeks to remain exterior to it, but that soon becomes merely a form of distraction and entertainment. Perhaps nowhere other than in the United States could so demanding and so radically innovative (and yet so contextually embedded) an ensemble of philosophical texts become familiar enough to allow this discourse to take on the narrative, allegorical, and even anthropomorphic dimensions that "French Theory" rapidly acquired—in a process that always clearly indicates that something has succeeded in penetrating the American imagination. For, as we have seen, the panopticon and the simulacrum became familiar conceptual characters, the floating signifier or the body without organs became cultural refrains, and the very names of Foucault and Derrida became heroic patronyms. This is precisely what made this adventure not merely a banal episode of transatlantic intellectual history, but a veritable *prosopopoeia*, in which the history of concepts, of authors, of texts, and of procedures are all personified, in situ, one after another.

Once extracted from its academic matrix, dislodged from its campuses, or at least freed from the grip of its professional commentators, theory can still offer its users a way to decipher all of the operations of power and the imposition of norms at work in the dominant discourse. Moreover, as a dream of a *theoretical grasp of the world,* an old academic dream but also an activist ambition, this history of French Theory is exemplary both of the process of modernity's retreat (with which it is contemporary), the postmodern process of placing into discourse what remains of life,[10] but also of a call to life, that pure desire for heroism that mediating intellectuals, anonymous transmitters of ideas, and all the commentators have always maintained, but without daring to take the risk it requires. For, in the university and beyond, French theory also embodies the hope that discourse might be able to restore life to life and provide access to an intact vital force that would be spared from the logic of the market and the prevailing cynicisms.

One must not overlook the authentic desire for heroism that is in fact manifest here, as in all radical or radicalized thought: the dream of activity through which all discourse would be annulled, dream of a resistance through action, or of a definitive sacrifice. No more than the other, this dream is not the property of a caste of American professors cozily installed in the ivy-shrouded buildings of a campus without borders. For in reality it is also the inheritance of all young Westerners dispossessed by history—revolutionary activists of thirty years ago who (unlike the preceding generation) did not have to make the choice between collaboration and resistance; minoritarian activists of today who, coming of age as the horizon of "real" Communism receded, did not have to dream the dream of revolution; neo-third-worldists of all ages who did not have to take the risks of decolonization. It is a belated heroism, a theoretical *faute de mieux* type of heroism for those who will always be obsessed by the experiences, and experiments, that have preceded them. However, each one of these authors, in his own peculiar ethic of *affirmation*, deploys the same war machine against the logic of ressentiment, nostalgia, and guilt, a machine by them programmed to dismantle self-hatred and the feeling that one has arrived too late, and in vain—*wrong place, wrong time*—a feeling that too many contemporary intellectuals have refined to the point of intimate cruelty. This *ethical* machine they provide us is more precious today than ever before, in Paris no less than at Harvard.

We must reconcile heroism with the here and now and free its motives from suspicion and guilt. Or, more precisely, we must keep heroism and its beautiful ecstatic energy, but free it from a certain submission to negative concepts (the reference, the Father, action considered as *other* and always to occur in the future), bringing it instead to the side of positive betrayal, such as Deleuze described in terms of being a "traitor," in his writing on Jean Genet or T. E. Lawrence, rendering the concept positive by associating it with the exile of the subject and a creative *erring*, a certain power of shame, and the fundamental suppleness of ethics.[11] For treachery is always what occurs when a text, a work of art, or a concept travels to faraway places and *becomes* something completely different from what it was at its source, within its context of origin. These are felicitous acts of betrayal, productive changes of sense. Misprision, misreading, and misuse are the three virtues of cultural exchange. At the dawn of the twentieth century, Oswald Spengler recognized as much.

Behind his pessimism and his debatable partitions, Spengler, the first to diagnose an inexorable "Decline of the West," also noted the importance of intersections and influences, of this *"art of deliberate misunderstanding"* indissociable from each culture's pure essence: "The more enthusiastically we laud the principles of an alien thought, the more fundamentally in truth we have denatured it"—something he already seemed to celebrate, praising the "trace" of Plato in Goethe's thought to illustrate his point, as well as "the history of the 'three Aristotles'—Greek, Arabian and Gothic."[12]

Much more could be written about the history of this type of felicitous misreading, of this kind of creative, even performative misprision. It is a vast zone in which both political *and* cultural virtues can be discovered, as well as the cross-pollinations and borrowings that are so numerous throughout history: the Western formalization of Arab mathematics, the humanist appropriation of ancient moral philosophy in the poetry of the Renaissance, borrowings from European engraving in Japanese prints, French readings of Heine or Hegel under the Third Republic provide only a few examples. Today, these intersections have their counterparts in phenomena such as the Indian programmers who are influencing the design of American software, Chinese DJs remixing already hybrid music from the West, or, once again, that combination of antinomian forces characteristic of the border cultures of Istanbul or Hong Kong.[13] One could also mention the amazing frescoes that Indian workers painted in the homes of their masters in sixteenth-century colonial Mexico, blending their ancestral pictorial tradition with newly arrived elements of Italian painting and references to the stories of the navigators or even to Ovid's *Metamorphoses*.[14]

LIVING THOUGHTS are sensitive surfaces, skins lightly touched, dark folds—less a *body* of thought, compact and muscular, than a zone of contact between eroded borders. A single citation may be enough to communicate them, or an argument taken up once again, a book mentioned in passing, or even an entire oeuvre whose unifying proper name is gradually being effaced. Their circulation, their *détournement*, their transferral far from the context in which they were born, and the very audacity of using them in ways that contradict any textual didactics—all of these taken together, after such texts have left their authors behind but before they have been embalmed within a corpus, make up an entire *erotics* of thought, wayward and unpredictable. Placing these terms in contact seems to stir up dust from a bygone era. Yet the idea of a *theoretical libido* (not a *jouissance* of words, of course, but a certain *libidinal* relationship to theory) did not wait for the 1970s to remind us of the ancestral prostitution of texts, their flirtatious glances moving along the sidewalks of history, seductions all the more promising in that they escape the control of their pathetic pimps, their official heirs, or their scholastic exegetes. This flirtation of texts is not simply a metaphor; the issue is to oppose desire as *play* (in the mechanical sense)—as delay and unhindered movement—to the interdiction against any deviation and to the inspection of well-organized compartments, which, for their part, preside over legitimate interpretations. For these latter postulate a magical, dominant source of meaning, a textual essence with its monosemic truth. And by this measure they bring a harsh judgment to bear on any strange or foreign readings, on the gleanings of students, on fragmentary reevaluations, and on every form of instrumentalization—all of which can be felicitous distortions, and yet their blasphemous character is said to render them invalid. In contrast, the desire I am referring to heats up in contact with texts, whether taken whole or in fragments, and in proportion to the primary interval to which we owe the *life* of texts—the interval between the emergence of writing and its canonical normalization, between the logics of the intellectual field and the unpredictabilities of posterity, between the effects of fashion and the subterranean paradigm shifts. Thus opens a lawless zone between the original appraisers of meaning and value and future owners, a zone formed completely of interstices, within which, far from the guardians of the Work, texts themselves will be put to work. They will embed themselves along various paths, will tattoo the body, will invest practices, and will bring together new communities. It is within such an interval that the invention of French theory began to play out in the United States around the beginning of the 1980s; this interval is still open, and in this open space it has kept its strength intact.

Acknowledgments

THIS BOOK WOULD NOT HAVE BEEN POSSIBLE without the generosity, the personal insights, and the graciously offered words of all those who, having participated in and observed the history related in this book, agreed to share their version of it with me by kindly granting one or several interviews, in France and in the United States. I would like to express my tremendous gratitude to them here:

Jean Baudrillard, Richard Bernstein, Leo Bersani, Sara Bershtel, Tom Bishop, George Borchardt, Peter Brooks, Fulvia Carnevale, Mary-Ann Caws, Sande Cohen, Antoine Compagnon, Régis Debray, Michel Delorme, Michael Denneny, Jacques Derrida, Joël des Rosiers, Elie During, Eric Fassin, Michel Feher, Stanley Fish, Jim Fleming, Todd Gitlin, Stephen Greenblatt, Peter Halley, Jeanine Herman, Denis Hollier, Dick Howard, Laurent Jeanpierre, John Kelsey, Fram Kitagawa, Chris Kraus, Lawrence D. Kritzman, Sanford Kwinter, Michèle Lamont, Knight Landesman, Bruno Latour, Jean-Jacques Lebel, Sylvère Lotringer, Masuda Matsuie, Jeffrey Mehlman, Nancy Miller, J. Hillis Miller, Paul Miller aka DJ Spooky, Claire Parnet, John Rajchman, Willis Regier, Carlin Romano, Edward Said, Marc Saint-Upéry, André Schiffrin, Eve Kosofsky Sedgwick, Richard Sieburth, Thomas Spear, Gayatri Chakravorty Spivak, Allucquere Rosanne Stone, Enzo Traverso, Bernard Tschumi, Jorge Volpi, Moriaki Watanabe, Lindsay Waters.

TRANSLATOR'S ACKNOWLEDGMENTS

I WOULD LIKE TO THANK Josephine Berganza and Marlon Jones for their skillful and substantial contributions to the work that went into translating this book. I would also like to thank Blake Ferris for his much appreciated work on chapter 14 and the Conclusion. Finally, many thanks to François Cusset for his patience and helpfulness in handling my numerous queries.

NOTES

Preface to the English Edition

1. To echo the words with which Jean Hyppolite opened his lecture at the famous 1966 symposium on structuralism held at Johns Hopkins University: "Isn't it too late to speak of Hegel in our age?"

2. Pierre Bourdieu, "The Social Conditions of the International Circulation of Ideas," in *Bourdieu: A Critical Reader,* ed. Richard Shusterman (Oxford: Blackwell, 1999), 223.

3. The fact that Stanley Fish's classical essays on "interpretative communities" have finally been translated into French today, after twenty-five years, is indeed a sign of the times (see Stanley Fish, *Quand lire c'est faire: Sur l'autorité des communautés interprétatives* [Paris: Les prairies ordinaires, "Penser/Croiser" series, 2007]).

Introduction

1. Alan Sokal and Jean Bricmont, *Impostures intellectuelles* (Paris: Le Livre de Poche, "Biblio essais" series, 1999 [1997]). The authors wanted the French to be the first to hear the news and therefore published the book first in France; an English version appeared the following year under the more heavy-handed title *Fashionable Nonsense* (New York: St. Martin's Press, 1998).

2. Sokal and Bricmont, *Fashionable Nonsense,* 21, 5, 7, and 14.

3. Ibid., 1–3.

4. Ibid., 13, 16, and 7.

5. Ibid., 5, 37, 148, and 6.

6. Marion Van Renterghem, "L'Américain Alan Sokal face aux 'imposteurs' de la pensée française," *Le Monde,* September 30, 1997.

7. "Sokal contre les intellos: La pensée du k.o.," *Libération,* September 30, 1997. ["La terre est bleue comme une orange" (the earth is blue like an orange) is the well-known first line of an untitled poem by Paul Éluard.—*Trans.*]

8. Jean-François Kahn, "Morgue scientiste contre impostures intellectuelles," *Marianne,* October 13–19, 1997.

9. Jean-Marie Rouart, "Fumée," *Le Figaro,* October 16, 1997.

10. Angelo Rinaldi, "La comédie française vue d'Amérique," *L'Express,* October 16, 1997.

11. Jean-François Revel, "Les faux prophètes," *Le Point,* October 11, 1997.

12. "Les intellectuels français sont-ils des imposteurs?" *Le Nouvel Observateur,* September 25–October 1, 1997.

13. "Les agités du Sokal," *Le Canard enchaîné,* October 8, 1997. [*On les colle partout:* the phrase also implies posting bills or putting up adverstising posters.—*Trans.*]

14. Philippe Petit, "Voilà où en est la philosophie au pays d'Astérix," *Marianne,* October 13–19, 1997.

15. Van Renterghem, "L'Américain Alan Sokal face aux 'imposteurs' de la pensée française."

16. This was the title of a special section of *L'Événement du Jeudi,* March 27–April 2, 1997.

17. Michel Pierssens, "Sciences-en-culture outre-Atlantique," in *Impostures scientifiques: Les malentendus de l'affaire Sokal,* ed. Baudoin Jurdant (Paris: La Découverte/Alliage, 1998), 106–17.

18. Alan Sokal, "Transgressing the Boundaries: Toward a Transformative Hermeneutics of Quantum Gravity," *Social Text,* no. 46–47 (spring–summer 1996): 217–52.

19. Alan Sokal, "A Physicist Experiments with Cultural Studies," *Lingua Franca* (May–June 1996): 82–84.

20. Janny Scott, "Postmodern Gravity Deconstructed, Slyly," *New York Times,* May 18, 1996.

21. See the excerpts from the press collected in the volume *The Sokal Hoax: The Sham That Shook the Academy,* ed. *Lingua Franca* (Lincoln: University of Nebraska Press, 2000). Quotes are from (respectively) George F. Will, "Smitten with Gibberish," *Washington Post,* May 30, 1996; Ruth Rosen, "A Physics Prof Drops a Bomb on the Faux Left," *Los Angeles Times,* May 23, 1996; and Linda Seeback, "Scientist Takes Academia for a Ride with Parody," *Contra Costa Times,* May 12, 1996.

22. Scott McConnell, "When Pretention Reigns Supreme," *New York Post,* May 22, 1996.

23. Stanley Fish, "Professor Sokal's Bad Joke," *New York Times,* May 21, 1996.

24. Bruno Latour, "Y a-t-il une science après la guerre froide?" *Le Monde,* January 18, 1997.

25. Pierre Bourdieu, "The Social Conditions of the International Circulation of Ideas," in *Bourdieu: A Critical Reader,* ed. Richard Shusterman (Oxford: Blackwell, 1999), 222.

26. What in German is called *Neostrukturalismus;* see Manfred Frank, *What Is Neostructuralism?,* trans. Sabine Wilke and Richard T. Gray (Minneapolis: University of Minnesota Press, 1989); first published in Germany in 1983.

27. This refers to a well-known article published under this title: "Les grands prêtres de l'université française," *Le Nouvel Observateur,* April 7, 1975.

28. Luc Ferry and Alain Renaut, *La Pensée 68: Essai sur l'antihumanisme contemporain* (Paris: Gallimard, collection "Folio essais," 1988 [1985]); English translation: *French*

Philosophy of the Sixties: An Essay on Antihumanism, trans. Mary H. Cattani (Amherst: University of Massachusetts Press, 1990).

29. Cited in Didier Éribon, *Michel Foucault,* trans. Betsy Wing (Cambridge: Harvard University Press, 1991), 120–21.

30. Gilles Deleuze, "Discussion," in *Nietzsche aujourd'hui?,* Colloque de Cerisy (Paris: Union Générale d'Éditions/10-18, 1973), 2:186.

31. See Jean Baudrillard, *Forget Foucault* (New York: Semiotext(e), 1987); Foucault quoted in Éribon, *Michel Foucault,* 275.

32. Jean Baudrillard, *Simulacres et Simulation* (Paris: Galilée, 1981), 34 and 109. English: "Simulacra and Simulations," in *Selected Writings,* ed. Mark Poster (Stanford, Calif.: Stanford University Press, 1988), 178.

33. Jared Sandberg, "PC Forum Attendees Hear Fighting Words on High Technology," *Wall Street Journal,* March 26, 1997.

34. Steven Moore, "Deconstructing Ralph," *Washington Post,* November 28, 1999.

35. "C'est la guerre" (interview with Bernard-Henri Lévy), *Tel Quel,* no. 82 (winter 1979): 19–28.

36. Bernard-Henri Lévy, *Barbarism with a Human Face* (New York: Harper and Row, 1979), 120 and 189. First published in French in 1977.

37. Pierre Nora, "Que peuvent les intellectuels?" *Le Débat,* no. 1 (May 1980): 3–19.

38. Ferry and Renaut, *La Pensée 68,* 17 [This reference is for the phrase "philosophies of difference," which appears in French in the preface to the Gallimard Folio edition; this preface is not included in the English translation.—*Trans.*]; *French Philosophy of the Sixties,* 16, 13, and 14, respectively [i.e., for the last three phrases quoted—*Trans.*].

1. Prehistories

1. Vincent Descombes, *Le Même et l'autre: Quarante-cinq ans de philosophie française (1933–1978)* (Paris: Minuit, 1979), 14; English: *Modern French Philosophy,* trans. L. Scott-Fox and J. M. Harding (Cambridge: Cambridge University Press, 1980), 5 (translation modified).

2. Edward Said, "Intellectual Exile: Expatriates and Marginals," in *The Edward Said Reader,* ed. Moustafa Bayoumi and Andrew Rubin (New York: Vintage, 2000), 380–81.

3. Jean-Paul Sartre, "New York, ville coloniale," in *Situations III* (Paris: Gallimard, 1949), 121.

4. "An interview with Stephen Riggins," *Ethos,* vol. 1, no. 2 (fall 1983): 5; reprinted in *Essential Works,* vol. 1, *Ethics: Subjectivity and Truth* (New York: New Press, 1997), 123.

5. Julia Kristeva, *Étrangers à nous-mêmes* (Paris: Fayard, 1988), 113–38.

6. Cited in Philippe Roger, *The American Enemy: The History of French Anti-Americanism,* trans. Sharon Bowman (Chicago: University of Chicago Press, 2005), 407–8.

7. Motherwell, Greenberg, and Schapiro quoted in Lazare Bitoun, "Intellectuels et écrivains du Village à Harlem," in *New York 1940–1950,* ed. André Kaspi (Paris: Autrement, 1995), 128. See also Martica Sawin, *Surrealism in Exile and the Beginning of the New York School* (Cambridge: MIT Press, 1995).

8. Quoted in J. Hoberman, "Madmen across the Water," *Village Voice Literary Supplement,* April 1996. See Dickran Tashjian, *A Boatload of Madmen: Surrealism and the American Avant-Garde* (London: Thames and Hudson, 1996).

9. Quoted in Guy Ducornet, *Le Punching-Ball et la Vache à lait: La critique universitaire nord-américaine face au surréalisme* (Angers: Actual/Deleatur, 1992), 9. See Herbert J. Muller, "Surrealism: A Dissenting Opinion," in *New Directions in Prose and Poetry* (Norfolk, Conn.: New Directions, 1940), 549.

10. Ducornet, *Le Punching-Ball et la Vache à lait,* 18 and 29.

11. See Roger Shattuck, "Introduction: Love and Laughter: Surrealism Reappraised," in Maurice Nadeau, *History of Surrealism,* trans. Richard Howard (New York: Macmillan, 1965), 11–34.

12. Ducornet, *Le Punching-Ball et la Vache à lait,* 34–47.

13. According to whom "the Surrealists used women . . . to work out their rebellion against the Father" (quoted in ibid., 108).

14. Ibid., 68–102.

15. Janet Flanner, "Paris Journal," *New Yorker,* December 15, 1945, 116.

16. Roger, *The American Enemy,* 441 (emphasis in original).

17. See Ann Fulton, *Apostles of Sartre: Existentialism in America 1945–1963* (Evanston, Ill.: Northwestern University Press, 1999), particularly chapter 1, "Importing a Philosophy."

18. Norman O. Brown, *Love's Body* (New York: Random House, 1966), 130–42.

19. See Ronald Laing, *Self and Others* (New York: Pantheon, 1969 [1961]).

20. See Frieda Fromm-Reichmann, "Notes on the Development of Treatment of Schizophrenics by Psychoanalytic Psychotherapy," *Psychiatry* 11 (1948): 273, and Gregory Bateson, *Steps to an Ecology of the Mind* (Chicago: University of Chicago Press, 2000 [1972]).

21. François Dosse, *History of Structuralism,* vol. 1, *The Rising Sign, 1945–1966,* trans. Deborah Glassman (Minneapolis: University of Minnesota Press, 1997), 316.

22. Gilles Deleuze, *Logic of Sense* (1969), trans. Mark Lester with Charles Stivale, ed. Constantin V. Boundas (New York: Columbia University Press, 1990), 71.

23. Jacques Derrida, *Writing and Difference* (1967), trans. Alan Bass (Chicago: University of Chicago Press, 1978), 6.

24. Claude Lévi-Strauss, *The Savage Mind,* no trans. (Chicago: University of Chicago Press, 1966); and see *Yale French Studies,* ed. Jacques Ehrman, nos. 37/38 (1966).

25. Richard Macksey and Eugenio Donato, eds., *The Structuralist Controversy: The Languages of Criticism and the Sciences of Man* (Baltimore: Johns Hopkins University Press, 1972 [1970]), xii–xiii.

26. Ibid., ix.

27. See Jean Hyppolite, "The Structure of Philosophic Language according to the 'Preface' to Hegel's Phenomenology of the Mind," in ibid., 157.

28. Jacques Derrida, "Structure, Sign, and Play in the Discourse of the Human Sciences," in *Writing and Difference,* 278–79.

29. Ibid., 284–89.

30. Ibid., 289–90 (translation slightly modified).

31. Ibid., 292.

32. Hashem Foda, "The Structuralist Dream," *SubStance*, no. 20 (winter 1978): 133.

33. Richard Moss, "Review," *Telos*, no. 6 (winter 1971): 355.

34. See Fredric Jameson, *The Prison-House of Language: A Critical Account of Structuralism and Russian Formalism* (Princeton, N.J.: Princeton University Press, 1972).

2. The Academic Enclave

1. Helen Lefkowitz Horowitz, *Campus Life: Undergraduate Culture from the End of the Nineteenth Century to the Present* (New York: Alfred A. Knopf, 1987), 271.

2. Christopher J. Lucas, *American Higher Education: A History* (New York: St. Martin's Press, 1994), 200.

3. Gerald Graff, *Beyond the Culture Wars* (New York: W. W. Norton, 1992), 8.

4. Simone de Beauvoir, *America Day by Day,* trans. Carol Cosman (Berkeley: University of California Press, 1999 [original French publication 1948]), 307, 309, and 348.

5. Stanley Fish, *Professional Correctness: Literary Studies and Political Change* (New York and London: Oxford University Press, 1995), 118 and 126.

6. W. H. Cowley and Don Williams, *International and Historical Roots of American Higher Education* (New York: Garland, 1991), 101–3.

7. Quoted in Lucas, *American Higher Education,* 133.

8. Ibid., 135–36.

9. Ibid., 144–45.

10. Ibid., 188.

11. Benjamin Barber, *An Aristocracy of Everyone: The Politics of Education and the Future of America* (New York: Ballantine, 1992), 205.

12. Clyde Barrow, *Universities and the Capitalist State* (Madison: University of Wisconsin Press, 1990), 124.

13. See M. Devèze, *Histoire contemporaine de l'université* (Paris: SEDES, 1976), 439–40.

14. Lucas, *American Higher Education,* 226.

15. C. B. Hulbert, *The Distinctive Idea in Education* (New York: J. B. Alden, 1890), 34.

16. Ibid., 212–14.

17. Jonathan Culler, *Framing the Sign* (Norman: University of Oklahoma Press, 1988), 78.

18. Bill Readings, *The University in Ruins* (Cambridge: Harvard University Press, 1996), 70–71.

19. Ibid., 55.

20. Ibid., 166.

21. Alain Touraine, *The Academic System in American Society* (New York: McGraw-Hill, 1974), 115.

22. Hannah Arendt, "The Crisis in Education," in *Between Past and Future: Eight Exercises in Political Thought* (New York: Penguin Books, 1993), 182.

23. Quoted in Lucas, *American Higher Education,* 268.

24. Stanley Aronowitz and Henry Giroux, *Education under Siege: The Conservative, Liberal and Radical Debate over Schooling* (Boston: Bergin & Garvey, 1985), 171–75.

25. These are the final two lines of Archibald MacLeish's poem "Ars Poetica" (1926).

26. Gerald Graff, *Professing Literature: An Institutional History* (Chicago: University of Chicago Press, 1987), 188–89.

27. Quoted in Jonathan Arac, Wlad Godzich, and Wallace Martin, eds., *The Yale Critics: Deconstruction in America* (Minneapolis: University of Minnesota Press, 1983), 177.

28. Quoted in Graff, *Professing Literature,* 247.

29. Jacques Derrida, *Of Grammatology* (1967), trans. Gayatri Chakravorty Spivak (Baltimore: Johns Hopkins University Press, 1997), 158.

30. Wlad Godzich, *The Culture of Literacy* (Cambridge: Harvard University Press, 1994), 16–17.

31. See Lazare Bitoun, "Intellectuels et écrivains du Village à Harlem," in *New York 1940–1950,* ed. André Kaspi (Paris: Autrement, "Mémoires" series, 1995), 118–20.

32. Wlad Godzich, "The Domestication of Derrida," in Arac, Godzich, and Martin, *The Yale Critics,* 24.

3. The Seventies

1. See Paul Goodman, *Growing Up Absurd: Problems of Youth in the Organized System* (New York: Random House, 1983 [1960]).

2. Helen Lefkowitz Horowitz, *Campus Life: Undergraduate Culture from the End of the Nineteenth Century to the Present* (New York: Alfred A. Knopf, 1987), 223.

3. Quoted in ibid., 229.

4. Ibid., 231.

5. Quoted in Todd Gitlin, *The Twilight of Common Dreams* (New York: Henry Holt, 1995), 69.

6. Quoted in Horowitz, *Campus Life,* 238–39.

7. Ibid., 249–50.

8. Ibid., 236.

9. Ibid., 258.

10. Alain Touraine, *The Academic System in American Society* (New Brunswick, N.J.: Transaction Publishers, 1997), 191.

11. Ibid., 239.

12. Quoted in François Dosse, *History of Structuralism,* vol. 2, *The Sign Sets, 1967–Present,* trans. Deborah Glassman (Minneapolis: University of Minnesota Press, 1997), 155.

13. Ibid., 156.

14. Mark Poster, "Review," *Telos,* no. 18 (winter 1974): 171–78; Jean-François Lyotard, "Adorno as the Devil" and "Michel Foucault on Attica: An Interview," *Telos,* no. 19 (spring 1974): 128–37 and 154–61.

15. Dominick LaCapra, *Rethinking Intellectual History* (Ithaca, N.Y.: Cornell University Press, 1983), 20-21.

16. George Steiner, "The Mandarin of the Hour," *New York Times Book Review,* February 28, 1971; this was followed by Michel Foucault, "Monstrosities in Criticism," and George Steiner, "Steiner Responds to Foucault," in *Diacritics* vol. 1, nos. 1 and 2, respectively (1971).

17. Gayatri Chakravorty Spivak, "*Glas*-Piece: A *Compte Rendu*," *Diacritics*, vol. 7, no. 3 (fall 1977): 22.

18. Text by Vera Lee, *Diacritics*, vol. 3, no. 2 (summer 1973).

19. The Editors, "About October," *October* 1 (1976): 3.

20. Gilles Deleuze, *Logic of Sense*, trans. Mark Lester with Charles Stivale, ed. Constantin V. Boundas (New York: Columbia University Press, 1990), 153n4.

21. The last party that Foucault had at his home, in April 1984, was held in honor of William Burroughs.

22. Richard Goldstein, "Nietzsche in Alphaville," *Village Voice*, December 11, 1978.

23. Harry Blake, "Le post-modernisme américain," *Tel Quel*, nos. 71–73 (1977): 171ff.

24. Quoted in Sylvère Lotringer, "Doing Theory," in *French Theory in America*, ed. Sande Cohen and Sylvère Lotringer (New York: Routledge, 2001), 140.

25. See "Avant-garde Unites over Burroughs," *New York Times*, December 1, 1978.

26. Julia Kristeva, Marcelin Pleynet, and Philippe Sollers, "Pourquoi les États-Unis?" *Tel Quel*, nos. 71–73 (1977): 4.

27. According to François Dosse, *Michel de Certeau: Le marcheur blessé* (Paris: La Découverte, 2002), 412.

28. Gilles Deleuze and Claire Parnet, *Dialogues* (1977), trans. Hugh Tomlinson and Barbara Habberjam (New York: Columbia University Press, 1987), 139.

29. The expression is from Andreas Huyssen, "Mapping the Postmodern," *New German Critique*, no. 33 (fall 1984): 16.

30. See Greil Marcus, *Lipstick Traces: A Secret History of the Twentieth Century* (Cambridge: Harvard University Press, 1989).

31. *Semiotext(e)*, vol. 3, no. 1 (1978): "Nietzsche's Return."

32. Sande Cohen and Sylvère Lotringer, "Introduction: A Few Theses on French Theory in America," in Cohen and Lotringer, *French Theory in America*, 1.

33. Kathy Acker, "Introduction," in *Young Lust* (London: Pandora, 1989). Acker is referring to Patti Smith's song "Rock 'n' Roll Nigger," which is itself a takeoff on the "Bad Blood" section of Rimbaud's *A Season in Hell*.

34. Cohen and Lotringer, "Doing Theory," 126. In another irony, Cage's book *For the Birds* was published in French (as *Pour les oiseaux*) before appearing in English.

35. Jean Starobinski, "Introduction," *Semiotext(e)*, vol. 1, no. 2 (1974): "The Two Saussures," 10.

36. See *Recherches*, no. 16 (September 1974): "Les deux Saussures."

37. Jacques Derrida, "From Restricted to General Economy: A Hegelianism without Reserve," in *Writing and Difference* (1967), trans. Alan Bass (Chicago: University of Chicago Press, 1978), 253.

38. Sylvie Merzeau, "La voix du livre," *Littérales* (fall 1986): 55.

39. Sylvère Lotringer and Christian Marazzi, "The Return of Politics," *Semiotext(e)*, vol. 3, no. 3 (1980): "Autonomia," 8.

40. M. Corrigan, "Vive Las Vegas," *Village Voice*, November 12, 1995.

41. "Schizo-Culture," *Soho Weekly News*, December 7, 1978.

42. Sylvère Lotringer, "La découverte de l'Amérique" (interview), *Artpress* (April 1999).

43. "Agent de l'étranger" (interview), in *Imported: A Reading Seminar*, ed. Rainer Ganahl (New York: Semiotext(e), 1998), 216.

4. Literature and Theory

1. Antoine Compagnon, *Literature, Theory and Common Sense,* trans. Carol Cosman (Princeton, N.J.: Princeton University Press ["New French Thought" series], 2004), 3. [In France, the term *dissertation* refers to brief formal papers written by students on a specified topic.—*Trans.*]

2. Michèle Lamont, "How to Become a Dominant French Philosopher? The Case of Jacques Derrida," *American Journal of Sociology,* vol. 93, no. 3 (November 1987): 602–4.

3. Michèle Lamont and Marsha Witten, "Surveying the Continental Drift: The Diffusion of French Social and Literary Theory in the United States," *French Politics and Society,* vol. 6, no. 3 (July 1988): 20.

4. Edward Said, "The Franco-American Dialogue: A Late Twentieth-Century Reassessment," in *Traveling Theory: France and the United States,* ed. Ieme van der Poel, Sophie Bertho, and Ton Hoenselaars (Teaneck, N.J.: Fairleigh Dickinson University Press, 1999), 143.

5. Randall Collins, *The Sociology of Philosophies* (Cambridge: Harvard University Press, 1998), 783–84.

6. Excerpts from an unpublished interview published in Roger Pol Droit, "Foucault, passe-frontières de la philosophie," *Le Monde,* September 6, 1986.

7. Michel Foucault, "The Thought from Outside," in *Foucault/Blanchot,* trans. Jeffrey Mehlman and Brian Massumi (New York: Zone Books, 1987), and "Le Mallarmé de J.-P. Richard," *Annales ESC,* no. 5 (September–October 1964); published in English as "Richard's *Mallarmé,*" trans. Arthur Goldhammer, in *Literary Debate: Texts and Contexts,* ed. Denis Hollier and Jeffrey Mehlman (New York: New Press, 1999), 226–34.

8. André Brink, *The Novel: Language and Narrative from Cervantes to Calvino* (New York: New York University Press, 1998), 10–28.

9. Peggy Kamuf, "Penelope at Work: Interruptions in *A Room of One's Own,*" *Novel: A Forum on Fiction,* vol. 16, no. 1 (fall 1982).

10. D. A. Miller, *The Novel and the Police* (Berkeley: University of California Press, 1988), 16–17.

11. Simon During, *Foucault and Literature: Towards a Genealogy of Writing* (New York: Routledge, 1992).

12. Bill Readings, *Introducing Lyotard: Art and Politics* (New York: Routledge, 1991), 71.

13. Gilles Deleuze and Félix Guattari, *Kafka: Toward a Minor Literature* (1975), trans. Dana Polan (Minneapolis: University of Minnesota Press, 1986).

14. See in particular Ross Chambers, *Room for Maneuver: Reading (the) Oppositional (in) Narrative* (Chicago: University of Chicago Press, 1991), and Louis Renza, *A White Heron and the Question of Minor Literature* (Madison: University of Wisconsin Press, 1988), 41.

15. See Allan Megill, *Prophets of Extremity* (Berkeley: University of California Press, 1985).

16. Antoine Compagnon, "The Diminishing Canon of French Literature in America," *Stanford French Review,* vol. 15, nos. 1–2 (1991): 106–8.

17. Quoted in Gerald Graff, *Professing Literature: An Institutional History* (Chicago: University of Chicago Press, 1987), 248.

18. Ibid., 254.

19. See, for example, Stanley Aronowitz, *Science as Power: Discourse and Ideology in Modern Society* (Minneapolis: University of Minnesota Press, 1988).

20. Dudley Andrew, "The 'Three Ages' of Cinema Studies and the Age to Come," *PMLA,* vol. 115, no. 3 (May 2000): 343–44.

21. Ibid., 344.

22. See David Bordwell and Noël Carroll, eds., *Post-Theory: Reconstructing Film Studies* (Madison: University of Wisconsin Press, 1996). In a rather unflattering acronym, the editors condemn the effects of the old French "package" they call SLAB (Saussure-Lacan-Althusser-Barthes).

23. Peter Brooks, *Troubling Confessions: Speaking Guilt in Law and Literature* (Chicago: University of Chicago Press, 2000).

24. Gayatri Chakravorty Spivak, *In Other Worlds: Essays in Cultural Politics* (New York: Routledge, 1998), 213.

25. See the recent contribution by Richard Delgado and Jean Stefancic, eds., *Critical Race Theory: An Introduction* (New York: New York University Press, 2001).

26. Mark Taylor, *Deconstructing Theology* (Minneapolis: Crossroad, 1982) and *Erring: A Postmodern A/theology* (Chicago: University of Chicago Press, 1984).

27. J. Richard Middleton and Brian Walsh, *Truth Is Stranger Than It Used to Be: Biblical Faith in a Postmodern Age* (Westmont, Ill.: Intervarsity Press, 1995).

28. See Charlotte Allen, "The Postmodern Mission," *Lingua Franca* (December 1999): 55–59.

29. Michel de Certeau, *The Mystic Fable,* vol. 1, *The Sixteenth and Seventeenth Centuries,* trans. Michael B. Smith (Chicago: University of Chicago Press, 1992), 129.

30. See Julia Kristeva, *Revolution in Poetic Language,* trans. Margaret Waller (New York: Columbia University Press, 1994).

31. *Foucault/Blanchot.*

32. *Forget Foucault/Forget Baudrillard* (New York: Semiotext(e), Foreign Agents Series, 1987).

33. Michel Foucault and Gilles Deleuze, "Les intellectuels et le pouvoir," *L'Arc,* no. 49 (second trimester, 1972): 3–10; English translation: "Intellectuals and Power: A Conversation between Michel Foucault and Gilles Deleuze," in Michel Foucault, *Language, Counter-Memory, Practice: Selected Essays and Interviews,* ed. Donald F. Bouchard (Ithaca, N.Y.: Cornell University Press, 1977), 205–17.

34. Gayatri Chakravorty Spivak, "Can the Subaltern Speak?" in *Marxism and the Interpretation of Culture,* ed. Cary Nelson and Lawrence Grossberg (Chicago: University Press of Illinois, 1988), 274–75.

35. Collins, *The Sociology of Philosophies,* 74.

36. Michel Foucault, "Preface," in Gilles Deleuze and Félix Guattari, *Anti-Oedipus: Capitalism and Schizophrenia,* trans. Robert Hurley, Mark Seem, and Helen R. Lane (Minneapolis: University of Minnesota Press, 1983), xiii.

37. Michel Foucault, "Theatrum Philosophicum," in Foucault, *Language, Counter-Memory, Practice,* 165.

38. De Certeau, *The Mystic Fable,* 1:162.

39. Quoted in *The Sokal Hoax: The Sham That Shook the Academy,* ed. Lingua Franca (Lincoln: University of Nebraska Press, 2000), 224.

40. Ian R. Douglas, "The Calm before the Storm: Virilio's Debt to Foucault," online article: http://proxy.arts.uci.edu/~nideffer/_SPEED_/1.4/articles/douglas.html.

41. Gayatri Chakravorty Spivak, "Translator's Preface," in Jacques Derrida, *Of Grammatology* (Baltimore: Johns Hopkins University Press, 1976), xxxvii–xxxviii and xxxvi.

42. Jean-René Ladmiral, *Traduire: Théorèmes pour la traduction* (Paris: Payot, 1979), 168–69, 19, 246, and 145, respectively.

43. See Gilles Deleuze, "Letter to a Harsh Critic" in *Negotiations: 1972–1990*, trans. Martin Joughin (New York: Columbia University Press, 1995), 6, and Michel Foucault, *The Order of Things: An Archaeology of the Human Sciences*, no trans. (New York: Pantheon, 1970), 387.

44. Antoine Compagnon, *La Seconde main, ou le travail de la citation* (Paris: Seuil, 1979), 351 and 356.

45. See his analysis of the "academic" construction of Lévi-Strauss, in Pierre Bourdieu, *Homo Academicus*, trans. Peter Collier (Oxford: Polity Press, 1998), 21–23.

46. As we are invited to do, not without irony, in the chapter "What Was Structuralism?" contained in a guide to literary *savoir-vivre* and cultural splash by Judy Jones and William Wilson, *An Incomplete Education* (New York: Ballantine, 1987).

47. Paul de Man, *Resistance to Theory* (Minneapolis: University of Minnesota Press, 1986), 12 and 19–20.

48. Dominick LaCapra, *Rethinking Intellectual History* (Ithaca, N.Y.: Cornell University Press, 1983), 18.

49. See Dominic LaCapra and Steven L. Kaplan, eds., *Modern European Intellectual History: Reappraisals and New Perspectives* (Ithaca, N.Y.: Cornell University Press, 1982).

50. Peter Novick, *The Noble Dream: The "Objectivity Question" and the American Historical Profession* (Cambridge: Cambridge University Press, 1988).

51. Lynn Hunt, "History as Gesture, or, the Scandal of History," in *Consequences of Theory*, ed. Jonathan Arac and Barbara Johnson (Baltimore: Johns Hopkins University Press, 1991), 91–107.

52. Didier Éribon, *Michel Foucault,* trans. Betsy Wing (Cambridge: Harvard University Press, 1991). [The quoted sentence was omitted from the English translation, where it would have appeared on p. 313.—*Trans.*]

53. Quoted in John Rajchman, ed., *The Identity in Question* (New York: Routledge, 1995), 255.

54. See, for example, Nicholas Fox, *Postmodernism, Sociology and Health* (Toronto: University of Toronto Press, 1993).

55. Lamont and Witten, "Surveying the Continental Drift," 21.

56. Gilles Deleuze and Claire Parnet, *Dialogues* (1977), trans. Hugh Tomlinson and Barbara Habberjam (New York: Columbia University Press, 1987), 74.

57. Pascal Engel, "French and American Philosophical Dispositions," *Stanford French Review,* vol. 15, nos. 1–2 (1991): 165–81.

58. Quoted in ibid., 168.

59. John Rajchman, "Philosophy in America," in *Post-Analytic Philosophy,* ed. John Rajchman and Cornel West (New York: Columbia University Press, 1985), xi.

60. Judith Butler, *Subjects of Desire: Hegelian Reflections in Twentieth-Century France* (New York: Columbia University Press, 1987), 7, 180, and 209.

61. Rajchman, "Philosophy in America," xiv.

62. Graff, *Professing Literature*, 252.

63. Hiram Corson, "The Aims of Literary Study," in *The Origins of Literary Studies in America,* ed. Gerald Graff and Michael Warner (New York: Routledge, 1989), 90.

64. Quoted in Theo d'Haen, "America and Deleuze," in van der Poel, Bertho, and Hoenselaars, *Traveling Theory,* 45.

65. Pradeep Dhillon and Paul Standish, eds., *Lyotard: Just Education* (New York: Routledge, 2000), 110, 54, 97, 215, and 194, respectively.

66. Ibid., 10.

67. Ibid., 20–22.

68. The English version was first published as the leading essay in a volume edited by Tom Cohen, *Jacques Derrida and the Humanities: A Critical Reader* (Cambridge: Cambridge University Press, 2001), 24–57. Reprinted as "The University without Condition," in *Without Alibi,* trans. Peggy Kamuf (Stanford, Calif.: Stanford University Press, 2002), 202–37.

69. Jacques Derrida, *Memoirs for Paul de Man,* trans. Cecile Lindsay, Jonathan Culler, Eduardo Cadava, and Peggy Kamuf (New York: Columbia University Press, 1989), 16.

70. David Kaufmann, "The Profession of Theory," *PMLA,* vol. 105, no. 3 (1990): 520 and 528.

71. Steven Knapp and Walter Benn Michaels, "Against Theory," reprinted in *Against Theory: Literary Studies and the New Pragmatism,* ed. W. J. T. Mitchell (Chicago: University of Chicago Press, 1984), 11.

72. Stanley Fish, "Consequences," in ibid., 107.

73. W. J. T. Mitchell, "Introduction," in Mitchell, *Against Theory,* 2.

74. Ibid., 7.

75. Wlad Godzich, *The Culture of Literacy* (Cambridge: Harvard University Press, 1994), 31.

76. Peter Brooks, "Aesthetics and Ideology: What Happened to Poetics?" *Critical Inquiry,* vol. 20, no. 3 (spring 1994): 521.

77. See Martin Heidegger, "Science and Reflection," in *The Question concerning Technology and Other Essays*, trans. William Lovitt (New York: Harper and Row, 1977), 155–82.

78. Roland Barthes, "Sur la théorie," in *Œuvres complètes* (Paris: Seuil, 1994), 2:1031–36.

79. Camille Paglia, "Junk Bonds and Corporate Raiders: Academe in the Hour of the Wolf," in *Sex, Art and American Culture: Essays* (New York: Vintage, 1992), 221.

5. Deconstruction Sites

1. *Deconstructing Harry* (1997) appeared in France as *Harry dans tous ses états* (Harry beside himself), since the verb *déconstruire* would have meant very little to French moviegoers.

2. This is the title of an article by Rebecca Comay on the "nonidentity" of deconstruction in the United States; see "Geopolitics of Translation: Deconstruction in America," *Stanford French Review,* vol. 15, nos. 1–2 (1991): 47–79.

3. Jacques Derrida, *Memoirs for Paul de Man,* trans. Cecile Lindsay, Jonathan Cullter, Eduardo Cadava, and Peggy Kamuf (New York: Columbia University Press, 1989), 18.

4. Gayatri Chakravorty Spivak, "Translator's Preface," in Jacques Derrida, *Of Grammatology* (Baltimore: Johns Hopkins University Press, 1976), xvi and xxii.

5. Ibid., xvii, xxi, xxix, liv, and l, respectively.

6. Ibid., xxxv.

7. Ibid., lvii–lix.

8. William Fleisch, article titled "Deconstruction," in *A Companion to American Thought,* ed. Richard Wightman Fox and James Kloppenberg (Cambridge: Blackwell, 1995), 170–71.

9. Quoted in Arthur Danto, "Philosophy as/and/of Literature," in *Post-Analytic Philosophy,* ed. John Rajchman and Cornel West (New York: Columbia University Press, 1985), 71–73.

10. Quoted in Bill Readings, *The University in Ruins* (Cambridge: Harvard University Press, 1996), 123–24.

11. William Pritchard, "The Hermeneutical Mafia, or, After Strange Gods at Yale," *Hudson Review,* no. 28 (winter 1975–76).

12. Harold Bloom, Paul de Man, Jacques Derrida, Geoffrey Hartman, and J. Hillis Miller, *Deconstruction and Criticism* (New York: Seabury Press, 1979).

13. Wlad Godzich, "Foreword," in Paul de Man, *Blindness and Insight: Essays in the Rhetoric of Contemporary Criticism* (Minneapolis: University of Minnesota Press, 1971; 2d ed. 1983), xvi.

14. Paul de Man, *Resistance to Theory* (Minneapolis: University of Minnesota Press, 1986), 8–9.

15. See Paul de Man, "Conclusions: Walter Benjamin's 'The Task of the Translator,'" in ibid., 103–4.

16. Wlad Godzich, "The Domestication of Derrida," in *The Yale Critics: Deconstruction in America,* ed. Jonathan Arac, Wlad Godzich, and Wallace Martin (Minneapolis: University of Minnesota Press, 1983), 39.

17. Harold Bloom, *The Anxiety of Influence: A Theory of Poetry* (New York: Oxford University Press, 1973).

18. Harold Bloom, *The Western Canon* (New York: Harcourt Brace, 1994), 517–18.

19. Harold Bloom, *Shakespeare: The Invention of the Human* (New York: Riverhead Books, 1999).

20. Denis Donoghue, "Deconstructing Deconstruction," *New York Review of Books,* June 12, 1980, 38–41.

21. See R. V. Young, *At War with the Word* (Wilmington, Del.: Intercollegiate Studies Institute, 1999), 58.

22. Jacques Derrida, "From Restricted to General Economy," in *Writing and Difference* (1967), trans. Alan Bass (Chicago: University of Chicago Press, 1978), 253 (translation modified).

23. Jacques Derrida, "Structure, Sign and Play in the Discourse of the Human Sciences," in ibid., 281 (translation slightly modified).

24. Jacques Derrida, *Specters of Marx,* trans. Peggy Kamuf (New York: Routledge, 1994); "Force of Law," trans. Mary Quaintance, in *Acts of Religion,* ed. Gil Anidjar (New York: Routledge, 2001); *Archive Fever,* trans. Eric Prenowitz (Chicago: University of Chicago Press, 1996).

25. Hannah Arendt, "The Crisis in Education," in *Between Past and Future: Eight Exercises in Political Thought* (New York: Penguin Books, 1993), 182.

26. Mary Cicora, *Modern Myths and Wagnerian Deconstructions: Hermeneutic Approaches to Wagner's Music Dramas* (Westport, Conn.: Greenwood Press, 2000), 1–3.

27. Robert Mugerauer, *Interpreting Environments: Traditions, Deconstruction, Hermeneutics* (Austin: University of Texas Press, 1995), 30.

28. David Wood, *The Deconstruction of Time* (Amherst, Mass.: Prometheus Books, 1990).

29. Meyer Abrams, "The Deconstructive Angel," *Critical Inquiry,* vol. 3, no. 3 (spring 1977): 425–38.

30. Andrew Boyd, *Life's Little Deconstruction Book: Self-Help for the Post-Hip* (New York: W. W. Norton, 1998).

31. Michel de Certeau, *The Mystic Fable,* vol. 1, *The Sixteenth and Seventeenth Centuries,* trans. Michael B. Smith (Chicago: University of Chicago Press, 1992), 129 (translation slightly modified).

32. Jacques Derrida, "The Law of Genre," trans. Avital Ronell, *Glyph* 7 (1980): 202–32. [See also *Parages* (Paris: Galilée, 1986), a collection of Derrida's writings on Blanchot.—*Trans.*]

33. Drucilla Cornell, "Gender, Sex and Equivalent Rights," in *Feminists Theorize the Political,* ed. Judith Butler and Joan Scott (New York: Routledge, 1992), 286–87.

34. Judith Butler, *Bodies That Matter: On the Discursive Limits of "Sex"* (New York: Routledge, 1993), 29.

35. Judith Butler, "Preface" (1999), in *Gender Trouble: Feminism and the Subversion of Identity* (New York: Routledge, 1999 [1990]), xiv.

36. Homi K. Bhabha, *Nation and Narration* (New York: Routledge, 1990), 291ff.; *The Location of Culture* (New York: Routledge, 1994), 139ff.

37. Gayatri Chakravorty Spivak, "Can the Subaltern Speak?" in *Marxism and the Interpretation of Culture,* ed. Cary Nelson and Lawrence Grossberg (Chicago: University of Chicago Press, 1988), 292–94.

38. Nancy Fraser, "The French Derrideans: Politicizing Deconstruction or Deconstructing the Political?" *New German Critique,* no. 33 (autumn 1984): 129–30.

39. Vincent Descombes, *Modern French Philosophy,* trans. L. Scott-Fox and J. M. Harding (Cambridge: Cambridge University Press, 1980), 151.

40. Derrida, *Specters of Marx.*

41. Ibid., 88.

42. See Pierre Macherey, "Marx dématérialisé ou l'esprit de Derrida," *Europe,* no. 780 (April 1994).

43. Michael Sprinker, ed., *Ghostly Demarcations: A Symposium on Jacques Derrida* (London: Verso, 1999).

6. The Politics of Identity

1. Todd Gitlin, *The Twilight of Common Dreams* (New York: Henry Holt, 1995), 162.

2. Bill Readings, *The University in Ruins* (Cambridge: Harvard Univeristy Press, 1996), 89 and 103.

3. Raymond Williams, *The Long Revolution* (London: Chatto and Windus, 1961); Richard Hoggart, *The Uses of Literacy* (London: Chatto and Windus, 1957).

4. See the debates that divided the University of Pittsburgh over whether the interdisciplinary program created in 1986 should be titled "Institute of *Cultural Studies.*"

5. Andrew Ross, *No Respect: Intellectuals and Popular Culture* (New York: Routledge, 1989), 11.

6. See Marjorie Ferguson and Peter Golding, eds., *Cultural Studies in Question* (London: Sage, 1997), xiv–xv.

7. Lawrence Grossberg, Cary Nelson, and Paula A. Treichler, eds., *Cultural Studies* (New York: Routledge, 1992).

8. Dick Hebdige, *Subculture: The Meaning of Style* (New York: Methuen, 1979).

9. Cathy Schwichtenberg, ed., *The Madonna Connection: Representational Politics, Subcultural Identities, and Cultural Theory* (Boulder, Colo.: Westview Press, 1993).

10. E. Ann Kaplan, *Rocking around the Clock: Music Television, Postmodernism and Consumer Culture* (New York: Methuen, 1987), 117.

11. Timothy Murray, ed., *Mimesis, Masochism and Mime: The Politics of Theatricality in Contemporary French Thought* (Ann Arbor: University of Michigan Press, 1997), "Introduction."

12. Abigail Bray and Claire Colebrook, "The Haunted Flesh: Corporeal Feminism and the Politics of Embodiment," *Signs,* vol. 24, no. 1 (fall 1998).

13. Ian Buchanan, "Deleuze and Cultural Studies," *South Atlantic Quarterly,* vol. 96, no. 3 (summer 1997): 487 and 491.

14. Michel de Certeau, *The Practice of Everyday Life,* trans. Steven Rendall (Berkeley: University of California Press, 1984).

15. François Dosse, *Michel de Certeau: Le marcheur blessé* (Paris: La Découverte, 2002), 419.

16. James Livingston, "Corporations and Cultural Studies," *Social Text,* no. 44 (fall 1995): 67.

17. See especially Henry Louis Gates Jr., "Whose Canon Is It, Anyway?" *New York Times Book Review,* February 26, 1989.

18. Patricia Williams, *The Alchemy of Race and Rights* (Cambridge: Harvard University Press, 1991), 256.

19. Martin Bernal, *Black Athena: The Afroasiatic Roots of Classical Civilization,* 2 vols. (Piscataway, N.J.: Rutgers University Press, 1987 and 1991).

20. Henry Louis Gates Jr., "Black Demagogues and Pseudo-Scholars," *New York Times,* Op-Ed, July 20, 1992.

21. Mary Lefkowitz, *Not Out of Africa: How Afrocentrism Became an Excuse to Teach Myth as History* (New York: Basic Books, 1996).

22. See, for example, Ramón Saldívar, *Chicano Narrative: The Dialectics of Difference* (Madison: University of Wisconsin Press, 1990).

23. Alfred Arteaga, ed., *An Other Tongue: Nation and Ethnicity in the Linguistic Borderlands* (Durham, N.C.: Duke University Press, 1994). See in particular Norma Alarcón, "Conjugating Subjects: The Heteroglossia of Essence and Resistance," 125–38, and Cordelia Chávez Candelaria, "Différance and the Discourse of 'Community' in Writings by and about the Ethnic Other(s)," 185–202.

24. Gilles Deleuze and Claire Parnet, *Dialogues* (1977), trans. Hugh Tomlinson and Barbara Habberjam (New York: Columbia University Press, 1987), 58.

25. Edward Said, "Yeats and Decolonization," in *The Edward Said Reader,* ed. Moustafa Bayoumi and Andrew Rubin (New York: Vintage, 2000), 291ff.

26. The theme of his most famous work: Edward Said, *Orientalism* (New York: Pantheon, 1978).

27. Jacques Derrida, "Force and Signification," in *Writing and Difference* (1967), trans. Alan Bass (Chicago: University of Chicago Press, 1978), 4.

28. Cited in Dosse, *Michel de Certeau,* 427.

29. Homi K. Bhabha, *The Location of Culture* (New York: Routledge, 1994), 20, 32, and 37.

30. Gayatri Chakravorty Spivak, *In Other Worlds: Essays in Cultural Politics* (New York: Routledge, 1998), 202.

31. Gayatri Chakravorty Spivak, "Can the Subaltern Speak?" in *Marxism and the Interpretation of Culture,* ed. Cary Nelson and Lawrence Grossberg (Chicago: University Press of Illinois, 1988), 280–81 and 290–91.

32. Gayatri Chakravorty Spivak, "French Feminisms Revisited: Ethics and Politics," in *Feminists Theorize the Political,* ed. Judith Butler and Joan Scott (New York: Routledge, 1992), 57.

33. *Subaltern Studies,* vol. 1, no. 1 (1982).

34. Spivak, "Can the Subaltern Speak?"

35. Ranajit Guha and Gayatri Chakravorty Spivak, eds., *Selected Subaltern Studies* (New York: Columbia University Press, 1988).

36. Adrienne Rich, *Of Woman Born: Motherhood as Experience and Institution* (New York: Bantam, 1977).

37. Kate Millett, *Sexual Politics* (New York: Doubleday, 1970).

38. Meryl Altman, "Everything They Always Wanted You to Know: The Ideology of Popular Sex Literature," in *Pleasure and Danger: Exploring Female Sexuality,* ed. Carol Vance (Boston: Routledge, 1984).

39. Gayle Rubin, "Thinking Sex: Notes for a Radical Theory of a Politics of Sexuality," in ibid.

40. Butler and Scott, *Feminists Theorize the Political,* xiii.

41. See Sandra Harding, *The Science Question in Feminism* (Ithaca, N.Y.: Cornell University Press, 1986).

42. Cited in *Traveling Theory: France and the United States,* ed. Ieme van der Poel, Sophie Bertho, and Ton Hoenselaars (Teaneck, N.J.: Fairleigh Dickinson University Press, 1999), 19.

43. Butler and Scott, *Feminists Theorize the Political,* xvi.

44. Spivak, "French Feminisms Revisited," 58–59.

45. See Elaine Marks and Isabelle de Courtivron, eds., *New French Feminisms: An Anthology* (Amherst: University of Massachusetts Press, 1980).

46. Hélène Cixous, "Le rire de la Méduse," *L'Arc*, no. 61 (1975): 39–54. English translation: "The Laugh of the Medusa," in Marks and de Courivron, *New French Feminisms*, 245–64.

47. Cited in John Mullarkey, "Deleuze and Materialism: One or Several Matters?" *South Atlantic Quarterly* (1997): 455.

48. Elizabeth Grosz, "A Thousand Tiny Sexes: Feminism and Rhizomatics," and Rosi Braidotti, "Toward a New Nomadism: Feminist Deleuzian Tracks, or Metaphysics and Metabolism," in *Gilles Deleuze and the Theater of Philosophy*, ed. Constantin Boundas and Corothea Olkowski (New York: Routledge, 1994).

49. Deleuze and Parnet, *Dialogues*, 43.

50. Christian Descamps, "Entretien avec Félix Guattari," *La Quinzaine littéraire*, August 28, 1975.

51. Irene Diamond and Lee Quinby, eds., *Feminism and Foucault: Reflections on Resistance* (Boston: Northeastern University Press, 1988), ix and xiii–xv.

52. Michel Foucault, *The History of Sexuality*, vol. 1, *An Introduction*, trans. Robert Hurley (New York: Vintage, 1980), 131.

53. Ibid., 114.

54. Kaja Silverman, *Male Subjectivity at the Margins* (New York: Routledge, 1992).

55. Teresa de Lauretis, "Queer Theory: Lesbian and Gay Sexualities. An Introduction," *Differences (Journal of Feminist and Cultural Studies)*, vol. 3, no. 2 (summer 1991).

56. Eve Kosofsky Sedgwick, *Epistemology of the Closet* (Berkeley: University of California Press, 1990).

57. Ibid., 1.

58. Foucault, *The History of Sexuality*, 1:43.

59. David Halperin, *One Hundred Years of Homosexuality* (New York: Routledge, 1989), 8–12.

60. See Alex Callinicos, *Against Postmodernism: A Marxist Critique* (New York: St. Martin's Press, 1989).

61. Terry Eagleton, *Literary Theory: An Introduction* (Minneapolis: University of Minnesota Press, 1983).

62. Todd Gitlin, "The Anti-Political Populism of Cultural Studies," in Ferguson and Golding, *Cultural Studies in Question*, 30.

63. Stanley Aronowitz and Henry Giroux, *Education under Siege: The Conservative, Liberal and Radical Debate over Schooling* (Boston: Bergin & Garvey, 1985), 177.

64. Butler and Scott, *Feminists Theorize the Political*, xiv (emphasis in original).

65. Stanley Fish, *Professional Correctness: Literary Studies and Political Change* (New York and London: Oxford University Press, 1995), 123–24 (emphasis in original).

66. Sedgwick, *Epistemology of the Closet*, 23.

67. Jean-François Lyotard, *Libidinal Economy*, trans. Iain Hamilton Grant (Bloomington: Indiana University Press, 1993), 116. (Originally published in French in 1974.)

68. Amiel Van Teslaar, "Un Structuralisme, mais à l'américaine," *La Quinzaine littéraire*, no. 330.

69. Catherine Gallagher and Stephen Greenblatt, *Practicing New Historicism* (Chicago: University of Chicago Press, 2000), 17 and 19.

70. Ibid. 10–11.

71. Stephen Greenblatt, *Hamlet in Purgatory* (Princeton, N.J.: Princeton University Press, 2001).

72. Stephen Greenblatt, *Shakespearean Negotiations: The Circulation of Social Energy in Renaissance England* (Berkeley: University of California Press, 1988), 142.

73. The title of his contribution to Gerald Graff and James Phelan, eds., *The Tempest: A Case Study in Critical Controversy* (New York: Bedford/St. Martin's Press, 2000), 113.

74. Roger Chartier, "Greenblatt entre l'autre et le même," *Le monde des livres,* November 29, 1996.

7. The Ideological Backlash

1. Pierre Bourdieu, *The Rules of Art: Genesis and Structure of the Literary Field* (1992), trans. Susan Emanuel (Stanford, Calif.: Stanford University Press, 1996), 147.

2. James Atlas, *The Book Wars: What It Takes to Be Educated in America* (New York: Whittle Books, 1990).

3. See William Henry III, *In Defense of Elitism* (New York: Doubleday, 1994).

4. Henry Louis Gates Jr. "Whose Canon Is It, Anyway?" *New York Times Book Review,* February 26, 1989.

5. Quoted in Christopher J. Lucas, *American Higher Education: A History* (New York: St. Martin's Press, 1994), 274.

6. Quoted in Michael Bérubé, "Public Image Limited," *Village Voice,* June 18, 1991.

7. The topic even reached Public Television stations, as in the debate "Do We Need the Western Canon?" on PBS on October 30, 1997.

8. Edward Said, "Secular Criticism," in *The Edward Said Reader,* ed. Moustafa Bayoumi and Andrew Rubin (New York: Vintage, 2000), 236.

9. Richard Goldstein, "The Politics of Political Correctness," *Village Voice,* June 18, 1991.

10. See Michael Bérubé and Cary Nelson, eds., *Higher Education under Fire* (New York: Routledge, 1995), 82–83.

11. Eric Fassin, "La Chaire et le canon: Les intellectuels, la politique et l'université aux États-Unis," *Annales ESC,* vol. 48, no. 2 (March-April 1993): 300.

12. John Taylor, "Are You Politically Correct?" *New York,* January 21, 1991.

13. Camille Paglia, "Ninnies, Pedants, Tyrants and Other Academics," *New York Times Book Review,* May 5, 1991.

14. Pierre Nora, "Les Nouveaux maîtres censeurs," *Le Nouvel Observateur,* August 29–September 4, 1991.

15. "Le crépuscule de l'Europe sur les campus américains," *Le Messager européen,* no. 5 (1991).

16. Tzvetan Todorov, "Crimes against Humanities," *New Republic,* July 3, 1989, 28–30.

17. Werner Hamacher, Neil Hertz, and Tom Keenan, eds., *Paul de Man: Wartime Journalism 1939–1943* (Lincoln: University of Nebraska Press, 1989), 45.

18. Quoted in David Lehman, "Deconstructing de Man's Life," *Newsweek,* February 15, 1988. The article's author also wrote an acerbic book on the affair: *Signs of the Times: Deconstruction and the Fall of Paul de Man* (New York: Poseidon Press, 1991).

19. Bérubé, "Public Image Limited."

20. Allan Bloom, *The Closing of the American Mind* (New York: Simon and Schuster, 1987).

21. Dinesh D'Souza, *Illiberal Education: The Politics of Race and Sex on Campus* (New York: Vintage, 1991).

22. Roger Kimball, *Tenured Radicals: How Politics Has Corrupted Our Higher Education* (Chicago: Ivan R. Dee, 1998 [1990]), xi–xiv.

23. Ibid., 7.

24. Ibid., for example, xvi–xvii.

25. Ibid., 46–47.

26. Ibid., 236.

27. We might note a conference in 1988, "The Politics of Liberal Education," reprinted later in *South Atlantic Quarterly,* no. 89 (winter 1990).

28. Quoted in Goldstein, "The Politics of Political Correctness."

29. Quoted in Lucas, *American Higher Education,* 296.

30. Quoted in Fassin, "La Chaire et le canon," 290.

31. Russell Jacoby, *The Last Intellectuals: American Culture in the Age of Academe* (New York: Basic Books, 1987).

32. Arthur Schlesinger, *The Disuniting of America: Reflections on a Multicultural Society* (New York: W. W. Norton, 1991).

33. Quoted in Kimball, *Tenured Radicals,* 17. See William Bennett, *To Reclaim a Legacy: A Report on the Humanities in Higher Education* (Washington, D.C.: National Endowment for the Humanities, 1984).

34. Bourdieu, *The Rules of Art,* 280.

35. Ibid.

36. Adam Begley, "Souped-up Scholar," *New York Times Magazine,* May 2, 1992.

37. Robert Westbrook, "The Counter-Intelligentsia: How Neoconservatism Lived and Died," *Lingua Franca* (November 1996): 69.

38. Wlad Godzich, *The Culture of Literacy* (Cambridge: Harvard University Press, 1994), 2.

39. Francis Fukuyama, *The End of History and the Last Man* (New York: Free Press, 1992).

40. Quoted in Fassin, "La Chaire et le canon," 289–90. For the original quotes, see Eugene Genovese's (largely positive) review of Dinesh D'Souza, *Illiberal Education:* "Heresy, Yes—Sensitivity, No," *New Republic,* April 15, 1991, 32; see also Genovese's contribution to "The American Eighties: Disaster or Triumph? A Symposium," *Commentary,* vol. 90, no. 3 (September 1990): 49.

41. Mark Gerson, *The Neoconservative Vision: From the Cold War to the Culture Wars* (New York: Madison Books, 1997), 31.

42. Shadia Drury, *Leo Strauss and the American Right* (New York: Palgrave Macmillan, 1997), chapter 3.

43. James Wilson and George Kelling, "Broken Windows: The Police and Neighborhood Safety," reprinted in Mark Gerson and James Wilson, eds., *The Essential Neoconservative Reader* (Washington, D.C.: Perseus Press, 1996).

44. See Alain Frachon and Daniel Vernet, "Le stratège et le philosophe," *Le Monde,* April 16, 2003.

45. This is the title of chapter 5 in Gitlin, *The Twilight of Common Dreams,* 126–65.

46. Ibid., 165.

47. Michael Walzer, "The Lonely Politics of Michel Foucault," in *The Company of Critics: Social Criticism and Political Commitment in the Twentieth Century* (New York: Basic Books, 1988), 195 and 200–204.

48. Lindsay Waters, "The Age of Incommensurability," *Boundary 2,* vol. 28, no. 2 (2001): 147.

49. Gitlin, *The Twilight of Common Dreams,* 147.

50. Paul de Man, *Resistance to Theory* (Minneapolis: University of Minnesota Press, 1986), 5.

51. André Schiffrin, *L'Édition sans éditeurs* (Paris: La Fabrique, 1999), 77.

52. Gerald Graff, *Beyond the Culture Wars: How Teaching the Conflicts Can Revitalize American Education* (New York: W. W. Norton, 1992).

8. Academic Stars

1. Cited in Christopher J. Lucas, *American Higher Education: A History* (New York: St. Martin's Press, 1994), 180.

2. Pierre Bourdieu, *Homo Academicus,* trans. Peter Collier (Oxford: Polity Press, 1998), 105.

3. "La Lecture, une pratique culturelle" (debate between Pierre Bourdieu and Roger Chartier), in *Pratiques de la lecture,* ed. Roger Chartier (Paris: Payot, 1993), 275.

4. Michel Foucault, "What Is an Author?" in *Essential Works of Foucault 1954–1984,* vol. 2, *Aesthetics, Method, and Ideology,* trans. Robert Hurley et al. (New York: New Press, 1998), 217, 222, and 210.

5. In 1998 she won the so-called Bad Writing Contest, an annual (and parodic) award staged by the academic journal *Philosophy and Literature.*

6. Judith Butler, *Bodies That Matter: On the Discursive Limits of "Sex"* (New York: Routledge, 1993), 230.

7. Judith Butler, *Subjects of Desire: Hegelian Reflections in Twentieth-Century France* (New York: Columbia University Press, 1987), 178, 216, and 213, respectively.

8. Judith Butler, *Gender Trouble: Feminism and the Subversion of Identity* (New York: Routledge, 1999 [1990]), particularly chapter 3.

9. Judith Butler, *La Vie psychique du pouvoir* (Paris: Léo Scheer, 2002). English: *The Psychic Life of Power: Theories in Subjection* (Stanford, Calif.: Stanford University Press, 1997).

10. Butler, *Bodies That Matter,* 19.

11. Louis Althusser, "Ideology and State Ideological Apparatuses," in *Lenin and Philosophy and Other Essays,* trans. Ben Brewster (New York: Monthly Review Press, 1971), 127–86.

12. Butler, *The Psychic Life of Power,* chapter 4, "'Conscience Doth Make Subjects of Us All': Althusser's Subjection," 107 and 130.

13. Judith Butler, "Preface (1999)," in *Gender Trouble,* xxvi.

14. See, for example, Gayatri Chakravorty Spivak, *In Other Worlds: Essays in Cultural Politics* (New York: Routledge, 1998), 209–11.

15. Gayatri Chakravorty Spivak, "French Feminisms Revisited: Ethics and Politics,"

in *Feminists Theorize the Political,* ed. Judith Butler and Joan Scott (New York: Routledge, 1992), 58.

16. Julia Kristeva, *Des Chinoises* (Paris: Éditions des Femmes, 1974). English translation: *About Chinese Women,* trans. Anita Barrows (New York: Urizen Books, 1977).

17. Gayatri Chakravorty Spivak, "French Feminisms in an International Frame," *Yale French Studies,* no. 62 (1981): 158–60.

18. Barbara Johnson, "Introduction: Truth or Consequences," in *Consequences of Theory,* ed. Jonathan Arac and Barbara Johnson (Baltimore: Johns Hopkins University Press, 1991), xii.

19. Gayatri Chakravorty Spivak, "Can the Subaltern Speak?" in *Marxism and the Interpretation of Culture,* ed. Cary Nelson and Lawrence Grossberg (Chicago: University of Chicago Press, 1988), 280–82.

20. Ibid., 271.

21. Colin MacCabe, "Foreword," in Spivak, *In Other Worlds,* xii.

22. David Lodge, *Small World: An Academic Romance* (Harmondsworth, UK: Penguin, 1985).

23. Stanley Fish, *Surprised by Sin: The Reader in Paradise Lost* (Berkeley: University of California Press, 1972).

24. Stanley Fish, "Is There a Text in This Class?" in *The Stanley Fish Reader,* ed. Aram Veeser (Oxford: Blackwell, 1999), 41–48.

25. Ibid., 54.

26. Stanley Fish, *There's No Such Thing as Free Speech: And It's a Good Thing, Too* (New York: Oxford University Press, 1994).

27. Stanley Fish, "Consequences," in *Against Theory: Literary Studies and the New Pragmatism,* ed. W. J. T. Mitchell (Chicago: University of Chicago Press, 1984), 113.

28. Adam Begley, "Souped-up Scholar," *New York Times Magazine,* May 2, 1992.

29. Stanley Fish, *Professional Correctness: Literary Studies and Political Change* (New York and London: Oxford University Press, 1995), 140.

30. See his recent *Israël-Palestine, l'égalité ou rien* (Paris: La Fabrique, 2001). [This collection of essays first appeared in English in various places, so there is no corresponding English edition to cite.—*Trans.*]

31. Edward Said, *Orientalism* (New York: Vintage, 1978). French translation: *L'Orientalisme: L'Orient créé par l'Occident* (Paris: Seuil, 1980), preface by Tzvetan Todorov.

32. Ibid., 172.

33. Edward Said, *Representations of the Intellectual: The 1993 Reith Lectures* (New York: Vintage, 1996).

34. The title of Eric Hobsbawm's overview of the end of the nineteenth century, *The Age of Empire 1875–1914* (New York: Vintage, 1989).

35. Edward Said, *Culture and Imperialism* (New York: Alfred A. Knopf, 1993).

36. Ibid., 210.

37. Chapter 12 of Gilles Deleuze and Félix Guattari, *A Thousand Plateaus: Capitalism and Schizophrenia,* trans. Brian Massumi (Minneapolis: University of Minnesota Press, 1987 [French version first published in 1980]), 351–423.

38. Said, *Culture and Imperialism,* 331–32.

39. Edward Said, *The World, the Text, and the Critic* (Cambridge: Harvard University Press, 1983), 244.

40. Edward Said, "Traveling Theory," in *Imported: A Reading Seminar,* ed. Rainer Ganahl (New York: Semiotext(e), 1998), 178–79.

41. Edward Said, "Introduction to Orientalism," in *The Edward Said Reader,* ed. Moustafa Bayoumi and Andrew Rubin (New York: Vintage, 2000), 89.

42. Edward Said, "Opponents, Audiences, Constituencies and Community," in *The Anti-Aesthetic: Essays on Postmodern Culture,* ed. Hal Foster (Port Townsend, Wash.: Bay Press, 1983), 135–58.

43. Edward Said, "Secular Criticism," in Bayoumi and Rubin, *The Edward Said Reader,* 241.

44. Ibid., 242. See Raymond Williams, *Politics and Letters: Interviews with New Left Review* (London: New Left Books, 1979), 252.

45. Richard Rorty, *Philosophy and the Mirror of Nature* (Cambridge: Cambridge University Press, 1979), 4.

46. Richard Rorty, *Contingency, Irony and Solidarity* (Cambridge: Cambridge University Press, 1989).

47. Richard Bernstein, *The New Constellation: The Ethical and Political Horizons of Modernity/Postmodernity* (Cambridge: MIT Press, 1992).

48. Cf. Herman Saatkamp, ed., *Rorty and Pragmatism: The Philosopher Responds to His Critics* (Nashville: Vanderbilt University Press, 1995).

49. Deleuze and Guattari, *A Thousand Plateaus,* 148.

50. Michel Foucault, "La philosophie analytique de la politique" (conference in Tokyo), published in *Dits et Écrits, 1954–1988,* vol. 3, *1976–1979* (Paris: Gallimard, 1994), 540–41.

51. Richard Shusterman, *Pragmatic Aesthetics* (Lanham, Md.: Rowman & Littlefield, 1998).

52. Cornel West, *The American Evasion of Philosophy: A Genealogy of Pragmatism* (Madison: University of Wisconsin Press, 1989).

53. As François Dosse, in particular, notes, in *Michel de Certeau: Le marcheur blessé* (Paris: La Découverte, 2002), 414.

54. Fredric Jameson, *Fables of Aggression: Wyndham Lewis, the Modernist as Fascist* (Berkeley: University of California Press, 1979).

55. Fredric Jameson, *The Prison-House of Language: A Critical Account of Structuralism and Russian Formalism* (Princeton, N.J.: Princeton University Press, 1972).

56. Fredric Jameson, *Marxism and Form* (Princeton, N.J.: Princeton University Press, 1974).

57. Fredric Jameson, *The Political Unconscious: Narrative as a Socially Symbolic Act* (Ithaca, N.Y.: Cornell University Press, 1981).

58. Fredric Jameson, *The Ideologies of Theory: Essays 1971–1986,* 2. vols. (Minneapolis: University of Minnesota Press, 1988).

59. See Fredric Jameson, *Postmodernism, or, The Cultural Logic of Late Capitalism* (Durham, N.C.: Duke University Press, 1991).

60. Ibid., 39–44 and chapter 4.

61. Ibid., 224–27.

62. Fredric Jameson, "Reification and Utopia in Mass Culture," *Social Text,* vol. 1, no. 1 (winter 1979).

63. Jameson, *The Ideologies of Theory,* vol. 2, *Syntax of History,* 195.

64. Jameson, *Fables of Agression,* 7n6.

65. Fredric Jameson, "On Cultural Studies," in *The Identity in Question,* ed. John Rajchman (New York: Routledge, 1995), 284, 291.

66. Jameson, *Postmodernism, or, The Cultural Logic of Late Capitalism,* 337–38.

67. See Fredric Jameson, "Periodizing the Sixties," *Social Text,* 9/10 (1984): 178–209; this issue was reprinted as *The Sixties without Apology,* ed. Sohnya Sayres, Anders Stephenson, Stanley Aronowitz, and Fredric Jameson (Minneapolis: University of Minnesota Press, 1984).

68. William Dowling, *Jameson, Althusser, Marx* (Ithaca, N.Y.: Cornell University Press, 1984), 10.

69. Peter Sellars, interviewed by Stephen Holden, "The Avant-Garde Is Big Box Office," *New York Times,* December 16, 1984.

70. Richard Wightman Fox and James Kloppenberg, eds., *A Companion to American Thought* (Cambridge: Blackwell, 1995), 534.

71. An example of a few of the *posts* invoked by critic Leslie Fiedler in the 1965 essay "The New Mutants," in *A Fiedler Reader* (New York: Stein & Day, 1977), 182–210.

72. Jean-François Lyotard, *The Postmodern Condition: A Report on Knowledge,* trans. Geoff Bennington and Brian Massumi (Minneapolis: University of Minnesota Press, 1984).

73. Ihab Hassan, *The Dismemberment of Orpheus: Toward a Postmodern Literature* (New York: Oxford University Press, 1971).

9. Students and Users

1. Gerald Graff, *Professing Literature: An Institutional History* (Chicago: University of Chicago Press, 1987), 248.

2. David Kaufmann, "The Profession of Theory," *PMLA,* vol. 105, no. 3 (1990): 529.

3. Anne Matthews, *New York Times Magazine,* February 10, 1991, 43.

4. Peter Brooks, "Aesthetics and Ideology: What Happened to Politics?" *Critical Inquiry,* vol. 20, no. 3 (spring 1994): 512.

5. Edward Said, "The Franco-American Dialogue: A Late Twentieth-Century Reassessment," in *Traveling Theory: France and the United States,* ed. Ieme van der Poel, Sophie Bertho, and Ton Hoenselaars (Teaneck, N.J.: Fairleigh Dickinson University Press, 1999), 146.

6. Ibid., 152.

7. Gustave Lanson, *Trois mois d'enseignement aux États-Unis: Notes et impressions d'un professeur français* (Paris: Hachette, 1912), 157–58.

8. See www.rhizome.org.

9. See www.hermenaut.org.

10. Quoted in Scott McLemee, "Meet the Hermenauts," *Lingua Franca* (October 1999): 18.

11. http://intermargins.net/intermargins/TCulturalWorkshop/academia/scholar%20and%20specialist/Baudrillard/Baudrillard%20on%20the%20Web.htm.

12. http://www.hydra.umn.edu/derrida/glas1.html.

13. Daniel White, "Dreams in Rebellion: The Battle of Seattle. The City of Disney, Book IV: Augustine of Epcot," *Ctheory:* http://www.ctheory.net/articles.aspx?id=123.

14. Michel de Certeau, *The Practice of Everyday Life,* trans. Steven Rendall (Berkeley: University of California Press, 1984), 71.

15. Lanson, *Trois mois d'enseignement aux États-Unis,* 144.

16. See Maxwell McCombs and Donald Shaw, "The Agenda-Setting Function of Mass Media," *Public Opinion Quarterly,* no. 36 (summer 1972): 176–87.

17. "La lecture, une pratique culturelle" (debate between Pierre Bourdieu and Roger Chartier), in *Pratiques de la lecture,* ed. Roger Chartier (Paris: Payot, 1993), 279.

18. See http://www.tranquileye.com/mirrors/panop/home.htm.

19. R. A. Brinckley and Robert Dyer, ". . . returns home (Mythologies, Dialectics, Structure): disruption," *Semiotext(e),* vol. 2, no. 3 (1977): 159–70.

20. See Jean Baudrillard, *The Gulf War Did Not Take Place* (Bloomington: Indiana University Press, 1995).

21. Paul Ricoeur, *Temps et Récit,* vol. 1, *L'intrigue et le récit historique* (Paris: Seuil, "Points" collection, 1983), 150–51.

22. Ibid., 151.

23. Ibid., 152.

24. Michel Foucault, *History of Sexuality,* vol. 2, *The Use of Pleasure,* trans. Robert Hurley (New York: Vintage, 1985), 8.

10. Art Practices

1. Howard Becker, *Art Worlds* (Berkeley: University of California Press, 1982), 34–38.

2. Jacques Rancière, "Le ressentiment anti-esthétique," *Magazine littéraire,* no. 414 (November 2002): 19.

3. Robert Storr, "Le grondement de courants nouveaux [The rumbling of new currents]," *Artpress,* no. 284 (November 2002): 39. [This article was published in French.—*Trans.*]

4. From the wall text to a Cy Twombly painting presented in the exhibit "Roland Barthes," Centre Georges-Pompidou, Paris (co-organized with Institut Mémoires de l'Édition Contemporaine [IMEC]), November 27–March 10, 2003.

5. Clement Greenberg, "'American-Type' Painting," in *Art and Culture* (New York: Beacon Press, 1961), 226.

6. Jean Baudrillard, "Le snobisme machinal," *Cahiers du Musée national d'art moderne,* no. 34 (winter 1990): 35–43.

7. Bernard Blistène, *Une histoire de l'art du XXe siècle* (Paris: Beaux-Arts Magazine/ Centre Pompidou, 2002 [1997]), 108.

8. Pierre Bourdieu, *The Rules of Art: Genesis and Structure of the Literary Field* (1992), trans. Susan Emanuel (Stanford, Calif.: Stanford University Press, 1996), 157 and 372n25.

9. See Gary Indiana, "Crime and Misdemeanors," in "The East Village 1979–1989: The Rise and Fall of an Art Scene," *Art Forum* (October 1999).

10. Kathy Acker, "Devoured by Myths," in *Hannibal Lecter, My Father* (New York: Semiotext[e], 1991), 10.

11. Jean Baudrillard, *Simulacres et Simulation* (Paris: Galilée, 1981), 218.

12. Cited in Sylvère Lotringer, "La théorie, mode d'emploi," *TLE,* no. 20 (spring 2002): 96.

13. Wolfgang Max Faust, "With It and Against It: Tendencies in Recent German Art," *Art Forum* (September 1981).

14. Achille Bonito Oliva, *The Italian Trans-avant-garde* (Milan: Giancarlo Politi Editore, 1981).

15. Thomas Lawson, "Last Exit: Painting," *Art Forum* (October 1981).

16. Benjamin Buchloh, "Figures of Authority, Ciphers of Regression," *October,* no. 16 (autumn 1981); quoted in Sylvère Lotringer, "Doing Theory," in *French Theory in America,* ed. Sande Cohen and Sylvère Lotringer (New York: Routledge, 2001), 142.

17. Sylvère Lotringer, "Third Wave: Art and the Commodification of Theory," *Flash Art* (May–June 1991): 94–95 and 97 (reprinted in Richard Hertz ed., *Theories of Contemporary Art* [Englewood Cliffs, N.J.: Prentice Hall, 1985], 93–103).

18. Lotringer, "Third Wave."

19. Peter Halley, *Collected Essays 1981–1987* (Zurich: Bruno Bischofberger Gallery, 1989), 95.

20. Françoise Gaillard, "D'un malentendu," in *Sans oublier Baudrillard,* ed. Jean-Olivier Majastre (Brussels: Éditions de la Lettre volée, 1996), 48–50.

21. Cited in ibid.

22. Ibid., 49.

23. Halley, *Collected Essays,* 164–65 and 132–37, respectively.

24. Theodor Adorno, *Théorie esthétique* (Paris: Klincksieck, 1989), 434.

25. David Pagel, "From Mysteries of Wonderland to the Realities of Modern Life," *Los Angeles Times,* December 18, 1998.

26. Gilles Deleuze, *Francis Bacon: The Logic of Sensation,* trans. Daniel W. Smith (Minneapolis: University of Minnesota Press, 2003), 48.

27. Jacques Derrida and Peter Eisenman, *Chora L Works* (New York: Monacelli Press, 1997).

28. James Wines, *De-architecture* (New York: Rizzoli, 1988), 14.

29. Peter Eisenman, "Preface," in *Houses of Cards,* ed. Peter Eisenman (New York: Oxford University Press, 1987), v.

30. Mark Wigley, *The Architecture of Deconstruction: Derrida's Haunt* (Cambridge: MIT Press, 1993).

31. Bernard Tschumi, *Architecture and Disjunction* (Cambridge: MIT Press, 1995), 174–78, 65–80, and 267n6, respectively.

11. Theoretical Machinations

1. Quoted in Philippe Roger, *The American Enemy: The History of French Anti-Americanism,* trans. Sharon Bowman (Chicago: University of Chicago Press, 2005), 381.

2. Bernard Stiegler, *Technics and Time,* vol. 1, *The Fault of Epimetheus,* trans. Richard Beardsworth and George Collins (Stanford, Calif.: Stanford University Press, 1994), 137 (translation slightly modified).

3. Bruce Sterling, *The Hacker Crackdown: Law and Disorder on the Electric Frontier* (New York: Bantam, 1992), chapter 2.

4. Hakim Bey, *The Temporary Autonomous Zone: Ontological Anarchy, Poetic Terrorism* (New York: Autonomedia, 1991), 108 and 115–16.

5. Ibid., 108 and 36–38.

6. Gilles Deleuze and Félix Guattari, *What Is Philosophy?*, trans. Hugh Tomlinson and Graham Burchell (New York: Columbia University Press, 1994), 71 (translation modified).

7. Félix Guattari, *Chaosmose* (Paris: Galilée, 1992), 130–31.

8. Ibid., 17.

9. "Baudrillard on the New Technologies: An Interview with Claude Thibaut"; see www.uta.edu/english/apt/collab/baudweb.html. [This site appears to have been taken down; the article can be found at: http://www.egs.edu/faculty/baudrillard/baudrillard-baudrillard-on-the-new-technologies.html.—*Trans.*]

10. "The Deleuze and Guattari Rhizomat"; see www.bleb.net/rhizomat/rhizomat.html.

11. See www.hydra.umn.edu/fobo/index.html.

12. Charles Stivale, *The Two-Fold Thought of Deleuze and Guattari: Intersections and Animations* (New York: Guilford Press, 1998), 74–78.

13. Gilles Deleuze and Félix Guattari, *A Thousand Plateaus: Capitalism and Schizophrenia,* trans. Brian Massumi (Minneapolis: University of Minnesota Press, 1987), 3.

14. Jaron Lanier, "Programmes Informatiques, programmes politiques (entretien)," *Cahiers de médiologie,* no. 3 (first semester 1997): 233–34.

15. Arthur Kroker and Marilouise Kroker, eds., *Digital Delirium* (New York: St. Martin's Press, 1997).

16. Istvan Csicsery-Ronay, "The SF of Theory: Baudrillard and Haraway," *Science-Fiction Studies,* vol. 18, no. 55 (November 1991).

17. Sylvère Lotringer, "Doing Theory," in *French Theory in America,* ed. Sande Cohen and Sylvère Lotringer (New York: Routledge, 2001), 153.

18. Erik Davis, "After the Deleuze," *Voice Literary Supplement,* September 1994, 29.

19. Rudy Rucker, Queen Mu, and R. U. Sirius, eds., *Mondo 2000: A User's Guide to the New Edge* (New York: HarperCollins, 1992).

20. Keith Ansell-Pearson, ed., *Deleuze and Philosophy: The Difference Engineer* (New York: Routledge, 1997).

21. Donna Haraway, "A Cyborg Manifesto: Science, Technology and Socialist Feminism in the Late Twentieth Century," in *Simians, Cyborgs, and Women: The Reinvention of Nature* (New York: Routledge, 1991), 149–82.

22. Chris Hables Gray, ed., *The Cyborg Handbook* (New York: Routledge, 1995).

23. Allucquere Rosanne Stone, "Virtual Systems," in *Incorporations* (Zone 6), ed. Jonathan Cracy and Sanford Kwinter (New York: Zone Books, 1992), 618, 621.

24. See Allucquere Rosanne Stone, *The War of Desire and Technology at the Close of the Mechanical Age* (Cambridge: MIT Press, 1995).

25. Sherry Turkle, *Life on the Screen* (New York: Simon and Schuster, 1995), especially chapter 8.

26. Ibid., 17–18.

27. One of the few texts that attempts a systematic use of this type of language is, unsurprisingly, an academic article, but it could just as easily have been written under the influence of ecstasy: Robin Mackay, "Capitalism and Schizophrenia: Wildstyle in Full Effect," in Ansell-Pearson, *Deleuze and Philosophy,* especially 248–56.

28. See www.djspooky.com/articles.html.

29. Michael Agger, "And the Oscar for Best Scholar . . . ," *New York Times,* May 18, 2003.

30. Peter McQuaid, "Midnight at the Oasis," *New York Times,* April 14, 2000.

31. Hillary Chute, "More, More, More," *Village Voice,* December 22–28, 1999 (ellipses in original).

32. Percival Everett, *Glyph* (Minneapolis: Greywolf Press, 1999).

33. Patricia Duncker, *Hallucinating Foucault* (New York: Ecco Press, 1997).

34. Robert Grudin, *Book: A Novel* (New York: Random House, 1992).

35. Saul Bellow, *Ravelstein* (New York: Viking, 2000), and Philip Roth, *The Human Stain* (New York: Vintage, 2001).

12. Theory as Norm

1. I am referring to the title of a polemical book by Neil Postman, *Amusing Ourselves to Death: Public Discourse in the Age of Show Business* (New York: Viking, 1985).

2. Herman Rapaport, *The Theory Mess* (New York: Columbia University Press, 2001).

3. Hannah Arendt, "The Crisis in Education," in *Between Past and Future: Eight Exercises in Political Thought* (New York: Penguin Books, 1993), 193.

4. Camille Paglia, "Junk Bonds and Corporate Raiders: Academe in the Hour of the Wolf," in *Sex, Art, and American Culture: Essays* (New York: Vintage, 1992).

5. Ibid., 216.

6. Ibid., 174, 187, 197, 216, and 224.

7. Ibid., 180, 211, 215, and 213.

8. Ibid., 215.

9. M. G. Lord, "This Pinup Drives Eggheads Wild," *New York Newsday,* October 6, 1991.

10. James Miller, *The Passion of Michel Foucault* (New York: Simon and Schuster, 1993).

11. Tony Judt, *Past Imperfect: French Intellectuals, 1944–1956* (Berkeley: University of California Press, 1992) and *The Burden of Responsibility: Blum, Camus, Aron and the French Twentieth Century* (Chicago: University of Chicago Press, 1998).

12. Robert Hughes, "The Patron Saint of Neo-Pop," *New York Review of Books,* June 1, 1989.

13. From a conversation with Sylvère Lotringer.

14. Bill Readings, *Introducing Lyotard: Art and Politics* (New York: Routledge, 1991), xi–xii.

15. Pierre Bourdieu, *The Rules of Art: Genesis and Structure of the Literary Field* (1992), trans. Susan Emanuel (Stanford, Calif.: Stanford University Press, 1996), 159–60.

16. Quoted in Bertram Gordon, "The Decline of a Cultural Icon: France in American Perspective," *French Historical Studies,* vol. 22, no. 4 (fall 1999): 627.

17. Jacques Derrida, "Deconstructions: The Im-possible," in *French Theory in America,* ed. Sande Cohen and Sylvère Lotringer (New York: Routledge, 2001), 16–17.

18. Tom Cohen, ed., *Jacques Derrida and the Humanities: A Critical Reader* (Cambridge: Cambridge University Press, 2001).

19. Rhonda Lieberman, "Jacques le Narcissiste," *Art Forum* (October 2002).

20. Program for the seminar "After Theory" (2002–3) at the CUNY Graduate Center.

21. See Jean-Philippe Mathy, *Extrême-Occident: French Intellectuals and America* (Chicago: University of Chicago Press, 1993), for a rich analysis of this aging "rhetoric of America."

22. Alexis de Tocqueville, *Democracy in America,* trans. Harvey C. Mansfield and Delba Winthrop (Chicago: University of Chicago Press, 2000), 403–4.

23. André Breton, "Interview with Jean Duché (Le Littéraire, October 5, 1946)," in *Conversations: The Autobiography of Surrealism,* trans. Mark Polizzotti (New York: Paragon House, 1993), 199.

24. Jean-Paul Sartre, "Individualism and Conformism in the United States," in *Literary and Philosophical Essays,* trans. Annette Michelson (New York: Criterion Books, 1955), 101.

25. Philippe Sollers, "Un Français à New York," preface to Paul Morand, *New York* (Paris: Garnier-Flammarion, 1988), 10.

26. Michel Foucault, "Le Triomphe social du plaisir sexuel: Une conversation avec Michel Foucault," in *Dits et Écrits, 1954–1988,* vol. 4, *1980–1988* (Paris: Gallimard, 1994), 308–14. This interview was originally conducted in English. See "The Social Triumph of the Sexual Will: A Conversation with Michel Foucault," *Christopher Street,* vol. 6, no. 4 (May 1982): 36–41.

27. Julia Kristeva, Marcelin Pleynet, and Philippe Sollers, "Pourquoi les États-Unis?" *Tel Quel,* nos. 71–73 (1977): 5.

28. Edward Said, "The Franco-American Dialogue: A Late Twentieth-Century Reassessment," in *Traveling Theory: France and the United States,* ed. Ieme van der Poel, Sophie Bertho, and Ton Hoenselaars (Teaneck, N.J.: Fairleigh Dickinson University Press, 1999), 156.

29. Richard Wolin, "Where Have All the French Intellectuals Gone?" *Dissent* (summer 1998): 123.

30. Gayatri Chakravorty Spivak and Michael Ryan, "Anarchism Revisited: A New Philosophy," *Diacritics* (summer 1978): 69–70.

31. Jane Gallop, "French Theory and the Seduction of Feminism," in *Men in Feminism,* ed. Alice Jardine and Paul Smith (New York: Methuen, 1987), 111.

32. Erving Goffman, *Forms of Talk* (Philadelphia: University of Pennsylvania Press, 1981); *Façons de parler* (Paris: Minuit, 1987), 194.

33. Paul Watzlawick et al., *Une Logique de la communication* (Paris: Seuil, "Points" collection, 1979), 211–13.

34. Yves Winkin, ed., *La Nouvelle Communication* (Paris: Seuil, 1981), 42.

35. Laura Epstein, ed., *Reading Foucault for Social Work* (New York: Columbia University Press, 1999).

36. Lydia Filligham, ed., *Foucault for Beginners* (New York: Writers and Readers, 1993).

37. Doug McEachern, "Foucault, Governmentality, Apartheid and the 'New' South Africa," in *Post-Colonialism: Culture and Identity in Africa,* ed. P. D. Ahluwalia and Paul Nursey-Bray (Commack, N.Y.: Nova Science, 1997).

38. John Rajchman, *Michel Foucault: The Freedom of Philosophy* (New York: Columbia University Press, 1986).

39. Hubert Dreyfus and Paul Rabinow, *Michel Foucault: Beyond Structuralism and Hermeneutics* (Chicago: University of Chicago Press, 1983).

40. Vincent Descombes, "Je m'en Foucault," *London Review of Books,* March 5, 1987.

41. Michel Foucault, *History of Sexuality,* vol. 1, *An Introduction,* trans. Robert Hurley (New York: Vintage, 1980), 94–95.

42. Michel Foucault, *The Archaeology of Knowledge,* trans. A. M. Sheridan Smith (New York: Pantheon, 1972), 17.

43. Quoted from a conversation with Edmund White.

44. "Sexual Choice, Sexual Act," in *Foucault Live,* ed. Sylvère Lotringer, trans. John Johnston (New York: Semiotext(e), 1989), 229–31.

45. Lee Quinby, *Freedom, Foucault, and the Subject of America* (Boston: Northeastern University Press, 1991), 3–6.

46. Jacques Derrida, *Of Grammatology* (1967), trans. Gayatri Chakravorty Spivak (Baltimore: Johns Hopkins University Press, 1997), 62.

47. Derrida, "Deconstructions," 20 (ellipses in the original).

48. Robert D'Amico, "Introduction to the Foucault–Deleuze Discussion," *Telos,* no. 16 (winter 1973): 102.

49. Brian Massumi, "Becoming Deleuzian," in *The Deleuze Reader,* ed. Constantin Boundas (New York: Columbia University Press, 1993), 401.

50. Gilles Deleuze and Félix Guattari, *A Thousand Plateaus: Capitalism and Schizophrenia,* trans. Brian Massumi (Minneapolis: University of Minnesota Press, 1987), 22.

51. Élie During, "Deleuze, et après?" *Critique,* no. 623 (April 1999): 292 and 301.

52. Chris McAuliffe, "Jean Baudrillard," in *The Judgment of Paris: Recent French Theory in a Local Context,* ed. Kevin Murray (North Sydney: Allen and Unwin, 1992), 98–101.

53. Jean Baudrillard, *L'Autre par lui-même: Habilitation* (Paris: Galilée, 1987), 84–85.

54. Susan Sontag, "Writing Itself: On Roland Barthes," in *A Barthes Reader,* ed. Susan Sontag (New York: Hill and Wang, 1982), iii.

55. Quoted in Steven Ungar, *Roland Barthes: The Professor of Desire* (Lincoln: University of Nebraska Press, 1983), xiii–xv.

56. Ibid., xi–xii.

13. Worldwide Theory

1. Jean Baudrillard, *America,* trans. Chris Turner (London and New York: Verso, 1989).

2. Gilles Deleuze, *Proust and Signs,* trans. Richard Howard (New York: George Brazillier, 1972), 167.

3. See Kevin Murray, ed., *The Judgment of Paris: Recent French Theory in a Local Context* (North Sydney: Allen and Unwin, 1992).

4. Gayatri Chakravorty Spivak, *In Other Worlds: Essays in Cultural Politics* (New York: Routledge, 1998), 100.

5. Alvin Gouldner, *The Future of Intellectuals and the Rise of the New Class* (New York: Seabury Press, 1979).

6. Pierre Bourdieu, "The Social Conditions of the International Circulation of Ideas," in *Bourdieu: A Critical Reader,* ed. Richard Shusterman (Oxford: Blackwell, 1999), 223.

7. ["White overalls," named for the hooded outer garment they wear at demonstrations.—*Trans.*]

8. Michael Hardt and Antonio Negri, *Empire* (Cambridge: Harvard University Press, 2000).

9. Michael Hardt, *Gilles Deleuze: An Apprenticeship in Philosophy* (Minneapolis: University of Minnesota Press, 1992).

10. See Giorgio Agamben, *Stanzas: Word and Phantasm in Western Culture,* trans. Ronald L. Martinez (Minneapolis: University of Minnesota Press, 1993); *The Coming Community,* trans. Michael Hardt (Minneapolis: University of Minnesota Press, 1993); *State of Exception,* trans. Kevin Attell (Chicago: University of Chicago Press, 2005).

11. See, for example, Slavoj Žižek, *Everything You Always Wanted to Know about Lacan (But Were Afraid to Ask Hitchcock)* (New York and London: Verso, 1992).

12. This follows the title of one of Slavoj Žižek's essays: *The Ticklish Subject* (New York and London: Verso, 1999).

13. Slavoj Žižek, *Welcome to the Desert of the Real: Five Essays on September 11 and Related Dates* (London: Verso, 2002).

14. The following quotations are taken from Édouard Glissant, "Le chaos-monde, l'oral et l'écrit," in *Écrire la "parole de la nuit": La nouvelle littérature antillaise,* ed. Ralph Ludwig (Paris: Gallimard, "Folio" collection, 1994), 111–29.

15. Quoted in François Cusset, "Écritures métissées," *Magazine littéraire,* no. 392 (November 2000): 41.

16. Françoise Lionnet, *Postcolonial Representations: Women, Literature, Identity* (Ithaca, N.Y.: Cornell University Press, 1995), 170–71.

17. Michael Dash, "*Haiti and the United States: National Stereotypes and the Literary Imagination* (New York: Macmillan, 1988).

18. Edward Said, "Secular Criticism," in *The Edward Said Reader,* ed. Moustafa Bayoumi and Andrew Rubin (New York: Vintage, 2000), 228.

19. Quoted in Jean-Philippe Mathy, "The Resistance to French Theory in the United States: A Cross-Cultural Inquiry," *French Historical Studies,* vol. 19 (fall 1995): 347.

20. See Meera Nanda, "The Science Wars in India," *Dissent* (winter 1997).

21. See Jesús Martín-Barbero, *Communication, Culture and Hegemony: From the Media to Mediations* (London: Sage, 1993).

22. Néstor García Canclini, *Transforming Modernity: Popular Culture in Mexico* (Austin: University of Texas Press, 1993).

23. Jorge Volpi, *La Fin de la folie,* trans. Gabriel Iaculli (Paris: Plon, 2003); original: *El fin de la locura* [The end of madness] (Barcelona/Mexico City: Seix Barral, 2003).

24. Tomás Abraham, *Vidas Filosóficas* (Buenos Aires: Prometeo Libros, 1999).

25. See Tomás Abraham, *El presente absoluto* (Buenos Aires: Editorial Sudamericana, 2007).

26. See Martin Hopenhayn's contribution to Manfred Max-Neef, ed., *Desarrollo a escala humana* (Montevideo: Nordan-Communidad, 2001).

27. José Guilherme Merquior, *Foucault ou le nihilisme de la chaire* (Paris: Presses universitaires de France, 1986). Brazilian edition: *Michel Foucault, ou o niilismo de cátedra* (Rio de Janeiro: Editora Nova Frontera, 1985).

28. Olavo de Carvalho, "Sokal, parodista de si mismo," *Folha de São Paulo,* October 21, 1996.

29. See Yue Daiyun, *To the Storm: The Odyssey of a Revolutionary Chinese Woman* (Berkeley: University of California Press, 1985).

30. An observation made by Harvard University Press editor Lindsay Waters after returning from a conference in Beijing.

31. See Shinichi Nakazawa, "Gojiro no Raigou," in *Chuo Kóron,* 1983 (quoted in Yoshihiko Ichida and Yann Moulier-Boutang, "La fin de l'histoire: Un jeu à trois," *Multitudes,* no. 13 [summer 2003]: 18).

32. Karatani Kôjin, *Architecture as Metaphor: Language, Number, Money* (Cambridge: MIT Press, 1995).

33. Hiroki Hazuma, "Two Letters, Two Deconstructions," *Hiyho Kukan,* vol. 2, no. 8 (1993): 77–106.

34. See Yoshi Oida, *L'acteur invisible* (Arles: Actes Sud, 1998).

35. Akira Asada, "Infantile Capitalism and Japan's Postmodernism: A Fairy Tale," in *Postmodernism and Japan,* ed. Miyoshi Masao et al. (Durham, N.C.: Duke University Press, 1989), 273–78.

36. Félix Guattari, "Tokyo l'orgueilleuse," *Multitudes,* no. 13 (summer 2003): 58.

37. These phrases are from the final sentence of Luc Ferry and Alain Renaut, *French Philosophy of the Sixties: An Essay on Antihumanism,* trans. Mary H. Cattani (Amherst: University of Massachusetts Press, 1990), 229.

38. Denis Donoghue, "Deconstructing Deconstruction," *New York Review of Books,* June 12, 1980, 37.

39. Louis Pinto, *Les Neveux de Zarathoustra: La réception de Nietzsche en France* (Paris: Seuil, 1995), 154–56.

40. See Diane Michelfelder et al., eds., *Dialogue and Deconstruction: The Gadamer–Derrida Encounter* (Albany: State University of New York Press, 1989).

41. This dialogue was continued between Lyotard and Richard Rorty (see their contributions and their debate that appeared in *Critique,* no. 456 [May 1985], "La traversée de l'Atlantique," 559–84).

42. Manfred Frank, *What Is Neostructuralism?,* trans. Sabine Wilke and Richard T. Gray (Minneapolis: University of Minnesota Press, 1989).

43. Jürgen Habermas, "The Critique of Reason as an Unmasking of the Human Sciences," in *The Philosophical Discourse of Modernity: Twelve Lectures,* trans. Frederick Lawrence (Cambridge: MIT Press, 1989), 238–65.

44. Rainer Nägele, "Frankfurters and French fries," quoted in Andreas Huyssen, "Mapping the Postmodern," *New German Critique,* no. 33 (fall 1984): 32.

45. Albrecht Wellmer, *Zur Dialektik von Moderne une Postmoderne* (Frankfurt: Suhrkamp, 1985), 163.

46. Seyla Benhabib, "Reversing the Dialectic of Enlightenment: The Reenchantment of the World," in *Confronting Mass Democracy and Industrial Technology: Political and Social Theory from Nietzsche to Habermas,* ed. John P. McCormick (Durham, N.C.: Duke University Press, 2002), 347.

47. Yves Cusset, "Lutter pour la reconnaissance et/ou témoigner du différend: Le mépris, entre tort et reconnaisance," in *Où en est la théorie critique?,* ed. Emmanuel Renault and Yves Sintomer (Paris: La Découverte, 2003), 201–16.

14. Meanwhile, Back in France . . .

1. [We must now add to this list: Derrida in 2004, Lacoue-Labarthe and Baudrillard in 2007.—*Trans.*]

2. Cited in Philippe Roger, *The American Enemy: The History of French Anti-Americanism,* trans. Sharon Bowman (Chicago: University of Chicago Press, 2005), 425.

3. Bernard-Henri Lévy, *Barbarism with a Human Face* (New York: Harper and Row, 1979), 131.

4. Pierre Nora, "Que peuvent les intellectuels?" *Le Débat,* no. 1 (May 1980): 11.

5. Michael Löwy and Robert Sayre, *Révolte et mélancolie: Le romantisme à contrecourant de la modernité* (Paris: Payot, 1992), 224.

6. From the title of the essay by François Furet, Jacques Julliard, and Pierre Rosanvallon, *La République du Centre* (Paris: Calmann-Lévy, 1988).

7. Anne Godignon and Jean-Louis Thiriet, "Pour en finir avec le concept d'aliénation," *Le Débat,* no. 56 (September–October 1989).

8. François Furet, *Penser la Révolution Française* (Paris: Gallimard, 1979).

9. "La preuve du pudding" (interview with Bernard-Henri Lévy), *Tel Quel,* no. 77 (autumn 1978): 25–35.

10. Lévy, *Barbarism with a Human Face,* 112–18.

11. Christian Jambet and Guy Lardreau, *L'Ange: Pour une Cynégétique du semblant* (Paris: Grasset, 1976).

12. Cited in Didier Éribon, *Michel Foucault,* trans. Betsy Wing (Cambridge: Harvard University Press, 1991), 300 (translation modified).

13. See André Glucksmann, *Le XIe commandement* (Paris: Flammarion, 1991).

14. Gilles Deleuze, "On the New Philosophers (Plus a More General Problem)," in *Two Regimes of Madness: Texts and Interviews 1975–1995,* ed. David Lapoujade, trans. Ames Hodges and Mike Taormina (New York: Semiotext(e), Foreign Agents Series, 2006), 144–45.

15. Ibid., 139–42 and 147 (translation slightly modified).

16. Pierre Bourdieu, *The Rules of Art: Genesis and Structure of the Literary Field,* trans. Susan Emanuel (Stanford, Calif.: Stanford University Press, 1996), 163.

17. Luc Ferry and Alain Renaut, *La Pensée 68: Essai sur l'antihumanisme contemporain* (Paris: Gallimard, collection "Folio essais," 1988 [1985]); English translation: *French Philosophy of the Sixties: An Essay on Antihumanism,* trans. Mary H. Cattani (Amherst: University of Massachusetts Press, 1990).

18. See Luc Ferry, *L'Homme-Dieu, ou Le sens de la vie* (Paris: Grasset, 1996).

19. Ferry and Renaut, *French Philosophy of the Sixties,* xxviii.

20. Lévy, *Barbarism with a Human Face,* 190–91.

21. Nora, "Que peuvent les intellectuels?" 7.

22. Ferry and Renaut, *French Philosophy of the Sixties,* 65.

23. "Placer l'élève au centre du système est démagogique," interview with Luc Ferry, *Le Monde,* April 17, 2003.

24. To borrow the title of an incisive article by Gilles Châtelet ("Du chaos et de l'auto-organisation comme néoconservatisme festif," *Les Temps Modernes,* no. 581 [March–April 1995]).

25. Armand Mattelart, *La Communication-monde* (Paris: La Découverte, 1992), 255.

26. In an interview with a national magazine, Notat even brought out a citation of Foucault, using it out of context as though it were a question of the union negotiator's realism, as she denounced the "political regime . . . , indifferent to reality" ("La société qui veut savoir pourquoi bouger . . ." [an interview with Nicole Notat], *Le Point,* March 22, 2002).

27. François Ewald and Denis Kessler, "Les noces du risque et de la politique," *Le Débat,* no. 109 (March–April 2000).

28. François Ewald, Nicolas de Sadelee, and Christian Gollier, *Le Principe de précaution* (Paris: Presses universitaires de France, "Que sais-je?" series, 2001).

29. François Ewald, "Droit: Systèmes et stratégies," *Le Débat,* no. 41 (September–October 1986): 63–69.

30. François Ewald, *L'État providence* (Paris: Grasset, 1986), 530.

31. Michel Foucault, *The History of Sexuality,* vol. 1, *An Introduction,* trans. Robert Hurley (New York: Vintage, 1980), 144.

32. Ewald, *L'État providence,* 482–83 and 405–6, respectively.

33. Ibid., 10–11, 603, and 524–26, respectively.

34. Ibid., 527 (my emphasis).

35. Ibid., 10.

36. See Ulrich Beck, *La Société du risque: Sur la voie d'une autre modernité* (Paris: Aubier, 2001).

37. Michel Foucault, "Ariane s'est pendue," *Le Nouvel Observateur,* no. 229 (March 31–April 6, 1969).

38. Roger, *The American Enemy,* 374.

39. See Robert Harvey and Pascal Le Brun-Cordier, "Horizons," *Rue Descartes: Revue du Collège international de philosophie,* no. 40 (summer 2003): "*Queer:* Repenser les identités," 4. See also the polemical and high-profile books by French queer theorist and activist Marie-Hélène Bourcier.

40. Walter Benjamin, "Surrealism" (1929) and "The Present Social Situation of the French Writer" (1934), in *Selected Writings,* vol. 2, *1927–1934,* ed. Michael W. Jennings, Howard Eiland, and Gary Smith (Cambridge: Harvard University Press, 1999), 213, 752, and 755.

41. Peter Starr, *Logics of a Failed Revolution: French Theory after May '68* (Stanford, Calif.: Stanford University Press, 1995), 202.

42. [A reference to "Crise de vers," a prose text by Stéphane Mallarmé written between 1886 and 1896.—*Trans.*]

43. Marilyn August and Ann Liddle, "Beyond Structuralism," *SubStance*, 5–6 (spring 1973): 237.

44. Bruno Latour, "The Promises of Constructivism," in *Chasing Technoscience: Matrix for Materiality*, ed. Don Ihde et al. (Bloomington: Indiana University Press, 2003), chapter 2.

45. An *empirical* construct, because French epistemology (where one speaks of "constructing the facts") has in fact always seen the sciences as constructing *theory*, as Latour points out, but a theory that derives only from itself.

46. Latour, "The Promises of Constructivism."

47. Alan Sokal and Jean Bricmont, *Fashionable Nonsense* (New York: St. Martin's Press, 1998), 85.

Conclusion

1. Friedrich Nietzsche, *The Gay Science*, trans. Walter Kaufmann (New York: Vintage, 1974), aphorism 374, 336 (translation slightly modified).

2. Gilles Deleuze and Claire Parnet, *Dialogues* (1977), trans. Hugh Tomlinson and Barbara Habberjam (New York: Columbia University Press, 1987), 147.

3. Ibid. (translation slightly modified).

4. Maurice Blanchot, *The Unavowable Community*, trans. Pierre Joris (Barrytown, N.Y.: Station Hill Press, 1988), 55–56 and 11–12 (translation modified).

5. Alexis de Tocqueville, *Democracy in America*, trans. Harvey C. Mansfield and Delba Winthrop (Chicago: University of Chicago Press, 2000), 482.

6. See Luc Boltanski and Eve Chiapello, *Le Nouvel Esprit du capitalisme* (Paris: Gallimard, collection NRF Essais, 1999).

7. Tiqqun, "Echographie d'une puissance," *Tiqqun 2, "Zone d'Opacité Offensive"* (2001): 217.

8. Vincent Descombes, *Modern French Philosophy*, trans. L. Scott-Fox and J. M. Harding (Cambridge: Cambridge University Press, 1980), 188.

9. Pierre Bourdieu, "Deux impérialismes de l'universel," in *L'Amérique des Français*, ed. Christine Fauré et al. (Paris: François Bourin, 1992).

10. A process on which Theodor Adorno had already commented, noting that "life has become the ideology of its own absence" (see *Minima Moralia*, trans. E. F. N. Jephcott [London: Verso, 1974], 190).

11. See Gilles Deleuze, "The Shame and the Glory: T. E. Lawrence," in *Essays Critical and Clinical*, trans. Daniel W. Smith and Michael A. Greco (Minneapolis: University of Minnesota Press, 1997), 115–25.

12. Oswald Spengler, *The Decline of the West*, vol. 2, *Perspectives of World-History*, trans. Charles Francis Atkinson (New York: Alfred A. Knopf, 1928), 58–59 (Spengler's emphasis).

13. See Akbar Abbas, *Hong Kong, Culture, and the Politics of Disappearance* (Minneapolis: University of Minnesota Press, 1997).

14. A syncretic artistic tradition to which Serge Gruzinski has dedicated a very fine study: *La Pensée métisse* (Paris: Fayard, 1999).

INDEX

François Cusset, a writer and intellectual historian, teaches contemporary French thought at Institut d'Études Politiques and at Reid Hall/Columbia University in Paris. He is the author of several books, including *Queer Critics* and *La Décennie*.

Jeff Fort is assistant professor of French at the University of California, Davis. He has translated works by Maurice Blanchot, Jean Genet, Jean-Luc Nancy, and Philippe Lacoue-Labarthe.